The China Model

This book is part of the Peter Lang Regional Studies list.
Every volume is peer reviewed and meets
the highest quality standards for content and production.

PETER LANG
New York • Bern • Berlin
Brussels • Vienna • Oxford • Warsaw

Yongnian Zheng

The China Model

Experience and Challenges

PETER LANG
New York • Bern • Berlin
Brussels • Vienna • Oxford • Warsaw

Library of Congress Cataloging-in-Publication Data

Names: Zheng, Yongnian, author.
Title: The China model: experience and challenges / Zheng Yongnian.
Description: New York: Peter Lang, 2021.
Identifiers: LCCN 2021025146 (print) | LCCN 2021025147 (ebook)
ISBN 978-1-4331-7200-7 (hardback)
ISBN 978-1-4331-9020-9 (ebook pdf) | ISBN 978-1-4331-9021-6 (epub)
Subjects: LCSH: China—Politics and government—1949– | China—Economic policy—1949– | China—Foreign economic relations. | China—Social policy.
Classification: LCC DS777.75 .Z472453 2021 (print) | LCC DS777.75 (ebook) | DDC 951.05—dc23
LC record available at https://lccn.loc.gov/2021025146
LC ebook record available at https://lccn.loc.gov/2021025147
DOI 10.3726/b18592

Bibliographic information published by **Die Deutsche Nationalbibliothek.**
Die Deutsche Nationalbibliothek lists this publication in the "Deutsche Nationalbibliografie"; detailed bibliographic data are available on the Internet at http://dnb.d-nb.de/.

中信出版集团
CITIC Press Group

This edition is an authorized translation from the Chinese language edition
Published by arrangement with CITIC Press Corporation
B&R Book Program

Table of Contents

Preface

The China Model in New Circumstances

In 2009, I compiled some of my articles and lectures into a book entitled *The China Model: Experience and Challenges*. The book was published in the context of the 2008 global financial crisis.

After the crisis occurred, both China itself and many Western countries exhibited great interest in the China Model. The concept of "China Model" also began to become quite popular. But earlier discussions of the so-called "Beijing Consensus" were actually considerations of the China Model as well. The concept of Beijing Consensus was proposed in juxtaposition with the "Washington Consensus" that was popular at the time. Before the 2008 financial crisis, the Washington Consensus was widely promoted in the West, but the author of *The Beijing Consensus* observed the shortcomings in the Washington Consensus and pointed out some of the advantages of the Chinese model of reform. In China, however, the Beijing Consensus has often been interpreted for the inherent superiority of the Beijing Consensus over the Washington Consensus. In this understanding, the former should replace the latter. In the West, however, the China Model was beginning to be regarded as a threat to the Western Model (that is, the Washington Consensus). In other words, whether Chinese or non-Chinese, people had been overly politicizing their understanding of the Beijing Consensus.

After the 2008 global financial crisis, this antagonistic stance became even more apparent. Chinese were attracted to the China Model because China had more effectively withstood the financial crisis. Some even inferred from the China Model's success that the China Model was inherently superior to the Western Model. In fact, both everyday citizens and government officials began to lecture the West about the superiority of the China Model. At the same time, there were also Westerners who began to develop interest in the China Model. However, their interest in the China Model did not so much reflect an understanding of China as a disappointment with the Western Model. Like the Chinese, many Westerners observed both how the Western crisis occurred and how China effectively withstood the financial crisis, even making exciting achievements. For many years after the 2008 financial crisis, China has been one of the most important forces driving the development and growth of the world economy. Because of this, more and more Westerners have begun to discuss how the China Model may pose a threat to the Western Model.

As someone who has long studied China's reform and economic development, I felt at the time that discussions of both the Beijing Consensus and the China Model were too politicized, and that they brimmed with ideological prejudice. Regardless of whether they were supporters or opponents, too many people brought with them preconceived ideas that were inconsistent with China's actual experience. As a result, these discussions did not actually help people understand China.

In this context, I decided to collect my previous work on the topic and participate in the discussion by directly entitling the resulting book *The China Model.* However, as I was to go on to explain many times after the publication of the work, using the term "China Model" did not mean that I was praising or criticizing the China Model through the lens of moral judgments—as so many other theorists had done. Instead, I regarded the experience of China's reform and economic development as a social object, the experience of which I would make the focus of my research. Therefore, I added the subtitle "Experience and Challenges." Obviously, in my view, China's reform and development offer valuable experiences and enormous challenges.

This revised edition is not just a reprint for two main reasons. First, with changes in the international scene and the intensification of China's reform and development, questions about the China Model are growing increasingly important. At the international level, the status quo of China's development and reform has given rise to two completely different predictions. On the one hand, some predict that the "Chinese Century" is coming, while others argue that China's reform and development have entered their "end game." As a Chinese researcher,

I feel that I cannot simply choose between the two—yet must also clearly state my own views.

Second, over the past few years, I haven't ceased to think about this issue simply because I had published a book on it. I have continued to conduct more observations and done some deeper thinking—on which I've spilled quite a bit of ink. This new work may well answer the question about whether the world has entered the "Chinese Century" and whether China's economic reform and development has truly entered its end game. In this revised edition, I've added several new chapters to the original text. Of course, in order to control the book's length, I also had to remove several chapters of redundant content.

Over the years, the China Model has been controversial at home and abroad, but none of these debates have reached any consensus. Generally speaking, in this long-running debate, people have not been concerning themselves with the China Model's objective existence; rather, they have reduced the whole question to an up-down vote: "China Model, yes or no?" Undoubtedly, the debate has become too politicized—even moralizing. If this continues, people will have difficulty understanding the China Model.

Does a China Model exist? What does this model look like? What internal and external significance does it possess? Where did this model come from, and where is it going? Whether we're seeking to understand China's own development, or whether we want to know the impact of China's development on the world, we must answer these important questions. But answering these questions means we must first de-politicize them.

Everywhere, people have highly politicized illusions and fantasies about the China Model. In the West, three different but interrelated perspectives surround the China Model. The first is what I call the "Flatterers": those who gush with praise for the China Model, to the extent that some even hold that the China Model will soon replace the Western Model. Among the Flatterers, there are different reasons for flattering China. Many businesspeople have been optimistic about the China Model because their own interests are connected to China's. Because of these connected interests, they would like to believe that the China Model is sustainable. Others truly do want China to develop a model different from the West's. Such people tend to have lost confidence in the Western Model, and they question whether the Western Model can be sustained. For these people, China's success since Reform and Opening Up (*gaige kaifang*) has provided an inspiration. Some in China suggest that such people are simply flatterers and yes-men, but this is not necessarily so. Of course, it's easy to see that they frequently tally China's achievements without also considering the costs and constraints on future development that lie behind those achievements.

Over against the Flatterers stand the "Threatists." The "Threatists" not only observe that the China Model exists but also ruminate on the long-term impact of the China Model on the West. Threatists have observed that, while the Reform and Opening Up has indeed achieved decades of success, China has not developed in the direction that Westerners had hoped for, or in accordance with the Western logic. On the contrary, China has formed its own development model, one which has become quite competitive. These observers believe that, especially in developing countries, the China Model is placing great pressure on the Western Model. Some in the Threatist camp have seen in the China Model a reflection of fundamental values. They hold that the China Model represents values that differ from those held by the West—values that not only compete with Western values but which may even come to replace Western values.

Unlike the Flatterers or the Threatists, many Westerners do not acknowledge the existence of the China Model. We could label this group "Uncertaintists." Most Uncertaintists have observed the various problems and constraints involved in China's development, and they don't believe that China has actually formed anything that could be called a "model." They also remain skeptical about whether China's developmental model is sustainable. Some of the Uncertaintists have a greater awareness of China's development and are able to investigate China's problems at a deeper level. These Uncertaintists have observed China's various internal shortcomings and, on the basis of their observations, have assessed whether China may disintegrate or even collapse. However, some of the Uncertaintists are also ideologically hostile to China, and they actively wish for China's disintegration and collapse. For these, China is simply unworthy of producing a model.

Interestingly, over against the West, within China there are also three different perspectives on the China Model. The first lavishes praise on the China Model, holding not only that it exists but also that it is superior to the Western Model. We might label this perspective "Leftism." The Leftists are not hesitant to declare that a China Model has been established. Internationally, they want to contend with the West for discursive hegemony. But the conditions within Leftism are complex. Some find the origins of the China Model in Mao Zedong Thought; others find a theoretical basis in the New Marxism of the West; and others still approach the China Model from the perspective of comparative development. In a nutshell, although the Leftists have conducted a great deal of empirical research on the China Model, their evaluations of it are too ideological. As they approach questions from the perspective of a specific ideology, their objectivity is reduced, and their discourse on the China Model loses its ability to explain China.

In contrast with the Leftists, pro-Western Liberals do not recognize the existence of the China Model. For the Liberals, the China Model might not even be needed at all, since the success of China's development depends on whether China can develop Western-style political, economic, and social systems. When the existing systems aren't changing, why talk about a China Model? The Liberals therefore often use the West as a standard to measure China's development and progress. If China is an orange and the West is an apple, then for the Liberals, the *telos* of the orange is to transform itself into an apple, and when the orange does not become an apple, the orange itself is nothing.

The third viewpoint might be called "Indeterminism." The starting point for the Indeterminists, of course, is different from that of the Western Uncertaintists. Indeterminism is most prevalent among government scholars and officials, and Indeterminists hold that China is still in the process of development, and many problems still exist. It is simply too soon to talk about a China Model. However, the majority of Indeterminists have to deal with political considerations, so they follow Deng Xiaoping's policy of "hiding one's strengths and biding one's time" (*tao guang yang hui*), believing that China itself is not in a position to promote the China Model and fearing that doing so will leave a negative impact internationally.

Logically speaking, a China Model does exist. In building a house, a model must exist before the house can be built. The question is how to examine and evaluate the house. We could employ relatively scientific and objective methods in researching questions about the house. We could ask questions such as: What does the house look like? How was it built? Why was it built this way and not another way? Does the house have a firm foundation? How can it be renovated? But we could also approach the house from an aesthetic perspective. If we adopt an aesthetic approach, then it will become impossible to avoid politicization and moralizing. Unfortunately, up to the present, the vast majority of commentators on the China Model have conducted their investigations from an aesthetic perspective. There is no awareness of the objective existence of the China Model, while there are countless aesthetic criticisms.

Some either do not recognize or do not value the China Model because they see models as excessively idealistic in nature. But this is inconsistent with a historical viewpoint. Sociologically speaking, any given model has its own advantages and disadvantages; a 100% ideal model simply does not exist. Any given model has a historic quality, and this holds true for the Western Model, too. For instance, the Western democratic model represents long historical development. It began as an aristocratic democracy; during industrialization, it became the democracy of the commercial elite; and under current mass democracy, it has also experienced great changes. The West's model for a market economy is no different. It began as the primitive capitalism depicted by early Marxism, and it is now welfare capitalism. All the time it has undergone processes of evolution, improvement, and progress.

In other words, no model is static. In different historical stages, every model must reform itself to meet the demands of the times.

The China Model is also objective, but people from any country and any culture all have the right to investigate and interpret it. Because of this, the East-West debate over the China Model will never end. The same dynamic occurs as to Western democracies. Easterners often approach the Western democratic model from their own perspective, and the conclusions they draw are very different from those of Westerners approaching the same model. What's important here is that we distinguish the objective existence of the China Model from our aesthetic feelings about this model. Excessive aestheticism can lead to excessive politicization or moralization.

Since the China Model does in fact already exist, China needs to answer the question, "Who am I?" That is, China needs to explain what the China Model actually is. This task has become critical. Internally, more and more people within China are becoming increasingly unclear about what kind of state China actually is. Different social groups have begun to define their own understanding of Chinese identity on the basis of their own differing ideological perspectives. The positioning of various ideologies does not help the creation of a Chinese identity, for a Chinese identity must be grounded in an objective understanding of the China Model.

Externally, the China Model touches on questions of China's identity internationally. Neither traditional nor currently popular ideologies have helped explain to the international community the basic question, "Who am I?" The ambiguity surrounding this question is a major reason why the international community believes that China's future development is uncertain. At the same time, certainty can only come from an objective understanding of the China Model. Furthermore, if we can't answer the question "Who am I?", then we won't be able to discuss how China should deploy soft power within the international community.

Even more important are questions of improving the China Model. Failure to recognize the existence of the China Model will lead to neglect or disregard of the model's defects. Only by recognizing the objective existence of the China Model can we seriously study this model or locate its shortcomings and make improvements. In fact, just how to go about improving the China Model is the greatest problem China now faces.

It is my feeling that neither the earlier enthusiasm for the China Model nor the more recent suspicion of it will help us understand it better. In reality, the more we have discussed the China Model, the more confused people have become. I believe that the China Model may be discussed on at least three different levels.

The first is the relation of the China Model to Chinese civilization. I myself prefer to contextualize the China Model within a macroscopic view of history. It is not enough to examine thirty years of Reform and Opening Up; we need to consider the thirty years that came before—and, in fact, a study of those thirty years is still insufficient. We must consider China's national transformation during the entire modern period. I believe that, in order to study the China Model, we must first identify consistent structural elements. Quite simply, no matter how much China experiences change or reform, China remains China, and China cannot become the West or any other country. Then what elements keep China "forever China"? These elements are at the heart of the China Model. If we cannot identify them, then we will find ourselves unable to understand the China Model, and we certainly won't be able to identify the China Model's advantages or disadvantages. At this level, we must pay attention to the civilizational nature of the China Model.

And if we approach the China Model from the wide lens of history, it's not hard to observe not only the existence of the model but also its main implications. Although the China Model manifests itself in a variety of aspects, at its center is China's unique political and economic model. The political and economic aspects are interrelated and mutually reinforcing. China owes its achievements to this model, and if the many different elements within this model were imbalanced, the model itself might experience crisis or decline.

Economically speaking, China's model is a mixed economy. In the model, the state-owned sector and the non-state sector, the government and the market, must maintain balance. Once this balance is lost, a crisis is waiting in the wings. No economic model like China's exists elsewhere in the world. Over long historical periods, China has maintained a strong state-owned sector, and the state has played a direct role in key economic fields. The state-owned sector supports many of the state's functions, including the construction of public infrastructure, the response to various crises, and the power to balance the market. This is all very clearly expressed in the *Discourses on Salt and Iron* (*Yantie lun*) of the Han Dynasty, and such theories have been implemented throughout various dynasties. This economic function of the state does not find its replica in the West. Some commentators always link the state-owned sector with the planned economy of the Mao Zedong era, but this is to miss the bigger historical picture. Mao Zedong only pushed the state's role, one which it had held since ancient history, to the extreme.

Many evaluate China's economic model over against the Western economic model, as if the Western economic model were the *telos* for China's reforms. But if China can become the West, then there is in fact no China Model. The suggestion that China is a transitional economy, one that is moving from a planned economy to a market economy, and from a state-owned economy to a private economy, fails to take into account the essence of the China Model. For it is precisely because China has a strong state-owned sector that privatization like that experienced in the West will never happen in China. Historically speaking, private economies have always existed in China, but it is impossible for China to experience complete privatization on the scale of the West. Many economists have suggested that the way to solve problems is through privatization. But this would be a departure from the realities of China, where only part of the economy is privatized. Comprehensive nationalization and comprehensive privatization are not the norms for the Chinese economy, whereas a mixed economy is the norm. The problems facing the Chinese economy can only be resolved with a recognition of this normal state.

Mixed economies, however, often lose their equilibrium. It is frequently the case that when the state-owned sector and the government occupy a position of absolute dominance, the non-state sector and the market are squeezed. And when they lose their ability to play their normal roles, a crisis occurs. In contrast to China, the West experiences economic crises when the "invisible hand" completely dominates economic activities and the government's "visible hand" cannot effectively regulate the market.

Discussions of the China Model are more effective when they are confined to economics, since once we broach the political, discussions become quite difficult and are very sensitive. In reality, if we don't see the China Model, it's hard to understand China's economic model. We can even say that China's economic model is a product of China's political model, although discussing the political model has always been off-limits. Many Westerners devote their attention to criticizing Chinese politics, while Chinese scholars often lack confidence in their own political system.

Politically speaking, the Western democratic model means having a multiparty system and the separation of powers. China's politics is changing, and in differing institutions and to varying degrees, Chinese politics is accommodating Western democratic elements. The diversification of interests and representation of interests are also taking place. But no matter how much Chinese politics changes, China does not have, nor can it have, a model like that of the West.

Then what are the characteristics of the Chinese political model? Once again, we can answer this question with a larger historical perspective. After contact with the West in modern times, China tried to implement Western-style systems—but failed. Later, during wars and then a revolution that together lasted for more than a century, traditional imperial power slowly transformed into a fully modern party. It's not hard to see how traditional imperial power and modern party power have much in common. For example, imperial power and party power both serve as a force for integration within Chinese society; both are political manifestations of China's cultural emphasis on unification; and both are institutional vehicles of the government of the sage. However, party power also carries with it modern elements that traditional imperial power did not have. Imperial power could only be marginalized; it could not be democratized. The Party's power is not like this. The Party's power is the foundation of modern, centralized systems—but it can also be democratized.

Western political models often resolve problems by externalizing political issues; thus, there are opposition parties, and political opposition. In China this is not the case. Both traditional imperial power and modern party power resolve problems by opening up the political process and internalizing external issues. Party power is the heart of Chinese politics. Without an understanding of party power, Chinese politics cannot be understood.

Historically speaking, these two political models have their own advantages and disadvantages. In the West, a democracy built around multiparty politics has only become what it is after hundreds of years of evolution. In nations with balanced social and economic development, Western-style democracy can thrive. Although such nations feature shifts in which differing parties hold the reins of power, politically, they frequently possess the characteristics of single-party government. This is mainly due to the fact that there is an enormous middle class in the West. Regardless of which party is in power, every party must look to the interests of the middle class. It is often said that Western political parties integrate social forces. However, to a large extent, it is the Western middle class that has integrated political parties, and it is the middle class that has restrained the radicalization of party politics. This is especially true if we observe differentiation in party politics from the perspective of a developing society. Because of low levels of social and economic development in developing societies, social differentiation is severe, and the middle class is either weak or non-existent. In such societies, once multiparty politics is implemented, political parties become a force for social differentiation. Examples for this can be found throughout Africa, Latin America, and Asia.

In traditional China, the political process is also quite open. Although imperial power belonged to the emperor, administrative power (or the minister's power) is open to society, and it is also highly institutionalized (that is, bureaucratized). History shows that the more open administrative power is, the more a state's governance is effective. To the contrary, when administrative power is not sufficiently open, the relationship between imperial power and administrative power is poorly managed, and political crises occur. Party power has the same characteristics.

Effective governance depends on effectively opening the Party's power to every level of society and every interest. At the same time, the effectiveness of administrative power depends on both institutionalization and specialization.

On the following level, the term "China Model" refers to the model of the Reform and Opening Up. The so-called "Chinese Way" belongs to this level. The "Chinese Way" is the reason why China's reforms have come about. This means we must return to the questions of "Where did this model come from, and where is it going?" And at this level, China's reforms are clearly both gradualist and stage-based. I personally hold that China's reforms can be divided into three stages: economic reforms first, social reforms second, and finally political reforms. To state this is not to make a value judgment—that is, it is not to say that China should follow this path. Rather, it is an empirical observation. Advanced nations and regions including Europe, Japan, and Asia's "Four Little Dragons" all exhibited similar developmental characteristics; they have all gone through this process, as well. In addition, this model of reform is also in line with some of the general principles of development.

First of all, this process moves from easy to difficult. Economic reform is the easiest to perform. To put it bluntly, it means the mobilization of people's material consciousness; in other words, it means the liberation of what philosophers calls "evil in human nature"; it is to let people pursue their own material benefit. This is a liberation of instinct. Social reform is harder. If the subject of economic reform is production, then the subject of social reform is distribution. Social reform demands that people open their wallets and share a portion with the rest of society. Naturally, this is harder to do. Political reform is the most difficult to achieve. Political reform means that people must give up some power in order to let others share in that power. In China's political culture, power dominates everything. Thus, giving up power is more difficult than sacrificing money.

Second, this process touches on questions regarding the material basis for institutional reform. Economic reform takes priority because it can provide a material basis for the other reforms. The reason why economic reform takes precedence over social reform is simple: If there are no products, what can be distributed? After wealth has been created, then emphasis can be placed on distribution. Politically speaking, giving economic reform precedence over political reform has at least two advantages: From a social perspective, economic reform creates wealth and a middle class, which are the preconditions for rational political participation; and for political elites, economic reform provides them with an alternative. When politics dominates everything, losing power means losing everything. But if you can lose power and still enter the economic arena, then political reform is no longer a zero-sum game for political figures. This is true in Western societies: If politicians fail in political competition, this does not mean that there is nothing else left to them.

So why do economic and social reforms need to happen before political reform does? The primary issue here touches on questions regarding historical sequence in the construction of institutions. The state system of any nation manifests itself in aspects such as politics, economics, and society. If democracy is the product of social development, then without the support of a series of other systems, democracy will itself be weak. Democracy is only one of the many basic systems of a nation, and it cannot replace aspects of other systems. Historically, first there had to be a modern nation before the nation could be democratized. As far as China's political development is concerned, if elections become the focal point of democratization before economic and social systems are constructed, then the result is probably going to be a second-rate democracy. This is exactly what we can observe in countries that are both economically undeveloped and also feature democratic elections. At the very least, if a nation is lacking effective economic and social systems, no one can guarantee that the democracy itself will function well.

Finally, the China Model can be discussed at the level of specific policies. Thus it could well be called China's Policy Model. With such an approach, one can examine the China Model from a variety of differing areas—such as economic, social, and political reform. When people talk about the "case of China," I think this is what they are talking about. Since Reform and Opening Up, China has provided many policies for reform.

At present, many remain highly dissatisfied with this level of the China Model. In economic policy, dissatisfaction with reform policies can be approached from differing angles. Some employ Western standards to judge China's Policy Model. For example, some scholars hold that China only experienced reform in the 1980s and 1990s, and that it hasn't experienced any reform since. The early reforms were characterized by marketization and decentralization, while after the 1990s, reform has tended to exhibit the opposite trends. Other scholars hold that Chinese policy has been copied from the West and thus cannot be truly considered China's own model. In other words, there is no such thing as a China Model. However, these views are not very reasonable. Over against adherents of the first point of view, it seems to me that centralization can be a reform, while decentralization does not necessarily imply reform. If centralization means establishing and strengthening government regulation of the market, then it can also be reform. If decentralization only produces various administratively dominant local monopolies, and not markets, then it is not necessarily reform, but an oligarchic economy. As for the second view, the market does not belong exclusively to the West. Thousands of years of Chinese history have also exhibited developed markets. Some practices of a market economy first occurred in the West, but this does not mean that markets are Western. After the Reform and Opening Up, the obvious fact that China learned from the West does not mean that China cannot form its own model.

These three dimensions of the China Model are interrelated, but they can also be studied independently of each other. However, it is even more important that research be conducted in how to improve the China Model. Today, discussing how to improve the China Model is a work of extraordinary significance. To begin with, emphasizing improvement means emphasizing the gradualist nature of the model and avoiding any radical changes. Every model must improve itself in company with developments; otherwise, it will degenerate, lose its ability to adapt, and ultimately invite radical changes. Chinese history shows that radical change often involves no change, for radical change often means starting over from the beginning. In the long run, improvement or gradual progress means real change. Additionally, although China has already formed its own model, like all other models it has its own disadvantages, and thus these disadvantages must be identified. China will never be able to develop a truly perfect model, but having an awareness of the model's defects can help prevent decline. More importantly, an awareness of one's own defects can help one hold to one's strengths in the heat of competition with other models.

To truly understand the China Model, we must identify its defects. The heart of the China Model is China's political and economic systems; thus, the key to improving the China Model lies in identifying the flaws within China's political and economic systems. Flaws in the political and economic systems need to be corrected so that the flaws associated with the political and economic systems do not deal a fatal blow to the China Model itself.

In terms of its economic system, China has a relatively strong state-owned sector with its own advantages. This sector can effectively construct the nation's infrastructure and public works, and it can cope with major crises and bring balance to the market. But if the state-owned sector gains an absolute advantage and the government intervenes too much in the market, the disadvantages in the model will emerge.

Anything is problematic if carried to excess. If individualism is taken to excess, then the Western Model also becomes problematic. From the Great Depression to the current global financial crisis, the flaws in the Western Model can primarily be traced to the fact that key financial sectors were controlled by private individuals, while governments were incapable of sufficiently intervening. When there is insufficient regulation, the market can be manipulated by private individuals, and it becomes problematic. But what about China? The flaw in the China Model is that, once the state and the government secure absolute, monopolizing positions, the market's role cannot come into play, and problems arise. In other words, excessive statism will also produce economic crisis.

So how can we improve the model? For China, comprehensive privatization is not a realistic option. Solutions to China's problems must be found within, and improving the model means different things in different historical stages. Judging from the current environment, in which "the state sector advances while the private sector retreats" (*guo jin min tui*) and "the state is rich while the people are poor" (*guo fu min qiong*)—an environment created by placing a priority on economic development and allowing social development to stagnate—improving the China Model demands finding points of equilibrium in every aspect.

First of all, we must delineate the limits of the state-owned sector. The state-owned sector must operate within limits; it cannot be allowed to develop indefinitely, nor must it be permitted to endlessly infringe upon non-state-owned sectors. The two sectors should maintain relatively balanced and delimited spaces that allow them to compete with each other. Fair competition between the state-owned sector and the non-state-owned sector is critical.

Second, the respective functions and spheres of the government and the market should be clearly delineated. Where can the government play a role? And where can the government play a role where it hasn't yet played a role? Where should the government withdraw from influence but hasn't yet withdrawn? These issues need to be clarified. In areas of social policy, such as social reform, social security, health insurance, education, and environmental protection, the government clearly has not done enough.

Again, we need to find a balance between economic development and social development. The aims for "social construction" that have been proposed by China's leaders are good, but it is impossible to achieve these goals with the means actually being used. The government offers economic policies alone, while social policies remain quite lacking. On many occasions, economic policies have entirely replaced social policies. For example, in order to implement social construction, a series of social reforms must be executed—reforms of fields such as social security, healthcare, education, and housing. Across the globe, these aspects demand heavy state investment, but China does not do so. In fields like these, in which the state ought to have made major investments, the wealthy have moved in. When social policy is not firmly in place, society is frequently sacrificed for the sake of rapid economic development. This has launched Chinese society into a vicious cycle: As economic development has grown ever more rapidly, the more society has disintegrated; and the more society has disintegrated, the less sustainable economic development has become.

Lastly, it is even more urgent to address an environment in which "the state is rich while the people are poor." If this doesn't change, government at all levels will devolve into what the academy calls "predatory governments." Efforts such as poverty relief, improving incomes, changing industrial structures (like encouraging the development of small and medium-sized enterprises), and tax reforms could change the current climate and bring about social equity. Only a just society is a truly stable society; only a just society provides the government with a high degree of law-based governance.

The same applies to politics. During the Reform and Opening Up, China's political success stemmed from its openness, and past successes came from the formation of a relatively open political process. Political processes were open to all social classes and profit interests; they were first opened to farmers, and then opened to urban residents, all departments of government, and all levels of government. The openness of politics created a huge impetus for reform. Why has current political reform become so difficult? The reason is quite simple: Political processes are not sufficiently open. If the political arena is insufficiently open, interest groups can easily form, and vested interests will inevitably hinder further reforms.

So how can we continue to promote reform? The key lies in increasing openness. After the mid-1990s, the political arena was opened to private entrepreneurs. This was as it should have been, since as new social groups emerge, they need to be included in the political process—consolidating the Party's base in society. The problem is that, in this process, other social groups should not be ignored. In the economic sector, chambers of commerce are becoming stronger and stronger. But what about labor unions? If unions don't achieve sufficient strength, workers will find themselves in a weak position in relation to business owners. Vulnerable groups, such as farmers, should also be allowed to organize. If economically strong groups can organize and participate in politics, but disadvantaged groups are not allowed to organize, relationships between the two will fall out of balance. The ruling party and the government should play a major role in maintaining a balance between powerful social groups and disadvantaged social groups, for this is the only way to ensure social stability and social order.

The way things are now, the more you want reform, the more barriers you find put up by the system itself. If you want to reform a system, you find that, to a large extent, you end up destroying the system in question while failing to achieve institutional innovation.

What's at the root of the problem? Deng Xiaoping argued for "crossing the river by feeling for the stones," but no one dares to feel for the stones. At present, every time a policy is promoted, interest groups exploit it for personal gain. And with every change, interest groups exploit the people even more. In housing reform, for example, housing prices are climbing higher and higher. The original intentions of the policy were good, but with every change, interest groups are provided with an opportunity to make piles of money. Other aspects of reform, like healthcare and education, have experienced similar fates. No matter what the agenda for a reform is, once a policy is held hostage by interest groups, it ends up running counter to the original intention.

In this regard, Deng Xiaoping was indeed a great man. During the early stages of the Reform and Opening Up, many vested interests blocked reform. So, early on, Deng didn't touch vested interests, but instead worked on creating new interests that could be used to bring the old interests to heel. Urban reform was difficult, so rural areas were first reformed. Reforming state-owned enterprises (SOEs) was very challenging, so Deng did not reform them at first—instead went beyond SOEs to help nurture a non-state-owned sector.

This was essentially how the Reform and Opening Up played out. As a result, vast new interests were produced, which were then used to defeat the old interests. This was where Deng Xiaoping succeeded. Currently China has not been sufficiently reformed. Those new interests that played a big role in the reform of the 1980s are now vested interests which resist further reform. Without strong political power, how can we make any improvements to the China Model? The only way forward is political openness. In order to ensure political openness, we can look to other countries. Most Western nations achieve political openness through a multiparty system. But the multiparty system is not the only means; there are other means available for ensuring political openness. For example, although Singapore has always been dominated by a single party, the nation has also consistently guaranteed openness in the system. Only openness can keep pressure on the political process; once political processes become sealed, they automatically become corrupt. China's ruling party has learned many lessons from both its own history and that of the historical changes in the Soviet Union and Eastern Europe. How does a ruling party ensure perpetual openness? This will always be the most serious challenge. But it's also clear that if you want to avoid corruption and radical changes in society, the ruling party must confront this challenge.

In short, we should neither hold up the China Model as the best in the world, one that should never be improved upon, nor should we lose all confidence in the China Model. The China Model is open. History never ends. Hegel believed that the then-rising Western nation-state was the ultimate form of statehood, but it didn't take long for the nation-state to produce severe war among European nation-states. Similarly, in the 1990s, Fukuyama believed that Western democracy represented the ultimate form of government and the end of history. But since the beginning of the twenty-first century, Western democracies have experienced massive crises. China has a history of openness and inclusivity, and the China Model is open. But it is only through openness that the China Model will prove sustainable and achieve permanence.

Foreword

The Rise of China and the China Model

The rise of the China Model, it can be said, has been tremendous for international relations in the twenty-first century. The China Model is a product of the policies of the Reform and Opening Up, but the concept of a "China Model" was proposed and debated during the twenty-first century. Since the Reform and Opening Up included two interdependent aspects, internal reform and external openness, when we discuss the China Model, we must explore the significance of the Reform and Opening Up in the context of the two dimensions of China and international developments. In other words, the China Model is not merely an event in Chinese history but is also an event within world history.

In order to probe the global significance of the Reform and Opening Up, we must approach it with an understanding of changes within the international context. Since the Reform and Opening Up and the international context cannot be separated, the Reform and Opening Up naturally had a profound impact on the international community. In particular, China's reforms demonstrate that the Reform and Opening Up was, from the beginning, part of the world's developmental experience. This is precisely why, from the beginning, the international community has paid more attention to China's reforms than it has to even Chinese society.

What does the Reform and Opening Up mean for the world? The question has differing significance in differing periods of reform. This can be seen in the shifts in the discourse of some Westerners about the Reform and Opening Up. When China first began its reforms at the beginning of the 1980s, on the one hand, Western society welcomed China, believing that the reforms would soon transform China into another Western-style state. But when Westerners finally realized that China would not become just like them, from the beginning of the 1990s, the West saw wave after wave of endless discussion of the "Chinese threat." Such discussions have broached notions of the threat of the Chinese military, the threat of the Chinese economy, and the threat of Chinese political uncertainty. Of course, if China is viewed as a threat, such a view gives rise to a variety of policies—such as "containment," "suppression," "competition," "hedging," and "engagement." Once Westerners realized that China's rise could not be suppressed or contained, and that in fact China was already powerful, Westerners proposed theories for managing China, such as the "great power theory" and the "stakeholder theory."

Regardless of the various reasons behind Western worries and suspicions about China, the existence of these worries demonstrates that the Reform and Opening Up is connected with the interests of the West. But if we only approach the global significance of the Reform and Opening Up from the perspective of the West's reactions to it, our understanding will be too narrow. No matter how China is currently positioning itself or how other countries are positioning China, the fact that the Reform and Opening Up occurred within China as a developing country suggests that China's experience offers material significance and value for other developing countries.

The China Model has been discussed in the West for many years. Although the Chinese government itself takes a low profile on the issue, abroad the debate continues unabated. In general, the China Model holds different meanings for Western, developed countries, and other developing countries. For many "third world" developing countries, the significance of the China Model is whether it can serve as an alternative to other models that have been implemented in the past. After World War II, the world's developmental models were basically divided into the Soviet Model and the Western Model. Now the Soviet Model has collapsed, leaving only the Western Model—which primarily refers to the American Model. Although European countries often advocate their own values and models in international affairs, they have lost the power to promote the spread of their models on the world stage. And in many ways, Europe is currently separating itself from the United States and trying to find its own model. Clearly, in terms of internal affairs, Europe has more socialist elements than the United States. When after the close of the Cold War, and the United States became the world's only superpower, it promoted its own model, the "Washington Consensus." However, neither Europe nor the United States have found great success in promoting their models abroad. Many developing countries that have adopted the Western Model have found that democratic politics cannot achieve the stability necessary for economic and social development. Under such circumstances, the China Model offers tremendous significance for developing countries.

If it provides more developmental experience for developing countries, this leads to questions about Western values—particularly those of the United States. For many Westerners, the China Model both challenges and competes with Western values. Their concern is not only with the great interest that many developing countries have exhibited in the China Model but also with the high regard that many in the West hold for it, now that they have lost faith in the Western Model and the Washington Consensus. Regardless, the recent debate surrounding whether the so-called "Beijing Consensus" has replaced the Washington Consensus has its origins in the West, not in China.

The significance that the China Model holds for China's development itself cannot be ignored. It has now been more than thirty years since the beginning of the Reform and Opening Up. Numerically speaking, thirty years is but a drop in the bucket of China's millennia of history, but when placed in the context of China's past and future, many will feel that these thirty years stand as a milestone of historical significance. That is to say, these thirty years have injected elements into the long stream of Chinese history that had never been seen before, and will thus have a massive impact on China's future. Thousands of years is a long time, but such historical moments are quite rare. No matter how you approach it, these thirty years have become a critical link in the chain of history. Furthermore, if we don't understand the thirty years that led up to the Reform and Opening Up, it will become even more difficult to understand the achievements of the past thirty years. Those previous thirty years can be understood as a "trial and error" approach to development, one which offered a wealth of experience for the subsequent thirty years. Thus, an understanding of the China Model should begin with the People's Republic of China and its founding, sixty years ago.

In terms of China's great history, the most profound significance of the Reform and Opening Up lies in its approach to national development, one that includes approaches to economic, social, and political development. Before China entered modernity, while periods of time may have been long, it mostly experienced simple forms of repetition. An agricultural society and dynastic changes were the most continuous features for millennia. It was only when China made contact with modernity and the powerful nations of the West that it began to experience fundamental changes in all aspects of life. To put it simply, prior the

Reform and Opening Up, whether under the reform movements of the late Qing, Sun Yat-sen, or Mao Zedong, the Chinese were in a state of constant revolution. At the center of this was the search for the precise form of the state that was to be built. Although the Communists led by Mao Zedong eventually established the People's Republic, what sort of state the Republic ought to be has always been a thorny question, and the answers to many questions could only be found in practice. "Continuous revolution" could well be said to be the main feature of the Republic in the thirty years leading up to Reform and Opening Up.

In the first thirty years, owing to the international situation of the time, while China did achieve some institutional innovations (such as the establishment of socialism and the break with the Soviet Union), it was still primarily characterized by a Soviet-style planned economy and an impoverished socialism, and the country remained isolated (whether actively or passively) outside of the international system. Those previous thirty years laid the foundations for a sovereign and independent state. As far as how to go about building such a state, it can only be said that those thirty years left behind many valuable and costly lessons and experiences for future generations. At the same time, we must also realize that, without the sovereign state that was built during those first thirty years, the achievements of the second thirty years would have been difficult to realize. And it is precisely because Mao Zedong provided China with so many highly valuable social practices that the post-Mao leaders of China have been able to take a completely different approach.

Those first thirty years demonstrated that a planned economy, high degrees of centralization, a lack of freedom, isolation, and an impoverished socialism were unworkable; this led both leading classes and all of Chinese society to be willing to pursue values such as marketization, decentralization, freedom, openness, and wealth. Although Deng Xiaoping vividly portrayed the Reform and Opening Up as "crossing the river by feeling for the stones," what he meant was that the pursuit of these values had some uncertainty to it—for the actual course to be taken was quite clear. This is a major reason why the Reform and Opening Up has never retreated in the face of numerous crises—for example, when the 1990s saw the collapse of the Soviet Union and the Eastern Bloc.

At the same time, China's approach to development has not involved binary oppositions. After abandoning the Soviet Model, China has not considered it necessary to adopt the Western Model. In this respect, China has exhibited a different approach from that of Russia and other Eastern European countries. Here it should be said that this independent approach is a kind of value in itself. Russia and the Eastern European countries adopted the Western Model in the hope that, through the implementation of radical reforms, they too could become

Western countries—but most of them have experienced economic recession and social unrest.

After implementing the shock therapy of radical reforms, for some time Russia won high praise from the West. But it wasn't long until Russia discovered that both Western-style markets and Western-style democracy were not easily adapted to Russia's social and economic development. It wasn't until Putin came to power and began implementing reforms that Russia began to address the corrupt practices that the radical reforms had brought. Once Putin began to do this, however, Russia was seen as backsliding, and the West began to criticize Russia again. After many numerous setbacks, Russian politicians and the public both realized that while democracy was a value worth pursuing in itself, it could not guarantee social or economic development. And if democracy cannot promote social and economic development, it will generate social dissatisfaction, and political power will have low levels of legitimacy.

The rise of the China Model is not only of interest to China's future development but also serves as an outstanding reference for other developing countries. However, even though there is already great interest in the China Model both in the academy and among policy researchers, and while the media has widely popularized the concept of the China Model, as yet there has been no serious academic research into the China Model itself. A proper understanding of the China Model clearly demands a great deal of time and effort.

The articles collected in this book represent my reflections on the China Model over a period of many years. These reflections are undertaken on several different levels, that include what the China Model is, how it has evolved, and what its future holds. When many researchers discuss the China Model, they often focus on what the China Model ought to be. During many years of research, I have not concerned myself too much with questions of ideals, since the question of how to develop is difficult to answer, and if such discussions become too abstract, they will not prove beneficial in practice. The articles collected here primarily represent empirical observations—that is, observations of the actual practice of China's development. I believe that it is only by observing China's practice and experience that we can come to understand the China Model, and it is only by understanding where this model came from that we can explain where it is going. To explain where the model came from, we must have a historical perspective and a comparative perspective.

In other words, in these articles I am attempting to examine the China Model from China's perspective (that is, a historical perspective) and an international perspective (that is, a comparative perspective). It should be emphasized that any discussion of the China Model demands sustained effort from participants. This is true, first of all, because, as described above, the general understanding of the China Model does not have any depth to it. Second, the China Model itself is still in the process of development and change. I am publishing these reflections primarily in order to spark more, and deeper, discussions.

CHAPTER ONE

Globalization and State Transitions: The West, Asia, and China

The emergence and development of the China Model was performed in a state of openness; that is, the China Model was deeply influenced by the external environment. While globalization weakens sovereign states in the West, globalization has promoted transitions within the Chinese state in many ways, enabling the sovereign state to grow even stronger. In many respects, globalization has generated many positive results in the establishment of the Chinese state, but it also poses a tremendous challenge to China's political system, for a market economy is ultimately an economy under the rule of law.

Globalization and China

The topic of globalization and state transitions can be said to possess great significance in two aspects: historical and policy. We can approach this topic in regard to the following aspects.

The first is the historical experience of globalization and state transitions. Historically speaking, globalization has often led to transitions in state institutions. Globalization is not novel. History has experienced several large waves of globalization. With every wave, globalization has first of all been an economic globalization driven by capital. Marx observed that the economy is a society's base and that state systems—particularly political systems—are a society's superstructure. When the economic base has changed, sooner or later the systems of the state will experience change and transition. Thus, before the emergence of modern capitalism, trade with distant nations was often connected to forms of the imperial state. But after the rise of the modern capitalist market economy, there arose a state system that was compatible with the market economy, a system which is the modern state. The contradictions that globally exist today in political, economic, and social systems are connected with the most recent wave of globalization. Every country now faces the major challenge of just how to reconstruct state systems in accordance with the needs of today's globalization.

The second aspect is the nature of the crisis the West is experiencing under the impact of globalization. With this wave of globalization, the West is undergoing a severe economic and political crisis. After the collapse of the Soviet Union, optimism prevailed, prompting Fukuyama to suggest that humanity had reached the "end of history." For Fukuyama, a democratic politics based in free, capitalist economies was the optimal system available for humanity. This can now no longer be said. Western academic and political circles have become very pessimistic.

All of the West is facing problems regarding economic, social, and political reform. At the level of the economy, major problems have emerged in both the manufacturing industry itself and financial capitalism, and economic structures have become severely unbalanced. This kind of structural reform cannot be achieved within a short span of time, nor is it clear in which direction today's West should move in its reforms. At the level of society, income differentiation has led to social stratification, and the well-being of the traditional middle class has become increasingly difficult to maintain. It was the middle class that launched the Occupy Wall Street movement with its target squarely planted on financial capitalism. Social movements have expressed public dissatisfaction, but they have proved unable to solve underlying problems.

How are these problems to be solved? There is no obvious answer. On the level of politics, the West is also experiencing a new wave of democratic crises. Despite the fact that, in the era of mass democracy, Western democracies have become increasingly populist, no Western country has been able to produce a strong government. Both economic crises and social crises demand the intervention of a strong government. But contemporary Western democracies are becoming increasingly partisan; ruling parties and opposition parties are well matched and mutually veto each other's policies. To adopt a phrase from Fukuyama, democratic politics has evolved into a "vetocracy."

This brings up a key question: Is the contemporary crisis in the West ultimately a crisis in capitalism or a crisis in state power? In both the West and

China, everyone is talking about a crisis in capitalism. Increasingly large numbers of people are growing pessimistic about capitalism. The point I'm making here is that, although capitalism is facing serious challenges, at the heart of the modern crisis is a crisis of state power in the West. Capitalism is an economic behavior that uses market mechanisms to maximize profits. Globalization is the globalization of capital and the globalization of markets. In this process, capital also maximizes profits. Therefore, whether we approach the matter in terms of market expansion or profit maximization, it is not the case that capitalism has produced any sort of crisis. On the contrary, it is state power which is in crisis. This is to say, state power has been unable to cope with globalized capitalism. This means that there must be a transformation in state power. Historically speaking, every transition in capitalism has brought with it a transition in state power. The major transitions we have seen in democracy were also driven by capitalism. So how is democracy going to transition under this new wave of globalization? This question has no answer, but it does demand our consideration.

The third aspect is any question about China's state-building in the era of globalization. The developmental model we see today in China is also closely linked to globalization. China's development has been a product of the Reform and Opening Up, while China's reform has also been its globalization. In fact, the impetus for many of China's internal reforms has come from external reform and openness. On the one hand, we must join the international system. Modern Chinese history demonstrates that isolation does not offer a way forward. We must develop; thus, we must open up. On the other hand, openness has also brought with it many negative consequences. Thus, while we are globalizing, we must also erect a Great Wall of Steel to avoid being consumed by globalization. In this current wave of globalization, we have already experienced enough to prove that, if the negative effects brought about by globalization cannot be digested, not only will we fail to hold onto the fruits of globalization but also the state itself may easily descend into a crisis.

Globalization offers countries two choices. First, you can reject globalization. This means falling behind and failing to develop. Ultimately, it means putting yourself at the mercy of others. Here, North Korea is an example. In reality, with the exception of a few countries like North Korea, most countries cannot avoid this wave of globalization. The second choice is joining globalization. This choice offers both tremendous benefits and gigantic risks. The risks can be seen in the experience of Thailand and Indonesia during the 1997 Asian financial crisis and in the experience of the West during the 2008 financial crisis.

Which path should China choose? We have already chosen to join globalization. There is no backing out now. As Deng Xiaoping said at the time, we must grasp globalization "with both hands." In a new environment, we can understand these "two hands" a little differently. We must "grasp the economy with one hand and grasp politics with the other." In "grasping the economy," we must more actively integrate and promote globalization. In "grasping politics," we must pay careful attention to the building of state systems. We must not only ensure that globalization brings positive results but also utilize globalization to promote transitions in state systems. In other words, as in other countries, globalization in China demands a restructuring of state power.

This also touches on questions that have been under discussion in recent years. During this global economic crisis, China has, in comparison with the West, dealt with the crisis' impact on itself relatively well. And for many years, China has become the world's most effective force for recovery and growth. At home and abroad, debates over the China Model are both political and ideological. Although there is considerable debate in academia over the China Model, I still hold that the China Model truly exists. To put it simply, regardless of how it develops, China remains China, China's economy will not evolve into America's economy, and China's politics will not evolve into America's politics.

But even in the West, many people (mostly those politicians with a strong grasp of reality) have begun to realize that a China Model does exist, and that China therefore possesses valuable experience that others can learn from. The West has always looked down upon non-Western models; it has always viewed its own developmental model as universal in scope. But under the profound crisis occurring in the West, the West is beginning to have the motivation to consider non-Western models. With the rise of the non-West, this trend will prove unstoppable.

During this process, China's developmental model is playing a key role, and it is of particular importance for other developing countries. China has achieved so much economic success in such a short span of time, and this has piqued the interest of many developing countries. However, the China Model also faces daunting challenges. How should China go about improving its own developmental model? The improvement of the China Model has implications, not only for China itself but also for other nations. China must not only learn from other countries' successes with globalization but even more so from other countries' failures.

Of course, acknowledging the existence of a China Model does not demand advocating the China Model. I have always emphasized that the China Model is not the "Beijing Consensus." The theory of the "Beijing Consensus" was proposed in light of gathering doubts about the "Washington Consensus," and the theory implied that China had something to learn from the West, which it could then share with other countries. To my mind, if China had sought to emulate the West, the China Model would certainly have failed. But if other countries appropriate China's experience in accordance with their own local conditions, the China Model will prove workable. It's quite possible that the China Model could go global. The China Model is relevant for the rest of the world because it was produced and developed within a globalized environment. If the model had been produced in a state isolated from globalization, then the China Model would have little relevance for the rest of the world.

In a state of globalization, China has learned some of the best practices of other countries; this has enabled it to promote institution building in all aspects of its economy, society, and politics. Thus, the China Model is the product of globalization, and it also faces the challenges of globalization. For China, a serious question remains of how to continue integrating into the international community while avoiding the crises in state power that globalization can set off.

Capital, the State, and Globalization: A Short History

The modern state or modern nation-state originated in Western Europe. Previously, there were primarily two forms of states in the world: imperial and localized regimes. Imperial rule was relatively weak in character, and it lacked a complete set of state institutions. Empires contended primarily for either land or people, and they found their economic base in agriculture. Some studies have demonstrated that empires promoted "globalization" within their imperial territory. Historically speaking, empires often consisted of many localized regimes that could even be extended across several continents. After an empire was created, trade barriers within the empire were frequently eliminated. Thus, it has been said that empires were the first wave of globalization. But empires never had a complete set of institutions to support them. When empires disintegrated, localized forms of government returned.

In Europe, the market economy rose from the ruins of a disintegrated empire. The market economy worked from the small to the large, from one region to another. It was a bottom-up movement. The institution that is now called "capitalism" was born alongside market mechanisms. Once there is a market, capital can operate and function. In academic circles, there is no single definition of the concept of "capitalism." Everyone can agree, however, that capitalism has two major characteristics: One is the existence of market mechanisms, and the other is capital's pursuit of profit. The former is the condition, and the latter is the result. Once there are market systems, investors can pursue profits, and the expansion of profits can provide the impetus for capital to further expand the market.

Marx scientifically observed that capital is the pursuit of profit. Capital's infinite pursuit of profit means that, once unleashed, capital must necessarily become the major impetus for globalization. The globalization of capital begins within every country. Capital's first requirement is a unified domestic market. When the market itself fails to eliminate various highly localized regimes and thereby produce a unified market, capital looks to the aid of the state. In Europe, absolute monarchies rose in response to this demand. For a relatively long period of time, autocracies played extremely important roles, often employing force to destroy various isolated nations and creating unified domestic markets. This was the origin of the modern nation-state.

After capital unified national markets with the help of autocracies, it began to develop overseas markets. This was a period in which capital began to open up overseas markets. This was also a bloody process. China has personal experience of this process through the two Opium Wars. Politically speaking, the development of overseas markets was often accompanied by colonialist regimes. Colonialist regimes not only served to help develop overseas markets but also protected the overseas interests of colonial countries. The expansion and globalization of capital were both issues that were studied by Marx. Of course, there are differing interpretations of this process. For example, the British economist Adam Smith and others have interpreted this process from the perspective of comparative advantage. This is to say, every country has its own comparative advantage. Through free trade, one can use one's own comparative advantage to create wealth. And it cannot be denied that every country does have its own comparative advantages. But comparative advantage is not in itself powerful enough to drive globalization. If this process had primarily been driven by comparative advantage, then globalization would have been a peaceful process. Comparative advantage alone has difficulty explaining why globalization has been such a sanguinary process.

With the help of state power, the capitalists, or the bourgeoisie, unified national markets and opened up overseas markets. As markets grew larger, profits grew greater, and capital itself grew more powerful. As markets expanded, capitalists began demanding political power. They thus began to demand a share in the state's power that could stand alongside monarchs and aristocrats. The main objective of power-sharing was using laws to protect their interests and prevent political power from seizing their economic interests. These were the origins of Western democratic politics as well as the source of private property rights. The capitalists or the bourgeoisie were also the first social group to fight for democracy, and Marx thus described democracy as "bourgeois democracy."

The famous quip of the American historian Barrington Moore, "No bourgeoisie, no democracy," is an apt summary of this historical fact. The period of transition from monarchy and aristocracy to bourgeois democracy (or elite democracy) was the most important stage in the formation of Western society. In other words, before the advent of mass democratization in the West, most state systems, particularly legal systems, were already in place. These state systems also laid the institutional foundations for future mass democracies. This point will receive greater emphasis later.

Globalization and the "De-sovereignization" of Economic Activities

Following the close of the Cold War, the wave of globalization that we have experienced has represented a new form of globalization, and Western capital remains the main driver behind this wave of globalization. But why is this wave of globalization throwing the entire West into crisis? Here we need to find an adequate way to think about the development of both capitalism and its state systems. The question we need to answer is: "How has globalization led to a crisis in state power?" We can approach three different aspects of this question.

The first is a consideration of the tremendous changes within capitalism itself. This aspect can be divided into two further aspects. The first involves a change in the nature of capital, which primarily involved transitioning from an industrial capitalism centered on manufacturing to a financial capitalism centered on finance. The second aspect of changes within capitalism is the transition within manufacturing itself from industrial capitalism to post-industrial capitalism. Now, however, both financial capitalism and manufacturing capitalism operate in a globalized environment. The global capitalism we are discussing today is primarily financial and manufacturing capitalism.

So what is the difference between global capitalism and traditional capitalism? Phrased differently, what has been the ultimate impact that economic globalization has had on capitalism? Simply put, traditional capitalism is a sovereign economy, while global capitalism is an economy that transcends the borders of sovereign states. The economies we have previously discussed—whether localized economies, imperial economies, or modern economies—all have borders. In other words, their economic activities occur within defined boundaries. Even the economic globalization that occurred in Marx's time was mainly limited to trade—that is, products are exchanged for the products of others, products are produced by sovereign states, and trade transcends national borders. In other words, in sovereign economies, most factors in production can be controlled by the state. The main factors of production defined by classical economists include labor, land, and capital. All of these factors occur within the borders of a state and can be controlled by it. But globalization has changed everything dramatically, and it has had a vast impact on all aspects of society.

The first impact has been on economic ethics. Although the purpose of capital is profit, ethics has always been an important component of capital operation. Such an ethics proceeds from different aspects. In his *Theory of Moral Sentiments*, Adam Smith implied that, as humans have a moral dimension, entrepreneurs or capitalists have a moral dimension. The German sociologist Max Weber's *The Protestant Ethic and the Spirit of Capitalism* approached the moral aspects of capitalism from a religious perspective. Weber held that the virtues of traditional capitalism (such as thrift and industry) were connected with religion (primarily Protestant ethics). There, profit and money-making were only a means for personal salvation, since Christianity teaches that everyone is in original sin.

However, I personally think that the economic ethics of capital and sovereign states are connected. Regardless of whether we're investigating human moral nature or religious factors, all ethics arises from the interaction between differing people and differing social groups. The economic ethics of capital is generated by the interaction and exchange between capitalists and employees. Within sovereign economies, many factors facilitate the generation of ethics between capitalists and employees—factors such as the same religious beliefs, a unified nation, a unified language, and similar skin color. Marx observed the exploitative nature of capital, and he advocated an internationalism that called for a united rising of the whole world's working class or proletariat. He did not, however, achieve his aims. Some have said that in the contest between internationalism and nationalism, nationalism has come out on top. In other words, finding compromises between the bourgeoisie and the employees within one country is much easier than achieving cooperation among the proletariat of many countries. Here are some of my own observations.

A few years ago, when I conducted research in Guangdong and Zhejiang, I found that Guangdong had more foreign capital while Zhejiang had more domestic capital. At the same time, Guangdong had far more labor disputes than Zhejiang. I found that, in Zhejiang, relations were better between investors and hired workers, for most firms hired either local workers or workers from other parts of China, and thus it was much easier to produce a mutual understanding between management and labor. Management could not excessively exploit the locals; otherwise, the social reputation of management would be quite poor. In Guangdong, however, most foreign investment came from Hong Kong, Taiwan, South Korea, and Japan. It was difficult for management and labor there to have a sense of shared identity, and relations were often quite poor.

The example of Zhejiang shows how economic ethics plays out in sovereign economies, while the example of Guangdong demonstrates a decline in ethics in a globalized context. Globalization demonstrates that a global market has been formed, and the existence of this market shows that all the factors in production can be internationalized. It is the essence of capital to employ the global market in pursuit of maximum profits. The existence of cheap labor in international markets is an important driver in capital flows, but since foreign workers are the ones who are employed, the constraints of economic ethics on capitalists have been greatly reduced or have even completely disappeared.

It's easy to see how, as China became a center for international manufacturing, it necessitated becoming a center for "sweatshops." In academia, there has been quite a lot of research into this aspect. To put it simply, a "sweatshop" has a lack of worker rights. Such a lack is due not only to the absence or incompleteness of China's labor protection system but also to the absence of moral constraints in capitalists' dealings with foreign workers. In reality, in the absence of moral constraints, no legal or regulatory system can check the capitalist. Foxconn cannot easily treat mainland Chinese workers the same way it treats Taiwanese workers. A vast body of empirical research demonstrates that many well-known multinational companies, once they enter China, gradually reduce their corporate social responsibility—until it ultimately disappears.

Second, globalization also exerts a tremendous impact on employment. In the era of the sovereign economies, industrial development occurred within boundaries—that is, within the borders of sovereign states—and it generated employment. But globalization has brought dramatic changes to this dynamic. Globalization is the global flow of elements in production. For some technological industries, the technologies owned by corporations and the workers employed by corporations can be separated from one another. In a sovereign economy, "Made in Germany" means products manufactured using German technology and employing German workers, while "Made in Japan" means products manufactured using Japanese technology and employing Japanese workers. Here, technology produces two products: the first is industry, and the second is employment.

In the era of globalization, however, it often happens that a technology is owned by a company in Country A, while the product is manufactured by workers in Country B. Simply put, in an era of globalization, a technology can generate neither industry nor employment. During the era of sovereign economies, American technology created American industries and an American working class. Today, however, while the United States still owns technology, its industry and workers have moved to other countries. So where is American industry? And where is the working class? American industry is in the Pearl River Delta, and the majority of the American working class are Chinese migrant workers.

On the one hand, technology is not generating industry and employment, and on the other hand, manufacturing brings employment without products. For example, American technology can bring manufacturing or processing to China, but China does not keep anything that it has produced. In fact, China is the world's largest manufacturing center, but what products has China itself produced?

In terms of employment, although manufacturing has created a vast number of opportunities for China, since this employment does not possess the above-mentioned moral factors, employment can easily turn into a disguised system of labor slavery in sweatshops. In the era of sovereign economies, it could be said that manufacturing not only created a huge working class but also gradually created a vast middle class. As technology advances, wages constantly rise, eventually creating a middle class. Industrial workers are the most important segment of the Western middle class. Under the conditions of globalization, however, manufacturing has had difficulty in bringing industrial workers into the middle class, since capitalists either push to keep reducing wages or maintain permanently low wages. The Pearl River Delta has been employing migrant workers for decades, but how many of these migrant workers have transitioned into the middle class? It took about twenty years for the industrialization of Japan and Asia's "Little Dragons" to cultivate a huge middle class. But this has not happened in the Pearl River Delta.

One of the main reasons for this is the globalization of economic activity. The economic launch of the Little Dragons occurred in the era of sovereign economies, while China's economic launch occurred during the era of globalization. Globalization has also had a great impact on the taxation of sovereign states. From the foregoing discussion, we can see that economic activity has been globalized to the extent that there really are no sovereign borders.

Yet governments continue to exercise sovereignty. In fact, the popularization of democracy (that is, mass democracy) and the rise of nationalism have greatly strengthened the sovereignty of governments. In the past, sovereign states and sovereign economies overlapped with one another, but now the two are separate. When the two overlap, it's relatively easy for sovereign states to tax sovereign economies. Thus far, the tax systems of every state have also been products of traditional sovereign economies. In a globalized context, companies can evade taxes through a "transnational" approach. For some, one of the major goals of transnational companies, besides that of seeking investment objectives through cheap labor costs, is the evasion of the taxation of their own governments. After the globalization of economic activity, the tax base of governments representing sovereign states has been greatly reduced. Just how to design new tax systems for a globalized era is a major challenge facing all sovereign states. Some countries in the West, since they experienced economic globalization relatively early, at least have consciously levied taxes on globalized economic activities. For example, the United States, Canada, and European countries have differing taxation mechanisms. Nevertheless, these taxation mechanisms are problematic, and it has been difficult to effectively tax overseas economic activity. Even more seriously, globalized conditions have made it difficult for sovereign governments to levy high taxes on their own companies and wealthy classes, for once tax burdens are increased, these companies and wealthy individuals can choose to leave. This is a predicament that the American government is currently facing.

Globalization has impacted on taxation and thus income distribution within sovereign states. The market is the most effective mechanism for creating wealth, and the larger the market, the greater the wealth. Economic globalization has created a global market. Indeed, this wave of globalization has brought vast wealth to many countries. But at the same time when global wealth has grown dramatically, income disparities have also grown increasingly larger. One marked feature of globalization has been that, since the beginning of this wave of globalization, all countries and regions involved in globalization have seen growing disparities in income. In other words, rates of globalization and rates of growth in income disparity have been simultaneous.

As globalization has occurred with increasing speed, so have wage gaps. In Asia, this has been most obvious in the economies of the Four Little Dragons. During the process of modernization, the Four Little Dragons achieved both economic growth and equitable income distribution at the same time, and they have been considered a model of equitable economic growth by the international community. However, this is no longer the case. Globalization has also caused severe inequalities in the income distribution of these economies. So how has globalization influenced income distribution?

First of all, there has been a failure in the secondary distribution of income. The secondary distribution of income through taxation policies is the most important tool for resolving income disparities between social groups or regions. On the one hand, governments regulate economic development with their tax policies (for example, by offering tax incentives to increase investor motivation), while on the other hand governments can also guarantee basic social equity. As discussed above, however, companies can evade taxation through "transnational" forms, thereby effectively restricting the taxation functions of sovereign governments and leading to failures in the secondary distribution of income. Failures in the secondary distribution of income inevitably exacerbate a society's income distribution.

Second, globalization has led to a failure in primary distribution. Where has all the wealth generated by globalization gone? In any country, primary distribution is more important than secondary distribution, since primary distribution is structural in nature while secondary distribution is policy driven. For the most part, secondary distribution only serves as a supplement to primary distribution. When primary distribution fails, no efforts at secondary distribution can avail. Developed nations in Europe and North America have long striven to achieve basic equity in primary distribution through first promulgating antitrust laws and encouraging the development of small and medium-sized enterprises (SMEs) and then employing secondary distribution to improve equality. Japan and the Four Little Dragons have pursued similar policies. Then why has globalization led to a failure in primary distribution?

One reason is that antitrust mechanisms for domestic companies have become irrelevant. Today's transnational companies are getting bigger and bigger, and their economic activities are global in scope. But although these companies are enormous, in a geographic sense they are thinly distributed across differing sovereign states. The greater their monopolies, the more inequitable the distribution.

The second reason is that there have been changes in the relationship between ownership and management. Initially, ownership and management were one, and there were no issues in distribution. Later, as companies grew in size, the two separated so that owners hired professionals to manage their businesses. At this point, owners still retained greater power than their managers. But globalization has put managers in the driver's seat.

There have been at least three factors involved in this development. The first is a weakening in the power of ownership. In many cases, ownership is actually a collective—that is, one company has many shareholders. Investors in a corporation, for example, could be said to be its owners. As a collective of shareholders, the power of ownership is diffused. The second factor is the decentralization of corporate investment. Modern corporations, especially transnational companies, often invest in a variety of fields. The third factor is the globalization of corporate structures. On many occasions, the second and third factors overlap with each other. These environmental shifts have made modern corporations extremely complex. And this in turn increases a demand for managers with a professional background. Thus the modern economy has frequently seen "workers" (that is, managers) defeat owners in contests of power.

Recently, especially in the financial sector, managers in transnational companies have often received huge salaries and bonuses. On many occasions, these managers have continued to receive large bonuses even when the corporations themselves have been losing money. Despite the fact that this phenomenon has led to widespread dissatisfaction, it has persisted—for corporations cannot afford to lose these managers. Once these managers are lost, corporations are doomed. Under such circumstances (whether they are real or imagined), managers can easily hijack corporations. Massive amounts of the wealth of such corporations enter the pockets of managers and not ownership.

The third reason is that great changes have also taken place in labor relations. Earlier we discussed the separation of labor and capital within sovereign spaces (that is, how corporations can employ foreign workers). This is to say, because foreign workers do not need to be paid adequate wages, a large amount of the wealth created by foreign workers goes to employers and management. This has also exacerbated disparities in income distribution. This aspect will receive more treatment below.

Financial Capitalism and Its Globalization

The transformation of financial capitalism needs particular emphasis. It was emphasized above that globalization has always been driven by capital. The most recent wave of globalization has been no different. To a great extent, the globalization of manufacturing has also been driven by the globalization of financial capitalism. Here we must note that financial capitalism has taken the place of manufacturing (that is, industrial) capitalism as the main form of modern capitalism. Especially in countries such as Britain and the United States, as manufacturing has shifted to other countries, the financial industry has become the primary industry. Although other countries such as Germany, France, and Italy still retain manufacturing, they are being increasingly affected by financial capitalism.

Financial capitalism occupies a dominant position and exerts a tremendous impact on the real economy. Financial capitalism has a long history, but today's financial capitalism is quite different from traditional financial capitalism, although both pursue the maximization of profits. First of all, their scales are different. The scale of today's financial capital cannot be compared with the financial capital of the past. In addition, traditional financial capitalism provided a service for substantial entities, that is, industrial capitalism; it also provided financing for corporations. But the goal of today's financial capitalism is self-inflation—that is to say, finance exists in order to gather more capital. The purpose of capital is capital itself, "making money from money." Of course, financial capital is still invested in the real economy, but here financial capital is the subject, and the real economy has become the object. In the past, financial capital was more dependent on the real economy, but the contemporary situation is the reverse. The real economy is highly dependent on financial capital, and financial capital can exist independently of the real economy.

Financial capitalism has also produced the series of negative effects that we discussed above. One of these is a theoretical problem. Financial capitalism has proved far more demoralizing than manufacturing. In fact, the financial industry has always been seen as speculation. The global financial crisis that began in 2008 demonstrated just how far financial capitalism had developed: it had created countless derivative instruments to produce self-inflation, and opportunism or speculation has become a central value of financial capital.

The second negative effect is that financial capital does not generate employment. This has also proved worse than conditions under manufacturing. It is because of globalization that today's manufacturing does not generate employment, while the modern financial industry essentially lacks employment opportunities. The traditional financial industry generated a vast number of employment opportunities, primarily in the form of intermediaries. In the West, professionals in the financial industry were an important source of the middle class. Today, however, this vast number of professionals has been replaced by computers. In the financial world, there are only a few big bosses and a small number of staff who operate computers, the so-called "financial engineers." In some cases, the financial industry not only fails to generate employment but actually hinders employment. For example, some technological innovations could have been transformed into industries, thereby generating employment. But if financial capital believes that a certain technology will have a negative impact on the industry it controls, financial capital will deploy its enormous financial resources to buy out this technology and prevent it from creating jobs.

Third, the financial industry evades state taxation. This is really no different from the case of the manufacturing industry that was previously discussed, but in the financial industry the problem is even more acute. Financial capital is more globalized than manufacturing, with the power to flow to every corner of the world. Fourth, the financial industry has exacerbated income disparities. There can be no disagreement on this point: just look at Wall Street and everything becomes clear.

Even more significantly, global financial capitalism has produced a monetization movement that is global in scope. As Marx observed, it is the characteristic of capital to commoditize everything for the sake of trade. In order to maximize profits, financial capitalism desperately demands that everything be monetized. The reason is simple. Only through monetization can everything come under the domain of financial circulation. Financial capitalism therefore demands that sovereign states relinquish their control over all financial activities—for example, by demanding the opening of capital accounts. In fact, during this wave of globalization, financial capitalism has become the primary ideology of neoliberal economics. In order to monetize things, financial capital has not hesitated to work alongside authoritarian regimes to implement large-scale privatization efforts. Privatization is the necessary first step; for once privatization has occurred, private individuals can monetize objects.

Global financial capitalism has actually created immense financial empires. These financial empires control extremely vast amounts of money, which can vie with the funds held by any one sovereign state. As these empires constitute the heart of globalization, they pose a serious threat to more and more sovereign states. We can think of financial capitalism as an ever-growing river. If a sovereign state cannot link up with this river, then the river will never flow into a country, perhaps making it impossible for that country to develop. However, if a country is linked to the river, and there are no effective levees to prevent the river from flooding, then the country will be washed away in a flood. In other words, if a state lacks strong institutional mechanisms, financial capitalism can overwhelm a country's financial systems and cause wealth to be swept away by the flood.

Globalization and Weak Governments

Another observable phenomenon is the worldwide appearance of weak governments after the arrival of this current wave of globalization. Regardless of the systems countries may have previously adopted—whether democratic or authoritarian, whether unitary or federal—weak governments have been a widespread phenomenon. In North America and Europe, where some countries have traditionally been defined by democracy, contemporary democracies have had difficulty in forming strong governments or even effective governments. In the Arab world, movements of social protest (labeled by some as "democracy movements") continue to paralyze governments. In Asia, Japanese political turmoil is well-known (with five governments formed within six years). Countries like Thailand, the Philippines, and Malaysia are facing political instability. Even Singapore, which features one-party rule, is facing challenges, including those posed on social media.

How has globalization weakened the governments of sovereign states? Here the West is fairly representative. Globalization occurred first in the West, and the problems it has generated there are emblematic. Since the 1980s, many Western scholars have begun to observe the challenge that economic globalization poses to sovereign states. In fact, just as we previously discussed, the disappearance of economic sovereignty has weakened sovereign governments. All of the factors mentioned above—such as the disappearance of economic ethics, the difficulty of employment, and the reduction of taxes collected—have contributed to the weakening of sovereign governments. If these are economic factors, then transitions in Western democracy are serving to weaken sovereign governments politically.

Historically speaking, democracy in the West has gone through three major stages, or three major transitions, and each transition has not strengthened governments, but weakened them.

In the history of Western democracy, the first wave of democratization could be said to be the democratization of the bourgeoisie. Prior to democratization, the West mainly featured monarchy and aristocracy. The bourgeoisie were the first social group capable of sharing power with monarchs and the aristocracy. The first wave of democracy was what Marx called bourgeois democracy—that is, elite democracy. During the stage of bourgeois democracy, democracies and the economic system of capitalism cooperated very well—that is, governments and capital had a good relationship with one another. As Marx noted, regimes were themselves produced by the bourgeoisie, with the former being the representatives of the latter. Economically speaking, this rather long period in the history of democracy belongs to the stage of primitive capitalism. Governments and capital often worked together to exploit the working class (laborers). This kind of "dog eat dog" capitalism can be well seen in the depictions of writers such as Marx, Dickens, and Hugo.

The driver behind the second wave of Western democratization was the working class. In pursuit of profits, the bourgeoisie vigorously developed industry and broadly expanded markets. As a result, not only were vast amounts of wealth created but also a gigantic working class or proletariat was brought forth. In its early stages, this working class was exploited by the bourgeoisie, but as it grew increasingly organized, its popular strength grew ever greater. The working class began to share power with the bourgeoisie; they made demands for reforms, such as improved working conditions, and higher wages. The movements of the working class began to exert political influence. This influence on Western democracy cannot be overstated. We can examine it through the following aspects.

To begin with, Western democracies began to transition from elite (bourgeois) democracies to mass democracies. Leaning on their sheer political numbers, the working class demanded political participation and the right to universal suffrage. Following the bourgeoisie, the working class also became a social group involved in the political process. Second, the working class exerted its influence by making changes in labor relations. Previously, governments and capital worked together to exploit laborers. After the rise of the working class, governments began separating from capital. This separation was in the interest of both capital and workers. For capital, this separation helped governments play a more neutral role between capital and labor, serving to reduce conflict between labor and capital and helping find common interests between the two. This was particularly apparent in the institutional arrangements of corporatism.

Next, the separation of government and capital spurred the establishment of regulatory regimes in Western governments. This was highly significant. During the stage of primitive capitalism, the bourgeoisie were only interested in profit; they completely disregarded the interests of workers, consumers, and society. Everything we see in modern China once existed in the West: the pollution, the industrial accidents, the contaminated food, etc. But with the separation of government and capital, governments began to be able to create systems that could regulate the operation of capital. Obviously, once this separation had begun, governments had to base their power in the votes of workers, a trend which continued to reduce the dependence of political power on capital. Without this separation, and without the support of the working class for government power, Western regulatory governments would not have emerged.

Finally, in terms of social systems, the West began transitioning from primitive capitalism to welfare capitalism. The sole aim of capital is profit. The West's transition from primitive capitalism to welfare capitalism was not driven by capital itself; rather, it was a product of political and social reforms, and the movements of the working class played a major role.

It stands to reason that socialism originated in the West. Socialist movements aimed to establish social systems such as social security, healthcare, education, and public housing. Of course, these goals were not achieved all at once but were realized through long-term development. The early socialist movement was also limited to basic labor protections and wages. If the development of capitalism created a set of market systems in the West, then the development of socialism created a set of state social systems.

Marx was only half-right when he said that the bourgeoisie were their own gravediggers. The bourgeoisie produced and cultivated their own competitors—the working class—but the working class was not destined to become the gravedigger of the bourgeoisie. In the countries where capitalism first developed, the rise of the working class not only failed to bury the bourgeoisie but actually rescued and spurred the bourgeoisie to develop in another direction—namely, humanitarian capitalism. Socialist movements led to the establishment of social systems that safeguarded the basic interests of workers, thereby ensuring social stability, while social stability provided a social basis for the continued development of capitalism. At the same time, capital no longer relied solely on the exploitation of the working class; instead, it transitioned into relying on innovations in technology and management. Improvements in the technology and management of industrial capitalism also led to the transition of workers from unskilled to skilled workers. In this process, the proletariat of former days was transformed into a middle class. Social systems and a middle class are the buttress or foundations of a consumer society. Thus, Western economies also possessed sufficient capacity for continued development.

However, in countries like the Soviet Union and China, that developed later than the West, the working class became the gravedigger of the bourgeoisie. In these countries, state power did not act as a coordinator between capital and labor as it had in the West but rather stood in solidarity with labor. The integration of state power with labor constituted a tremendous force, one that eliminated capital and the markets on which it depended. Of course, in these countries, the power of capital had never been very strong—so once capital was eliminated, these countries were forced down the road of a planned economy. But once capital had been destroyed, who would develop the economy? Once markets had been destroyed, how could an economy be developed?

History would later demonstrate that planned economies ultimately lead to what the economist Hayek called "the road to serfdom." Without the heart and driving power for economic development, poverty was inevitable. It's not hard to understand how the planned economies of the Soviet Union, Eastern Europe, and China led to widespread poverty—impoverished socialism. Socialism was meant to make economic development fairer and more sustainable, but impoverished socialism was ultimately headed on a path of self-destruction. Sovereign states that achieved Soviet-style impoverished socialism were defeated in competition with Western countries. And in the late 1970s, China began to return to a market economy, thereby avoiding a fate like that of the Soviet Union. (This will be discussed in more detail later.)

The third wave of Western democracy is mass democracy. The bourgeoisie created a working class, and the working class entered the political process, making the mass democratization of Western democracy inevitable. Since then, many social groups, including women and minorities, have entered the political process through various social movements (such as the Civil Rights Movement in the United States), and the process of mass democratization has, in theory at least, been completed. Many today associate many rights with democratization.

Historically speaking, it is true that many rights—particularly the political rights of citizens—have emerged with democratization. However, we need to pay attention to two issues. To begin with, as has been previously discussed, many aspects of rights, especially economic and social rights, had been realized before democratization. Many aspects of the formation of social systems in the West occurred before mass democratization—even during the stage of authoritarianism. The most outstanding cases of this are the establishment of France's educational system during the Napoleonic Era and the creation of Germany's social security system under the oversight of "Iron Chancellor" Bismarck. It can be said that the vast majority of basic state systems in the West are not intimately connected to mass democracy.

Thus, I've always emphasized that the building of state systems occurs before democratization. Most state systems must be established before mass democracy. Otherwise, after democratization, it's highly likely that they will cease to exist. Democratization can generate tremendous political energy; but this political energy can effectively destroy existing systems, while it cannot build new systems with equal effectiveness. Historically speaking, democratic politics has not made many significant contributions to the construction of state systems. The United States offers an example that is a prototypical democracy. Most of its institutions were created by the political leadership of the Founders; subsequently, they were only tinkered with. It wasn't until the Great Depression, when social and economic turmoil threatened the survival of the regime, that the United States took advantage of the crisis and created a social security system.

After the financial crisis of 2008, the American government also attempted to establish a system for medical insurance, but the government encountered great difficulties and the project faces an uncertain future. Perhaps the crisis hasn't been sufficiently severe. When a crisis does not pose a serious threat to a regime, it is difficult for all the political forces concerned to compromise, and major reforms do not readily find success. In fact, democracy is an extremely conservative system. In democratic politics, the interests of all parties can be expressed, but it's extremely difficult for any of them to make major compromises. So a democratic system is very good at maintaining the status quo.

The second point I'd like to emphasize is that the rights granted by democratic politics are mostly theoretical and legal in nature, not actual. Democratic politics emphasizes a whole series of human aspirations such as equality, freedom, and political participation, but this does not mean that democracy will automatically realize these rights. The reason is simple. In order to achieve these rights, there must first exist many preconditions. Democratic politics guarantees equality of opportunity through its laws, but the reality remains one of inequality. While it is true that, after the advent of mass democracy, the various pre-existing state systems have become more egalitarian and have brought assistance to disadvantaged social classes, this has not meant that the rights of everyone are truly equal on the practical level. Democracy is a system that provides cover for *de facto* inequality with theoretical and legal equality. Therefore, even in the countries held to be the most democratic, we can observe various social groups demanding equal rights through social movements. The feminist movement and ethnic minority movements are two examples.

Mass democracy has exerted a tremendous influence on the economies and politics of the West. During the stage of elite (bourgeois) democracy, political and economic systems collaborated with each other without major conflict. In the early days of mass democracy, the government began to disassociate itself from capital and identify itself more with society at large, but governments could still transcend capital and society and serve as a mediator between the two. In the age of mass democracy, however, governments quickly identified themselves with society. At its core, mass democracy is a democracy in which everyone gets one vote. If politicians want political power, they must first get enough votes. Clearly, society will get far more votes than capital. This has made today's mass democracy increasingly populist in character.

In welfare states, mass democracy's negative impacts on the economy have become increasingly marked. To a large extent, democracy has evolved into an auction house for welfare policy. This leaves the question: Who will pay the bill? Regardless of their own country's particular economy, the West's politicians can no longer maintain the burdens of the welfare state; yet, they continue to commit to high levels of welfare in order to win votes. At the same time, most social groups are not taking a long-term view, and they are unwilling to surrender any of their interests. Where is the money for high levels of welfare going to come from? The West borrows money from the common people, other countries, or the future. High levels of welfare are at the root of the crisis in Europe.

What's absurd is that it is equally difficult for mass democracy to form strong governments—especially in the era of globalization. As has been previously discussed, in an era of globalization, government taxation policies have become problematic. One aspect of this is the globalization of domestic capital, but governments do not have effective mechanisms to collect tax from capital flowing abroad. Even worse, governments also have great difficulty levying taxes on the capitalists within their own countries, since high taxes force capitalists to flee overseas. The only thing that governments can do is continue to tax the middle class. At the same time, under the pressures of the globalization of manufacturing and finance, the life of the middle class has become strained. It's hard for governments to tax the middle class with their support. Furthermore, the development of Western democracy has been to this day a system of mutual vetoes. This is connected with the conservative nature of democracy. Because various interests can be mobilized, if interests are relatively balanced, then no one party will be able to form a majority, and mutual vetoes will result.

Globalization, capital outflows, underemployment, excessive welfare, and weak governance are all the results of structural imbalances and economic and political imbalances in the West. This shows that the economic and political systems of the West have reached a new stage of reform and transition.

Recently, the crisis in capitalism has become a topic of discussion both at home and abroad. Yet to a large extent, this crisis is one of political power and state power. For the West, the key question is how to rebuild state power. The West spent many years creating a regulatory system for industrial capitalism. How many years are needed now to create a regulatory system for financial capitalism and manufacturing capitalism in the context of globalization? Establishing the government's oversight over business first requires a strong government, but how can a strong government be built with a mass democracy? If a strong government is lacking, who will exercise oversight over the powerful forces of capital? And who will restrain the populism in democratic politics?

The East Asian Model Under Globalization

Japan and Asia's Four Little Dragons are classic examples of success in journeying toward market economies and political development; these nations have essentially taken the same path as that of the developed countries of the West. I summarize this path as follows: economy first, society second, politics third; development first, distribution second, democracy third. Japan was the first modern country in Asia. During the long period after the Meiji Restoration, Japan first carried out the creation of state systems, including a centralized political system and an economic system. Japan's democracy (to be precise, its electoral politics) was established during the American occupation after World War II, but it is understood that, while Japan's is an electoral democracy like the West, it is not the same kind of democracy as those in the West.

For a long stretch of history, Japan was dominated by one party, the Liberal Democratic Party (LDP), which firmly controlled state power. This was a highly centralized democracy. Despite factional rivalries within the LDP, the opposition was incapable of challenging the LDP's dominance. After the economy began to take off in the 1960s, it took a little over twenty years for Japan to create a large middle class. At the same time, due to increases in financial resources, the Japanese government began to make large-scale social investments, accelerating the formation of institutions like social security, healthcare, and education. Here it should be said that electoral democracy did play a positive role in social construction. In order to gain votes, politicians strove to invest large amounts of the state's financial resources in social projects. Capitalism and the market economy ensured Japan's long-term economic development, while, with the safety net of social systems, a vast middle class became the foundation for Japan's social stability. In the response of Japanese society to the earthquakes, tsunamis, and nuclear disasters, it's strength has been quite evident. In fact, today's Japan is a classic example of a strong society with a weak government. When the government fails, society will continue to operate normally.

Following Japan, the Four Little Dragons embarked on a road essentially similar to Japan's. The only difference has been in democratization. On the surface, democratization occurred in Japan before the economy took off. However, the main reason for democratization was the American occupation, and democracy remained an authoritarian-style electoral democracy characterized by one-party power. In the Four Little Dragons, economic development and social construction all occurred before democratization. The Four Little Dragons first created authoritarian regimes and then achieved rapid economic development. Once society accumulated a certain amount of wealth, the government engaged in the building of social systems. And the establishment of social systems and the existence of a middle class created the conditions necessary for peaceful political openness and democratization.

On the one hand, after the living standards of the middle class reach a certain stage, they begin to demand political participation—which serves as the driving force for democratization. On the other hand, the existence of both social systems and the middle class also ensures the peaceful nature of the democratization process—that is, the people can rationally participate in the political process. Of the Four Little Dragons, South Korea and Taiwan have been democratized, Singapore has recently been increasing its democratization, and Hong Kong's middle class has also been pursuing democratization. In any case, in comparison with the large-scale violence seen in the early democratic processes of European countries (particularly in the working-class movements), the democratization of East Asian society has appeared highly rational, orderly, and peaceful.

Judging from the relationships between state and market and between governments and the people, the success of the East Asian Model has been primarily owing to their opting for a "third way" that differed from the developed countries of the West and the Soviet Union with its Eastern Bloc. In comparison with the developed West, governments in East Asian economies have played a more important role. In the West, both economic development and social construction have undergone a relatively natural process. Economic development has been mainly driven by the market, and governments have not played a large role; they have mostly confined themselves to regulating economic activities. In terms of social construction, it was only when large-scale working-class movements have appeared and Western institutions have faced crises that governments began to get involved in the social sphere. That is, as has been previously discussed, governments began to separate themselves from capital, transitioning away from a political legitimacy based on capital to a democratic legitimacy that relies on votes.

In East Asia, and particularly with the Four Little Dragons, things have been quite different. Governments there have promoted economic development in a variety of ways; they have formed what the academic community has called "developmental states." Much literature has been written on this subject. Even more importantly, the government has actively adopted effective policies for implementing social construction and cultivating a middle class, thereby avoiding some of the violence characteristic of early working class movements in the West.

While the Japanese government was building its social systems, in the 1960s, it also began to pursue policies such as the raising of wages and supporting the growth of the middle class. South Korea, Hong Kong, and Taiwan have vigorously fostered private enterprise, especially SMEs, and they have created economic structures that are conducive to fair economic growth. Here, Japanese and Korean business conglomerates deserve special emphasis. As we have seen, large corporate groups have played a key role in the economic development of their respective countries—particularly in terms of their international competitiveness. The emergence and development of these large corporations is a result of an alliance between government and enterprise. Without strong government support, these private enterprises would have encountered great difficulty in their development.

Those who support this developmental model call it "East Asian Strategic Capitalism," but its critics (mainly Western scholars) call it crony capitalism. The former point to the advantages of a good relationship between governments and enterprises, while the latter point to the approach's disadvantages. The government of Singapore has proved an even more striking example of promoting economic growth and the creation of social systems. In terms of social change, it took much less time for a middle class to develop in East Asia than it did in the West. This was the fruit of the collaboration of governments with enterprises.

Unlike the socialist countries of the Soviet Union and Eastern Europe, East Asian governments not only allowed the market to play an important role but, even more importantly, also created systemic conditions for promoting the market's development and growth. As I mentioned earlier, the model of the Soviet Union and Eastern Europe was the integration of government and society, one that eliminated the bourgeoisie and market mechanisms and replaced both with a government-dominated planned economy. East Asian societies rejected this radical choice and embarked on a path of using market mechanisms with government intervention.

The governments of Japan and South Korea vigorously fostered private enterprise, mobilizing large amounts of resources and investing in industries with strategic significance so that their industries could compete with those of the developed West over the short run. Taiwan also adopted similar policies: The government vigorously strengthened strategic industries while supporting SMEs. While Hong Kong has a classical free market, its government also played an important role by protecting the operations of the market through the rule of law. Singapore is a special case. Singapore developed a vast government industry (that is, government-linked businesses and government-invested businesses). In this, Singapore differed from the other Little Dragons, but there was no major difference in the full implementation of the market. Singapore's SOEs differ completely from those in the planned economies of the Soviet Union and Eastern Europe. The reason is simple: In Singapore, business is business, and its operations must adhere to the rules of the market. The government does not protect its own businesses from market competition.

Owing to the full implementation of the powers of both the government and the market, East Asian economies were able to catch up to the West quite rapidly. Nevertheless, in an era of globalization, East Asian economies are facing a variety of severe challenges. All of the East Asian economies are facing problems—such as industrial transition, underemployment (with the exception of Singapore), increasing internal income disparities, serious social differentiation, and weak governments. Thus, as in the West, the economies of East Asia are also facing questions regarding how to further extend reforms.

Globalization and the China Model

Since the early 1990s, this current wave of globalization has rapidly reached its peak. While globalization has been driven by developed countries—particularly the United States—developing countries such as China have also taken the initiative. In this process, the West—primarily the United States—has busied itself in trying to push its own system on other countries, but it has forgotten that globalization has also been impacting their institutions.

Historical experience teaches that the West will need a long period of time to reform existing institutions and systems. But what about China? China has been a participant and promoter of this wave of globalization, and it has also been one of its beneficiaries. Because China has been a component of globalization, it has also suffered some of the effects of globalization. While China faces a host of problems connected to globalization, in comparison with other countries, it has effectively responded to the global economic crisis and has been able to maintain high rates of economic development, thereby providing ongoing power for the world economy. Because of this, the international community has been paying greater attention to the China Model.

There are several implications for a discussion of the China Model within the framework of globalization. First of all, of course, we can look to China's experience. China's transition within a few decades from a closed country in the Mao era to a major factor in globalization has in itself been a miracle. The experience here needs to be summarized. Next, there are problems facing the China Model. Where have these problems come from? Is the China Model itself capable of resolving these problems? If they can be resolved, then it's clear that the China Model is sustainable. But if they cannot be resolved, then the model has no future. Finally, at a deeper level, this discussion is about whether the China Model can serve as an alternative to the Western Model. The West is currently in crisis, and there is concern about whether the Western Model can right itself. Regardless, the Western crisis means that the Western Model is not perfect and that it needs to adjust itself to change. Since the Western Model is not universal in nature, it must be possible for other models to exist as well. Here, the China Model becomes highly relevant.

Of course, this does not necessarily mean that China will replace the Western Model; it only means that China is developing a model different from the West's. The existence of different models does not imply that the relationship between them must be mutually antagonistic; two models can coexist in a relationship in which each learns from the other. The emergence and development of the China Model was performed in a state of openness; that is, it was deeply influenced by the external environment. This demonstrates that the China Model is intimately connected to the outside world. Since the China Model has been successful, the outside world can learn something from it. This is true, not only for developing countries but for developed countries as well.

In terms of globalization, the emergence and development of the China Model has great significance. To begin with, the emergence of the modern Chinese system is a product of a kind of "anti-globalization." The Soviet Union, the socialism of the Eastern European states, and Chinese socialism were all products of anti-globalization. As discussed above, globalization began in the West and then spread to other regions—and globalization is first and foremost an economic globalization: As capitalists have pursued profit through the power of the market and the power of individual states, the entire world has become integrated. Marx observed this, and neo-Marxist scholars developed this observation into differing theories. The most celebrated have been center-periphery theory and dependency theory. The former analyzes the economic relations between the West and the non-West, between the North and the South. The latter was developed primarily by Latin American thinkers to explore how the dependence of Latin American economies on Western capitalism has led to economic stagnation in Latin America.

The globalization of capital has not only brought about the globalization of economic activity but also stimulated massive political changes in the non-Western world. Many states have evolved into colonies of the West, while others remain highly dependent on the West. Regardless of the precise causes, the non-West has seen underdevelopment and backwardness. The question is then: How can we break free from the globalization of capital? Lenin proposed that under-developed countries should liberate themselves by establishing new regimes through revolution, thereby throwing off the shackles of imperialism. This was the approach adopted by the celebrated October Revolution, and it became the approach of choice for many countries, including China. These countries formed political and economic systems different from those of the West.

This was the "historical choice" that is so emphasized today. Underdeveloped countries are subject to aggression and bullying by imperialist and developed countries. If one wants to reform societies characterized by colonialization, marginalization, and high degrees of dependency, one choice is to break away from that system—as the Soviet Union and China did. The other choice is to struggle for self-advancement within that system.

History can only explain; it cannot surmise. At that time, the political system in China dictated that it must adopt a revolutionary approach. It was an approach that was obvious to Sun Yat-sen, Chiang Kai-shek, and Mao Zedong. But we can still wonder what would have happened if China had not chosen the economic model selected by the Communist Party of China. Historical experience shows that China may have ended up following something like a Latin American model—that is, becoming marginalized and highly dependent on the West. It might also have become like India, which long remained an agricultural society. And, of course, it might have adopted a model like Japan's or that of the Four Little Dragons.

China chose to create a new state through revolution to avoid the political control of the West, but this does not mean that China needed to adopt a planned economy. In fact, after the founding of the New China in 1949, China was faced with a new set of choices. In the early years after the founding, the new-democratic state envisaged by Mao Zedong was far from the planned economy of the future. The problem was that Mao eventually went to extremes. When China adopted the line of "Continuous Revolution," the state's power and society's lower classes worked together to transform "the line of new democracy" within a brief span of time: Not only were private systems thoroughly eliminated but also entities in the private sector—that is, groups like capitalists and landlords—were also erased.

Without private enterprise, business owners, and a market, economic development would lose its impetus. What was to be done? Mao Zedong turned to political mobilization. The Great Leap Forward and the Cultural Revolution were two massive political mobilizations; they relied on decentralization between higher and lower government departments to gain economic and political control. Even though he also hoped to employ decentralization movements to adopt an economic approach different from that of the Soviet Union and Eastern Europe, since China lacked both capital and markets, Mao eventually had to embark on an impoverished socialism.

Since 1978's Reform and Opening Up, China has also made another choice. Whether China has been pursuing internal reform or opening up to the outside world, at the center has been a market economy, which has integrated China into the Western economic system and established connections with the West through various internal reforms. This established the foundations for a market economy.

The transformation from Mao Zedong's "disconnection" to Deng Xiaoping's "connection" was world-changing, but there is actually a strong relationship between the two positions, as it can be said that "disconnection" was the grounds for "connection." When it was disconnected, China built a powerful state apparatus. Without this powerful state, China would have had great difficulty in finding independence from the West. China has been able to take the world "with both hands" primarily because it has had a strong state.

It's been more than ten years since many Western scholars have demonstrated how globalization weakens sovereign states. When I was studying globalization in China, I observed the opposite phenomenon. If globalization has weakened sovereign states in the West, it has promoted transitions within the Chinese state in many ways, enabling the sovereign state to grow even stronger.[1]

What impacts has a globalization centered on the market economy had on China? The first was a transformation in ideology. From the May Fourth Movement to the Mao era, the mobilizations of long-term revolution (and "Continuous Revolution") transitioned China into a highly ideological society. Ideology directed and measured everything. Of course, this was an ideology of political mobilization that suited a planned economy. Then, reform was re-welcomed into the market.

1 See Yongnian Zheng, *Globalization and State Transformation in China* (New York: Cambridge University Press, 2004).

Formerly, the market was viewed as merely the product of capitalism. But Deng Xiaoping resolved this problem. For Deng, the market was not in itself ideological; it was simply a tool for enabling the creation of wealth. Thus, capitalism could employ the market, but socialism could also employ the market. This "de-ideologized" understanding of the market was certainly in accord with historical and material conditions. Historically speaking, Chinese tradition has existed for thousands of years, and for most of that time the market not only existed but was also quite developed. Materially speaking, in addition to the Soviet Union, Eastern Europe, and Mao-era China, markets also existed under differing political and economic systems.

In 1992, after Deng's Southern Tour, the 14th National Congress of the Communist Party of China formally proposed a "socialist market economy," writing it into the constitution.[2] This completed the ideological transformation of the ruling party. In terms of globalization, this transformation was both a product of globalization and a prerequisite for China's integration into the world. It is difficult to imagine how China could have possibly "connected" with the world or "go out" (*zou chuqu*) if China had still been operating under a planned economy.

The second impact of globalization has been the transformation of the ruling party. With a market economy, China has developed various economic components. After the end of the people's communes in rural areas, a non-collective economic sector was first formed in rural areas. Then, outside of the state-owned sector in the cities, there emerged a non-state sector—that is, a private sector. After the mid-90s reforms known as "grasping the large and letting the small go" (*zhua da fang xiao*), private enterprise gained the impetus for rapid development. The entry of foreign capital and the formation of various joint ventures also increased the diversification of all systemic components. These objective circumstances demanded a change within the ruling party.

As elsewhere, the traditional aim of the Communist Party of China has been the elimination of private ownership and the bourgeoisie. This was achieved during the Mao era. After the Reform and Opening Up, the ruling party kept up with the times and overcame resistance. First, it revised the constitution to give legal legitimacy to private property. Next it enacted the Property Law to provide legal protections for private property. At the same time, the ruling party also gradually liberalized political processes, allowing and encouraging private entrepreneurs to join the Communist Party. Thus the ruling party has, at least theoretically,

2 Henceforward, the National Congresses of the Communist Party of China will be referred to by their session: for example, the 14th National Congress of the Communist Party of China will be referred to as the "14th Congress."

transitioned from a closed party that represents a minority class to an open party that can represent the interests of most of society. This transition is a milestone for Chinese politics.

The third impact has been the transformation of society. During the Mao era, China used ideology to organize society. It's clear that different groups within a society are divided by political ideology; this is also the means by which they are managed and controlled. This control reached its peak during the Cultural Revolution. The so-called "Five Black Categories" of landlords, "rich peasants," counter-revolutionaries, "bad elements," and "rightists" were all highly politicized. After "de-ideologization," Chinese society returned to a more natural state and transitioned into a society oriented around interests. Though interest-oriented societies will generate many problems, they are still more compatible with human nature than ideologically oriented societies.

Globalization's fourth impact has been a transformation within the bureaucracy. The bureaucracy created after 1949 existed to serve the planned economy; it administered and supervised both society and various economic activities. This bureaucracy was incompatible with a market economy. From the 1980s through the end of the 1990s, China ushered in several bureaucratic reforms (or "institutional reforms") that created a bureaucracy suited for a market economy—the largest reform occurring when Zhu Rongji was premier. With the new century, reform in the bureaucracy has shifted to reform in the "super ministries" (*da buzhi*), and this is also a kind of "connection" with the world. With the super ministries, the government's functions must be transitioned from its previous direct interventions in economic activities to the regulation of economic activities. Today, this task is far from complete, but its aims are clear.

The fifth impact of globalization has been the transformation of the economy. Under the planned economy, the trinity of politics, society, and enterprise constituted a system of tight controls. A business was also a social and political entity. In the absence of distinct organizational functions, China lacked a basic state system. After the start of the market economy, the "trinity system" soon became unsuitable for the needs of the times. To this day, while SOEs and the government have not separated from each other, Chinese society has essentially achieved functional separation—that is, businesses are distinct from their social functions, and the government's functions are distinct from economic functions. This has required the creation of an economic system that is compatible with a market economy.

And great progress has been made in this regard. China has created a basic state system with a tax-sharing system, a central bank, and a financial system that supports the market economy domestically. At the same time, by the beginning of the twenty-first century, China had also achieved a basic balance between the state-owned sector and the non-state-owned sector, between large SOEs and SMEs. This has enabled China to realize a basic balance between the government and the market.

In all of these aspects, globalization has exerted a positive influence on China's state-building. But globalization also poses tremendous challenges to China's political system. The market economy is ultimately an economy of the rule of law. In the West, as has been previously discussed, contemporary states are built on market systems. In other words, markets have pre-existed states. Thus, to a large extent, state legal systems serve the market. Observing this phenomenon, Marx held that the entire legal system of the West exists to serve capital, and that law is the embodiment of capital's interests.

Of course, since Marx's time, Western legal systems have undergone great changes. Politics and capital have separated, and many laws regulate capital and thus economic activities themselves. In China, however, the market was introduced through state power after the Reform and Opening Up; the market is subject to the state. Under such circumstances, Chinese law frequently serves as a tool for state power. Without the effective rule of law, China's market economy has no institutionalized foundation.

Today this challenge appears to be growing increasingly serious.

The Future of the China Model

At the beginning of the twenty-first century, just as China's economy was developing at a rapid and steady pace and the West's economies were encountering difficulties, Western scholars theorized about the existence of the "Beijing Consensus," one which stood in contrast to a pre-existing "Washington Consensus." While the idea of a "Beijing Consensus" is only a highly politicized concept, it has led to a great deal of discussion about the China Model. In the early stages of the discussion, many scholars struggled to understand exactly just what was the "China Model"—that is, exactly what content is contained in the term. But after the global financial crisis of 2008, discussions of the Chinese model quickly politicized. Some have observed how China effectively responded to the crisis and have decided that the China Model is superior to other models, including the Western Model. Among such thinkers, many interest groups are seeking to establish and institutionalize vested interests; many of these interest groups also loudly beat the drum for the superiority of the China Model. Others focus on the various difficulties that have arisen over the past few years, difficulties like the greatly expanding state-owned sector, wealth disparities, and social differentiation. These thinkers have pilloried the China Model, holding that the aim of Chinese reforms must be to eliminate the China Model. For these thinkers, the Western Model is universal, and the China Model has no *raison d'être*. Within this group, some see nothing extraordinary in China's development: It only represents the fact that China has copied the market economies of Western countries.

I was one of the earlier thinkers to broach the question of a China Model, and I particularly object to the concept of "Beijing Consensus," since it implies that China can export its developmental model to other countries. I believe that every country can find its own unique developmental model in accordance with its own national conditions, and that creating such a model does not exclude the possibility of learning from the experiences of other countries. At the same time, however, I think that the China Model does exist: It is China's experience of development.

Highly politicized discussions of the China Model obviously do not help us fully understand the advantages and disadvantages of the China Model. Those opinions that emphasize the China Model's superiority over other systems are beyond the scope of my discussion. What I want to explain is how the Chinese system ultimately works and the advantages and disadvantages of this system in dealing with various problems. If the China Model is considered superior to other models, and does not need to be developed or improved, then it is a model that can only be buried in the end. This is true for any system.

In the 1950s and 1960s, many also thought that the planned economy was superior, but within a few decades, the system had buried itself. In the same way, after the close of the Cold War, everyone in the West was optimistic that democratic systems based on free markets represented the "end of history"—that is, the last political system for all human development. But it didn't take long for an economic crisis to hit and endanger the rest of the world. If people don't want the China Model to end, then they must study its strengths and weaknesses and reflect on how to reform and improve the system.

On the other hand, the idea that the Western Model is universal is also outside my purview. I don't believe that market values are inherently Western or that the market only exists in the West. As was previously mentioned, in the thousands of years of Chinese history, the market was often highly developed. The Chinese also recognize the importance of the market for economic development and economic management. It is true that the era of the planned economy saw the destruction of the market economy, while the Reform and Opening Up saw the introduction of market mechanisms. But this does not mean that the concept of a market is Western. What's more, I don't believe that the Western market economy is the only possible market economy. Even though the Western model of a market economy recently experienced a massive crisis, many continue to use the Western

Model to criticize the China Model. Such an approach will not help us reflect on the basic nature of the Western Model and implement needed reforms, nor will it enable an understanding of the real problems that the China Model faces.

China's own developmental experience, and the predicaments faced by the Western Model, gives me even greater confidence in the existence of a China Model—one which emerged and was developed within a globalized environment. Nevertheless, like the Western Model, the China Model also faces challenges. Working with a grounding in defining existing problems in the China Model, we have a responsibility to improve the China Model.

A model is a structure. That is, a model is said to exist because it has a structure. Studying a model means studying its structure, not just the individual behaviors within this structure. There are several structures that support the China Model. The three primary structures here are the structure of the economy, the structure of the economy and society, and the structure of the state and society. To say that the China Model faces problems is to say that it is facing imbalances—that is, imbalances within the economic structure, imbalances between the economic and social spheres, and imbalances between the state and society. In order to reform and improve the China Model, it is necessary to strike a balance among these three aspects.

Balance in the Internal Structure of the Economy

Over the past few years, I've been conducting research on comparative political economics. This has led me to propose two different concepts. I hold that China is a market-in-state, while the United States is a state-in-market. That is to say, in China, the market must submit to the principles of the government, while in the United States, the government must submit to the principles of the market. Of course, to borrow the phrasing of Max Weber, these are only two "ideal types" in theory. In real life, there is no market that is completely dominated by the government, nor is there any government that is completely dominated by the market. In fact, even under a planned economy, the market will always exist to a certain extent, as with black markets or underground markets. And even in the most prototypical market economy, like Hong Kong, the government still exerts a certain influence on the economy. But we can be sure that, if the market occupies a position of absolute dominance in the West, and the state and society do not have sufficient strength to balance the market, then a crisis will occur. This was true in both the crisis of the 1930s and the global financial crisis of 2008. Conversely, if the state comes to occupy a position of absolute dominance in China, and the market and society do not have sufficient strength to balance the state's power, then a crisis will also occur.

The problem for every country is how to find a point of equilibrium in the relationship between the government and the market. In the West, the government is subordinate to the market. Although, broadly speaking, the government's role in the economy is constantly growing—the government is still ultimately part of the market. No matter whether the state is regulatory (the state regulates the market) or interventional (Keynesian), there is still a clear demarcation between the government and the market, and neither can take the place of the other. In China, however, the market is subordinate to the government. Even though, since the Reform and Opening Up, the market has been expanded and its functions have been constantly reinforced, the market remains a part of the government. To a great extent, the market is only a tool of the government to achieve its economic and social objectives (or political engineering). Seen in this light, it is fundamentally impossible, as some economists have suggested, for China to be Keynesian. The Chinese government's intervention in the economy goes far beyond Keynesianism; it could be said to be a classic kind of economic nationalism.

Within a market economy, the lines between the government and the market are clearly delineated, although, in different countries, the lines are going to be drawn differently. This is one thing that distinguishes those countries that developed earlier from those which developed later. Generally speaking, the role of the government in a country which has developed later is going to be greater than that in a country which developed earlier. In Europe, for example, the United Kingdom was the very first to develop, and the space its free market occupies is much larger than those of Germany and France, which developed later. Economists from different schools have differing ideas about where this line should be drawn, as can be seen in the variety of opinions advocated by Adam Smith, Marx, Keynes, and different contemporary economic schools. But none of this has erased the distinction between the government and the market. Thus, in the West, every time an economic crisis occurs, the role of the government is always emphasized, while after every crisis, there is always an emphasis that the government must exit the market in a timely manner and allow the market to occupy its rightful place. In fact, the experience of recent years demonstrates that, in the West, the market economy is considered normative, while government economies are considered aberrations. Even though the economic crisis is not yet over, many are already busy looking for a way to get the government out of the market.

It must also be noted that, owing to the boundary between the government and the market, governments are trying to find and develop various institutional mechanisms for effectively relating to the market. On the one hand, governments must develop effective systems for ensuring the highest possible security in the market and efficiency in production. On the other hand, governments must also develop equally effective systems for absorbing sufficient taxes from the market while still regulating the market and preventing markets from experiencing a crisis. In recent years, many of the innovations in Western economic systems have been carried out within this dynamic.

In contrast, in China the market exists within the boundaries established by the government, and there is no line drawn between the government and the market. After the Reform and Opening Up, China learned from the West's experience and established modern taxation and financial systems. The primary force behind these systems has been the government. With the improvement in the government's institutional capabilities in these areas, the government's ability to regulate the market has also increased. This explains how it is that, after Reform and Opening Up, while China's market has greatly expanded, the government's power over the market has not only failed to weaken but has actually grown. In the West, governments control the tax system, but the private sector often dominates the financial sector. In China, however, the government itself remains the main driver of economic activity—that is, the government still has a large state-owned sector.

Some economists have described China's market economy as crony capitalism. This is not very accurate. In fact, there are three forms of "capitalism" currently in China: "market capitalism," "crony capitalism," and "state capitalism."

Market capitalism exists at the bottom rung of the economy; it is most prevalent at the local level, and it is not large in scale. It is mainly seen in various trading markets or private networks. Such markets also exist in traditional societies. Even before the Reform and Opening Up, these markets had an "illegal" existence, particularly in the southeastern and coastal areas. After the Reform and Opening Up, during the 1980s, this market began to expand. In the 1990s, particularly during the period of "grasping the large and letting the small go," market capitalism made great progress. The markets of market capitalism are largely beyond the government's control. While tolerating the existence of market capitalism, the government does not offer it substantive support like legal, fiscal, or financial support. Without the government's support, such markets are bound to be subject to many restrictions, such as geographical restrictions, and without legal support, credit will be difficult to establish, preventing such markets from developing into national markets. Another form of restriction is economic in nature. The state does not allow private individuals to develop the financial industry or other fields, for once private individuals monopolize an economic field within a country, the country faces huge economic risk.

In comparison with market capitalism, the latter two forms of capitalism, crony capitalism and state capitalism, have experienced massive expansions. In other East Asian economies, the development of many private enterprises has been strongly supported by the state; these developments have occurred because these enterprises were dependent on the state. This is where the concept of crony capitalism comes from, and the practice has been more positively framed as "strategic capitalism." China has followed suit. In this field, many private enterprises have been developed with the support of the state. Many of these have evolved through privatization, away from SOEs. These companies are highly dependent on their relationship with the government. Without the government, they might not survive.

But because companies in this field are often much larger than those in the field of market capitalism, the state does not let them become completely independent. Instead, the state tries to control them and ensure that they will not pose a threat. In recent years, crony capitalism has only grown. In regions where private enterprise is relatively well developed, some private enterprises have begun to snuggle up to the SOEs of the central government, hoping that they could form various alliances with them. For these private companies, as long as they are protected by politics, they can share some of the benefits of the political and administrative power that the central government's SOEs have. For the central government, on the other hand, this ensures that these private companies will not pose a threat to the state. In the short term, this might look like a win-win situation, but over the long term, it might be lose-lose.

The capitalism that has seen the fastest expansion has, of course, been state capitalism. The 1990s strategy of "grasping the large and letting the small go" enabled the SOEs of the previous planned economy to wriggle out of their difficulties. Today, China's SOEs, especially those owned by the central government, are some of the greatest in the world in terms of scale. But this does not mean that SOEs are actually healthy. Li Rongrong, the former director of the State-owned Assets Supervision and Administration Commission (SASAC), once said that China's SOEs are large but not healthy. I have discussed the problems in SOEs on many previous occasions, and I will not reiterate them here. What I want to emphasize is that SOEs are entirely at the service of China's so-called "whole-nation system" (*juguo tizhi*): They are primarily symbols of the state's power. It should also be noted that SOEs are already serving as instruments of the state in overseas markets. While SOEs have played a critical role in "going out," their "going out" has been driven more by politics and less by market-driven reasons.

In the West, China's SOEs have encountered strong political resistance from Western governments, and in non-Western countries (for example, in Africa and the Middle East), SOEs face the massive risks of governmental and social instability. Most of the West now sees China as an authoritarian political system dominated by state capitalism. As this new concept is taking shape, many countries are beginning to formulate a strategic response to China. Once this concept is expressed in the China policy of a Western government, it will certainly have a great impact on China and will constitute massive resistance to China's "going out."

Once state capitalism becomes the dominant economic form, the impact on China's internal development will be considerable. The wealth of a people can make their country strong. This has been the West's experience, and it is also the experience of Japan and the Four Little Dragons of Asia. Much of economic history is actually the history of how markets expanded and developed—and how governments learned to regulate markets. As discussed above, in the West there is competition between the state and the market, but the government can never get the market under its control. The government regulates the market, but it does not control it. Only after the market creates wealth can the government have the capacity to implement social reforms and protect the economic rights of society's members. The West's transition from primitive capitalism to welfare capitalism was not the result of developments in capitalism itself, but of the government's regulation of the market under pressure from social forces. But the state's leading role in the welfare system led to a massive expansion of the state and an accompanying contraction of the market, especially in the economic arena. This prompted a privatization movement, which was led primarily by President Reagan in the United States and Prime Minister Thatcher in the United Kingdom. In short, maintaining a balance between the market and the government has always been a key factor in the ability of Western economies to function effectively.

China's state capitalism can produce national wealth within a brief stretch of time. Today, in terms of the state's financial resources, China is the richest state in the world, but this has come at the expense of the people. It is a characteristic of state capitalism that the state or its agents effectively transfer wealth from the people to the state through a variety of mechanisms such as politics, administration, and markets. In the long run, however, the people's weakness will inevitably lead to the country's weakness. It should be noted that the state's wealth does not necessarily lead to the state's strength, especially in China. In China's institutional environment, SOEs do not belong to the state but to the state's agents. The wealth accumulated by so-called "state capitalism" is not allocated by the government but by a few select agents. In many cases, the actions of these agents have gone well beyond the government's control. In other words, the existence of this field has not only failed to make the government strong but has actually served as an effective brake on the government's actions. More importantly, state capitalism is rapidly leading to the exhaustion of social resources. Once social resources are exhausted, the government will first lose its economic base and then its political base.

Clearly, then, when there is a massive imbalance between the government and the market, the key task of China's economic reform is to regain a balance between the two. If the government (especially the state-owned sector) continues its indefinite expansion, the market will continue to shrink, and wealth will continue to flow to the state (or the state's agents) instead of to the people. This will mean that the state capitalism so beloved by some today will inevitably evolve into a system that "hoists itself by its own petard." Today many are worried that the private sector, so painstakingly developed after the Reform and Opening Up, will suddenly collapse, spawning a massive crisis.

These worries are far from unreasonable, and in this regard, China has much to learn from its own history. Before the founding of the People's Republic of China in 1949, the Communist Party supported and advocated the theory of new democracy as the way to state-building. Here it should be said that, as an economic structure, this theory is that of a mixed economy—one which includes private enterprise, public-private joint ventures, and state capitalism. In the early days of the founding, these three coexisted and were relatively balanced. So why was it that, after a few years, circumstances rapidly changed, with private enterprise and joint ventures collapsing? Many have said that this was due to the success of the ruling party in restructuring the old economy. Now, however, this looks like a failure. If China could have held to new democracy for a longer period of time, it might have followed in the steps of Japan and the Four Little Dragons and avoided impoverished socialism.

Unfortunately, the economic line of new democracy quickly evolved into a mere transition strategy—that is, a transition to state capitalism. With state capitalism soon coming to control the supplies and markets on which private capital depends, the death of the private sector became inevitable. Rather than demonstrating the success of the ruling party in transforming capitalism, this shows that private capitalism got hemmed in and then surrendered "peacefully." Once the private sector dies, the economic foundations of a planned economy are in place, and a country has no way back.

In today's China, relevant departments defend the expansion of the state-owned sector by denying that it is expanding or generating problems. The information these departments employ is primarily the proportion of SOEs and non-state-owned enterprises in overall GDP. But this simple ratio is meaningless. The reality is that the state-owned sector is now facing a variety of serious problems, such as the difficulty of obtaining loans from government-controlled banks, a lack of private financing institutions, and shrinking investment space.

These problems are all directly related to the rapid expansion of the state-owned sector.

For a long time, the relationship between private enterprise and the state-owned sector has been less characterized by competition and more by intertwining. Private enterprise has a fixed amount of power with which it can withstand the expansion of SOEs. But this has changed rapidly in the aftermath of the 2008 financial crisis. The government's four trillion in bailouts went primarily to the state-owned sector. Since then, SOEs have grown dramatically. The policy mistake here is obvious. It's understandable that the government would deploy SOEs to save the economy. But the government did not clearly instruct SOEs on which fields they could enter and which they had to leave alone. As a result, SOEs have entered every field where money was to be made—especially those that had been previously occupied by private enterprise. This quickly led to an imbalance in economic structure. Since China's SOEs are often large in size, and private enterprises are either medium-sized or small, the growth in SOEs has also led to imbalances between big business and small business. Of course, this has ultimately led to an imbalance between the government and the market. When SOEs and the government work together, the market cannot restrict any of the actions of the former.

Just like the 1950s, China's private businesses are beginning to "surrender." There are two ongoing phenomena that deserve our attention and consideration. The first is the aforementioned cozying up of private enterprise to state-owned enterprise. Even in regions like Zhejiang with a highly developed private sector, private enterprises are one by one wedding themselves to SOEs. Some of these marriages are voluntary, but others are forced. Why are they having to make this choice? To survive—or at least survive a little longer.

Riding the coattails of state-owned enterprises is buying political insurance at a high economic price. Without a legal system that can effectively protect private enterprise, private entrepreneurs feel very unsafe. In reality, no matter how large a private enterprise is, once power fixes its eyes on it, the private enterprise is in a bind. Sometimes it folds, and other times it's imprisoned. The second phenomenon is that, for a long time, a large number of entrepreneurs in China's private sector, along with their capital, have been forced to escape from the deteriorating domestic environment. Some of these people felt that the cost of currying favor with SOEs was too high, while others simply couldn't successfully do so—so they chose to run. Is China going to repeat the 1950s? If current trends aren't reversed, history will repeat itself. This will not be changed by sheer effort. And once it happens, China's economy will suffer a major crisis.

If the problem in the United States is Wall Street, China's problem is SOEs. So, what's to be done? In general, China needs to find a balance among the three aforementioned forms of capitalism.

First, as far as state capitalism goes, currently there are two policy ideas. One is economic liberalism—that is, comprehensive privatization. The second is socialism—that is, to have SOEs engaging in profit sharing. In both China and the West, economic liberals have been beating the drum for privatization because they regard private property rights as the most important element in economic development. Of course, we're not going to review the strengths and weaknesses of this theory here. Regardless, comprehensive privatization is not a viable option for China.

There are several factors which have enabled state capitalism in China. The first is that comprehensive privatization is not politically feasible. In other words, comprehensive privatization is too idealistic and impracticable. SOEs are now, just like Wall Street, "too big to fail." The second factor is the current international economic structure and the international situation. Generally speaking, China is still a developing country, and the state still needs to play a major role in improving the international competitiveness of Chinese companies. In other words, SOEs can strengthen China's international competitiveness. The third factor is the domestic justification for SOEs—that is, their role in internal economic operations. Since the Han Dynasty's *Discourses on Salt and Iron*, China has seen the formation of a consensus on the functions of SOEs. SOEs must play a key role in important fields such as national defense, the construction of infrastructure, and crisis response. And those functions continue at present.

The idea of profit sharing reflects Chinese society's recent frustration with SOEs. According to this line of thought, while SOEs can still continue to grow and develop, their profits must be shared with society at large. But this is simply just slicing a cake, and it will not effectively reform SOEs. This is the case, first of all, because it means a total compromise with the vested interests of SOEs; profit sharing will not affect vested interests. Some of their interests could be sold off, true, but this would not do anything to improve the overall distribution of benefits to society as a whole. Second, the approach will not effectively improve the structure of China's economy, which requires a balance between SOEs and private enterprise, and between big business and small business. Third, this approach will ultimately lead to impoverished socialism, as the growth of SOEs and motivation mechanisms will become inversely proportional. As SOEs grow, they will grow increasingly monopolistic. And the greater their ability to transfer wealth, the less incentive will there be to create wealth through innovation.

So how do we introduce a series of reforms to state capitalism that can prevent it from becoming an important source of economic crisis? There is another way forward here: the East Asian Model. First of all, China could implement what Chen Yun has called a "birdcage economy," that is, to draw distinct boundaries for SOEs. Zhu Rongji's strategy of "grasping the large and letting the small go" means assigning SOEs to fields that are of strategic importance to the country. This primarily means learning from the corporate strategies of Japan and South Korea.

After Zhu Rongji, however, this approach was abandoned. But SOEs need to be placed within a cage. They must surrender those fields that belong rightfully to private enterprise, and those fields that either SOEs or private enterprise could both perform should also be surrendered to private enterprise.

Second, competition needs to be introduced into the state-owned sector. China is a big country. In some areas, there should be multiple SOEs so that competition between them can be encouraged. Without competition, there is no progress. Finally, marketization needs to be introduced. In this regard, China can learn from Singapore's experience. SOEs must accept the test of marketization. In fact, China's SASAC was originally founded along the lines of Singapore's "Temasek System," but China only copied the structure and didn't learn from its spirit—one that includes corporatization, marketization, openness, and corporate supervision.

It's also important to prevent the internal privatization of SOEs. Today's SOEs are no longer the SOEs of the planned economy, and nowadays they mostly belong to their management. When SOEs make a profit, they can distribute profits however they like, but when they incur a loss, they can ask the state for help. At the same time, income differentiation within SOEs has grown excessively severe. Nothing really distinguishes their management from Wall Street, and their average workers are underpaid. This is a classic case of internal privatization. In this sense, SOEs do need to do profit sharing. To put it simply, reform in SOEs can be divided into three steps: first, a birdcage economy must be implemented; second, SOEs need to be marketized; and finally, SOEs need to be supervised and to engage in profit sharing.

Second, the state must vigorously support large private businesses. Here we can learn from Japan and South Korea. As has been previously discussed, Japan and South Korea's success was mainly owing to the implementation of a "strategic capitalism" in which the state strongly supports the development of large private businesses in a variety of ways, allowing them to grow rapidly and increase their international competitiveness. Without government support, Japanese and South Korean companies wouldn't have such strong international competitiveness.

In China, the government's behavior has been exactly the opposite—it has directed large amounts of resources to SOEs while restricting the development of private enterprise. It's going to be hard for China's SOEs to "go out." As discussed above, with the West's strategic response to China's state capitalism, "going out" will become increasingly difficult. China needs to learn from Japan and South Korea and vigorously support a large number of internationally competitive enterprises in key areas. Another option is the "public-private joint ventures" implemented in the 1950s.

Third, greater efforts must be made to develop market capitalism. Market capitalism was the foundation for the survival and development of today's Chinese small businesses. For any country, SMEs are always the most effective mechanism for solving problems in distribution. Most employment is assumed by SMEs. At the same time, in a developed society, SMEs distribute their income relatively equitably and fairly. There are many other benefits to the development of SMEs—including innovation. Most of the innovation in the world today comes from SMEs. In theory, whether ideologically or constitutionally, China has also been emphasizing the importance of SMEs, but various practical policies have not been conducive to the development of SMEs. If the development of SMEs does not become one of the government's policy priorities, the environment will become increasingly difficult for SMEs, and China itself will find it hard to achieve balance in its economic structure.

How should private enterprise be supported? There is not much clarity here. Government at all levels recognizes the importance of private enterprise, but many of their initiatives do not so much help private enterprises, but undermine their long-term interests. Government officials at all levels have long assisted private enterprise with measures such as offering cheap or even free land, reducing labor wages, and relaxing safety and environmental regulations. But such measures are not conducive to the healthy development of private enterprise. The problems in food safety, the environment, and production safety that are now endemic in China are cancers afflicting private enterprise. This was the case in the formula powder industry. Safety issues in Shanxi's private mining industry eventually doomed it, and it was returned to public hands. Similar problems exist in many other industries.

While covertly undermining the long-term interests of private enterprises, the government at all levels has also directly restricted private enterprises. Because of the state's monopoly, private enterprises with insufficient funds do not have effective financing available, and sufficiently funded private enterprises lack the room to invest. In addition, the state does not allow private financing to fix the problem. If private financing were allowed, then there could be a flow in funds from over-funded sectors to under-funded sectors. But at all levels of government, private financing is still illegal. Of course, this is ultimately related to the problem of the state's monopoly. Yet, in an era of globalization, if surplus private capital cannot find a domestic outlet, it will naturally flow overseas. This trend is already pronounced.

It's obvious that, if private enterprise is to be effectively supported, the government must establish effective supervisory mechanisms for private enterprise while simultaneously ensuring its free development—and a level playing field. Without freedom, there can be no development, while without regulation there can be no sustainable development.

Balance Between the Economy and Society

The second major structural balance is the balance between economy and society. Everyone understands why coordinated economic and social development is necessary, but such an approach is rarely reflected in actual policy. In previous discussions, we emphasized that these circumstances also occurred early on in the West, with economic development occurring without any accompanying social construction. But after the rise of working-class movements, the ruling class faced challenges, and Western governments turned to social reforms—working hard to create social welfare systems like social security, healthcare, education, and public housing. Of course, these systems were not built in a short span of time, but underwent a long and painful process. Even in developed countries, this process is not complete—for example, in the United States. Regardless, creating these social systems, which are part of the basic state system, laid the institutional foundation for sustainable development in the West. It is difficult to imagine how the West could have built a consumer society without these social systems.

We also emphasized that, in comparison with developed countries in the West, the governments in Japan and the Four Little Dragons have played a more proactive role in the construction of social systems, helping them to avoid large-scale social unrest. This has not only created a stable social environment for sustainable development but has also laid the social foundation for peaceful democratic reforms.

What about the situation in China? In short, there is a serious imbalance between economic reforms and social reforms. Government officials at all levels have long obsessed over GDP. Economic growth based on GDP figures has long been given the highest priority in policy. To this day, China still faces over-investment in basic economic construction and a serious deficiency in social investment. This poses a stark contrast with the West. In Europe, owing to the existence of welfare states, a large amount of government investment is directed to social areas such as social security, healthcare, education, and public housing. In China, however, most of the government's investment is economic, going to the construction of bridges, highways, railways, and docks. Of course, since China is a developing country, these investments are crucial for the early stages of development. Without investment in infrastructure, the economy cannot be easily developed. The problem is that, in recent years, these areas have seen over-investment. Bridges are being demolished, rebuilt, and then demolished again. The GDP is there, but such practices not only represent massive waste but also do nothing to improve the people's standard of living.

In fact, for Chinese reformers, a distinction has long been made between the economy and society, or economic policies and social policies. This has had serious consequences. The most serious has been the tactic of generating GDP by destroying society. Many countries regard fields like healthcare, education, and public housing as social fields, and there are many restrictions on investment in these fields, with governments acting as the primary investor. But in China, these areas are sometimes seen as economic in nature, and thus economic policies have inundated these areas.

After the mid-90s, the medical sector was the first to introduce economic policies, and hospitals became generators of vast wealth. During the Asian financial crisis of 1997, some suggested that education be commercialized in response to the crisis. While the government never formally advocated the commercialization of education, China's education has since embarked on a radical path of commercialization. After the 2008 financial crisis, economic policy was introduced into another highly social area—that is, real estate. Reform, development, and stability—these should be the markers of a positive developmental route for China. But the reality is that, the faster the development, the more unstable society becomes.

This is primarily because government at all levels pursues development by disrupting these social spheres. In any country, if highly social fields like hospitals, education, and real estate become fields for massive wealth, social stability will be hard to achieve. However, it should be pointed out that saying that these social fields should not introduce economic policies does not mean that they should completely exclude the market. In many countries, market mechanisms have also been applied to these fields—mainly to avoid excessive bureaucratization in these public areas and to improve efficiency in the government's provision of social services. Market mechanisms in the public sector and mechanisms in the economy should be two different things that are clearly distinguished.

While the social sphere is overly marketized, the economic sphere lacks sufficient marketization. The economic sphere should be fully marketized. Efficiency and productivity should be the main concerns in the economy, but this has not happened in China, particularly among SOEs. After neoliberal economics arrived in China, it was applied to the wrong places. In the West, neoliberal economics has occurred primarily in the economic sphere. During the 1980s, Reagan and Thatcher strove to privatize the public sector (in areas such as education, healthcare, and social security). But they failed because they encountered strong resistance from democratic governments. In China, however, neoliberal economics has encountered strong resistance from SOEs. As was discussed earlier, the marketization of SOEs has thus far been insufficient. However, neoliberal economics has successfully entered the social sphere because Chinese society offered no resistance to it.

During the transition from a planned economy to a market economy, the social systems built under the planned economy naturally collapsed, for they no longer met the needs of the new environment. Most of these systems were established during the Mao era. They fit perfectly with the planned economy, and they played a very important role at the time. But these systems had difficulty adapting to conditions under the market economy. In fact, with the arrival of the market economy, the collapse of old systems was inevitable. It needs to be said here that social systems under a planned economy can provide very few public services, and that the distribution of those services among different social groups is also inequitable. The only option left was to rebuild these systems through social reforms. Not only did the reformers put insufficient emphasis on social construction but they also tolerated or even encouraged high degrees of marketization in the social sphere. This set off a whole series of social problems. The social problems we experience today have a lot to do with the absence of the construction of social systems.

Therefore, we must work on building social systems—and systems like social security, healthcare, education, and public housing still need to be built. Yet some officials look at social construction as nothing more than "slicing a cake." For them, economic development makes the cake, and social construction distributes pieces of the cake. This approach to policy is welcomed by some. But if it's simply a matter of slicing a cake, China's economic development will become unsustainable, and if the cake isn't sliced well, we'll repeat the mistakes of the Mao era. In fact, social reform means dividing the cake more equitably as the cake grows ever bigger. In other words, social reform means searching for new sources of achieving sustainable economic growth.

Why is it that social reform can guarantee sustainable economic development? The answer is mainly seen in the need to create a society with high domestic demand. China's policy of openness has created an externally oriented economy—that is, an export-oriented economy in which exports serve as the primary driver for economic growth. Since the outbreak of the global financial crisis in 2008, the impact of the world economy on China's economy has demonstrated that export-oriented economies have significant limitations and are easily affected by changes in the world economy. For many years, China has been under pressure from the West, whether in exports or imports. Given China's size, what China consumes and produces will have a large impact on the world economy.

In recent years, China's primary market for exports, the West, has begun to see a rise in protectionism. While China might not like this development, it is a development that is far beyond China's control. In the past, developed countries always advocated free trade, while developing countries engaged in protectionism. Times have changed. While China is a country that still has a very low per capita GDP, it has become a powerful advocate for free trade. Since the current international system of trade was created by the West, while China has chosen to join the system and integrate into it, its influence on the system is still quite limited. As a result, whenever it faces protectionism from the West, China feels powerless. This is to say, for an economy that is highly dependent on foreign trade, sustainable development is highly problematic.

China needs to build a consumer society that can rely on internal consumption to achieve sustainable development. But a consumer society has to have a basis in social systems. The West can be a consumer society, not only because of its level of economic development but more importantly because of social systems that were built through social reforms—systems that include social security, healthcare, and education. In China, a consumer society could not be built in the early days of reform because of a low level of economic development, and extremely low levels of consumption. But now the main reason China doesn't have a consumer society is the absence of a comprehensive social system. It is not that the Chinese people won't consume or do not wish to consume, but that they cannot consume. In the absence of social policies, it takes money to see a doctor or to go to school. Currently, the Chinese people are forced to rely mostly on themselves. Only with a set of social policies in place will there be hope for a Chinese consumer society.

Besides achieving goals for sustainable economic growth, building a consumer society can have other positive effects. To begin with, a consumer society can help with the fairness of income distribution. In China at present, the wage gap is too large, and society is overly divided. This has led to excessive consumption by a small minority, and inadequate consumption by the vast majority. If we want to build a consumer society, we must first achieve fairness in income distribution. This requires both the government and society working hard to improve mechanisms for income distribution. Only when a majority of people enter the middle class will China become a consumer society. In fact, owing to the absence of social policies and social systems, China's already small middle class is in danger. When the middle class are all "mortgage slaves" (*fang nu*) or "slaves to their children" (*hai nu*), such a middle class has no systematic safety net. Without this safety net, today's middle class could well become tomorrow's poor.

Second, building a consumer society can help create basic social equity and eliminate many of the factors that lead to social instability. In addition, a consumer society can encourage sustainable economic development through innovation—particularly innovation in science and technology. China's current labor force only accounts for a fraction of its GDP. Capitalists or business owners primarily profit by reducing wages (this includes cheap land). To build a consumer society, we must increase wages. This will put pressure on management and drive innovation. Without any pressure of this kind, management has no incentive to innovate. In addition, building a consumer society can also reduce international pressure and enable China to truly rise. Once China becomes a consumer society, the pressure on exports will naturally decrease. At the same time, a consumer society will demonstrate just how much the outside world depends on China, just as today's China depends on the West. A consumer society will also have external pressures, but then China will have the initiative, just as the initiative today lies with the West.

Social construction is highly critical and also inevitable. But as we are engaging in social construction, it is even more important that we avoid applying social policies to economic fields. In China we have the terms "anti-leftist" (*fan zuo*) and "anti-rightist" (*fan you*). Deng Xiaoping once emphasized that it is more important to be "anti-leftist" than "anti-rightist." There is reason for this. After experiencing the practices of the Mao era, leftism had become deeply ingrained in China. A salient feature of the left is an overemphasis on the role of government in the economic process. Because social reforms require that governments play an extremely important role or even a major role, some believe that the government must play an equally large role in the economy. It was emphasized above that China's reformers mistakenly applied economic policies to the social sphere. If we apply social policies to the economy now, we'll be making the same mistakes again.

In fact, over the long run, the government needs to get as far away from economic activities as possible and shift its focus to managing society. Since there is a giant state-owned sector—constituted primarily by SOEs—the government will continue to play an important role in the economy for a long time to come. But the ultimate goal of government reforms should be the creation of a regulatory government. In other words, the government must transition from direct intervention in economic activities to indirect regulation of economic activities. When the government itself was directly active in the economy, regulatory government was difficult to achieve, for regulation frequently devolved into a situation in which "the left hand regulates the right hand." As world economic history shows, separation between the government and the economy is the systemic condition for a regulatory government.

It was emphasized earlier that China's state-owned sector needs to be placed in a "cage" and given designated boundaries. As it is emphasized in China's economics classic, *Discourses on Salt and Iron*, the state's economic monopoly should be restricted to a tiny handful of fields like national defense, national security, large-scale infrastructure, public engineering, and disaster prevention and response. Only when the government withdraws from the vast majority of economic activities and returns these activities to society at large can the government avoid "competing with the people" (*yu min zheng li*). This is also a precondition for building a harmonious society. It involves the government's social construction and social management—that is, questions of the relationship between the state and society.

Balance Between the State and Society

Whether in the design of political systems or economic systems, the aim is the construction of society—that is to say, society is the ultimate goal of politics and economics.

So, in terms of the relationship between the state and society, how can we build a good society? Above I used the image of a market-in-state to describe the relationship between the Chinese government and the economy. In reality, there is a similar relationship between the state and society. We could well say that there is a society-in-state—that is, China is a government-dominated society, and the size of the social sphere depends on the government.

In recent years, China's ruling party has struggled to break away from its former "GDPism" and has begun to emphasize the importance of social construction. In February 2011, Hu Jintao, then general secretary, advocated social policies such as "social management" and "managerial innovation" at a seminar on social management and social innovation for leading cadres at the provincial and ministerial levels. Since then, every province and municipality in China has created leading groups for innovation in social management in order to refine and implement new policies. This has been the overriding trend. However, the content of social management still needs to be enriched and developed. Historically speaking, social management has been both the continuation of past policies and a reflection of the demands made by previous policy transitions.

For many years, with the unavoidable emergence of instability in Chinese society, government at all levels has made "maintaining stability" (*wei wen*) the ultimate priority. From the central government to local governments, a large institution has been created, and government at all levels has invested a vast amount of resources. Yet a lack of innovation in maintaining stability has not only resulted in extremely high costs but has also appeared increasingly unstable as stability is increasingly "maintained."

In order for there to be innovation in social management, there must first be a rational understanding of the concept of social management. Effective social management has historically depended on a balance between the state and society or between the government and the people. There are two specific methods of social management: One is society's self-management, and the other is society's "being managed." Both situations exist in any society. In China, most people tend to give little consideration to the former—that is, self-management. China has traditionally been a paternalistic society. China has always emphasized order, but this order is often imposed from the top down. This tradition has not only failed to change with developments in society but has actually gotten stronger. To this day, when one speaks of social management, government officials at all levels understand what is being meant as top-down control.

If society is to develop into a self-managed order, the state and the government will need to give society much more room to operate. Only with greater space can China develop into a true society, and only with society can China develop an autonomous or bottom-up order for society. Many developed countries have such an order.

China currently has a poor relationship between the state and society—that is, it has not formed a virtuous circle for interactions between the state and society and between the government and the people. Government officials frequently regard society antagonistically and rely on the government's power to control society. When the state does not give society room for development, society will have difficulty in developing the effective capacity for self-government, making it impossible for China to produce an order of conscious morality. If a society lacks this capacity, it has to rely heavily on the government's management of all social affairs. Thus, in terms of social management, the burden on the Chinese government far exceeds that of many other countries. The government may manage everything, but it cannot manage society forever.

Regardless of whether society is self-managed or "being managed," a key issue at stake is always the relationship between the state and society, between the government and the people. In academia, this relationship is called a "regime." The "regime change" discussed in the West has been translated into Chinese as "regime replacement" (*zhengquan gengti*). What this translation means is not very clear. In some non-democratic countries, Western governments have deployed increasingly powerful NGOs to facilitate regime change. This has made the concept of a "civil society" politically sensitive in China. Some simply hold that the development of a civil society is not only detrimental to social stability but also poses a threat to the regime.

But "regime change" carries much greater significance than its translation into "regime replacement." If "regime change" is just "changing dynasties," then of course this is a sensitive concept. But this is actually not the case. This concept refers more to changes in the structure of power—that is, there must be changes in the relationship between the state and society, between the government and the people. This change is not a revolution, but a reform. It is a shift in the relations between the state and society, between the government and the people, and one that enables growth toward a better relationship and thereby proves beneficial for both the regime and society.

Many pit the state and society, the government and the people, against each other. This antagonistic understanding necessitates two extremes: (1) without the government, there can be no society; or (2) without society, there can be no government. Both appear to be zero-sum games. There was a time in China when there was only government, and no society. At the time, people theoretically regarded the relationship between the state and society as a zero-sum game. In practice, there was essentially no society. All the individuals in society were atomized and attached to the state through various personal restrictions.

At the other extreme, there is only society—there is no government. The worst case of this extreme is anarchy, while the best case is complete social autonomy or spontaneous organization. Historically speaking, however, there have never been any completely autonomous societies. Wherever there are people, there is government, regardless of which form government has taken.

Over the past few decades, there has been great debate in academia over the relationship between the state and society, between the government and the people. The basic relationship between the two can be summarized into four kinds of circumstances: first, a strong government and a weak society; second, a strong society and a weak government; third, a weak government and a weak society; and fourth, a strong government and a strong society. Obviously, the worst possible situation is a weak government and a weak society, while the fourth situation of a strong government and a strong society is the most ideal.

Which kind is China? Many will definitely say that China is a strong government and a weak society. In reality, however, this question is not easily answered.

On the one hand, China has exhibited a classic example of a strong government, both in theory and in practice. The government of China is very strong and has the social mobilization capacity to realize its policy agenda. It always seems able to deal with society's wide variety of challenges, and with ease. But, on the other hand, not only is China's society weak but its government is weak as well. The government manages everything, but its management is often not effective. While more and more policies appear theoretically sound, they are proving difficult to implement, and they often remain nothing more than words on a page.

The difficulties in executing policy and the weaknesses of society are related. It's difficult for society to exert influence on the government. The central government must rely on the bureaucracy to implement policies. But without pressure from society on the bureaucracy, the bureaucracy has no incentive to implement policy. And a weak society also does not have enough power to implement government policies. The Chinese government's great ability to mobilize comes from political mobilization. But overusing political mobilization can lead to many negative effects, one of the worst of which is to make an already weak system even weaker.

An example is the legal system. A legal system is the safeguard for the institutional capabilities of any country. But China's various forms of political mobilization often exceed or even undermine the legal system. In many regards, while some leaders may emphasize the rule of law, they are often much more enthusiastic about implementing policies through political mobilization. This makes bringing the rule of law to Chinese society ever more difficult to achieve. Whether in policy formulation or implementation, society has difficulty exerting influence. At the same time, society itself has not been given enough room to develop its capacity for self-management. This has created a situation in which both the government and society have been weakened.

When it comes to social management, clearly everyone should strive for the fourth situation, a strong government with a strong society. The state and society, the government and the people, do not need to be in a zero-sum game; they can be in a win-win situation. What China needs is a society capable of self-organization. Without society, the government lacks a foundation. If society is weak, the government will be weak, too.

So how can we achieve a strong government with a strong society? Experience teaches us that such a society needs to feature three kinds of order. The first and most vital level of such a social order is a self-managed society. If society cannot be self-managing, then everything has to depend on the government. And if the government manages everything, this will inevitably be beyond the government's ability to manage, and its management will be ineffective. For society to become self-managing, it must be given adequate room to develop. This means that the government must delegate power to society. The government must not only delegate to society those areas where society can be self-managing but also delegate those areas it fails to manage well. This is to say, the orientation and content of decentralization must change.

In the past, decentralization meant decentralizing power among different levels of government—it primarily referred to delegating power from higher-level government to lower-level government. Today it must be clearly stated that to decentralize to society means that the government delegates power to society, whether by returning power to the people or empowering the people. It should be emphasized, however, that the self-management of society is not laissez-faire, and the government must regulate social spheres that involve the public interest. This is the same reason why the government must regulate economic activities.

The second level of such a social order is a partnership between government and society. In those areas where the government must participate in management, it is not necessary that the government manage these areas itself; it can delegate management to social organizations. In other words, the government and society can form a partnership. Delegating social management can reduce management costs and make management more sustainable.

The third level of this society is the social order that is administered by the government. While the most salient characteristic of modern states is a monopoly on violence, one in which violent machinery is employed to maintain social order, in most advanced countries the government's role in social management is mainly reflected in system building, which includes the legal system and various social systems (social security, healthcare, education, housing, etc.). The use of violence to maintain social order is the last and ultimate resort, and governments should focus on institution building. Institution building is the platform for society's individuals, as well as group activities.

In China, the government is clearly focusing on the third level. As far as the first level is concerned, while social autonomy has ideological legitimacy—as seen in the concept of village autonomy—at the policy level, autonomy has a very narrow scope. Since society cannot be sufficiently empowered, it lacks room to develop. At its most basic level in rural areas, while the village electoral system has been in place for many years, party institutions still dominate. Relations between a village's party apparatus and the elected village assemblies have not been managed well.

So while we have the concept of autonomy, it has no real content. In some places, officials understand autonomy as a laissez-faire attitude and a lack of regulation, one which would lead to the rise of an underworld and anarchy. Just how to achieve real autonomy in rural areas remains a daunting task. At the second level, forming partnerships between the government and society is not part of the Chinese tradition. Traditionally, society has always been an accessory to the government, one that is the object of administration. It will take time for the concept of equality between the government and society to take root.

But the issues that the government highlights at the third level appear more serious. On the one hand, in maintaining stability, the government tends to employ excessively violent machinery. On the other hand, China has seen a "privatization" of the state's violence, which has become most glaring in the "black jails" (*hei jianyu*) that have been recently exposed. The privatization of violence has also contributed to the violent nature of maintaining stability.

The absence of social order in the first two levels and the marked usage of violent machinery in the third level have clearly produced antagonism between the state and society, between the government and the people. And this antagonism is a real source of social instability.

China does not need to go down this road, however, for there are other more humane and effective approaches. In fact, after the Reform and Opening Up, China gained significant experience in social management. During the 1990s, the ruling party administered society through political processes that incorporated social forces into political power. This was primarily reflected in allowing private entrepreneurs to join the Party and participate in politics. After the Reform and Opening Up, the most successful part of China's reforms has been in allowing the development of a non-state sector outside of the state-owned sector. By a variety of measures, the private economy rapidly surpassed the state-owned sector.

But this raised a question: What were private entrepreneurs to do? This was a vast, new, and rising social group, one that played a vital role in society. Despite controversy at the time, the ruling party brought this social group into the political process. Allowing private entrepreneurs to join the Party has been one of the Communist Party's most creative decisions. Throughout the history of the international communist movement, communism's goal has always been to eliminate both capitalism and capitalists. Allowing private entrepreneurs to join the Party was a pioneering initiative for the Communist Party of China, one which distinguishes China's Communist Party from communist parties of other regions. This practical approach has guaranteed the future health of the ruling party.

At the same time, the government has recently been working hard in the construction of social institutions in order to safeguard society. In administrative and management systems, reform of super ministries is being implemented all the way from the central government to local governments. This reform is designed not just to create a regulatory government and improve the government's efficiency but also to create "a small government and a great society" (*xiao zhengfu, da shehui*). In China in which society is within the state, it is only with a smaller government that society can grow. Super ministries exist for "small government"; thus, building them is an institutional prerequisite for a "great society." When government functions become integrated, government itself grows smaller. Since government must grow smaller, it must transfer many of its functions to society. In other words, the result of a smaller government will be a larger society. In which direction are state-society relations developing? This question can be answered easily.

If, with accelerating social reforms, power can be transferred to society, and the work done in the 1990s can be continued as emerging social forces are integrated into the political process, then social management will return to sustainability, relations between the government and the people will enter a virtuous circle, and we will ultimately see the creation of a strong government with a strong society.

CHAPTER TWO

The Chinese Experience from the Perspective of International Development

> If we approach the political reforms of developing countries like China from a purely democratizing perspective, many of the valuable aspects of these reforms will be easily ignored. China has still not yet entered the stage of reforms where political reform is in the driver's seat. The timing of that stage depends on progress in social reform and further economic reform. But the stage will certainly come.

That China's experience is important is self-evident. Despite the unique nature of some aspects of China's development over the past thirty years, this experience has still received widespread attention from an increasing number of developing countries. If China continues to develop well, it may well become an instructive model for other developing countries.

If China's experience is situated within the context of international development, China does offer considerable experience that other countries can draw from. An understanding of China's experience is inherently significant. At the same time, the relationship between political reform and economic development is an important issue, one that has been debated since the Reform and Opening Up. China has experience, but relations between political and economic development can be treated under the following five primary aspects.

It Cannot Be Said That China Has Seen No Political Reform

I do not agree with the idea, popular in the international academy and policy circles, that "China has had no political reforms, only economic reforms." Since the Reform and Opening Up, it's hard to imagine how China could have realized its achievements in economic development without any political reform. This idea also has difficulty in explaining the massive differences between today's government and the government of the period before the Reform and Opening Up. The key lies in how we define political reform. In different developing countries, different internal conditions lead to different political reforms. Political reforms will also be different within different stages of economic and social development, even within the same country. If we approach the political reforms of developing countries like China from a purely democratizing perspective, many of the valuable aspects of those reforms can be easily ignored. In fact, when people approach the politics of developing countries from only a democratizing perspective, they usually draw pessimistic conclusions, since democratizing reforms in developing countries are rarely straightforward.

It's understandable that Western countries want developing countries to carry out democratizing reforms, since, to the date, democracy has proven the most effective system at enabling people to realize their self-worth. But the vast majority of developing countries do not face questions of democratization alone—more importantly, they need to deal with building basic state systems. Through centuries of development, Western societies have created a set of effective, complete, and modern state systems, but most developing countries clearly have not created such systems. For developing countries, the primary task at hand is state-building. In the experience of many developing countries, democratization does not help them create a modern state—but after they build a modern state, democratization is possible.

State-building has been at the heart of China's political reform over the past thirty years. The organizational reforms that China's leadership has consistently been emphasizing fall into this category. Democratization is an objective for China's political reform, but it is not the only objective. Besides democratization, China has many other equally important objectives, such as economic development and social transitioning. A variety in transitions in fields such as the economy, society, and politics often place tremendous pressure on the leadership of developing countries. In some countries, governments have proved powerless in the face of many different pressures. In China, this multiplicity of pressures is mainly handled through two methods.

The first is taking reform gradually. Gradual reforms demonstrate that what is taking place is reform, not revolution. Instead of adopting radical reforms, as the Soviet Union and Eastern European countries did, China has insisted on a gradual approach—giving China enough time and space to make regular adjustments to its political system as well as adapt to an economy and society in perpetual change.

In the second method, China has divided reforms into different stages. In each stage, various aspects of reform take differing priorities. Simply put, from the late 1970s to the beginning of the twenty-first century, the main focus of China's reforms was economic reform. But this did not mean that there were no political reforms or social reforms; rather, this demonstrated that economic reform took the lead during this stage, while political and social reforms were subordinate. Without a variety of subordinated political and social reforms, economic reform would have been hard to carry out.

Since the 16th Congress (2002), China has entered a stage of reform in which social reform is at the fore. The focal points of social reform have included aspects such as social security, healthcare, and education. On the one hand, social reform serves to absorb the negative effects brought about by economic reform; on the other hand, social reform can create a stronger social foundation for further economic reforms. Of course, without political reforms, social reforms are not easily achieved or developed. Orderly social reform can only be ensured by political reform.

China has still not yet entered the stage in reform in which political reform is in the driver's seat. The timing of the stage's arrival depends on progress in social reform and further economic reform. But the stage will certainly come.

The Indispensability of the Sociopolitical Order

Economic development demands a basic sociopolitical order. Without this order, normal economic activities are difficult. This was one of the major points of Huntington's *Political Order in Changing Societies*[1], and this view still applies in today's globalized times. The harsh reality of the era of globalization is this: If a country is isolated, it will have great difficulty in developing itself. International capital is the driving force for development in many developing countries, but if a country remains isolated, international capital will not come in.

1 Samuel P. Huntington, *Political Order in Changing Societies* (New Haven and London: Yale University Press, 1968).

Simply participating in the international economy is not enough—order is needed. Order is the basic condition for capital and business—and this is even truer for international capital. In fact, as the experience of Indonesia during the Asian financial crisis shows, once a basic politico-social order is lost, the original results of development will also be scattered to the winds. To a large extent, the Soviet experience also illustrates this point. In China, after the Reform and Opening Up, while there have been various social movements and mass protests, the government has guaranteed the basic sociopolitical order. After Deng Xiaoping's 1992 Southern Tour, China has also been a leader among developing countries in attracting foreign investment.

This must be related to China's social order. It's hard to imagine that foreign capital will continue to unceasingly flow into China if its society loses its order.

Protecting Property Rights through Political and Administrative Means

Economic development requires the effective protection of property rights. Protecting property rights touches on the enthusiasm of investors. Without property rights, there is no motivation mechanism. Thus, various Western economic schools—particularly neoliberal economics—give special emphasis to the central role of the protection of property rights in economic development. The question is what kind of mechanisms should be employed to secure property rights. Here, China and other developing countries approach the matter differently than the West. Western countries place particular emphasis on relying on the rule of law to protect property rights. This is also easy to understand, for in developed political and economic systems, the rule of law is the most effective guarantee of property. But it is unfair for the West to criticize developing countries like China for failing to create an effective rule of law that can protect property rights. As with democracy, it has taken centuries of evolution for Western legal systems to develop to where they are today. Demanding that developing countries create an effective rule of law in a brief span of time is simply not realistic. The point is that, in the absence of an effective legal system, developing countries must find other mechanisms by which they can protect property rights.

In China, when reforms had just begun, it was proposed that a legal system be created. And at the 15th Congress in 1997, establishing the rule of law was made a major objective for political reform. Since the Reform and Opening Up, China has enacted countless laws and regulations, so it cannot be said that China does not attach much importance to the rule of law. But on the other hand, it should be noted that, since China lacks a good legal infrastructure, it remains difficult to implement many laws and regulations. This applies to protecting property rights as well.

If there is no protection of property rights, then what is the explanation for China's rapid and sustained economic development? In fact, China protects property rights primarily through political and administrative means. When the rule of law has not been established and the legal system cannot operate effectively, political and administrative means must be employed to protect property rights if economic development is to be pursued.

During the Reform and Opening Up, China created what can be called a "pro-business" or "pro-development" government. The Communist Party of China revised its constitution to allow private entrepreneurs to enter the Party and enjoy political rights. China's constitution was also amended with protections for property rights. At the empirical level, the protection of capital and property rights by government at all levels has greatly exceeded the rule of law. In order to manage competition and promote local economic development, local governments often provide extra protection and incentives for capital through political and administrative means, like lowering workers' wages and selling land at low prices. But it needs to be noted that protecting property rights through political and administrative methods has its own inherent disadvantages.

Owing to the involvement of political and administrative power, the power of government officials at all levels often goes unchecked. Excessive power often leads to violations of property rights and other rights. Capital's rights are protected, but the rights and interests of workers and farmers are frequently uninsured. And in some instances, excess power has also led to violations of the rights of capital. Deploying political and administrative means to protect property rights is unavoidable; what's more important is whether a transition to protection through the rule of law can be achieved.

Here, China's passage of the Property Law is of great significance. While there are many disputes within Chinese law, the passage of this law has been a great step forward. It shows that China's protection of property rights has begun to transition from a political and administrative approach to the rule of law.

Social Justice Is a Prerequisite for Sustainable Development

Sustained economic development requires basic social justice. No economic activity occurs in an abstract space; rather, each occurs within physical social spaces. Every economic transition is both interpersonal and "intergroup" in nature—in other words, economic life cannot be independent of social life. Rather, it is an important component of social life. Thus, the inherent significance of an economic activity must be located within social relations.

The normal operation of society is the most basic condition for economic development. The sociopolitical order mentioned earlier is an important aspect of this. The significance of basic social justice is also fundamental here, for without basic social justice, society will experience severe challenges. Economic activities can create the economic conditions for basic social justice, but the impact of economic activities on social justice is not necessarily a positive one.

If, in economic development, equal opportunities are not provided for various social groups, social justice cannot be guaranteed. If a large amount of the wealth generated by economic development is not equitably distributed among social groups, again, social justice cannot be guaranteed. And once society lacks basic justice, social instability or even chaos becomes a possibility.

Since World War II, the problem has not been that developing countries have failed to reach a certain stage of economic development, but that economic development has not continued. A major reason for this arrested development has been deficiencies in social justice, which have ultimately bred social disorder. Today, many countries in Africa and Latin America face challenges in achieving basic social justice.

China has experience in this regard as well. While economic development has brought many benefits to the people, in many aspects it has also led to many frustrations of social justice. Since China's economic development has been achieved through large-scale decentralization, local government at all levels, along with their officials, has controlled vast amounts of resources—and their power has been excessive and unrestrained, leading to widespread corruption.

While China has not undergone mass privatization like that experienced in Russia, various disguised privatizations have occurred. What the West calls the public sector includes healthcare, social security, and education; in these fields, excessive industrialization has distributed a massive amount of wealth to a small minority. At the same time, Deng Xiaoping's policy to first make some people rich (but not others) has failed to bring prosperity to society in general.

In comparison with global standards, Chinese income disparities have reached dangerous levels. Under such circumstances, China must naturally experience some symptoms of social disharmony. Recent years have seen a steady stream of mass disturbances, with some of them becoming steadily more and more politicized. Under such circumstances, China has recently been offered a guiding ideology of "scientific development" and "a harmonious society"—clearly in order to realize basic social justice.

For developing countries, there can be no social justice without economic development, but economic development cannot be equated with social justice. The key lies in whether effective measures can be taken to correct social injustices when they arise.

Social Diversity Promotes Political Reform

Democratization demands a specific socioeconomic infrastructure. In the twenty-first century, most states and peoples yearn for democracy. But it often appears that democracy is sought more frequently than found. It is not that developing countries do not have experience with democratization but that not all experiences with democratization have been positive. There have been both good and bad democracies. In some countries, democracy has provided their peoples with many positive experiences, but democracy has brought many negative experiences elsewhere.

As was discussed earlier, the overriding task for many developing countries is the building of basic state systems. Democratic systems are only one important component of many state systems; they do not represent them in its entirety. Democracy cannot replace all modern state systems, nor can it necessarily build every aspect of a modern state system.

Furthermore, while democracy and economic development can occur in parallel within Western societies, in many developing countries, democracy cannot necessarily promote economic development. Economic development requires order, but democracy cannot guarantee such an order. Nor can democracy lead to social harmony. In developing countries, democracy often causes the over-politization of national economic and social life. When the state is excessively politically mobilized, the political sphere grows too great, while the economic and social spheres grow too small. None of this is conducive to social harmony.

For China and other developing countries, the key question is not whether democracy should be adopted, but rather how a good democracy can be pursued while avoiding a bad democracy. In the experience of both developed and developing democracies, a good democracy needs a certain socioeconomic infrastructure. In other words, good democracies require a certain standard of social and economic development. Poor localities can develop democracy, but if the people are too poor, they will lack the capacity to resist those in power, regardless of whether those in power are elected or generated by other means. Too much historical experience warns that peasant rebellions and revolutions cannot produce democracy—in particular, good democracy. But "revolutions" by the middle class frequently lead to good democracy.

China's economic development is still in its early stages, and the country's middle class is still not large. And there are still many poor people in China. As in recent years, there have been many mass disturbances among the poor, so it is critical that China's leadership confronts the problem of poverty. Obviously, if China cannot eradicate extreme poverty, it will find it difficult to avoid the vicious revolutions that have repeatedly afflicted Chinese history.

China has great hopes for democratization. In some parts of China, the awakening of the middle class is just beginning. Some mass disturbances in developed regions have been related to the middle class—particularly those touching on environmental protection and similar issues. But economic development has spurred social diversity, which has in turn incited the fine-tuning of China's political system to adapt to socioeconomic realities. Thus, while China's political changes are defined by gradualness, one can remain optimistic about democratic politics. In every respect, democratization can be said to be the future.

CHAPTER THREE

China's Experience with Political Innovation and Its Global Significance

> Openness is gradually becoming an important feature of China's party system. Historically, any party that is not open will eventually become xenophobic and isolated, ultimately leading to its extinction. Only an open politics is truly inclusive. In China, political openness is achieved through a mechanism I call "internal pluralism"—the openness of the ruling party. When differing interest groups emerge in society, the ruling party is open to them and absorbs them into the political process; it also reflects their interests through various systems and mechanisms.

"Is China's political system innovative?" As China becomes increasingly important in the daily lives of people across the world, it seems like a political entity that has never before encountered. Chinese leaders have repeatedly stated on many occasions that China wants to pursue a politics different from what has been pursued elsewhere. In fact, this is what China has done. However, what has spurred me to explore this subject was two different articles that I read.

Factors Behind the Crisis in Democracy in the Contemporary West

The first article was published in *Forbes*. Its author was Eamonn Fingleton, and the title was "Upside-Down Propaganda: How China Keeps Fooling The New York Times, The BBC, And Other Wishful Thinkers."[1] In the article, the author states:

> For nearly two decades now, Beijing has worked through various witting and unwitting surrogates, many of them Westerners, to persuade the United States and Europe that China's rise is somehow an illusion. Beijing is playing on an apparently limitless capacity for wishful thinking in the West and, to anyone who has been following the story, the motive is obvious: to foster complacency and procrastination. The point is that the slower Westerners are to understand how profoundly the map of world power is changing, the less effective will be any Western efforts to moderate Beijing's ambitions.

Citing many mistaken predictions made in Western media outlets such as *The New York Times*, *The Economist*, and *Time*, the author argues, "We now know that the earlier predictions proved not only wrong but the diametric opposite of the truth. Instead of conveniently collapsing, China continued to grow faster than any other major nation in history."

I'm not so sure whether the Chinese government has gone to such an extent to intentionally fool Western media. Many members of the Chinese media have often been surprised themselves by the rapid development of this country. What I do know is that no one, including China's leadership, can predict China's future. But Fingleton is right in saying that all previous predictions of China's collapse have proven premature.

Personally, I think that it is the duty of scholars to explain the world. If the facts can be explained clearly, then the objective laws governing the development of things can be known. And then you can know the future. But many contemporary "China watchers" are like fortune tellers who often want to "predict" China. The prediction market is very large and attractive, and from time to time it has recruited many into its ranks. As a result, China research abounds in too much of what I like to call "pseudo-knowledge."

1 Eamonn Fingleton, "Upside-Down Propaganda: How China Keeps Fooling The New York Times, The BBC, And Other Wishful Thinkers," *forbes.com*, Forbes Media LLC, February 23, 2014, https://www.forbes.com/sites/eamonnfingleton/2014/02/23/a-lesson-in-propaganda-how-china-fooled-the-bbc-the-new-york-times-and-other-wishful-thinkers/#2f4686eb5d99.

The second article I'd like to talk about was published in *The Economist*, "What's gone wrong with democracy."[2] This article discusses the many difficulties that democracy is currently experiencing across the world, along with the origins of these difficulties. Indeed, just as the authors say, democracy is on the decline. Outside the West, democracies are moving toward collapse. The authors state: "Where autocrats have been driven out of office, their opponents have mostly failed to create viable democratic regimes. Even in established democracies, flaws in the system have become worryingly visible and disillusion with politics is rife." In the West, "democracy has too often become associated with debt and dysfunction at home and overreach abroad." The idea that democracy is in crisis is now widespread.

And, as the authors discuss, it's very clear that democracy is in crisis within developing countries. Since the collapse of the socialism of the Soviet Union and Eastern Europe during the 1990s, the world has entered an era of "color revolutions." A combination of internal and external factors can easily give rise to a cheap revolution—that is, in comparison with the early democratic revolutions, color revolutions are relatively effortless. Although it's generally believed that democracy follows in the wake of color revolutions, the facts have simply not borne this out. After color revolutions, there is anarchy.

In addition, developed countries—most of them democracies—are also facing another kind of color revolution. Unlike developing countries, color revolutions in developed countries involve peaceful regime change—which is an advantage of democratic politics. But the issue isn't with debt, as the authors of the *Economist* article hold, but rather with the failure of Western democracies to produce effective governments. I recently read a new book by two other editors of *The Economist*, John Micklethwait and Adrian Wooldridge, *The Fourth Revolution: The Global Race to Reinvent the State*. The authors hold that the reforms carried out by Prime Minister Thatcher in the United Kingdom and President Reagan in the United States were "half revolutions" for the modern West. For me, since Thatcher and Reagan, the West has not been able to produce strong leaders capable of implementing reform. Serious issues have emerged in democratic politics, but democracies have not produced any leaders capable of solving them. This is the dilemma that Western democracies face today.

My interest in the article published by *The Economist* lies in the two reasons the authors believe caused the current crisis in democracy. For the authors, the two main reasons for this crisis are the 2007–08 financial crisis and the rise of China. The financial crisis exposed fundamental weaknesses in Western economic and

2 "What's gone wrong with democracy," *economist.com*, The Economist Group, February 27, 2014, https://www.economist.com/essay/2014/02/27/whats-gone-wrong-with-democracy.

political systems, thereby weakening the confidence of Westerners in democracy—and this confidence had always been an important asset for the West.

Since the advent of modernity, the West has promoted Western-style democracy. It has spent vast amounts of human resources, wealth, and materials in this regard, and its self-confidence has been one of its great driving forces. Today, especially when governments use taxpayer money to bail out financial capital, and when financiers continue to pay themselves high bonuses while citizens helplessly stand by, many Westerners no longer entertain fantasies about their economic and political systems.

The financial crisis of 2008 happened at the heart of Western democracy; thus, it's easy to understand why the crisis has so negatively affected Western democracy. But why do the authors mention China as a separate threat? For the West, China is not part of the democratic world. Since this is so, how does China influence the world's democratization? How does China influence Western democracy? The authors of the *Economist* article argue that the reason is simple: China's economic rise. Here I'd like to quote at length:

> The Chinese Communist Party has broken the democratic world's monopoly on economic progress. Larry Summers, of Harvard University, observes that when America was growing fastest, it doubled living standards roughly every 30 years. China has been doubling living standards roughly every decade for the past 30 years. The Chinese elite argue that their model—tight control by the Communist Party, coupled with a relentless effort to recruit talented people into its upper ranks—is more efficient than democracy and less susceptible to gridlock. The political leadership changes every decade or so, and there is a constant supply of fresh talent as party cadres are promoted based on their ability to hit targets. China's critics rightly condemn the government for controlling public opinion in all sorts of ways, from imprisoning dissidents to censoring internet discussions. Yet the regime's obsession with control paradoxically means it pays close attention to public opinion. At the same time China's leaders have been able to tackle some of the big problems of state-building that can take decades to deal with in a democracy. In just two years China has extended pension coverage to an extra 240m rural dwellers, for example—far more than the total number of people covered by America's public-pension system. . . . China offers an alternative model. Countries from Africa (Rwanda) to the Middle East (Dubai) to South-East Asia (Vietnam) are taking this advice seriously.

The authors go on:

> But as China's influence has grown, America and Europe have lost their appeal as role models and their appetite for spreading democracy. . . . And why should developing countries regard democracy as the ideal form of government when the American government cannot even pass a budget, let alone plan for the future? Why should

> autocrats listen to lectures on democracy from Europe, when the euro-elite sacks elected leaders who get in the way of fiscal orthodoxy?

Thus, the authors conclude that, much more than previous forms of socialism, China poses a substantial threat to the Western notion that democracy is inherently superior and that it will ultimately triumph.

These two passages are thought-provoking. My first thoughts are that the mentality of today's Westerners bears many similarities to that of late Qing China. Contemporary systems are experiencing serious problems. Some still cling to an indefinable sense of superiority, while others embrace change in the environment—particularly in the external environment. It was only after their thorough defeat that China's political elites came to understand the principles of "radical change." Today's China is the product of the "radical change" of modernity. But the mentality in today's West may not change until it meets an even more severe crisis.

Why Is It that China's Political System Survives?

For me, a much more important question is: Since China has changed so dramatically over the past thirty years, why has its political system managed to survive? According to Marx, changes in the economic base will inevitably lead to changes in the political superstructure. If you believe Marx, then this is a problem you must address. In fact, this issue has also long been of interest in the West. Westerners have always held that China's reform model is "only economic reform, not political reform."

In a world-historical sense, Marx is right. Economic changes will lead to political changes. Working from this understanding, some have long predicted the disintegration and collapse of China. But the reality is that China's political system still survives and is actually thriving. How are we to explain this? There are two possible explanations. The first is that China is an exception: The logical relation that Marx identified between the economy and politics does not apply to China. In other words, China's experience has broken the "law" that Marx discovered. The second possible explanation is that China's politics are not, as some have said, without their own reforms, but have undergone tremendous changes through reforms, and thus have been able to survive and develop. I personally tend to prefer the second explanation.

Here, let me address the question of changes within Chinese politics. Many other questions could be asked in relation to this question: How has China's political system survived and managed to develop itself? What is the essence of

China's political system? How does it actually operate? What makes it different from other political systems? Does it exist in serious conflict with Western democracy, and pose a menace to the West? Does China's political practice hold global significance?

In fact, I've been reflecting on those questions for at least twenty years. These are questions that "China watchers" have also asked. In fact, it could be said that these questions have become "standard questions" for China research—if researchers don't mention these questions, they're held to be "politically incorrect."

In recent years, there have been a series of "color revolutions," and some regimes in the Middle East and North Africa have fallen. This has led many to believe that the Chinese Communist Party (hereafter, CCP) might collapse within a few years, months, or even days. In the past several years, high-profile corruption cases like that of Zhou Yongkang have been interpreted by outsiders as signs of an internal power struggle; this interpretation has strengthened a belief in the Party's imminent collapse.

This view is divorced, however, from China's political realities. Not only has the CCP not collapsed, but it has also survived and even grown. Today, it has become the world's largest political party, with more than eighty million party members. Some might say that the number of party members is not important. The Communist parties of the Soviet Union and Eastern Europe also had vast quantities of members, and yet their regimes collapsed. What matters is elite politics. If there is a problem at the level of the elites, then having lots of party members is not going to help. Experience has proven this to be the case.

If you want to understand the changes within the CCP, you also need to understand the massive changes that have taken place within elite politics. Since the CCP is facing increasingly more difficulties, it seems reasonable to ask this question, but a much more important and significant question is: Why does the Party survive and continue to develop? Before answering this question, first suppose that the "knowledge" about whether it will collapse is false. To understand why the CCP can survive and thrive, we must first understand how it can learn, adapt, and change. In other words, we must examine how the CCP keeps innovating and adapting itself to a changing environment.

In my book *The Chinese Communist Party as an Organizational Emperor: Culture, Reproduction and Transformation*, I focused on the idea that, although the concepts and theories of Chinese party politics have been heavily influenced by modern Western politics, the CCP is still essentially a product of Chinese culture. The greatest political change in modern China has been in the shift from a traditional emperorship based on an individual to a party government based on a group.

Today, I want to focus on China's political innovations, an issue that has long been ignored by most but which is pivotal for China. But before exploring this issue, I'd like to talk about China's economic development and changes in the Marxist understanding of the "economic base." After undergoing thirty years of impoverished socialism, the CCP finally understood, absorbed, and implemented the so-called "seven pillars" that contributed to the development of the West: adjusting internal approaches such as a free-market economy, science and technology, a pragmatic culture, and education in accordance with a country's pursuit of wealth and power.

No one can deny that these pillars have been factors behind China's remarkable economic success. According to an estimate of national GDP based on purchasing power parity (PPP) that was conducted by the World Bank's International Comparison Program, in 2011, China's total GDP had reached $13.5 trillion, far exceeding that of the previously estimated $7.3 trillion, while the total GDP for the United States in 2011 was $15.5 trillion. The World Bank therefore concluded that China's total GDP will exceed that of the United States, making China the world's largest economy.

For the vast majority of Chinese, this estimate doesn't make much sense. The report sparked a new round of controversy worldwide about China's rise, but in China itself it has not received much attention: The government does not accept it, and the common people don't believe it. China's economy still faces huge challenges like overinvestment, overcapacity, and excessive local debt. China is rapidly losing the competitive advantage it has in cheap labor, while it lags far behind developed countries in fields that are critical to sustainable growth such as managerial experience, technology, and finance.

This calm approach is both realistic and important. In recent years, China's policy makers and policy researchers have been debating whether China will fall into the "middle income trap." The idea of a "middle income trap" basically refers to an economic phenomenon in which, after a country reaches a certain level of development, it remains stalled at that level for long periods of time. When a country's economic growth reaches the level of middle incomes, it enters a plateau and eventually stagnates. Such a country has fallen into the middle-income trap. This problem often occurs because of rising wages, diminishing cost competitiveness, or inability to compete with advanced economies in high-tech innovation. It can also be due to the fact that industries that produce cheap products keep wages low, and thus developing countries are stuck with economic models built around low wages. I don't intend to discuss in detail whether China will fall into this trap, as this would deviate from the main topic of this chapter.

What I want to say is this: Chinese leadership is keenly aware of such a possibility. While China has shown some awareness of this trap, its vivid awareness has led China to begin looking for strategies to avoid this trap—strategies such as introducing new processes of industrial production and finding new markets to maintain export growth. More importantly, China is seeking to increase domestic demand. China is doing everything it can to avoid the hidden dangers that have snared Asian economies like Thailand, the Philippines, and Malaysia into the middle-income trap. China's neighboring economies, like Japan, South Korea, and Singapore—as well as Taiwan and Hong Kong—have provided good examples. The experience of these high-income economies demonstrates that, if an economy is to avoid the middle-income trap, it must shift from a reliance on cheap labor to achieving growth through high productivity and innovation.

Here China must create a high-quality educational system that can encourage innovation and support technological breakthroughs. As part of the East Asian Community, China is expected to maintain economic growth and become a high-income economy. If China can achieve an annual growth of 6% or 7% over the next fifteen years or so, China will be able to achieve this goal.

Openness is gradually becoming an important feature of the Chinese party system.

In my opinion, the greatest challenge facing China remains political—that is, whether the CCP can survive. As many have observed, the CCP may die from vast and deeply entrenched corruption, lawless intra-party competition, or large-scale social unrest. However, the Chinese experience since reform indicates that the many problems facing the CCP are essentially problems of the developmental process. Many other regimes in the developed world today experienced the same problems, although those problems may have differed in degree and complexity. But unlike those developing countries that lack an effective governmental mainstay, China's strength lies in the existence of the CCP.

Here I need to elaborate on the concept of "pillars of government" (*zhizheng zhizhu*). Everyone is familiar with Tocqueville's classic work on Western democracy, *Democracy in America*. In the book, Tocqueville discusses the main body of democratic institutions, which is a civil society. Civil society is the "pillar of government" for Western democracy—Western democracies are built around a civil society. Civil society is a special product of centuries of development after the dissolution of the Western Roman Empire. Huntington therefore said that Western democracy is not universal, for it is a product of Western-specific culture.

Indeed, outside the West, it is difficult to find in developing countries a civil society similar to the West. Then what are the pillars of government in developing countries? The vast majority of countries have two pillars—one is religious organizations, and the other is the military. Religious organizations are the products of a long history. Some religious organizations are national in scope and can influence the politics of an entire country. Militaries are the products of modern developments in all developing countries. Today, however, with the exception of some countries in which politics and religion are united, religion has lost its legitimacy. What about militaries? Militaries also lack the legitimacy to directly govern a country. So how is a government to find its pillar? What happens most often is that military leaders shed their uniforms to run the country.

Egypt is the best example of this. Mubarak's was a military regime disguised as a civilian government. After its overthrow, religion became a pillar, but it quickly lost its base and was overthrown. Now things have returned to the way they were, as the military disguises itself as a civilian government.

So what is China's pillar of government? Religion is off the table, since China has always been a secular country, and religion lacks the legitimacy to rule. The military is important, but in a modern society, it has no legitimacy. Today, many are talking about civil society. Civil society is indeed developing, but it can't be said that the government in China is built on the basis of civil society. I personally don't believe that China's civil society will evolve into one like the West's. The political role of civil society will become more and more important, but it's not going to become a pillar of government. Realistically speaking, the pillar of government in China is the CCP. (Of course, it should be noted that the CCP and civil society do not need to be mutually exclusive, as long as the CCP is open enough to allow civil society to enter the political process.)

Let's return to the subject of the CCP. Although many negative developments in China today can be blamed on the CCP, it cannot be denied that the CCP has also accomplished much good. Generally speaking, it is an organization that learns rapidly and constantly from both the experience of other countries as well as its own history. The current anti-corruption movement is a good example. Within a brief span of time, dozens of high-level party cadres and government officials have been investigated and detained. Due to rampant and widespread corruption, the CCP was widely considered to be a hopeless case, with the only option being to wait for its inevitable death. Yet waves of anti-corruption campaigns over the past few decades have shown that, as long as leadership maintains a strong political will, this organization can mobilize its considerable power in order to realize its vision.

The ruling party neither expects corruption nor does it need it for its survival. On the contrary, an anti-corruption attitude is only the most basic requirement for the survival of the CCP. The survival and development of the CCP must be revived through the establishment of new systems. Self-renewal is produced, not only by an ever-changing environment but also by self-awareness among leadership. Since the Reform and Opening Up, the CCP has not survived and thrived by accident—it has all happened for a reason. If one word can be used to describe the self-renewal of the CCP, it is: openness.

Over the past thirty years, the CCP has transformed itself into an increasingly open party system. This differentiates the CCP from the Communist parties that fell from power in the Soviet Union and Eastern Europe—and it also differentiates the CCP from multiparty systems in post-socialist societies. After the collapse of socialism, Eastern European countries adopted a Western approach, allowing different interest groups to establish differing political parties. In order to avoid the death of the Party, the CCP has taken another course—that is, it has opened up the political process to all social and interest groups. As a result of this decision, China has gradually evolved into an "open party system" under a one-party rule.

Openness is gradually becoming an important feature of China's party system. Historically, any party that is not open will eventually become xenophobic and isolated, ultimately leading to its extinction. Only an open politics is truly inclusive. In the West, political openness is achieved through external pluralism, that is, a multiparty system. Theoretically speaking, every kind of interest can be represented in a specific political party. And if you can't find a means to express your interests, you can create your own party.

Do multiparty systems really represent the various interests that exist in society? This is an important question, but it is outside the scope of this chapter. Research by many Western scholars does reveal, however, that this hypothesis has only been demonstrated theoretically—not empirically. In China, political openness is achieved through a mechanism I call "internal pluralism"—the openness of the ruling party. When differing interest groups emerge in society, the ruling party is open to them and absorbs them into the political process; it also reflects their interests through various systems and mechanisms.

While it is often said that China has experienced no political reform, systemic changes in the CCP cannot be said to not be fast-moving. Since opposition parties have no legitimacy, a social group can most effectively express its own interests by entering the political process led by the CCP. At the start of the twenty-first century, the "Three Represents" (*san ge daibiao*) proposed by Jiang Zemin, the then General Secretary of the Central Committee of the CCP, reflected the typically pragmatic attitude of the CCP. Leadership realized that, with changes in the economic base, the ruling party had to represent differing social interests. And as the middle class grows increasingly larger in size (primarily through private enterprise), it has recently been showing a strong need for political participation. This is why the ruling party needs to keep up with the times. It must not only provide constitutional protections for private enterprise in the non-state-owned sector but also allow and encourage private entrepreneurs to enter a political process dominated by the ruling party. Changes in party membership are an important indicator.

During the Mao era, workers, farmers, and the Chinese People's Liberation Army constituted the vast majority of Communist Party members. However, since the Reform and Opening Up, the proportion of intellectuals, professionals, and emerging social classes within the Party has been growing greater and greater. After successfully bringing private entrepreneurs into the Party organization and the political process, the CCP has now begun to focus on social governance. In the past few decades, social forces have achieved significant growth and development, and the CCP must expand its governing base by being open to them.

As the social base for the CCP expands, that is, as more social forces enter the political process, the demand for democracy within the Party is also increasing. This is why the ruling party has been pursuing diverse forms of intra-party democracy for more than a decade. Some scholars have labeled China's political development as "corporatism." Under this institutional arrangement, the expanding middle class—particularly private entrepreneurs—become allies of the state, rather than an independent civil society outside of the state.

If anyone cares to look closely, the openness of this internal diversity will not seem much worse than any other system. Internal pluralism sets China apart from the Arab world, in which most regimes are closed, as one family (in a monarchy) or a few families monopolize political power and govern the state for long stretches of time. Many countries in Asia, while they may carry the forms of democracy, often actually function as aristocracies. In China, the number of people entering politics from the lower classes of society far exceeds that of many other countries, including democracies. So far, the CCP has not been based in one ruling family. It is a mass party with highly diversified interests.

Institutional Innovation Guarantees the Peaceful Transfer of Power

A central characteristic of the Chinese party system is that political openness has spurred the political elite to achieve peaceful transitions with increasingly institutionalized methods. It is the essence of Western democracies to achieve peaceful transitions of the political elite through regular elections. China has refused to follow the West, and has instead formed a very effective system of power transfer. The late Deng Xiaoping successfully established a series of important political systems to ensure the peaceful transfer of power. The most important of these include four systems: term limits, age limits, a selection system for elites, and collective leadership.

The first is term limits on leadership positions. Term limits are crucial. Generally speaking, leaders can serve a maximum of two consecutive terms, which means ten years. Included in these limits are the General Secretary of the Central Committee of the Communist Party of China, the President, the Premier, and other important positions. This isn't much different from the office of the presidency in many Western countries. Obviously, term limits are an effective method for preventing dictatorship. In other words, while China does not have a Western-style presidency that is based in democracy, it has created an alternative approach that prevents dictatorship. When one individual or one family rules a country for decades, political systems inevitably incline toward fraud and abuse. One of the principal factors in the color revolutions of many countries has been the long-term autocratic rule of individual leaders. In contemporary society, many, especially the young, are averse to particular leaders dominating the political stage for decades.[3]

Second, age restrictions are also highly important. Such restrictions provide a retirement system for senior political leaders and bureaucrats. In other political systems, retirement systems have been created for civil servants, that is, for bureaucrats. In China, however, mandatory retirement applies for all party and government officials, including political leaders, civil servants, congressional delegates, and the leaders of social organizations and all other important government and quasi-governmental organizations. Let me give a few examples. In the Political Bureau Standing Committee, up until the 18th Congress, the "seven up and eight down" (*qi shang ba bu*) rule was implemented—that is, officials aged sixty-eight and above had to retire regardless of term limit, while officials aged sixty-seven and below could stay in office. (Of course, at this level, retirement ages are not fixed, but change according with needs.) In ministries and commissions, mandatory retirement is at sixty, and at the departmental level, officials aged fifty-five and above must retire from leadership positions.

Term limits and age restrictions force China's political elite to renew itself at rapid rates, thereby enabling it to effectively reflect generational changes and changes in interests. Compared with many other political systems, China's political

3 There has been one important change since this paper was written. The Party's 19th National Congress in 2017 removed the term limit, and this move has been interpreted as the abolition of the system. But this is not necessarily true. In his meetings with foreign dignitaries and Chinese officials, Xi said that he is "personally opposed" to life-long rule, and foreign observers have "misinterpreted" the constitutional amendment that revoked the two-term limit on the state presidency and vice state presidency. See, Tom Mitchell, "China's Xi Jinping says he is opposed to life-long rule," *Financial Times*, April 16, 2018.

system can better achieve the rapid and large-scale replacement of government officials. Because of the strict enforcement of age restrictions, tens of thousands of officials step down from office every year, and an equal number of officials take their place. Despite its shortcomings, this rapid flow certainly does help the government reflect changes in the times.

The third system is a ruthless meritocracy. In many political systems, particularly in democratic systems, if you want political power, you have to get enough votes. In fact, China is also starting to implement intra-party voting, and voting is becoming increasingly important in the evaluation of the popularity of a potential leader with his or her colleagues and the public at large. Before the vote, however, there is an additional process of selection. The candidate must satisfy requirements such as education, work experience (with work in different regions and at different levels), and many other criteria. In Chinese politics, there can never be a "dark horse" candidate, as is sometimes seen in other political systems. Candidates are already part of the system, and have already met the necessary requirements for the position. In fact, China has a long history of elitism, and traditionally "scholars" (*shi*) were a class of specialized administrators. These days, the CCP is increasingly inclined to make use of helpful aspects of a system that has existed for millennia.

The fourth system is what China calls the "collective leadership system," or "intra-party democracy." This system was designed by the late Deng Xiaoping and was then implemented after his death. In this system, members of the Political Bureau Standing Committee collectively exercise political leadership. This is a system that is characterized by internal diversity. At the highest leadership levels of the CCP, Committee members have strict restrictions and balances. As the highest decision-making body, the Political Bureau Standing Committee is often regarded by the outside world as a symbol of a highly centralized political system—or of authoritarianism. But its members have almost equal power; they are each responsible for decision-making in one area and have the largest say and power to make policy within that area. Some scholars have called this system a "collective presidency," which means that major national decisions are made collectively.

In addition, another important feature of China's party system is worth mentioning here—that is, this particular system can help promote changes in policy. In theory, the obstacles to policy changes in a multiparty state should be relatively small, as policies can change with a change in the ruling party. When a new party comes to power, it can discontinue the policies implemented by the preceding party. But this is often not the case. In many democracies, opposition parties no longer play a constructive role; rather, they oppose simply for opposition's sake. With political parties mutually vetoing the other, no party can make significant decisions. Under such circumstances, major changes in policy are often difficult to achieve. This is not the case in China.

Although Chinese society frequently complains that the ruling party makes changes in policy too slowly, China has been implementing policy changes at a rate that is much faster than that of other political systems. From the 1980s through the 1990s, and into the twenty-first century, China has implemented several significant changes in policy. Failing to consider the ruling party's ability to respond to shifting circumstances with appropriate policy shifts makes it much harder to understand China's tremendous changes.

The CCP's innovations are not limited to these four areas, but in themselves they have been enough to enable the CCP to distinguish itself from other Communist parties. The survival and development of the CCP cannot be separated from these institutional innovations. At the same time, emphasizing these innovations does not imply that the system is free of serious flaws. In fact, the system still faces many problems and tremendous challenges.

What needs to be emphasized here is that this system is in the process of change, and it must improve itself through more change. The system is indeed changing, and the direction of change is clear—toward more openness, more competition, and more participation. As a result, the general characteristics of China's political system (characteristics toward which the system is also moving) are openness, competition, and participation. And these are the political changes that are happening today.

Relatively Centralized Authority Ensures Political Responsibility

In theory, the Chinese political system truly is highly centralized—or at least the upper ranks of leadership are provided with a strong institutional basis, for the upper echelons control the three most important positions in the system, namely, the General Secretary of the Central Committee of the Communist Party of China, the President, and the Chairman of the Central Military Commission. In reality, however, controlling these three positions does not mean that you have enough power to implement major reforms. As each member of the Political Bureau Standing Committee is only responsible for his or her own particular area and has the largest say in this area, the division of labor within the Political Bureau Standing Committee has become decentralized. Effective coordination does not exist.

As a result, the collective presidency often leads to the absence of a president, collective decision-making often leads to no decisions, and collective responsibility leads to a situation in which no one is responsible. This system is highly akin to feudalism, in which the person who occupies a certain territory has the final say in what occurs within it. It is this institutional feature that has given rise to the "Zhou Yongkang Phenomenon" seen today. To put it simply, the Zhou Yongkang Phenomenon is the transformation of economic oligarchs into political oligarchs.

Moreover, this system does not truly prevent retired politicians from interfering in politics. China does have mandatory retirement for its leaders, but it doesn't have a system for ensuring that its leaders withdraw from political involvement. Politicians frequently "retire without retiring" (*tui er bu xiu*): after their retirement, they continue to meddle in politics. In other words, the constraints on current leaders come not only from the system of collective leadership but also from the informal interventions of retired leaders.

This touches on the survival and development of the Communist Party itself. As far as deepening reforms goes, since the Third Plenary Session of the 18th Central Committee, high-level leadership has created four new major organizations for strengthening the institutional basis of high-level power, organizations which should bring corrections to the overly decentralized nature of high-level power.

The first organization is the Central Leading Group for Comprehensively Deepening Reform Commission, which is responsible for the overall design and implementation of reforms. This measure demonstrates Xi Jinping's determination to advance comprehensive reforms. After the 2008 financial crisis, China's process of comprehensive reform had almost stagnated.

The second organization is the National Security Commission. This new organization is primarily based on the American model, and it includes a team of national security experts who can stand at the controls of the country's vast security apparatus. But this agency differs from America's National Security Council in one key aspect: The Chinese version has dual responsibilities for both domestic security and foreign policy. Prior to the establishment of the National Security Commission, the power for determining high-level policy in foreign relations and national security was scattered among military committees responsible for the armed forces and two independent but sometimes overlapping leading groups, which were the Central Foreign Affairs Leading Small Group (FALSG) and the National Security Leading Small Group (NSLSG). As China's foreign and domestic security decision-making has become dramatically diversified, decentralized, and fragmented, the power of these two leading groups has continued to weaken in horizontal competition with other powerful institutional players.

During Hu Jintao's tenure, most of the domestic security work was carried out by the powerful Central Political and Legal Affairs Commission. At the time, the Secretary for the Political and Legal Commission was Zhou Yongkang, who was also one of the members of the Political Bureau Standing Committee. The CCP currently faces an increasingly resource-intensive situation in domestic security. China has experienced a series of terrorist attacks, including the Tiananmen Square attack and the knife attacks in the Kunming Railway Station and the Urumqi Railway Station. In order to cope with a deteriorating situation in domestic security, China needs a more centralized system.

In foreign affairs, as China becomes more and more integrated into the globalized world, the number and types of agencies and departments involved in security and foreign policy decision-making have increased significantly. Throughout the process, most national ministries, military and intelligence departments, large-scale enterprise units, media, local governments, NGOs, and even individuals have played an increasingly important role. As the highest-ranking decision-makers in diplomacy, high-ranking leadership before Xi Jinping tended to rely more on negotiation than those who had held office before them. At the same time, however, in the face of a much more complex international and domestic environment, today's central leadership bears many additional responsibilities and needs to rely on others to help plan and implement China's foreign policy and national security policy.

This will further reduce personal influence and increase the impact of multiple internal forces on the entire process. The two leaders before Xi Jinping considered creating an agency that could provide comprehensive coordination like that of the U.S. National Security Council, but, owing to a variety of factors, an agency was not created. Xi Jinping now has enough strength to formally establish such an organization. The new National Security Commission will guarantee Xi Jinping's authority among the members of the Political Bureau's Standing Committee. This change grants Xi Jinping a level of authority that his two predecessors, Jiang Zemin and Hu Jintao, did not have, and it reverses the trends toward collective leadership that had been in place since Deng Xiaoping.

The third important organization is the Central Leading Group for Cybersecurity and Informatization. As the commander-in-chief of China's military—that is, as the Chairman of the Central Military Commission—Xi Jinping created a fourth important leading small group: the Central Military Commission's Leading Group for Military Reform.

Many observers have noted that, with the establishment of these new institutions, Xi Jinping now has unparalleled power. On the surface, this new power may gradually weaken the collective leadership mechanisms in the CCP, but in fact these changes create a more rational distribution of high-level power. China's development still requires a concentration of power that can overcome the resistance of vested interests, avoid policy deadlocks, and implement drastic reforms. Moreover, while these changes do strengthen the power of the paramount leader, this is not a matter of individual power but of institutional power.

It should be noted that, in the past, China also had various leading groups, but they were often informal and could not operate openly and transparently. Thus, they often became political instruments by which a non-institutional approach undermined the formal system. These four agencies are all formal institutions that can operate openly and transparently. As long as they remain formal in nature, these agencies can gradually increase their institutionalization, while they can also be handed on to a new generation. Furthermore, in addition to his role in the Central Leading Group for Military Reform, Xi Jinping is the head of three other new agencies, Premier Li Keqiang is the deputy chief of these agencies, and other members of the Standing Committee are distributed among various groups. This can help avoid a dynamic in which the internal powers of the Standing Committee are overly restricted.

Even more important are questions surrounding political responsibilities. Intra-party democracy is important, but intra-party democracy should not stand in the way of political responsibility. The most important issue for any political system is the allocation of political responsibilities. If high-level power is overly decentralized, political responsibilities become confused. Excessive restraints on power in the previous system of collective leadership led to a situation in which no one takes responsibility. This is a dangerous situation for single-party governance.

Vietnam can be taken as an example. In recent years, many believed that intra-party democracy within the Communist Party of Vietnam had far outstripped China, so waves of people traveled to Vietnam to learn from the Vietnamese experience. But what about the situation on the ground? Today's Vietnam has four cooks in the kitchen—namely, the offices of the Party's General Secretary, the President, the Premier, and the Chairman of the National Assembly are filled by four different leaders. Among these leaders there are differing ideological orientations, differing interests, and different philosophies for foreign affairs. In addition, behind these leaders are differing vested interests or economic oligarchies. Unless Vietnam is ready to abandon one-party rule and move toward multiparty politics, I personally think that this mechanism of "polyarchy" faces a difficult future. Judging from Vietnam's current levels of economic and social development, if the country undergoes democratization, it will probably fall into the middle- or low-income trap.

After the 18th Congress, China has embarked on the opposite track—improving intra-party democracy by undertaking relative centralization. With the formation of the aforementioned agencies, China's top leadership can now overcome excessive decentralization of power and establish clear lines of political responsibility. So far, all of these changes have allowed the CCP to ensure openness. Through these newly designed systems, particularly the ruthless approach to promoting elites, China is developing a political system that is in keeping with the spirit of Chinese culture. It's worth mentioning that, while the CCP continues to oppose any form of Western-style democracy, it has adopted various democratic elements such as intra-party elections, decentralization, and political consensus.

The success of Asian countries has come through integrating some elements of Western democracy into their own political systems, while those countries that have been unsuccessful have frequently tried to copy their systems from Western democracies.

Exploring China's Own Approach

Emerging social forces are equally critical to promoting change in China's politics. In fact, without the pressure applied by society, the top-down political changes discussed previously probably would never have happened. Of course, the Chinese do not have Western-style political freedom. But this should not obscure the fact that individual freedoms have dramatically increased.

For example, during the Mao era, the Chinese people could not choose how they would dress, where they would live or work, what kind of research they could perform, or how they would perform their research, and obviously they could not choose to travel abroad. Nowadays, these freedoms are enjoyed by everyone. As a result, nearly one hundred million opt to travel abroad every year, and practically all of these freely return to China after their trips.

Another example of greater freedom is the widespread use of new information and communication technologies (ICT). ICTs have not only brought greater freedom but also posed a greater challenge to the ruling party and its government. Nearly half of the Chinese people today are Internet users, and 75% of them access the Internet through their mobile phones. Public opinion formed online is exerting increasingly greater influence on the Party and the state, and in some cases it has even led to changes in policy.

Every year in China there are hundreds of thousands of protests, strikes, and other mass disturbances (180,000 in 2010), and some of these are organized online—on blogs, Internet forums, Weibo, and by e-mail. Public opinion formed on cyberspace has created pressures that have often dislodged corrupt officials or forced the ruling party and its government to make adjustments in policies. Compared with the traditional media, the Chinese Internet is relatively less controlled by the CCP's publicity departments and is much more driven by the commercial interests of major online content providers. At the same time, the unique nature of information flow on the Internet—immediate, interactive, and unlimited—has weakened the effectiveness of traditional publicity methods.

As they strive for equal treatment, Chinese very much hope to obtain Western-style freedoms and rights. But China has been deliberating over the realization of human rights for a long time. China's leadership does not believe that rapid democratization can help China realize freedom and human rights. In this sense, China is part of the East Asian Model. In East Asia and particularly the Four Little Dragons, freedom and human rights have been realized gradually. Economic rights were achieved first, then social rights, and only then political rights.

Even though democracy has many problems today, it still has many advantages. As the authors of the *Economist* article observed: "Democracies are on average richer than non-democracies, are less likely to go to war and have a better record of fighting corruption. More fundamentally, democracy lets people speak their minds and shape their own and their children's futures. That so many people in so many different parts of the world are prepared to risk so much for this idea is testimony to its enduring appeal."

It is certainly true that democracy does have a certain appeal. However, democracy does not fall ready-made from the sky. Another passage from the same editorial:

> All this has demonstrated that building the institutions needed to sustain democracy is very slow work indeed, and has dispelled the once-popular notion that democracy will blossom rapidly and spontaneously once the seed is planted. . . . Western countries almost all extended the right to vote long after the establishment of sophisticated political systems, with powerful civil services and entrenched constitutional rights, in societies that cherished the notions of individual rights and independent judiciaries.

This is precisely what China has learned from the success stories of Western democracies and the tragedies of failed democratization in developing countries. In the post-Mao era, China was held to be a country that was learning from others—"learning from other countries" has become the main source of China's progress. Of equal importance is the fact that China has been learning from the failures of other countries.

China's economic reforms are market-oriented, but China does not want the market to control the entirety of the economy. The state has ruthlessly used the market to promote economic development, but the market still remains under the control of the state. From a Western perspective, China's state-owned sector is either a symbol of China's low productivity or a nightmare that should be quickly done away with. But from a Chinese perspective, the state-owned sector is a powerful tool that enables the government to promote growth, balance the market, and respond to economic crises.

The West has taught China how to develop social policy, but China does not want to become a Western-style welfare state. Similarly, as has been previously mentioned, China is currently implementing some democratic mechanisms from the West—but it does not want to give up its long-standing tradition of elitism. China selectively introduces components of Western states and integrates them with its own traditions.

China has also been quite innovative in the reform of its political system. Dramatic changes in society and the economy must be accomplished by similarly dramatic changes in politics. But Marx is still right, and I hold that China must be allowed to explore its own political approach. This will prove beneficial, not only for China but also for other countries, particularly those in the developing world. In an era of a crisis in democracy, both in the developed West and the developing world, China's institutional experience offers particular significance, and this experience may provide useful inspiration to other countries.

Finally, it is my view that we do not need to interpret China's experience as an attempt to weaken political systems in other regions. As has been previously discussed, China has learned from both the positive and negative experiences of Western political systems, and it has combined this experience with its own traditions. The primary driving force for this learning and adaptation has been the pressing need for China to design a set of political entities that can adapt to changing circumstances. This is the fundamental aim of China's political innovations. China is not trying to change the world.

In the same way, the world will benefit from China's successful experiments; the failure of these experiments in China would probably exert a tremendously negative impact on the rest of the world. And a China that goes its own way is more likely to become a stable, prosperous, and peaceful China. This, in its turn, will provide more opportunities for other countries to grow and reap benefits alongside China.

CHAPTER FOUR

Human-Centered Socialism, Political Party Transition, and the China Model

> The question of how to improve governing capacity is actually a question concerning a second transition in the Party—that is, how to transition from a party that emphasizes administration to a party that governs through political means. This transition is related, not only to the development of the Party itself, but also to the overall direction of human-centered socialism in the country.

If you want to study the China Model, the heart of your study must be the Chinese Communist Party (CCP). The CCP is China's only ruling party; it is the medium for China's overall socioeconomic transition; it is the maker of the China Model. The transformation of China's society and economy and the transformation of the Party itself are two tightly interlinked aspects of the China Model. Although discussions of the China Model tend to emphasize social and economic development, the China Model cannot be discussed without a discussion of transitions within the Party itself. This is because, on the one hand, if the Party is to promote social and economic transition, any developmental policy determined by the Party must be promoted by the Party itself; and on the other hand, the Party itself must be reformed in accordance with this new orientation—in other words, it must constantly change itself in order to adapt to this transition. Only thus can the Party continue to lead the country under new conditions. In other words, the Party must maintain its position as the driver of reform by effecting a transition within itself.

The Party's transition includes two major aspects: the direction of the transition and the methodology of the transition. The issue of the Party's transition is not a new one. Since Deng Xiaoping implemented the policies of the Reform and Opening Up, transition has long been on the table. In thirty-plus years of reform, the CCP has, I believe, undergone tremendous change, not only in terms of its internal organization and ideology but also in the relationship of the political life of the Party to the country itself.

For during the era of Deng Xiaoping and Jiang Zemin, the CCP transitioned from a revolutionary party into a ruling party. This was the first major transition within the Communist Party. This transition has transformed the Party from a party that employed revolutionary methods to govern the country before the Reform into a party that governs the country by administrative means. It is a transition that has generated a series of positive effects, but there have also been significant shortcomings. Since the beginning of the twenty-first century, the Party's leadership has determined that its governing capacity is an issue that needs to be discussed. The question of how to improve governing capacity is actually concerning a second transition in the Party—that is, how to transition from a party that emphasizes administration to a party that governs through political means. This transition is related, not only to the development of the Party itself but also to the overall direction of human-centered socialism in the country.

Political Parties, State-Building, and Democracy

In discussing transitions in the Party, we must first address the unique nature of the CCP. Although we can refer to it as a "party," this concept differs from the concept of a "party" in Western politics. Thus, we need to discuss the differences between political parties in China and in the West.

The concept of "political party" itself only came into use during the nineteenth century, and it was a product of the development of representative systems and universal suffrage in Europe and the United States. Initially, political parties were organizations that obtained public office by participating in elections; the concept was later applied to political organizations that did not intend to participate in elections, and even sought to eliminate electoral systems entirely. It can be said that modern politics is party politics.

Any discussion of politics inevitably touches on political parties, especially when the discussion involves democratic politics, for party politics and democratic politics are practically twin brothers. Moore once summarized the development of Western democracy with a quip: "No bourgeoisie, no democracy." However, the bourgeoisie used party politics to share power with monarchies and aristocracies. Similarly, after the rise of the working class, the working class used party politics to enter the political sphere. The importance of political parties in democratic politics forces us to employ the term when discussing the political democratization of China.

Many Chinese and international scholars associate democratization with lifting bans on alternative political parties, implementing a multiparty system, and competition among parties. Undoubtedly, this point of view is obtained by comparing the differences in the operational methodologies of the Chinese political system and the Western political system. Regardless, since these studies only approach political parties from an understanding of the operational methodology of democratic politics, a political party is therefore narrowly defined as a mechanism for integrating and expressing the interests of various social groups.

And, at least as far as this definition applies to the operations of democratic politics, it is an accurate one. But the main flaw in this understanding is that it has not taken a historical perspective on the role of political parties in state-building. Modern political parties originated in the West and gradually spread to other countries. The role that political parties played in the state-building of Western societies is obviously different from their role in later developing countries—particularly in "third-world" countries. Here we need to briefly discuss the role of political parties in different countries.

In developing countries, political parties often serve as the founders of their states. But in many developed countries, particularly in Western Europe, things have gone very differently. Political parties were not the founders of states, but only promoted transitions from non-democracy to democracy. Before the emergence of modern political parties, the West experienced a long period of authoritarianism, which long featured powerful state power. From the earliest beginnings of modern states in the Western Europe of the twelfth to fourteenth centuries to the maturity of the modern state in the nineteenth century, the growth and transformation of the state has gone through many historical stages. Despite its various permutations, the modern state has always maintained considerable continuity—and logical consistency.

Western political parties developed under authoritarian regimes in response to the needs of social and economic development, and they gradually altered the forms of a state's political power. In short, the origins of Western political parties and the origins of modern states do not share much with each other, although they are both inseparable from transitions within modern states.

Western Political Parties

It can be said that the rise of political parties is related not only to the original, irrational forms of state power but is also inseparable from the emergence and development of democratic politics. Western democracy did not begin as the mass democracy it is today. From its beginnings within monarchies to its flowering as mass democracy, democratic politics has undergone a long period of historical development. At the same time, political parties were not originally such loosely organized, mass parties. Simply put, the emergence of political parties in the modern sense was caused by a series of factors.[1]

Political parties have always been associated with parliamentary politics, and parliamentary politics is the essence of Western democracy. Weber once demarcated the development of political parties into three stages: the stage of the aristocracy, the stage of the elites, and the stage of mass democracy. Although the first political parties also sought power-sharing and political participation, to a large extent they were only clubs in which a select few could participate. In Europe, the earliest members of these party-like clubs were differing types of nobles. At the time, democracy was just power-sharing among the nobility; it had no organic relationship with the vast majority of social groups. Later on, as political parties faced external pressure for greater participation in politics, they gradually expanded the class of people who could participate in politics, allowing representatives from various members of society—that is, social dignitaries and elites could participate in and share political power. While these political parties did not yet demonstrate truly popular characteristics, they demonstrated an open attitude and began to exhibit a kind of egalitarianism—that is, by including elite figures from differing social groups.

If, in the stages involving the nobility and social elite, political parties already had the openness of modern political parties, then in the stage of mass democracy modern political parties reached maturity.[2] Thus, the political scholar Maurice Duverger linked the emergence of political parties with electoral politics, holding that electoral politics drove the development of political parties and their democratization.[3] It is the characteristic of electoral politics to be politically universal. This universality does not mean that everyone in a society has the right to vote,

1 Joseph LaPalombara and Myron Weiner, eds., *Polities and Political Development* (Princeton: Princeton University Press, 1966), chapter one.

2 Max Weber, "Politics as a Vocation," in *From Max Weber: Essays in Sociology*, eds. Hans Gerth and C. Wright Mills (New York: Oxford University Press, 1946), 102–7.

3 Maurice Duverger, *Political Parties* (New York: John Wiley and Sons, 1955).

but that those who have the right to vote have equal opportunity to share political power.

The historical logic connecting political parties and democratic politics is borne out by the history of the development of major Western democracies. Researchers have discovered that, in Britain, modern political parties emerged from the 1832 reforms;[4] in France, mass organizations with the characteristics of political parties appeared during the 1848 revolution; in America, political parties did not appear until the 1830s;[5] in Japan, political parties did not appear until after the 1867 Meiji Restoration—and in their modern substance not until World War I.[6] Here it must be pointed out that, in all of these developed countries, political parties certainly did promote transitions in national politics—that is, from non-democracy or partial democracy to democracy—but political parties emerged later than modern nation-states. Before the emergence of political parties, modern-style states were already up and running. To summarize, these political parties were born and lived within the systemic framework of existing states. Political parties have played a large role in the transformation of the state, but this does not mean that they created the forms of the modern state.

As far as the relationship between political parties and democracy is concerned, in contemporary democracies, democratic politics is partisan politics. Democracy is realized through an electoral system, and elections are organized by political parties. Joseph Schumpeter defined democracy as a political process in which political elites compete for political power through elections. For Schumpeter, the party system is implicit within an electoral system. For effective elections, there must be electoral organizations and forums, and political parties serve to organize and provide forums. Ideology and the ability to organize have also become the basis for the survival of political parties.[7]

Why is it that political parties play an extremely vital role in a nation's transition? One important aspect is that the emergence of political parties can help a country resolve deep and serious political crises. Scholars have found that a variety of political crises often occur during political development. These crises come in

4 Samuel H. Beer, "Great Britain: From Governing Elite to Organized Mass Parties," in *Modern Political Parties*, ed. Sigmund Neumann (Chicago: University of Chicago Press, 1956); R. T. McKenzie, *British Political Parties* (New York: St. Martin's Press, 1955).

5 V. O. Key, *Politics, Parties and Pressure Groups* (New York: Crowell Publishers, 1958); William N. Chambers, *Political Parties in a New Nation: The American Experience 1776–1809* (New York: Oxford University Press, 1963).

6 Robert Scalapino, *Democracy and the Party Movement in Prewar Japan: The Failure of the First Attempt* (Berkeley and Los Angeles: University of California Press, 1953).

7 Joseph A. Schumpeter, *Capitalism, Socialism and Democracy* (New York: Harper Torchbooks, 1975).

three major kinds: a crisis of legitimacy, a crisis of political integration, and a crisis of political participation. Any of these three crises provides the objective conditions for the emergence of political parties. In other words, political parties serve as the most effective organizational means for resolving, or at least alleviating, these three kinds of political crises.[8]

In resolving these crises, political parties have helped state systems adapt to modernization. Economically speaking, a modern state differs from a pre-modern state in that a pre-modern state primarily draws its economic resources from society without inquiring into how society's economic resources can be increased. In other words, pre-modern states were consumers, not producers. In contrast, while modern states do draw on the economic resources of society, they also strive to create economic resources, whether directly or indirectly. The economic life of a modern country exists, not only for those in power but also for the people.

However, while a state is promoting economic development, it will also face political crises generated by economic development—crises such as changes in the legitimacy of state power and in the social base, the production and improvement of a people's political awareness and participation, and the differentiation of interests. Historically, political parties have been the most effective political tool at resolving these crises. In Weber's aforementioned theory of political participation, the different stages of a political party's development actually reflect a party's legitimacy and social base across differing periods. This is because socioeconomic development often leads to the multiplication of interests and a high degree of differentiation, and different interests in turn require differing political parties to represent and express them. This is also why many believe that political parties are primarily a mechanism for uniting and expressing interests.

In the twenty-first century, political parties are at the heart of modern politics in every society, regardless of whether it is democratic or non-democratic. As the most important organization in modern politics, political parties, on the one hand, organize public opinion and communicate the demands of the people to the seats of government power and policymaking, while on the other hand, they convey the ideas of a party to its members and society at large. Moreover, modern politics requires political parties because modern politics is highly complex. A complex politics requires more complex organizations to handle it, and this is what political parties can do. Regardless, in modern societies, the ultimate basis for the politics of power is political parties.

8 We will not offer a detailed discussion here of how such crises can be dealt with; see Leonard Binder et al., *Crises and Sequences in Political Development* (Princeton: Princeton University Press, 1971).

Political Parties in Developing Countries

When we examine the development of political parties in developing countries, we need to get past the somewhat simplistic idea that "political parties are election machines," since this applies primarily to Western societies. In developing countries, we must not only study the function of political parties within democratic politics but also the functions of political parties in state-building and participation in managing social change. It can be said that in developing countries democratic politics cannot do without political parties, but political parties do not exist only for the sake of democratic politics.

Within developing countries, political parties often act as the founders of new states. If it is true that, in advanced Western countries, the main function of political parties is to serve as a means for political participation while politicians' objective is to share political power, then in developing countries politicians face a more arduous task—namely, state-building, economic development, and social transition.[9] In the developed countries of the West, political parties and the state are two different things. In developing countries, however, the relationship between the two is ambiguous, to the extent sometimes of being inseparable. This is so, not only because the survival of a state often largely depends on the survival of a political party but also because socioeconomic development depends much more on the decisions made by a political party.

Broadly speaking, political parties in developing countries have a completely different historical mission from that of their Western counterparts. We can consider this with the following aspects.

To begin with, political parties either promote or limit political participation. The promotion of political participation can be seen in how political parties mobilize people to enter the political processes of a state. In other words, political parties are a means for enabling people to participate in national politics. But political parties can also restrict the people's participation in politics. In some states, especially in single-party states, political parties are used to control the people's political participation. Political elites frequently use their control of political parties to prevent the people from fully participating in politics; rather, they bring the people into political processes to a limited extent, that varies in accordance with political needs. In Asia, Malaysia and the Indonesia of Suharto feature this kind of party. These political parties no longer serve to encourage political participation, but just the opposite. In certain historical periods, there is a political rationale behind this.

9 Henry Bienen, *Tanzania: Party Transformation and Economic Development* (Princeton: Princeton University Press, 1967).

Limited and gradual participation not only ensures that the need for political participation is being met but also provides for social stability. Asia has learned that high levels of political mobilization and full political participation often lead to social instability.

Second, political parties help create political legitimacy. In modern societies, legitimacy comes from the relationship between a government and the people—this is the frequently discussed relationship between the state and society. Whether a government possesses legitimacy largely depends on whether the people identify with it. Moreover, this identification is mainly established through elections or other forms of political participation. A political party is both a means for facilitating elections and also the most important instrument for political participation, and thus it can create the government's legitimacy. In addition, political parties actually serve to tie the government to the people, while the government's image is largely shaped by political parties—especially by the ruling party. This is particularly true in countries with a single-party system or single-party dominance, for, in these circumstances, it is difficult to make a clear distinction between the party and the government, and the legitimacy of the government depends on the legitimacy of the ruling party.

A close relationship between a political party and the government means that political parties can exert a negative influence on a government's legitimacy. Problems within the political party can easily turn into problems for the government. When this happens, "the death of the party halts the government" (*dang wang zheng xi*). In the case of Suharto-era Indonesia, the government relied entirely on the ruling party to survive. All important policymakers were members of the ruling party. As a result, when the ruling party collapsed, the entire government stopped functioning and was left in a state of paralysis.

Third, political parties serve to improve a country's integration. Political parties' work in integrating a country can be seen in how parties provide political elites. Where party politics is more developed, the elites of various parts of society can often be absorbed into political parties, thereby coordinating the interests of different parts of society within one political party. This reduces the open conflict between social interests and makes a country more integrated. This can be clearly seen in Singapore. Although a small nation, Singapore is also a classic example of a multi-ethnic country, and the ruling party, the People's Action Party, has never made racial questions part of its public policy. In Singapore, problem-solving depends on negotiation among various ethnic elites within the party.

Finally, political parties serve as political socializers. Political parties are the bridge between a government and a society. On the one hand, they convey society's demands to the government, while on the other hand, they implement policy on the government's behalf and communicate a government's intentions to the people. People participate in national politics by participating in either political parties or activities organized by political parties. It is in this way that parties serve as political socializers.

In addition to performing some of the functions mentioned above, the CCP has its own unique features. The difference is found primarily in the tendency of parties in other countries to rule indirectly—that is, to perform the functions of government by organizing the government—while the CCP rules directly. This unique characteristic is rooted in the historical trajectory of Chinese party politics. To put it simply, the traditional political heritage of China is one of "building the state with the Party" (*yi dang jianguo*), "ruling the country with the Party" (*yi dang zhi guo*), and "the unity of Party and state" (*dang guo heyi*).

First, China saw "building the state with the Party"; then there was "ruling the country with the Party"; and now we have a political regime in which the "Party and the state are one." This is not a historical trajectory that began with the CCP. Political elites starting with Sun Yat-sen did not have many options available other than this particular historical trajectory. And whether it has been "building the state with the Party" or "ruling the country with the Party," both the Kuomintang and the CCP have embraced Sun Yat-sen's approach.

Of equal importance is the fact that both the KMT and the CCP claimed the mantle of a revolutionary party, and revolution means overthrowing the existing government and creating a new government. All of this has made modern Chinese political parties extremely revolutionary. The revolutionary nature of political parties has also profoundly influenced the socioeconomic composition of political parties. After 1949, Mao Zedong held to a policy of "continuous revolution," and he employed revolutionary methods to launch wave after wave of sociopolitical movements to build his ideal state. If a party wants to build its own state, it cannot tolerate the existence of an independent government; quite the contrary, the government or the entire bureaucracy must be rebuilt in accordance with the party's vision.

The First Transition in the CCP

Since the Reform and Opening Up, the CCP has transitioned from a party that uses revolutionary methods into a party that uses administrative methods to govern the country, and it is now beginning to transition into a party that governs through political methods.

The Three Means of Governance

What are revolutionary methods of governance? As the word "revolution" implies, a revolution is effected in order to implement radical changes to the existing system of governance. This objective also determines the specific characteristics of a party's social relations and intra-party relations. In terms of social relations, revolutions are often a class struggle in which some classes revolt against other classes. Before political power was achieved, there was a revolution of the workers and peasants against the ruling capitalists, landlords, and other classes. After taking power, there was a revolution against designated class enemies. Since these were revolutions of class against class, political mobilization was necessary. In order to achieve political mobilization, the CCP relied on certain classes, and this reliance could be seen in the Party's internal operations. Revolution and its attendant political mobilization also objectively demanded a highly centralized structure of political power. Political power was first concentrated away from various social and political groups into the Communist Party, then from the lower echelons of the Party into its leadership, and finally into the hands of the Party's highest-ranking leaders.

If it can be said that revolutionary methods aim at changing existing systems, then the focus of administrative methods is on reforming the existing system while maintaining it. In terms of the Communist Party's relations with society, large-scale political mobilization no longer occurs. When it was operating with revolutionary methods, the Party—particularly the Party's leadership—used political mobilization to unite itself with the support of social forces. But when the Party operates with administrative methods, the Party and its leadership have a relative degree of separation from social forces, and the Party employs relatively independent and autonomous means to manage the "object" of society.

The Party's power base is also different from that of the revolutionary era: Revolutionary methods require the Party to base itself directly in social support, but when it employs administrative methods, the Party's power comes directly from the Party's own elite. While the most salient feature of the Party's internal power structures is still the concentration of power, the Party's primary objective is to develop the economy—that is, to govern by developing the economy. Thus, the Party emphasizes the efficiency of its governance. This in turn demands that the Party's power remains relatively concentrated. When the Party employed revolutionary methods, power was concentrated for the sake of political mobilization, but under an administrative methodology, power is concentrated in order to make decision-making more effective. The concentration of power does not necessarily mean that there is autocracy. Technocratic leaders can generally reach a consensus for decision-making. This consensus makes it possible to attain a certain degree of collective leadership, but the overall power structure has not experienced fundamental changes.

The third method of governance, political governance, has just begun to be implemented, and its characteristics cannot be easily summarized. But judging from current trends in its development, we can note several features. First of all, political methods do not involve some classes ruling other classes; rather, they involve cross-class reconciliation and the coordination of interests. A political methodology is not exclusively in the hands of the existing professional class and the technocracy; instead, it involves the political participation of all classes in governance. Second, with a political methodology, political parties serve as a means of limited government over society—that is, a party's sphere of control contracts, allowing social groups more space to exercise autonomy. Finally, relations between the party and the government gradually shift from direct governance to indirect governance—in other words, the party influences the government by participating in government, rather than by directly dominating the government. In terms of the Communist Party's internal power structures, since the Party accommodates the interests of different classes or social strata, the Party needs to develop democratic mechanisms within the Party that can express, represent, and coordinate the interests of various classes and social strata. As a result, the concentration of power will be greatly reduced, and many problems will be resolved through political debate rather than through hierarchies of power. In addition, coordination, reconciliation, and political debate are the primary features of a political methodology.

The Transition from a Revolutionary Party to an Administrative Party

The reforms initiated by Deng Xiaoping not only promoted change within China's economic system but also changes within the CCP itself. This latter point has often been overlooked. Generally speaking, while the Party's institutions still exist, and while the entire system of government still depends on the Party's institutions, it cannot be denied that the Party's behavior is poles apart from how it behaved thirty years ago. This transition within the Party is a transition from a revolutionary methodology to an administrative methodology; this is the first major transition of the Party. This transition has been achieved through great efforts in many aspects like organization, ideology, and the institutionalization of leadership succession.

The most important characteristic of this first transition has been the emergence of technocracy, or system of expert governance. The technocracy of governing institutions can primarily be seen in the fact that the country's managers are not produced through bottom-up elections by the people but are instead generated by an appointment system run by the CCP. In this appointment system, cadres are selected on the basis of their education backgrounds and work experience. This is what has been termed "technocracy."[10]

In comparison with the older generation of revolutionaries, technocrats have obvious advantages. The older revolutionaries often made ideology both the starting point and criterion for observing and resolving problems, and they often politicized issues that were not originally in themselves political, thereby making it even more difficult to resolve problems. In addition, they had an intense emotional attachment to the political system that they themselves created, and this made it impossible for them to implement thoroughgoing reforms in the old system.

The newly formed technocrats comport themselves differently. What is most striking about them is that they do not behave ideologically. When they investigate and resolve problems, they are not overly constrained by ideology, nor do they take ideology as the starting point for their work. Instead, they take a professional, factual approach, one that seeks to solve problems by reforming systems. This is why third-generation leadership has devoted more attention to making institutions more rational—that is, to promoting changes in the national political system at the level of institutional operation.

This approach has created the gradualism and stability of Chinese politics. Of course, it can also be said that technocrats cannot produce a more radical approach to political reforms, since they mostly diagnose and solve problems from a professional perspective. They will never conduct revolutionary reforms or overthrow systems in the way the first generation of revolutionaries did.

Owing to these characteristics, the rise of technocracy has exerted a tremendous impact on China's political economy. This can be seen in a variety of ways.

To begin with, technocracy provides a stable environment for economic development. The technocracy responds to challenges by emphasizing gradualism in the system and continuity in policy. Working under this emphasis, the technocracy then finds solutions to problems. It is an approach that is highly conducive to political stability. From a democratic perspective, technocracy may appear conservative and less aggressive, but technocrats undoubtedly ensure, to some extent, the political stability necessary for economic development.

10 For example, Jean Meynaud, *Technocracy* (New York: Free Press, 1969).

Second, during more than thirty years of operating as technocracy, the CCP has essentially completed its transition from a radical revolutionary party to an administrative party or a managerial party. Revolutionary elites have essentially left the stage of Chinese politics. While Deng Xiaoping personally called China's reforms "the Second Revolution," the main participants in this revolution were not revolutionaries but technocrats. Scholars often use the term "developmental state" to describe those governments that are committed to promoting economic development. In fact, we could say that the CCP is a "developmental political party"—at least in an economic sense.

Third, to a certain extent and for certain periods of time, technocracy is largely a superior alternative to popular democracy. In democratic countries, elites are mostly selected through democratic elections. Thus, democracy implies not only elections but also a mechanism for connecting political elites with the market. In democracy, political elites must remain sensitive to the market—they must remain sensitive to the needs of the people in order to win more votes and to be elected. Of course, political elites in democratic countries cannot always promote economic development and satisfy the people's needs. This is evidenced by the fact that many countries have relatively well-developed democracies, yet they have underperforming economies. Since China neither has a democracy nor plans to develop one within the short term, the CCP has to find an alternative that can play a somewhat democratic role—and this is technocracy. In contrast with revolutionaries, technocrats are more sensitive to the country's problems, and they can use a more scientific approach to gather information about society and discover methods for meeting the people's needs within a timely manner. In other words, technocrats can serve as a better bridge between the state and the people than revolutionaries can.

In contrast with tradition, technocracy represents a major political advance. Since the Party's current focus remains on economic development, the Party needs a massive contingent of technocrats who understand the economy. In addition, since the CCP's institutions are in a transitional period, the old system needs to be reformed at the institutional level. The achievements of China's economic reforms in the 1990s were largely due to the contributions of the technocracy. Over the long run, however, technocracy is itself only a transitional system of governance, for economic development is currently causing dramatic levels of differentiation within Chinese society, and the conflict between various interests is not something that a technocracy can resolve.

A more democratic method of governance is needed. Again, not all political issues can be reduced to technical issues. Many major problems in society can only be resolved with a political methodology. During the 1960s and 1970s, the

Soviet Union developed a technocracy that made the mouths of Western scholars water. In every regard, Soviet technocracy was more developed than China's is now, yet it was still unable to resolve the political issues that the Soviet Union faced. Technocracy can promote economic development and make some systemic adjustments in accordance with the demands of economic development, and this enables China's system to include more democratic elements. On the other hand, economic development is currently generating an ever-increasing number of political problems that cannot be solved by technocrats. Thus, to a large extent, the technocracy is currently laying the institutional and material foundations for China's future democratic politics.

The second feature of the first transition was the reconstruction of ideology. The CCP has two primary pillars: One is its organization, and the other is ideology. Organization can be described as hard power, while ideology can be depicted as soft power. These two aspects are mutually complementary, not only in their support of the Party but also in their support for the political system of the entire country. In the words of the American scholar Schurmann, organization and ideology are the foundation of China's state system.[11]

During the Mao era, everything in China was overly politicized and ideological. No matter how much reason there may have been to Mao's actions at the time, the waves of political movements launched by Mao's CCP—particularly the Anti-Rightist Campaign, the Great Leap Forward, and the Cultural Revolution—were a series of disasters. During the late 1970s, after the CCP officially announced the end of the Cultural Revolution, a pragmatic spirit became the ideology for the major reforms implemented by the CCP's leadership. Ideology began to shift away from the "offense" to the "defense." While ideology ought to guide the developmental orientation of political parties and even society itself, the ideology of the 1980s' CCP obviously no longer maintained this.

Ideology shifted from playing a leading role in formulating policy to serving to buttress policy. In the past, the CCP's leaders used ideology to guide material policymaking. If material policy and ideology didn't coincide, then material policy had to be changed to maintain ideological purity. The opposite is now true. Ideology is at the beck and call of reality; it is called upon to explain the reasonableness of reality and demonstrate the reasonableness of practical policies. When ideology doesn't match up with reality, what needs to be corrected is ideology; reality should not be sacrificed.

11 Franz Schurmann, *Ideology and Organization in Communist China* (Berkeley: University of California Press, 1968).

In the 1990s there occurred a series of events which accelerated changes within the ideology of the CCP; these included the collapse of the Soviet Union and the demise of the Eastern Bloc. The CCP's leaders recognized that the root cause of the collapse of the Soviet Union and the disintegration of the Eastern Bloc lay in those countries' failures at economic reform. Economic failures caused the Soviet and Eastern European Communist regimes to lose their basic governing legitimacy, while their peoples lost confidence in both the Parties and their governments. At the same time, radical political reforms opened a door for dissatisfied opposition parties and governments. Thus, if the CCP wanted to avoid the fate of the Communist parties of the Soviet Union and Eastern Europe, it had to carry out economic reforms and promote economic development—which would shore up the government's power and provide the people with sustainable economic benefits. In other words, economic methods were deployed to improve and consolidate the governing legitimacy of the CCP.

The movement from the "over-ideologization" of the Mao era to "de-ideologization" reflected to a great extent not only the psychological needs of the great mass of society but also the need for economic development. In practice, de-ideologization has been proven to have positive effects on China's development. But negative consequences have also come with it, which can mainly be seen in the following aspects:

First of all, as a form of soft power, ideology serves to demonstrate the legitimacy of the CCP. With a decline in the traditional ideology, ideology's power to shore up legitimacy has also diminished. Since soft power has declined, hard power has become much more prominent. Formerly, the behavior of cadres was controlled by ideology, and it could generally be ensured that the CCP's leadership could be controlled without institutional intervention—they would "consciously" submit themselves to the Party's control. Now that ideology can no longer control and regulate the behavior of the cadres; the Party can only control them with institutional means, leading to a great reduction in the effectiveness and efficiency of its control.

Second, the decline of ideology has led some cadres to lose their sense of party identity and loyalty. Since the Party's dominance is largely assured through ideology, ideology's decline has confused the Party's positions in the minds of cadres. They do not know what the Party is doing or what the Party wants them to do. As a result, many are disoriented.

Third, the most serious consequence of ideology's decline has been wide-scale corruption within the Party. There are many factors behind this corruption, but the decline of ideology is undoubtedly one of the most important. When ideology first went into decline, the Party was no longer able to offer positive guidance for cadres' behavior. Subsequently, the Party's ability to control cadres was reduced. This ultimately meant that cadres lost standards for behavior, and personal interest became the ultimate behavioral criterion. Corruption in the Party has grown to the point that many within Party leadership are saying that corruption will prove "the death of the Party and the country" (*wang dang wang guo*).

Fourth, the decline of ideology has also had an extremely negative influence on social behavior. The CCP is China's only ruling party, and the Chinese people aren't provided with many other ideological alternatives. Thus, the CCP's ideology can also offer the people a certain amount of "spiritual energy." The decline of ideology has meant that the Party can no longer provide spiritual sustenance, yet it is impossible for any society to do without spiritual needs. Thus, ideology's decline has led to a rise in various unofficial quasi-ideologies that include extreme nationalism, various religions and even cults, and intellectual movements that have played an ideological role but have taken on various forms.

The third feature of the first transition was the institutionalization of the process of leadership succession. The CCP is unique in its approach to resolving the problem of succession, a political issue that can be approached from at least two angles. On the one hand, succession touches on the "political exit" of high-ranking politicians—that is, how current leaders can leave the political stage. On the other hand, the problem of succession deals with how successors should be trained and selected, and how political power should be transferred from the hands of older politicians to a newer generation. The problem of succession is the most important and also the most difficult in Chinese politics, but the Party's highest leadership has also begun to implement a managerial solution to this problem.

First of all, there is the creation of political exit mechanisms. Without political exits, there can be no successors. When current leadership exits politics and new leaders take the helm, this is the succession of power. Without political exits, leadership will inevitably age, and the CCP has learned many lessons in this regard. Before Deng Xiaoping, the leadership of the CCP adhered to a system of life tenure for leadership, which had grave consequences for the Party and the government. In view of the situation, Deng Xiaoping committed himself to institution-building, and in 1980 he abolished life tenure for leading cadres. Later, however, Hu Yaobang and Zhao Ziyang did not make normal exits from the political stage. Thus, while it is true that Deng Xiaoping made great strides in rejuvenating leading cadres, he did not successfully ensure that senior leaders would exit the political arena.

With the death of the older generation of revolutionaries, this is a problem that the new generation of leadership within the CCP will have to face. To solve this problem, they must work hard at systemic innovations and fine-tuning the rules of the political game. There is a high level of consensus here among the third generation of leadership, and leadership is striving to cultivate the core of the next generation, seeking to regularly provide various political stages for future leaders to gain experience. In addition, progress has been made at achieving political exits and institutionalizing procedures for political exits at the most senior levels. Important progress can be seen in the 17th Congress, in which the Party began to introduce substantive mechanisms for intra-party democracy that can solve the succession problem.

Why Discuss a "Second Transition" in the Party?

The Party's administrative methodology of governance has also generated a series of serious political problems. We can approach these problems under the following headings.

Challenges to Administrative Governance

The decline of ideology has led to uncertainty about the direction of the Party's future development. Sun Yat-sen once remarked that a party should govern "with principles" (*zhuyi*). From the Reform and Opening Up to the end of the 1990s, the Party's leadership has busied itself with specific economic and administrative tasks, paying less attention to the development of ideological aspects and failing to adequately consider the future direction of the Party. Employing administrative means of governance has also led to some highly negative effects on the government's administrative capacity.

Originally, administrative tasks were assigned to the government, but now the Party often replaces the government in implementing policy and in management. The Party has become the *de facto* top-tier of government, while the government is completely subordinate to the Party—it is second-tier government. Under such circumstances, the administrative capacity of the government has not only not been developed or strengthened but has also been greatly weakened. It's increasingly clear that the administrative capacity of China's government has not been greatly improved, and this development cannot be separated from the Party's usurpation of the government's executive functions.

Political friction between the Party and governmental departments has only exacerbated this situation. With the rapid development of the economy and society, Chinese society is becoming ever more complex, which is making it ever more difficult to govern. Such circumstances demand that the administrative capacity of government departments be greatly improved and strengthened. If the Party continues to usurp the government's role, it will be difficult to improve the government's administrative capacity.

Regarding the Party's internal power structure, many positive changes within the Party have already been discussed, as above, but generally speaking, the problems pointed out by Deng Xiaoping in 1982 still exist. At the time, Deng Xiaoping observed: "The excessive concentration of power has been exacerbated under the pretense of strengthening the unity of Party leadership. This process has improperly and uncritically concentrated all power in Party committees, and power within Party committees is often concentrated with a few secretaries, particularly with the First Secretary. Everything needs the First Secretary's support and approval. Unification in Party leadership often thus turns into individual leadership."[12] While intra-party collective leadership and democracy have been developed, either they are far from being institutionalized, or their institutionalization is so low that it varies from person to person. Such power structures have also generated a series of negative consequences, the most disturbing of which are situations in which "the Party lives or dies with one person" (*ren cun dang wang, ren wang dang xi*).

Why is this happening? First of all, under these strictures, the Party often becomes the personal weapon of individual Party leaders; it becomes a tool for the pursuit of power and personal interests—even the interests of friends and relatives. The Central Committee has repeatedly demanded that the Party serve the people, but in many locales, the Party lacks institutional mechanisms for ensuring that local Party leaders do so. Second, this system makes it difficult for a political party to become institutionalized, and if we want to avoid the Party "living or dying with one person," the Party must be institutionalized. Leaders come and go. Only institutions persist. But because the Party has become a personal weapon for some of its leaders, institutionalization is impossible. And because it is a personal weapon, the Party is easily manipulated by individuals. Such conditions have happened before in both the Soviet Union and Indonesia. So far, the CCP has managed to avoid this, but it's doubtful whether the Party has found systemic mechanisms that can prevent this from happening. Finally, this system elevates the upper echelons in the Party far above lower ranks, and upper and lower ranks do not usually have close relationships with each other. Lower ranks in the Party do not have much

12 Deng Xiaoping 邓小平, "Dang he guojia lingdao zhidu de gaige" "党和国家领导制度的改革" [The Reform of the Party and State Leadership Systems], in *Deng Xiaoping wenxuan* 邓小平文选 [The Selected Works of Deng Xiaoping], vol. 2 (Beijing: People's Publishing House, 1994), 328–29.

input into policy or decision-making, and depends on leaders exerting their will to enact policy in a top-down manner. As a result, implementation and enforcement of the Party's central policies have been greatly reduced.

Together, the Party's centralized system and its administrative approach to governance have made the Party itself an interest group that pursues and seeks to maximize its own interests. The Party was originally part of the people—it was an organic component that came from the people and served the people. The Party is an organization with its own organizational interests, but the original objective of the Party was to represent the interests of the people and pursue the best interests of the people. If the Party becomes an organization that pursues its own interests, it will no longer be the party it was intended to be; it will no longer be able to represent the interests of the people, and it will have difficulty in leading society. Expert governance and technocracy do incorporate members of society's professional classes both into the Party and into leadership positions within the Party, but in many cases society is only the object of management and administration, not the main driver of national politics.

Governing the country with administrative methods has thus created a gulf between the Party and society. Treating society as some object to be managed can make the Party complacent, which will make it difficult for the Party to absorb good, fresh blood from society. When the Party's base and society itself cannot invest in the Party's policies, society's investment in the Party will also decrease. It will become difficult for society to identify with or feel close to the Party, and it will become impossible to discuss any conscientious service on the Party's part.

Transition to a Political Methodology

All of this requires a second major transition in the Party's approach to governance—namely, the transition from administrative governance to political governance. The CCP's leadership has been aware of all of these problems arising from the methodology of administrative governance. In fact, some aspects of this transition already began to be realized during the 1990s. Proposing the theory of the "Three Represents" certainly provided the impetus for such a major transition. Just as a transition from a revolutionary methodology to an administrative methodology is comprehensive in nature, transitioning from an administrative methodology to a political methodology will also involve all aspects of the Party.

First, a new "-ism" (*zhuyi*) and ideology need to be established. A new "-ism" must be established, one that not only Party members but all of society can identify with. Without such an "-ism," there can be no transition—for an "-ism" represents the direction of the Party's future development. As Sun Yat-sen said, a ruling party must not govern or administer a country with its members but must govern the country with the party's ideas. Ideology represents the developmental orientation of an entire country as well as the blueprint by which the Party intends to lead the people to those objectives. If the Party cannot build a new ideology, its governing capacity will continue to decline at the same rate at which the economy continues to develop.

However, rebuilding the Party's ideology does not mean revitalizing ideology's previous function as a means of control. The aim of this rebuilding is to prevent the Party and China's material reality from developing a total disconnect from each other; rather, the Party and Chinese society should develop in ways that are intimately connected with each other. A new ideology needs to be adapted to and offer guidance to the reality of social development; it must accommodate and transcend the pluralism of values in any modern society; it must clearly communicate to the people the Party leadership's mid-term and long-term objectives for national development, along with the means by which these objectives may be achieved. Only thus can the governing party revitalize society's identification with it; only thus can the Party once again strengthen its leadership.

The "Three Represents" can serve as a starting point for creating a new "-ism." While the second generation of Party leaders abandoned class struggle, they did not apply theoretical solutions to the issue of the Party's class base. Since the CCP is China's only ruling party, can it realistically situate itself over certain classes while excluding other classes? In theory, every class needs its own political representatives. This is true of the working class and farmers, and it is true of other classes as well.

Before the Reform and Opening Up, China had only one class, and the problem of representing interests was either non-existent or unimportant. But after decades of reform directed toward creating a market economy, class questions have become complex. Under such circumstances, the issue of the Party's class base needs to be revisited. If some classes cannot find representation within the CCP, they will eventually "save themselves," create their own organizations, or look for their own representatives. This reality requires that the Party incorporate various major socioeconomic interests into the Party. Clearly, if the CCP cannot represent their interests or they are excluded from the Party's political processes, they will form their own power and participate in politics in various ways.

This will eventually lead to their opposition to the Party. Furthermore, as the country's only ruling party, the Party must, to a certain extent, transcend the specific interests of various classes. Thus, the Party must not only represent the interests of these classes but must also mediate their conflicting interests. If the

Chinese Communist Party wants to consolidate and strengthen its position as the ruling party, it must develop along these lines.

Second, the ruling party must expand its class base through socioeconomic development. Here the required line of development is quite clear as well. The most important instance of this has been allowing private entrepreneurs to join the Party. This was a necessary step in expanding the Party's social base. In the past, the largest classes in China were traditional classes like workers and farmers, but after more than thirty years of reform, there have been great changes in the composition of the classes. The non-state-owned sector, which includes private companies, has come to occupy a large portion of society, and emerging entrepreneurs are playing a critical role. If the Party cannot incorporate these emerging forces into itself, its growth, development, and even survival will not have an adequate social base.

The Party needs the broadest possible social base, but this does not mean that it must directly interfere in social forces. Quite the contrary, if the Party is to improve its governing efficiency, it must adjust its relationship with other social forces. Because it needs to rule politically, the Party will not be able to directly control various social forces as it did before, or place various social forces under its power. Political governance ought to be selective in nature. While the Party strengthens its leadership over more politically inclined social forces, it also needs to withdraw from some of the less politically conscious social spaces and give social forces the chance to exercise self-governance.

Third, the relationship between the Party and administration must be redefined. Political governance means that the Party must gradually withdraw from the administrative domain and strengthen its political functions while strengthening the government's political functions. On the one hand, if the Party continues to perform administrative functions, its decline will become practically unavoidable. On the other hand, economic development has made Chinese society increasingly complex, thereby demanding continuous enhancements to the administrative capacity of the government. For the Party to be revitalized and the government's administrative functions to be strengthened, it needs to exit the administrative domain.

Furthermore, if the Party continues to perform administrative functions, either it will become harder for China to democratize or China will democratize and then experience disorder. Once democratization comes, administrative power will decrease sharply. Exiting administration does not mean that the Party does not play a leading role, but that it shifts away from its current approach of direct administration to an approach of indirect governance through political participation.

The CCP has learned many lessons in this regard. During the 1980s, "division of labor between the Party and the government" (*dang zheng fen gong*) and "separation between Party and government" (*dang zheng fenkai*) became the objectives of political reform. If these objectives could have been achieved, Chinese politics would probably have experienced major changes. However, these goals were too idealistic. Neither China's history as a "party state" nor the actual political relations between the Party and the government allowed these objectives to be realized. In other words, there was no institutional possibility for the division of labor—of a separation of Party and state.

A more pragmatic and effective approach would be for the Party to influence governance by participating in politics. Since the 1990s, there has been some momentum in the institutional development of the Party's political participation. This can primarily be seen in two aspects: the development of the institution of the presidency and the development of the system in which local party secretaries simultaneously serve as chairs of standing committees in people's congresses.

Let's begin with the first aspect, the consolidations within the presidency. The power of the presidency and the office's role in China's political life have experienced great changes under the third generation of leadership. From the perspective of political rule, changes within the presidency have carried manifold significance. These changes have the potential to resolve problems within the Party's high-level leadership. This is true, first of all, in the relations between the Party's general secretary and the president.

Every country must have a head of state such as a president or a prime minister. In China, the president is the head of state, but the actual power lies with the Party's general secretary, who is generally considered to be the *de facto* head of state. Many functions—particularly international functions—cannot be performed by the Party's general secretary. China is now implementing a system in which the general secretary and the president are united in one person. This system offers an extremely effective means for the Party's participation in governmental affairs. If this political practice is institutionalized, the Party might have an effective means of participating in governance. The Party need not intervene directly in government affairs; it can exercise political power by participating in the government.

The second aspect of the Party's influence on the government through political participation is that the secretaries of local party committees also serve in the standing committees of people's congresses. While this system of dual roles is still in development, and its future remains unclear, it is very conducive to the Party's transition from administrative governance to political governance, and it can also help create a more democratic relationship between the Party and the government.

This is true, first of all, because the arrangement can strengthen the role of the people's congresses. By having Party secretaries hold office in standing committees, the power of both functions is strengthened: The Party's leadership over the people's congresses is improved, while the powers and functions of the people's congresses themselves are also strengthened. The outside world has always described people's congresses as "rubber stamp congresses," and one important reason for this is that members of congresses are often celebrities rather than political figures. No matter how famous they might be, they don't understand how Chinese politics actually works. In comparison with celebrities or retired cadres, the Party committee secretaries serving in congresses have more influence over the government's decisions.

Regardless, one of the important roles of the people's congresses is to influence and monitor government policy. In addition, this measure helps build a more institutionalized bridge between the Party and representatives of public opinion. The people's congresses are a vehicle for the will of the people, but in the past, congresses have had difficulty in enabling the will of the people to influence government policy. As there was no formal, institutionalized channel for communicating the will of the people, there was only a unidirectional understanding of the people's interests—that is, the people's interests were often only interpreted or even determined by officials. If the Party's key members can personally participate in congress, at the least they will be forced to listen to the opinions of members of congresses and thus have to reflect the wishes of members of congresses to a certain extent in their policy decisions. More importantly, this can serve as an important step in straightening out relations between the Party and the government.

As has been previously discussed, an administrative methodology means that the Party exercises power directly, while a political methodology means that the Party exercises power indirectly by forming a government. Under the present circumstances, the Party is employing an administrative methodology, and the government is only one of the organs of the Party. Thus, direct Party intervention in the government is inevitable. After the Party's committee secretaries do concurrent service on the standing committees of the people's congresses, their leadership style will change. When this happens, the Party will be given a reasonable and institutionalized channel for participating in governmental affairs, thereby making it possible for the Party to shift from direct intervention in the government to indirect intervention through congresses. This is the only way that the Party can gradually be separated from administrative affairs and transform into a truly ruling party.

The fourth aspect of the Party's transition toward political governance is the establishment of democratic representation mechanisms within the Party. As far as various intra-party relations go, it is most important that mechanisms for democratic representation be established. Democratic mechanisms will solve major problems by preventing the aforementioned excessive concentrations of power and, even more importantly, by resolving the following two issues.

The first is the issue of preventing the Party from becoming an interest group in its own right. As a ruling party, the CCP should not have its own special interests but should reflect and represent the interests and needs of the vast majority of the people. But danger looms, for since the Party controls all important political resources, Party cadres and officials can obtain economic benefits in the exercise of political power. If sufficient attention is not devoted to this problem, the Party itself can easily become an interest group. As discussed above, this happened not only in the Soviet Union and in the Eastern Bloc but also in developing Asian countries that were ruled by one party—country like Indonesia.

From Mao Zedong to today, leadership has been aware of this issue, but it has been very difficult to find systemic means to prevent it from happening. Of such means, intra-party democracy appears extremely important, for only by creating democratic systems can various interests be represented. As the "Three Represents" theory demonstrates, the CCP has already stated that the interests of the majority must be represented—but just how to represent them is another matter altogether. Without a sound system that can represent differing interests, "representation" is hard to achieve. How to represent is not a simple question of allowing people of all classes and strata to enter the political process. Once people enter the Party, they will demand that the Party's policies reflect their voices and serve their interests. Building a mechanism that can represent varying interests is not easy, but no matter what, establishing mechanisms for democratic representation is the only way the Party can avoid sacrificing the interests of some weaker classes.

The second issue is the question of how to coordinate the interests of various classes. Every class seeks its own interests, and once within the Party, a party will continue to pursue its own best interests. While the interests of various classes may adhere together in some areas, to a large extent they conflict with each other. If the Party cannot coordinate interests among the classes and only represents in actuality the interests of one class, or if differing leaders within the Party represent the interests of differing classes, it will break up. In order to maintain a unified and strong ruling party, the differing interests represented by the Party need to be coordinated.

Preventing the Party from becoming an interest group and establishing mechanisms for representation and the coordination of interests both touch on a problem with democratic politics. In order to prevent the formation of interest groups, all classes and strata need to have freedom of speech and the right to determine policy, and the most effective mechanism for representing various interests is democratic institutions. Similarly, for the Party to transcend the interests of various groups, it needs some help from democracy, for only democracy can prevent the Party from representing only a portion of the nation's interests.

Human-Centered Socialism and the Second Transition of the Party

Since the beginning of the twenty-first century, the Party's fourth generation of leadership has, at least theoretically, made some preparations for the Party's second transition and has outlined the direction that transition will take. I term this direction a new wave of socialism. This new wave is reflected in three main areas.

First, it can be seen in the direction of development. What's most important is a tone that emphasizes "human-centeredness" (*yi ren wei ben*). Human-centeredness was originally at the heart of European socialist movements; this human-centeredness sought to correct the many problems generated by the capitalist system. For a long time, however, socialist practice in China has run counter to human-centered thinking. In the 1980s, human-centeredness was considered an inseparable component of bourgeois liberalization and so came under heavy criticism. At present it has become the keynote for directing China's social development. This is a major advance in politics.

Second, this new wave has been reflected in the level of policy. An important feature is that a "human-centered" focus has been placed on the majority of society. While protecting emerging social forces through legal means, the interests of the workers and farmers who account for the vast majority of society have been reaffirmed. "Human-centered" theory can also be seen in the proposals of new leadership, such as "The New Three Principles of the People" (*xin san min zhuyi*). In terms of specific policy, new leadership has also begun to pay more attention to pursuing social justice. The recently established system of a basic living allowance is one of such policies.

Lastly but perhaps most importantly, the new wave of socialism can be seen in the behavior of leadership. Leadership's behavior is very important in any country, and its importance is even greater in China. When the rule of law has not yet been completely established, the exemplary behavior of leadership has considerable political influence, and it can influence the behavior of lower officials more than specific policies. The "people-friendly" attitude that has developed within new leadership is closely connected to leadership's personal behavior.

This new wave of socialism can be called a rebuilt Chinese socialism. And simply put, socialism in China has now gone through three historical stages.

The first stage was the revolution and state-building conducted under the leadership of Mao Zedong. When socialism first entered China, it was not mainstream. Surrounded by various popular ideologies like liberalism, democracy, capitalism, nationalism, and anarchism, Mao Zedong and other first-generation leaders opted for socialism. But the primary objective at the time was the construction of an independent, sovereign state—not the social welfare emphasized in the Europe where socialism was born. Thus, in China, socialism and nationalism were combined. Since the founding of New China, the content of this approach to socialism has not experienced much change. Regardless of how it is assessed, the planned economy was employed at the time as a means of creating an independent, sovereign state. The focus was not on individuals, but on national power. With the added factor of the Cold War, leadership overemphasized the state-owned system and artificially separated the state from capitalism.

The second stage involved a reconsideration of socialism by second-generation leaders like Deng Xiaoping. Mao Zedong's extremist form of socialism created a country with strong national sovereignty but an impoverished people. Deng Xiaoping argued that "poverty is not socialism," and implemented the policy of "let some people get rich first." After the collapse of the Soviet and Eastern Bloc regimes, this stage comprehensively introduced the market economy and even borrowed approaches from capitalist economies. This was done so that, on the one hand, the economy could be built and the country could escape from impoverished socialism, and on the other hand, capitalist economic approaches could bring pressure on a rigid political system's restraints against economic reform.

This period achieved great successes in developing the market economy, and it also brought about the beginnings of comprehensive transformation within Chinese society. The old system was broken, and the establishment of a new system took some time, but high-level leadership never once announced that socialism would be abandoned.

Now China is entering the third stage, the new wave of socialism, because it is not a return to traditional socialism but a new synthesis. It inherits many reasonable ideas from traditional socialism, such as social justice and a human-centered and coordinated approach to development, but it employs completely different methods to realize those ideas. In many ways, this new wave of socialism has completely abandoned versions of socialism espoused by the Soviet Union and Eastern Europe during the Cold War, while it is much more similar to European versions of socialism.

The basis for the new wave of socialism is in China's social realities. Industrialization in the European sense has only just begun in China. To this are added factors such as globalization, social mobility, problems among farmers, and class differentiation. This means that China seemingly has an even stronger base for socialism. In a word, if the problems of workers and farmers, who account for the vast majority of society, cannot be resolved, then no ideology will long survive in China. This is why socialist concepts such as social justice and human-centeredness have rejuvenated socialism. In fact, there are many different currents of thoughts within contemporary Chinese society—intellectual movements such as liberalism and the New Left. While these movements have differing ideas, none of them have repudiated the central notions of socialism. These various factions are not divided by their ideas about society, but about the means to realize them.

The proposal of concepts like human-centeredness and the introduction of new methodologies in development have given Chinese socialism renewed vitality. This is a new political and economic system. Its direction is gradually becoming clear, but just how to create a socialist democracy faces both theoretical and practical questions. Socialism is a system that achieves social justice and realizes human-centered values through the people's participation in the political process. Now that an economy of diversified ownership has come into existence in China, more attention is being paid to establishing political democratization and social democracy. This is the challenge facing China.

The Key to Human-Centeredness: Democracy

If attention is paid to the major speeches of past generations of CCP leadership, it will be seen that a Chinese vision of democracy, or the direction of political development that has been identified by the CCP, has already been vividly laid out on paper. In this vision, China will not embark on a path of radical democratization.

What does Chinese democracy mean to leadership? In the past, there were two major markers of Chinese democracy: One was that a multiparty system would not be established, and the other was that there would be no separation of powers. Now a third marker has been established: China will not follow in the footsteps of the radical democratization of the Soviet Union and Eastern Europe.

Not pursuing Western-style democracy does not mean that political reform is not desired. At present, high-level leadership in the CCP has placed political reform at the top of its agenda. This is a move of historical significance. It demonstrates that top leadership is highly aware of the urgency of political reform within the ruling party—as without reform, there will be a crisis.

The CCP has learned enough from the changes experienced within the Soviet Union and Eastern Europe. After the collapse of the Eastern Bloc regimes, Deng Xiaoping believed it was mainly owing to the regimes' inability to develop the economy and provide the people with sufficient economic benefits. Seeing this, Deng Xiaoping argued that "development is the hardest principle" (*ying daoli*). At present the ruling party has learned another lesson from the rise and fall of other political parties—that is, a ruling party must not only be able to promote economic development but also learn how to govern an increasingly complex society.

China's decline in governing capacity can be reduced to two reasons: one internal, and the other external. The external reason is that socioeconomic changes can occur rapidly and thus pose a challenge to the ruling party. From the planned economy of the Mao Zedong era to today's market economy and globalization, Chinese socioeconomic life has undergone tremendous change. Yet although there have been some quantitative changes in the relationship between the ruling party and the people, there have been no substantial changes.

The internal reason lies in organizational and ideological problems that have arisen within the ruling party: The Party has been unable to control cadres and Party members, and this has given rise to severe levels of corruption and led to the decline of the Party's governing capacity. The problem is not that there have been no reforms within the ruling party, but that there have not been enough effective reforms. Anti-corruption is one such example. To date, high-ranking officials have launched countless anti-corruption political campaigns, but corruption is only getting worse.

How can governing capacity be increased? Here we need to find common ground between the ruling party and the people—and common ground is an important component of human-centered socialism. This aim, it should be said, is a reasonable one. Every political party ought to be an integral part of the people. Once a party loses contact with the people, its governing capacity will inevitably go into decline. Just how to establish organic relations with the people has become the key to increasing governing capacity. In the developed countries of the West, relations between the people and governing parties are established through elections. Since the CCP has rejected Western-style democracy, it must look for other ways to achieve reform.

The political reform priorities identified by the CCP can be ranked. First is the self-improvement of the ruling party through intra-party democracy. This approach comes first. In some regions and countries, ruling parties have failed to conduct intra-party reform and thus have proven incapable of managing social crises—leading to the eventual collapse of the ruling party. Thus, the CCP must strengthen itself through intra-party democracy. The second priority is the strengthening of the people's congresses' oversight of the government, gradually allowing congresses to become indirect channels for the people's participation in politics. At the same time, the people's congresses can also become a means by which the ruling party can transition from direct governance to indirect governance through participation in government organizations. The third is social democracy, which is often referred to as bottom-up sociopolitical participation.

Theoretically, this is a good ranking. After the ruling party's own capacity is strengthened, congresses can be allowed to monitor a government formed by the ruling party. At the same time, strengthening the ruling party's capacity is also conducive to opening the ruling party and its government, thereby allowing more members of society to participate in politics. If successful, this will provide a stable path toward democratization.

At the practical level, however, this prioritization faces major and perhaps even insurmountable difficulties. With the strengthening of the ruling party's capacity, it's possible that people's congresses might not be strengthened—or may even be weakened. There is only a highly institutionalized, political relationship between the Party and the government—that is, the Party controls the government. The legal relationship between the two—one in which the Party itself would be subject to the law—is still extremely weak. In many circumstances, it does not even exist. The ruling party generates a government in a top-down fashion. When the people do not have an effective mechanism for producing a government, how can people's congresses provide governmental oversight? And would the ruling party consciously submit itself to the law?

In democratized countries, bottom-up political participation is the primary driver of political democratization. The people participate in politics, elect their own leaders, and influence government decisions. It is the people's participation that creates an organic connection between the ruling party and the people—that constitutes external restraints and pressure on governments, and that drives ruling parties and governments to serve the people. But in China, top-down incentive mechanisms are used to achieve the ruling party's stated objectives and promote China's democratization.

When we discuss the governing capacity of the ruling party, we are not discussing governance for the sake of governance. The meaning of governance lies in the direction the Party is taking. Without direction, there is no point in discussing governance. Without direction, the problems facing the ruling party will not be resolved on a fundamental level. But it is not a simple matter to externalize a new "-ism." We are discussing the ruling party's governing capacity today so that we can realize a system that can reflect this new "-ism."

CHAPTER FIVE

A China Model of Democratization

As China is unwilling to pursue a Western-style, multiparty politics, it must absorb a diversity of socio-political interests by "internalizing" these various interests—that is, by accommodating this external diversity of interests within the Party and by achieving the expression of those interests, the representation of those interests, and the coordination of those interests within the system. This is the most direct source of intra-party democracy.

The Universality and Particularity of Democracy

In recent years, China's intellectual community has widely debated democratization. The report of the 17th Congress made democratic politics an important item on the agenda, and, at least theoretically, it established a roadmap for China's democratization: Intra-party democracy must promote the development of social democracy (or people's democracy). But at the social level, China's intellectual community has begun to rethink Western democracy. I would like to begin by discussing my views on this issue.

This debate has tended to drift in two directions: Some have emphasized that democracy has universal value and thus is a political value worth pursuing; others have held that democracy is not universal in nature. Many polemics have also argued that democracy is a product of the West. These have held that the West is constraining the development of non-Western countries by exporting democracy to them, and this can be seen in the "color revolution" movements that the United States has ignited in recent years. Thus, the West's attempt to promote democracy within China is an attempt to box in China and permanently weaken China.

Some have equated the democratic crises faced by many developing countries in Asia, Africa, and Latin America with a crisis within democracy itself. Such thinkers have begun to question the inherent value of democratic politics. Obviously, this recent reconsideration of Western democracy is essentially opposed to the democratization of Chinese politics itself. Since democracy is Western, then, the thinking goes, democratization means Westernization. Since the West can use democracy to effectively control and weaken non-Western countries, there is some validity to the anti-democratic attitude.

In my opinion, our consideration of democracy should go back to the principle that Deng Xiaoping used to launch the first wave of intellectual emancipation in the early 1980s: Practice is the sole criterion for measuring truth. Democracy should be investigated in terms of human experience; it should not be held as some pure value, in and of itself. In experience, democratic politics has its positives and negatives, and it has had differing effects within differing countries and regions. It's also clear that democratic countries and regions tend to have more highly developed economies and societies. In other words, in democratic societies, economic society has already been developed to a certain extent, and economic development is relatively stable and sustainable. This is particularly visible in North America, in Europe, and in Asian countries like Japan and South Korea.

In countries and regions that practice democracy, politics is also relatively stable. The structure of democratic politics is often formed through compromise and the coordination of various interests. Once these systems and structures have been formed, the overall political system will not be shaken, no matter what specific social and political disputes occur. In other words, democratic politics is relatively adept at absorbing socioeconomic contradictions. At the same time, while corruption can also occur under democratic politics, it's generally true that countries with a developed democratic politics are less corrupt than non-democratic countries.

On the other hand, however, democracy is often correlated with the weakness of a country, and a bad democracy might well be the worst form of government. In many developing countries in Asia, Africa, and Latin America, democracy frequently coexists with long-standing internal political and social conflicts. Politicians focus on political struggles, corruption is rampant, socioeconomic development remains at low levels for extended periods of time, and living standards do not improve. In these places, democracy is to some extent synonymous with the extant social disorder, and it has become a grievous political burden on the people. The recent crisis within Asian democracy also illustrates this problem.

Democracy offers excellent political advantages in developed countries, but in underdeveloped countries it frequently surfaces as a political disadvantage. Why is it that democracy can be both good and bad? First of all, problems have arisen in the development of democracy away from the West, in non-Western countries. But one should not equate the problems that have arisen with the expansion of democracy with those inherent to democracy itself. Compared with all other political systems, democratic politics itself still has great vitality.

Democracy itself means a government that is open—that is subject to change in the external environment. After the close of the Cold War, and with the decline in traditional political parties and ideologies, Western democratic politics is facing a variety of challenges. Every aspect of Western democracy, including its institutions themselves, is adjusting to the times and making constant changes. For example, when many young voters have lost interest in traditional political parties, various NGOs have emerged in response. From its organizations to its ideologies, from its districting to its election methodologies, Western democracy is continuously making adjustments. It should also be emphasized here that democracy has developed away from the West to non-Western countries, which does not mean that democracy belongs only to the West. For example, industrialization first occurred in the West, but this does not mean that industrialization belongs only to the West.

In many developing countries, problems that have emerged with democratic politics have primarily been caused by radical democratization. The healthy functioning of democratic politics requires the previous existence of every aspect of institutional infrastructure, as well as a considerable level of socioeconomic development. Democracy experiences problems in developing countries because their peoples, whether through external forces like Western colonialism or through the disregard of their political elites for socioeconomic and institutional conditions, uncritically introduce democratic systems.

That is, the negative effects or failures of democratic politics in a country or region are not owing to democratic politics itself, but to the specific approach and local conditions that are necessary for the emergence and development of democratic politics. On the other hand, while democracy originated in the West and has been exported from the West to other countries and regions, democracy is not a "specialty" of the West. Even the Western democracies that are visible today did not emerge simultaneously. In the West, democracy is found among countries that developed earlier and those that developed later, but no one talks about "Frenchization," "Britishization," "Germanization," or "Americanization."

Even in the process of spreading democracy to the former Soviet Union and Eastern Bloc countries, there was no such thing as "Westernization." At the same time, in countries where democracy has been developing in a healthy manner, no one is keen to discuss questions surrounding political models. The issue here is a simple one: Countries where democracy has succeeded have been those that built democracy on the basis of their level of socioeconomic development, political institutions, and cultural conditions. Because of this, it can be said that democratic politics takes on a different model in every country. In other words, there is no prototype for democracy. Every country can develop a democratic politics in accordance with its own cultural, economic, and social conditions. But there are "pirated versions" of democratic politics. These are those democracies—primarily in developing countries—that have been too heavily influenced by the United States and have ignored their own conditions.

From the beginning, the spread and development of democracy in Asia has been fraught with value conflicts. One of the biggest misunderstandings in the history of modern Asian thought happens when the developmental process of introducing to and developing within Asia the processes of modernization and democratization (processes that first began in the West) is labeled as "Westernization." While such an approach is quite popular in both Japan and China, in China "Westernization" has taken on politico-ethical significance. Since the cultural traditions of China and the West differ from one another, it's not hard to understand why modernization and Westernization are made equivalent. But this has become a major obstacle to progress in China.

The main reason why wave after wave of democracy can spread throughout the world is that the West's strength is driving it. As has been previously mentioned, there have been few successful examples of forcefully introduced democracies. The emergence and development of democracy in different countries and regions occurs primarily in order to meet the demands of socioeconomic development and political progress in these countries and regions. The given extent of socioeconomic development in any country will result in demand for political change—especially for democratic politics. In every country and region that possesses certain socioeconomic conditions, democratic politics has a great chance of success. And it's not hard to notice that market systems, democracy, and the rule of law are all interconnected. Yet in this case, there is no convincing case to be made for equating the market economy, democracy, and the rule of law with "Westernization." Let me state it clearly: Democracy is the product of socioeconomic development within any given country, and not the product of "Westernization."

Another negative result of equating democratization with "Westernization" is that it leads people to misunderstand democracy—and this is particularly so in developing countries. Many neglect the essence of democratic politics, and only simplistically focus on some Western institutional expressions of democracy—expressions like a multiparty system and the separation of powers. Democracy has so many different forms of institutional expression that the model practically changes from country to country. Institutional expressions are important, but they are not essential. The essence of democratic politics is competition, transparency, participation, and political responsibility. It is in this sense that democratic politics is a universal value for humanity. Because these essential aspects are most in tune with human nature, people yearn for political systems that embody these essentials.

Building State Systems Precedes Democratization

Democracy is the product of a country's economic and social development. In this sense, democracy is universal. But democracy must be implemented within a specific cultural context. In this sense, democracy is particular. When building a democratic politics within a specific cultural context, the most important thing is to build for democratic politics a set of state systems.

At home and abroad, democratic politics are widely understood as basically being elections for all levels of office and multiparty systems. But this is only a simplistic generalization of Western democratic politics: It is a generalization about the results of development, not a summary about the process of democratic development, and it certainly cannot explain the variety of approaches to democratic development and the probability of diversity within democratic politics. The election of officials at all levels is an important part of social democracy, but it does not represent the entirety of democratic politics. It needs to be emphasized here that the essence of democracy is not the quantity of political parties. There are no fundamental differences between a two-party democracy and other multiparty democracies with three or more parties. Similarly, competition can also occur within single-party systems or under single-party dominance (as in Japan and Singapore). The quality of competition depends on the state systems that help keep democracy going.

Across the globe, any effective democracy must be built on the foundations of an effective, modern state system. Democratic politics can be used to classify modern state systems into three categories. The first must be built before democratization occurs—for once democratic politics occurs, it is either difficult or impossible to establish this kind of system. The second is established before the arrival of democratic politics, but after democratization, it will also experience changes. The third must occur after democratization.

The first category of system is the basic systems of modern states. Without these systems—which include national defense, international diplomacy, law, taxation, government finance, commercial finance, distinctions in central and local relations, medical insurance, social welfare, education, etc.—no country can claim to truly have a state. In countries with developed democracies, these basic systems were established before the emergence of democratic institutions, and some of them have undergone great changes after democratization. In developing countries, it has not been easy to build effective systems. In some countries, democratization has been ongoing for many years, but these countries have still not established these basic systems of the modern state. A country might be democratic, but this does not mean that it is strong. If these basic state systems are in place, democracy often serves to promote integration; without these systems, democracy often becomes a force for differentiation. And the third category of system, such as democratic elections, should not experience significant development until after democratization. Yet even this category of system may turn into a chaotic process if there are no specific systems and rules in place before democratization.

Seen in this light, I have always argued that China needs to build state systems before it pursues a democratic politics. State systems must be built through various reforms. I classify China's overall reforms into three fields: economic reform, social reform, and political reform. But this does not mean that these three fields are independent of one another. In China's political environment, these three fields are not easily separated. But at each different stage, only one kind of reform can be the driver.

From the Reform and Opening Up to the beginnings of the twenty-first century, economic reform was in the driver's seat, and it was supported by political and social reforms. In the 1990s, the government's focus was on economic reform, and China made great strides in economic development and the building of economic systems, while a basic market economy was established. But the costs were also high. China paid a price in environmental degradation, excessive income disparities, moral decline in society, and official corruption. If this situation cannot be fundamentally changed, China's economic development will become unsustainable, and social instability will become a major problem. Of course, these elements have also led the international community to demonstrate anxiety over the "uncertainty" of China's development, and as a result, China is also facing tremendous international pressure.

Seen in this light, the 17th Congress was a watershed moment. To say it was a watershed moment does not mean that the reforms advocated by the 17th Congress had nothing to do with the past, but that the Congress identified a new model for reform. Although this model differs from previous models, its objectives remain the same. The 16th Congress officially advocated the creation of a "prosperous society" (*xiao kang shehui*), while the 17th Congress also advocated a "prosperous society." Here there is continuity. But when the 17th Congress also advocated a "harmonious society," this represented a shift. A prosperous society is achieved by continuing economic reforms. Without continued development, overall social development will stagnate, and it's possible the nation could return to an impoverished socialism. Thus, development remained a top priority for the 17th Congress.

But while the 17th Congress emphasized that development is still the number one priority, establishing the concept of a harmonious society indicates that social reform has officially become a high priority. On the one hand, social reform should serve as a corrective to the previous models of economic development, and make economic development more sustainable. Doing so will deepen economic reform. On the other hand, social reform must also create the conditions for future reforms centered on politics. Every democratic politics needs an effective sociopolitical infrastructure that includes social security, health insurance, education, and environmental protection. This infrastructure is built through social reform.

If, during the stage of economic reform, the government's power is primarily based on promoting economic development and improving living standards, then during the stage of social reform, this power base is transferred to providing government services for society—that is, a development-oriented government transitions into a service-oriented government. In fact, with the rise of various problems and social conflicts brought by the corporatization of government, the demand for a service-oriented government has become palpable.

Reforming society means building basic state systems. This is very important. The central government must assume responsibility for building systems at a national level; it cannot shift that responsibility to local governments. If China cannot establish systems that can provide the services of a modern state, it may not become a modern state. Naturally, both transitions to a service-oriented government and establishing modern social systems must be carried out through political reform. But here political reform does not necessarily mean electoral politics. Electoral politics is not capable of building these systems. These systems are often successfully built through bottom-up pressure and top-down, systemic innovation.

Success in social reform can not only provide the basis for proceeding to political reform but can also serve as a driving force for democratization. Similar processes have also occurred in Western countries. Transitions from early primitive capitalism to welfare capitalism (or to a capitalism with socialist elements) were all achieved through social reform. And the impetus for social reform came from society itself. While China will not exactly repeat the Western experience, current developmental trends indicate that it will also go through a similar process.

Here we must note the recent "reform fatigue" in China. Chinese government officials at all levels have been lauding reform and their lofty aspirations to realize reform, but once reform is expressed at the level of policy or action, effective measures for reform are seldom seen. In fact, as far as reform itself is concerned, many feel as if reform has become bogged down in many ways.

Every aspect of reform has been discussed for many years, but no great strides have been made. This has been true, for example, with the reform of government agencies, transitions in governmental functions, the building of a regulatory government, adjusting economic structures in accordance with the economic needs of the people, health insurance, social security, education reform, and the building of an environmentally friendly society.

In promoting social reform, the most important thing is building good relationships between the central and local governments. For thousands of years in traditional China, relations between central and local government have never been adequately addressed. Emperors ruled without governing, and central power never truly reached local government. After the founding of the People's Republic of China, central power reached every corner of the land for the first time in history. But while this central power was in theory massive, at the local level it sometimes totally disappeared. Owing to disparities among specific locales, no reform initiated by the central government, no matter how reasonable it may have been, could readily be implemented in each locale.

In my opinion, the relationships between China's central and local government are theoretically that of a unitary and centralized state, while in reality they are actually federal. The actual power of China's provinces exceeds that of any state government under a federal system. This is to say, China's power has been decentralized. The central government holds nominal power, while local governments enjoy actual power. Because of the decentralized nature of power, a unitary state is required to hold the country together.

In the 1980s, what was most discussed was the contradiction between decentralization and centralization—that is, "Once you let free the reins, you get chaos; once you get chaos, you pull in the reins; once you pull in the reins, you smother with control; once things are too smothered with control, you let free the reins."

A lot has happened since then. But the problem continues to persist. In fact, it's actually getting worse. If the problem of central-local relations is going to be resolved, selective centralization must be implemented. After Deng Xiaoping's Southern Tour, China experienced a movement of radical decentralization, one that resulted in problems of macroeconomic regulation. Zhu Rongji effected selective centralization in economic fields, implementing a tax-sharing system and reforming the central bank. But in the political arena, apart from strengthening the Party's oversight over cadres, selective centralization has not been implemented. In recent years, various centralization movements have taken place in order to strengthen macroeconomic regulation.

To break out of the vicious cycle between centralizing and decentralizing power, and to build effective central-local relations, there must be additional selective centralization in the field of economics, while political and legal systems also need selective centralization. China's geographic size, multiplicity of ethnicities, diversity amongst locales and other factors all need a central government with sufficient power. Power over national defense, foreign affairs, nationally significant laws, and overall economic regulation needs to be centralized in the central government.

The central government needs to hold onto this power at all costs. But local governments cannot be viewed as the mere local branches of the central government. Local governments are also governments, and as such, they also need space for their own autonomy. That is, local governments must also have sufficient political and legal power to effectively govern their local jurisdictions. In areas touching on local affairs, the central government must delegate power to local governments. In some areas, the workload will not be managed well if the central government issues policies that the local government has to pay for. In these areas, it's better if power is delegated to local government as well. Under the status quo, in those areas where there is money to be made, the central government's bureaucracy has come up with a variety of ways of centralizing power, but in those areas that are vital to the country and also need heavy expenditures, the central bureaucracy has no incentive to centralize power, and it does everything it can to pass the buck to the locales. Competition between the central government and local government is a major source of problems in central-local relations.

When power is delegated to locales, it's highly likely that corruption will occur at the local level. What can be done? While power does need to devolve to the local level, power must also be delegated to society. Without the empowerment of society, it will become impossible to stop corruption at the local level. In China, anti-corruption now mainly relies on the central government. There is no bottom-up motivation, nor is there any external restraint on corruption from society. The restraining power of the central government is also a form of internal constraint. Without constraints imposed by external society, internal constraints will become ineffective.

Over the years, many studies have shown that the central government holds far greater legitimacy in the eyes of ordinary people than the local governments do. One of the important reasons for this is that local governments interact directly with the people, and the people are extremely dissatisfied with local corruption. If this problem is to be solved, the social democracy mentioned above will need to become very important. Social democracy will put effective pressure on local governments, increase transparency in local governments, and make local governments accountable to the people who are under their jurisdiction. Obviously, in this sense, social democracy is highly beneficial for central power.

The problem is not that the concerned parties are unaware of the importance of empowering society, but that many are afraid of society's power. This is owing to the fact that many pit society's power against the government's power, as if their co-existence were a mutual contradiction. But this is not the case. During the Tang dynasty, Liu Zongyuan clearly saw that the power of the people can serve as a basis for the power of the emperor. This is even truer today. If the central government wants power and authority over local governments, it needs to base its power in society's power. Some also worry that increasing society's power will lead to social disorder. But here we are emphasizing the institutionalized power of society.

Society's power refers not only to society's legal right to participate in politics but also to society's right to participate in economic life. For example, society's power must replace the economic monopoly of local government at all levels. Monopolies at the central level are justified because some economic sectors are of strategic importance. But the farther down the chain you go, the more monopolies themselves change. When you get to the local level, monopoly simply means competition for profit between the government and the people. And where there is money to be made, that's where you find government monopolies.

This is why there must be determined effort to reform central monopolies and break up the monopolies of various local governments. Even when the central government's monopoly is necessary, the smaller it is, the better. In some areas, society could be empowered, and there could be established partnerships between the government and society, like those in developed Western societies. Furthermore, at the local level, the economy arena must be completely handed over to society. Only in so doing can China create an economic environment that is conducive to the development of SMEs. SMEs are the economic foundation of the people's well-being, and they are the most effective economic means of resolving income disparities.

China's Gradualist Democratization

While China's democratic politics is still facing major problems, and it has not been possible to form a consensus about various aspects of democracy on the theoretical level, at the experimental level the basics for a model for the development of Chinese democracy have already taken shape. To a large extent, Chinese democratic theory lags far behind its democratic practice.

It can be argued that China's model for democratic development has already basically taken shape on the evidence of the two following facts: First, the basic impetus for the development of democratic politics in China has already emerged; second, China has already found a more workable approach to achieving democracy. These two facts are critical for the development of democracy in any country. If democratic development lacks a basic impetus, democracy will forever remain only at the level of ideals. Even when certain factors such as radical reforms or external forces produce the forms of a democracy, such a democracy can only be superficial and insubstantial. The democratic practice of "third world" countries after World War II illustrates this problem.

The second element is equally important. If there are no practical means of implementing a democracy, it will remain only an ideal. Political reality is often thus: While no one can deny the importance of democracy, there may be no good means of effecting it; or, while democracy is being implemented, it may not be the democracy that had been originally anticipated.

Chinese democratic politics already has an impetus primarily because socioeconomic development has provided an objective external environment for democracy. This can be discussed under the following aspects. First, China's economic development is market-oriented and export-oriented. Marketization and globalization have created a Chinese economy that is open. Second, an open economy has created an open society. This can be seen in two aspects: One is that an open economy provides infrastructure for an open society such as markets, transportation, and communications systems; the other is that an open economy has created a rational and open mindset within society. A particular political value is no longer assessed in terms of ideals but with an eye for its practical benefit. The same is true of democracy. Third, in direct relation to democratic politics, socioeconomic development has led to the diversification of socioeconomic interests. Globally speaking, democratic politics is the product of socioeconomic development, for the diversification of socioeconomic interests must ultimately manifest itself within the political sphere.

The impetus already exists; all that is needed is to identify a viable path for democratization. The report of the 17th Congress emphasizes that "democracy in the people must be driven by democracy within the Party." There are two forms of democracy here: "intra-party democracy" and "people's democracy." Furthermore, the report also emphasized the rule of law and the authority of the law. If we consider the existence of concepts like intra-party democracy and people's democracy along with concurrent practices, a developmental model for Chinese democracy is already on paper.

Regarding intra-party democracy, two points need to be emphasized. First, intra-party democracy is also a reflection of the diversification of socioeconomic interests. As China is unwilling to pursue a Western-style, multiparty politics, it must absorb a diversity of sociopolitical interests by "internalizing" these various interests—that is, by accommodating this external diversity of interests within the Party and by achieving the expression of interests, the representation of interests, and the coordination of interests within the system. This is the most direct source of democracy within the Party.

Second, intra-party democracy can help cultivate democratic rules and a democratic culture among political elites. While so-called democratic rules can be found in various textbooks, these rules represent a summary of the experience of already extant democratic politics—and they are not easily transferred to other countries. The democratic rules of any country can only be produced through the interactions among that country's political elites. Without some basic democratic rules or cultural identity, a democratic politics will collapse into disorder. This has been demonstrated by the balanced development of democracy in democratic countries and the democratic practice of many developing countries and regions.

If intra-party democracy emphasizes the top-down coordination of interests, then a people's democracy emphasizes bottom-up political participation. Theoretically speaking, "people's democracy" is more appropriately labeled "social democracy." In China, social democracy can be seen in the various ways the people can participate in politics, such as representation in people's congresses, the Political Consultative Conference, basic-level democracy, and community organizations. In this sense, democracy has already achieved considerable development.

Social democracy also exhibits the characteristics of openness, which means that various new types of participation are constantly emerging—for example, participation in NGOs. NGOs used to be a highly sensitive topic, but in recent years they have developed extremely rapidly. While NGOs have differing space to develop, depending on their particular fields, their participation in political affairs has already become quite pronounced. For another example, the democratic practice of negotiation (or "agreements") has already become quite developed in many areas.

Social democracy is primarily occurring at the local and departmental levels, and it is connected with the direct interests of its participants. As with intra-party democracy, social democracy can also help develop democratic rules and a democratic culture among members of society and various social groups. The formation of democratic rules and a democratic culture at the local level are highly conducive to the progress of democracy at the national level.

But both intra-democracy and social democracy need to be implemented within a legal framework. This means that democracy needs to be granted legal supremacy. This point can be examined under several aspects. First of all, regardless of how intra-party democracy is carried out, the ruling party needs to obey the Constitution and the law. In other words, intra-party democracy also needs to accept the restraints of the Constitution and the rule of law. With the passage and implementation of laws such as the Supervision Law (*Jiandu fa*), this has become quite clear. Second, social democracy must be implemented within the scope of the Constitution as well, since this will guarantee the orderly development of democracy. Finally, intra-party democracy and social democracy have developed independently of each other up to the present. While, at the local level, intra-party democracy and social democracy have begun to interact with each other, as for example in the "two-vote system" (*liang piao zhi*) that has been produced by rural basic-level democracy (in this system, both the Party's basic-level leadership and the villages' autonomous organizations are determined by the votes of villagers), this interaction has not yet begun at the national level. And true democratization in China means direct interaction between intra-party democracy and social democracy at the national level. It's conceivable that this interaction might become large-scale.

What will a future Chinese democracy look like? I personally feel that it will be a combination of selections with elections. The selection of officials is a Chinese tradition, while elections are a form of modern democracy. Elections cannot guarantee the quality of leaders; leaders must first be selected and then chosen by election. This is precisely the direction in which China is developing. Judging from the development of various forms of democracy at this present stage, we can reasonably predict that the future China will combine three primary elements: top-down party selections (intra-party democracy), bottom-up social approval (social democracy), and the orderly interaction of the ruling party and society within a legal framework (the rule of law). If the former two represent the motivation for democracy, the latter is the systemic guarantee for interaction between the Party and society.

CHAPTER SIX

The Centrality and Popularity of State Power: Relations Between Central and Local Government in China

There is a necessary institutional connection between the centralization of state power and the popularity of the government. To put it differently, power comes from the people and is implemented among the people. This is the essence and significance of modern state power. A direct connection between the paramount leader and the people is crucial to the authority of the central government, for without such a direct relationship the central government's power cannot reach every part of society.

The Problem of Central-Local Relations

China's locales are vast in size, and there are also enormous differences in the various aspects of the provinces. Without sufficient power, it's difficult for the central government to manage affairs. In the same way, if the local level is not given enough initiative in its own right, every aspect of development will experience major problems. Thus, just how to manage the relationship between centralization and decentralization involves not only developmental questions for many aspects of China but also China's state-building itself. In fact, whenever Mao Zedong, Deng Xiaoping, or the third generation of collective leadership discussed China's state-building, they always touched on the relationship between the central government and local governments.

The relationship between the central government and local governments is undoubtedly an important aspect of China's political reform. In order to understand how this aspect of political reform should be carried out, we need to begin with understanding the existing problems in central-local relations. Since the Reform and Opening Up, while the government has made herculean efforts at managing central-local relations and has achieved some successes, it cannot be denied that many serious problems still exist. To summarize, these problems have two major systemic manifestations: (1) centralized power lacks sufficient power, and (2) decentralized power lacks sufficient democracy.

To begin with, centralized power lacks sufficient power. It cannot be denied that, on paper, China's current regime is one of a small minority in the world that has highly concentrated power. Politically, the CCP is the only ruling party. There are democratic parties, but the Chinese system does not feature Western-style multiparty competition. Rather, it is a system of multiparty cooperation—that is, the democratic parties do not contend for power with the CCP, but cooperate with and monitor the power of the CCP. Within the systems of governance, the Party's central leadership is obviously powerful, and power flows top-down in the legislative, executive, judicial, and other governmental systems. In a word, in the current Chinese political system overall, the source of all political power is the central government. At the beginning of the 1980s, Deng Xiaoping observed that the CCP's power structure was imbalanced: Power was concentrated in the hands of the Party, while the Party's power was also concentrated in top-level leadership, and this power was itself concentrated in the hands of a small minority of the Party's leaders.[1] Although this system has seen a few changes, its overall structure has not seen fundamental change.

Economically speaking, while the developmental goals of a socialist market economy have been established, and China's economic system has dramatically transformed itself from a planned economy into a market economy, none of this means that the government has withdrawn or will withdraw from the economic sphere. The government, and especially the central government, still controls a considerable amount of important economic resources. At the same time, the government's economic role is currently transitioning. Various macro-prudential regulatory mechanisms, such as systems for taxation, government finance, and financial management, are in the process of being established. We can be rest assured

1 Deng Xiaoping 邓小平, "Dang he guojia lingdao zhidu de gaige" "党和国家领导制度的改革" [The Reform of the Party and State Leadership Systems], *Deng Xiaoping wenxuan* 邓小平文选 [The Selected Works of Deng Xiaoping], vol. 2 (Beijing: People's Publishing House, 1994), 327–31.

that, in the economic sphere, the central government's power will continue to be strengthened with the establishment and improvement of various macro-prudential regulatory mechanisms.

From a social perspective, despite the rapid development of China's third sector since the Reform and Opening up, a so-called "civil society" is still taking shape. However, this civil society is fundamentally different from the West's civil society. In the West, civil society is independent of government. In a sense, it is a quasi-political entity that contends with the government as a comprehensive set of interests. In China, however, while the so-called civil society does play this role to a certain extent, at least at present it poses no challenge to the regime—largely serving as a collaborator with the government. Basically, the government can integrate various social forces into the system through various policy and institutional channels. In fact, as long as a powerful state apparatus can continue to exist and operate effectively, while there may be some institutional opposition outside the system, it will never pose a substantial threat to the ruling party's governance.

However, in such a highly centralized political system, many actually feel on a daily basis that the central government lacks sufficient power. The highly hierarchical nature of power does not guarantee the effective implementation of that power. Owing to reasons that will be discussed below, in many areas, no one is managing what the government should be managing, while many in the government are managing affairs that the government shouldn't be managing. Where political power is needed, no political power can be found, and in areas where there is money to be made, many government departments are engaged in competition with each other over management of these areas. The central government cannot control local governments, governments cannot control the people, and as a result, various underworld organizations and "evil forces" (*e shi li*) have emerged. They use violence in the pursuit of dominance, monopolize industry, and hoard wealth—while the basic living conditions and security of the people in some localities cannot be guaranteed. The gravity of these problems is reflected in the manner in which the government has engaged in anti-underworld campaigns. This has led some to wonder: Who exactly is leading the country?[2] Since the mid-1990s, the rise of various cults has also largely reflected a decline in the central government's power.

This decline in power has led to a paradox: The faster economic development grows, and the greater the people's wealth grows, the more they feel insecure. Some public opinion surveys conducted by a number of domestic academic institutions have shown that the people's sense of security is declining with the deterioration

2 *China Police Daily*, April 9, 2001.

of public security.[3] This shows that, to a certain extent, while the state has played a very large role in promoting economic and social development, it has not devoted enough attention to other aspects of state-building.

The second systemic problem in the relationship between the central government and local governments is that decentralized power lacks democracy. While China's political system remains highly centralized in theory, its actual decentralization of power has become an incontrovertible fact. If we can say that the waves of decentralization movements during the Mao era caused a certain amount of decentralization within overall political power in China, then it can be argued that the decentralization reforms of the Deng Xiaoping era further deepened that decentralization.

Delegation of power from the central government to local government at all levels and ultimately to society itself is an important feature of democratic politics. In some Western countries, decentralization reforms are often conducted along two lines: The first is the institutional decentralization of the central government to local governments, and the other is the strengthening of accountability mechanisms in local governments. Decentralization works because local government is closer to local people and is thus better able to serve the people in certain respects. In China, however, rapid decentralization has not been institutionalized, and an institutional democracy has not developed. Under these circumstances, on the one hand, the central government feels that its power is inadequate, since power is in the hands of local governments; and on the other hand, local governments also complain that they do not have any power, because in theory all power still belongs to the central government. Local governments may have power, but there is no systemic guarantee of this power, and the central government can take back power at any time. This loss of political power is extremely serious. Everyone knows that power has been lost, but no one knows where it has gone.

Even more worrisome, this non-institutional decentralization has weakened the central government's oversight over local governments, and it has also failed to strengthen mechanisms for ensuring local governments' accountability to the people. While local officials lack "sovereignty," and are only the representatives of the central government, they can deviate from central policy and do whatever they like. Some local officials have dominated the state apparatus and oppressed the people at will. Some have even preyed upon the people by colluding with the underworld and evil forces. In order to create some systemic pressure on local cadres and to allow the people to manage themselves, since 1987 China has gradually

3 See the annual report of the *Blue Book of China's Society* prepared by the Institute of Sociology at the Chinese Academy of Social Science.

established village-level direct elections, while the municipal- and township levels have also begun experiments with holding elections.[4] On the one hand, such efforts are far from sufficient; on the other hand, there are indications that evil forces and the underworld have seriously penetrated local governments in China.

These evil forces frequently manipulate elections through various methods, thereby using their agents to control power, or employ the power of money to corrupt authority and enter the sphere of local political power. Many cases show that an increasing number of criminal elements and underworld organizations have entered local congresses and consultative conferences—and have even penetrated the administrative system.[5] Obviously, without a strong central government that can ensure the normal operations of democracy, democracy cannot easily express and protect the interests of the people on its own. Thus, when the central government feels that its power is insufficient, what the people feel is insufficient democracy. The people welcome democracy, for it can give them the power to choose their own "rulers," but at the same time they also sense the weakness of local democratic systems and the inability of these emerging systems to protect their interests.

As the reformer Liang Qichao once observed, the disadvantage of Chinese politics is that both ends of power are often good, and that the problem lies with the middlemen. In other words, we can have a good emperor and a good people. The problem lies with the corrupt officials in between who cut off the connection between the emperor and the people. To a certain extent, this is also true today, but Liang Qichao's manner of expressing it is too simplistic.

This situation was not created by the central government, nor is the answer the eradication of middle management. Neither a central government nor the people themselves can form a complete system of governance—and this is especially true in China. Without strong local government, how can the central government implement its policies for promoting social, economic, and political development? The problem can only be solved through reforms at the systemic level—through using the system to force the middle levels to "do good" while curbing its own corruption. In order to achieve this political objective, we need to devote attention to the relations between the central government, local governments, and society. At

4 Wang Xu 王旭, "Xiangcun Zhongguo de jiceng minzhu: guojia yu shehui de quanli huqiang" "乡村中国的基层民主：国家与社会的权力互强" [Basic-Level Democracy in Rural China: The Mutual Support of State and Society], *Twenty-First Century*, April 1997, no. 40; Zheng Yongnian 郑永年, "Xiangcun minzhu he Zhongguo zhengzhi jincheng" "乡村民主和中国政治进程" [Rural Democracy and China's Political Process], *Twenty-First Century*, June 1996, no. 35.

5 Zheng Yongnian 郑永年, "Jingti minzhuhua guocheng zhong de zhengzhi fubai" "警惕民主化过程中的政治腐败" [Watch out for Corruption During Democratization], *Hong Kong Economic Journal*, December 15, 2000.

the center of these there are three levels of people: central officials, local officials, and the common people. If it is true that "human nature is inherently good," then it is society and the institutional environment that makes people "bad"; or if it is true that "human nature is inherently evil," then a lack of institutional restraints gives people the chance to pursue "evil." No matter how you look at it, systems come first, while people come second. What we want in political reform is the creation of a system that "suppresses evil and promotes good."

The Root Causes of Problems in Central-Local Relations

What should relations between central and local government look like? How can China create an effective system for managing the relations between the central government and local governments? Beginning with Mao Zedong's "On the Ten Major Relationships," continuing with Deng Xiaoping's statements on the topic, and also including Jiang Zemin's "Properly Managing Important Relationships in the Construction of Socialist Modernization" (or "On the Twelve Major Relationships"), there has already been a thorough discussion of relations between the central government and local government. I do not need to supply copious quotations from these analyses here. We want to analyze the current problems in central and local relations from another related angle—that is, questions of the centrality and popularity of state power, questions which also correspond to the "democratic centralism" that Mao Zedong and other CCP leaders already developed.

We hold that the root causes of the problematic phenomena occurring in the relationship between central and local governments are the lack of centrality and the lack of popularity in state power. In other words, state power lacks both concentration and democracy. The CCP has always emphasized democratic centralism, which is the centralization of power based on democracy. And this is important indeed, for the state power of every modern country must undergo such a political process. Western democracies in fact are characterized by a kind of "democratic centralism." However, China's current political system does not reflect an effective combination of "centralization" with "democracy."

To a certain extent, China lacks both an institutional approach to centralization and an institutional approach to democracy. In order to develop a modern state power that is both centralized and democratic, we need to discuss centralization and democracy—that is, we need to discuss the relations between centrality and democracy in power. We will discuss the meaning of these two aspects separately, for in China democratic centralism means at least two different things. The first is democratic centralism at the institutional level. On October 25, 1937, when Mao Zedong was talking with a British journalist and was asked about the meaning of democracy, he offered an interpretation of democracy and centralization:

> There is no impassable gulf between democracy and centralism, both of which are essential for China. On the one hand, the government we want must be truly representative of the popular will; it must have the support of the broad masses throughout the country and the people must be free to support it and have every opportunity of influencing its policies. This is the meaning of democracy. On the other hand, the centralization of administrative power is also necessary, and once the policy measures demanded by the people are transmitted to their own elected government through their representative body, the government will carry them out and will certainly be able to do so smoothly, so long as it does not go against the policy adopted in accordance with the people's will. This is the meaning of centralism. Only by adopting democratic centralism can a government be really strong.[6]

In 1945, Mao returned to the meaning of democratic centralism, in "On Coalition Government," in which he argued:

> The organizational principle of the new-democratic state should be democratic centralism, with the people's congresses determining the major policies and electing the governments at the various levels. It is at once democratic and centralized, that is, centralized on the basis of democracy and democratic under centralized guidance. This is the only system that can give full expression to democracy with full powers vested in the people's congresses at all levels and, at the same time, guarantee centralized administration with the governments at each level exercising centralized management of all the affairs entrusted to them by the people's congresses at the corresponding level and safeguarding whatever is essential to the democratic life of the people.[7]

The second thing democratic centralism means concerns the political life of the country. In 1957, Mao Zedong applied democratic centralism to the task of managing contradictions among the people:

6 Mao Zedong 毛泽东, "He Yingguo jizhe Beilante de tanhua" 和英国记者贝兰特的谈话 [Interview with the British Journalist James Bertram], in *Mao Zedong xuanji* 毛泽东选集 [Selected Works of Mao Zedong], vol. 2 (Beijing: People's Publishing House, 1991), 383. Translation from "Interview with the British Journalist James Bertram," *marxists.org*, https://www.marxists.org/reference/archive/mao/selected-works/volume-2/mswv2_05.htm.

7 Mao Zedong 毛泽东, "Lun lianhe zhengfu" 论联合政府 [On Coalition Government], in *Mao Zedong xuanji* 毛泽东选集 [Selected Works of Mao Zedong], vol. 3 (Beijing: People's Publishing House, 1991), 1057. Translation from "On Coalition Government," *marxists.org*, https://www.marxists.org/reference/archive/mao/selected-works/volume-3/mswv3_25.htm.

> Within the ranks of the people, we cannot do without freedom, nor can we do without discipline; we cannot do without democracy, nor can we do without centralism. This unity of democracy and centralism, of freedom and discipline, constitutes our democratic centralism. Under this system, the people enjoy broad democracy and freedom, but at the same time they have to keep within the bounds of socialist discipline. All this is well understood by the masses.[8]

In 1962, Mao Zedong further extended this principle to the working methods of leading cadres. He argued that the working method of leading cadres "is a democratic centralist method; it is a mass-line method. First democracy, then centralism; coming from the masses, returning to the masses; the unity of the leadership and the masses." He also commented that, when "putting democratic centralism into effect," "we must conscientiously bring questions out into the open, and let the masses speak out. Even at the risk of being cursed we should still let them speak out."[9]

It should be said that when Mao Zedong discusses centralization and popularity at an institutional level, he does so in a very clear manner. A strong government must meet two conditions—centralization and popularity—and popularity is the foundation of centralization. In the terms of modern political theory, without popularity, it is hard to achieve centralization. Centralization itself is meaningless, for its end is the people: Centralization is the concentration of power during the government's implementation of policies among the people. An effective centralization must be grounded in the people. In other words, there is a necessary institutional connection between the centralization of state power and the popularity of the government. To put it differently, power comes from the people and

8 Mao Zedong 毛泽东, "Guanyu zhengque chuli renmin neibu maodun de wenti" 关于正确处理人民内部矛盾的问题 [On the Correct Handling of Contradictions Among the People], in *Jianguo yilai Mao Zedong wengao* 建国以来毛泽东文稿 [Mao Zedong's Manuscripts Since the Founding of the People's Republic of China], vol. 6 (Beijing: Central Government Documents Publishing House, 1992), 321. Translation from "On the Correct Handling of Contradictions Among the People," *marxists.org*, https://www.marxists.org/reference/archive/mao/selected-works/volume-5/mswv5_58.htm.

9 Mao Zedong 毛泽东, "Zai kuoda de zhongyang gongzuo huiyi shang de jianghua" 在扩大的中央工作会议上的讲话 [Talk at an Enlarged Working Conference Convened by the Central Committee of the Communist Party of China], in *Jianguo yilai Mao Zedong wengao* 建国以来毛泽东文稿 [Mao Zedong's Manuscripts Since the Founding of the People's Republic of China], vol. 10 (Beijing: Central Government Documents Publishing House, 1992), 18. Translation from "Talk At An Enlarged Working Conference Convened By The Central Committee Of The Communist Party Of China," *marxists.org*, https://www.marxists.org/reference/archive/mao/selected-works/volume-8/mswv8_62.htm.

is implemented among the people. This is the essence and significance of modern state power.

In the second level of the political life of the country, Mao Zedong emphasized working methods—that is, the ways that power operates within a certain system. This mode of operation itself contains a certain rationality and legitimacy. In fact, working methods have always been regarded as an organic component of the traditions of the CCP. But in the actual operations of power, some leaders often confuse the democratic centralism of one level with the democratic centralism of the other, and they use democratic centralism as a working method instead of as an institution. In so doing, the building of democratic systems is objectively diluted, and a theoretical basis is provided for the "non-democratic" behavior of some cadres. In order to return to democratic centralism at the institutional level, we must examine how this system manifests itself within a modern state system. In other words, we must determine which institutional elements the modern state employs to express this principle.

The Centralization and Popularity of Power in Modern States

What is a modern state? Modern state theory can be approached from the perspective of various ideologies like Marxism and liberalism that define modern states from their differing perspectives. If we are to define the characteristics of modern states in empirical terms, of how they were produced and developed, we cannot do better than Weber.[10] Working from a comparative analysis of the development of state power in various countries, Weber summarized some of the main characteristics of modern states, and his summary has gone on to exert influence on all scholarship after him. The American scholar Gianfranco Poggi offered the following summary of Weber's analysis: The modern state is defined as a political organization that exists within specific territory. It has several primary characteristics: First, it is distinct from and separated from all other organizations within that territory (that is, the state is a unique political organization); second, it is autonomous (that is, the state's decision-making can be entirely reduced to responses to the demands of various political forces at home and abroad); third, its power is centralized (that is, in comparison with other political organizations, the state's power is relatively concentrated); fourth, various departments within the state exhibit coordination.[11]

10 Weber's discussion of the subject can be found in his book *Economy and Society*.

11 Gianfranco Poggi, *The State: Its Nature, Development and Prospects* (Stanford: Stanford University Press, 1990).

Many scholars including Poggi hold that what is now called a true, mature modern state did not appear until the nineteenth century. Poggi divided the nearly thousand years of the state's development in the West into three major stages: From the late twelfth century to the early fourteenth century, it began to transform into a hierarchical state system; from the sixteenth to the seventeenth century, it transitioned from a hierarchical state system into a system of absolutist rule; and the early eighteenth century saw the rise of civil society and the decline of absolutism, which continued into the nineteenth century, when liberal democracy began to rise and effect a transition to democratic states.[12]

We can reinterpret this definition under our own terms. A mature, modern state must be both centralized and popular in nature. Before the nineteenth century, no state possessed both of these characteristics. Previously there were feudal social structures, and regimes were only localized, and not centralized. The formation and rise of modern states cannot be separated from the development of hierarchical states and authoritarian states. After centralization of power was achieved, states gradually began to become more popular in nature. This popularity is different from the localization of earlier periods. It is the popularity of the central government, not the localization of central power. This both centralized and popular state power is possible only after a modern democratic politics has emerged.

How then does a modern state achieve a transition from a decentralized, localized government to a centralized government, and from that to a both democratic and centralized government? There are both economic and political factors at play here. The most powerful explanation of this transition is offered by Marxism, which emphasizes that the emergence and development of the political forms of the state is connected with the economic forms of differing historical periods.

To summarize, as a political organization, the state has heretofore experienced three major forms. The first is various forms of localized organizations, which include primitive societies, feudal societies, and a variety of forms of a state in societies with simple commodity production.

In these social forms, economies were small-scale, and the primary economic driver was the survival of the individual producer. These were subsistence economies, and the economic forms made it impossible for central power to be centralized. A decentralized economy cannot provide economic support for central power, for the decentralization of the economy determines the localization and decentralization of political power.

12 Gianfranco Poggi, *The Development of the Modern State* (Stanford: Stanford University Press, 1978).

The second form of a state is an imperial system, which is a product of socioeconomic forms in an agricultural society. In an empire, the economy is mostly a controlled economy, with the state dominating and controlling all social wealth. The economy serves the needs of bureaucrats and nobles. In other words, the economic activity of an empire exists in order to increase the wealth and power of these classes and enhance their status. In all empires, economic activity is subordinate to the state and the ruling class.

In an empire, the state's wealth and power depend primarily on controlling farmers. Before the large-scale agricultural and economic production of modern times, empires achieved surplus value primarily through controlling territory and imperial tribute. The greater the expansion of an empire's territory, the more surplus product an empire could obtain, and thus the stronger the empire. In another respect, however, an empire's economic wealth was also affected by international commerce, and controlling trade was a major objective of imperial politics.

Empires as a state system seemed quite powerful, but they eventually disappeared. Why was this? There are three main reasons. First, the rise of the modern nation-state replaced the political form of the empire; second, industrialization promoted economic transition; and third, the world saw the formation of a global market system.

The third form of the state is the modern state. As a form that was inevitably going to replace empires, the modern state can be regarded as an institutional innovation for coping with environmental changes that pre-modern political organizations could not cope with. In an empire, there is no organic connection between the state and society. While empires were vast and sometimes featured strong military power, they only gained the political loyalty of one portion of the residents within their territories; many residents never felt that the empires under which they lived held legitimacy. As a result, under pressure from foreign enemies and internal strife, imperial governments could not garner strong support from their residents. The most salient characteristic of modern states, on the other hand, is their ability to obtain the political loyalty of most of their residents. In an imperial system, the actual loyalties of their residents were often local political bodies, while in modern nation-states, the loyalties of residents lie with the state. Thus, after the formation of nation-states, ideological nationalism strengthened cohesion within modern states and the loyalty of residents to the state.

Industrialization, the development of a market economy, and revolutions in military technology have also greatly promoted the development of modern nation-states. Development in both trade and economies provided vast amounts of fiscal revenue for modern states, while military technology and organizational innovations improved the effectiveness of the control of a central government over its territory. A modern state means that a strong central government occupies a place above all other sociopolitical organizations, and its central authority covers all the land and residents within its territory. At the same time, the modern state is the only political organization that can legally monopolize violence and can employ an effective system of bureaucracy and various other methods (such as law) to control the residents of its territory. In addition, the objectives of the modern state are often the promotion of economic development, the construction of domestic infrastructure, the elimination of various elements that hinder the unified development of a domestic market, and the utilization of various effective means to promote economic growth. The economist Schumpeter holds that a modern state, first of all, needs to emancipate its people and give them adequate freedom to create wealth. Then it needs to deploy various means, especially taxation, to gather that wealth, improve the overall levels of welfare within its territory, and increase national strength.[13]

Another important factor that has influenced the development of modern states is the formation of a global economy. On the one hand, national economies and an international economy have replaced the local and imperial economies of the pre-modern era; on the other hand, the interdependence of various countries' economies has steadily increased, and a global economic system has gradually taken shape. The formation of an international economy has also increasingly influenced the roles and functions of states.

The brief discussion provided above illustrates how a modern state is achieved. The most important factor in the replacement of various pre-modern forms of the state with the modern state was the need for economic development. While empires did feature concentration of power, their goals were not economic development but the seizure of economic resources. With the emergence and development of capitalist factors, the people need the government, not only to unify the domestic market but also to develop markets overseas. This objective requires a highly centralized central government. For both unifying domestic markets and opening up overseas markets cannot be achieved by economic factors on their own. State power, at the very least, can accelerate this process. Thus, Marx held that the early autocracies were reasonable polities under the economic conditions of their time. Markets require centralized power, and centralized power in turn promotes market development. This shows that economic factors are driving modern states to become ever more centralized.

13 Joseph A. Schumpeter, *The Economics and Sociology of Capitalism* (Princeton: Princeton University Press, 1991).

How then is this centralization of state power legitimized? The first way to legitimize state power, of course, is the economic factors mentioned above. This is true, not only because centralized systems meet the needs of contemporary economic development but also because unlike empires that seized economic resources, the aim of centralized autocracy is to create more economic wealth, thereby benefiting all the people within the nation, regardless of whether they constitute a minority or a majority. Another source of legitimacy is nationalism. With the disintegration of the imperial system came the rise of forms of the nation-state. The new nation-states certainly needed highly concentrated political power, for this could ensure the state's sovereignty externally and provide political order for the people internally. In other words, a centralized system met not only the economic needs of the people but also the political needs of the people. But when the nation-state began to expand outward, nationalism provided greater legitimacy for centralized power.

Where then did the popular nature of state power come from? The answer is connected with the development of democratic politics. Since the French Revolution, the two themes of nationalism have been national sovereignty and popular sovereignty. The principle of nation-state sovereignty proves the need for centralized state power, while the principle of popular sovereignty proves the need for the popular nature of the state's power. But we have discussed this topic elsewhere.[14] Simply put, popularity changes in accordance with changes in class relations, and the development in class relations has experienced several major stages. The first was the political contest between the bourgeoisie and autocratic monarchies. Autocratic monarchies arose and developed in response to the needs of the bourgeoisie, but while autocratic monarchies provided services for the bourgeoisie, they also paved the way for their exit from the stage of history. The bourgeoisie demanded shared power with monarchs and the ruling class. Economic power ultimately overcame political power, and this triumph manifested itself in the politics of bourgeois democracy. The rise of the bourgeoisie also created a working class. The working class used its numerical strength to win the right to vote and enter power-sharing with the bourgeoisie. After the working class entered the political process, democracy had theoretically transitioned from a democracy for the few to a democracy for the many. Since then, the development

14 See Zheng Yongnian 郑永年, *Zhongguo minzuzhiyi de fuxing: minzu guojia xiang hechu qu* 《中国民族主义的复兴：民族国家向何处去？》 [The Revival of Chinese Nationalism: Where Is the Nation-State Headed?], Hong Kong: Joint Publishing, 1997; and "Zhengzhi gaige yu Zhongguo guojia jianshe" 《政治改革与中国国家建设》 [Political Reform and State-building in China], in *Strategy and Management* 2 (2001): 1–12.

of democracy has primarily been a question of expanding its popular base. The twentieth-century Civil Rights Movement in the West did not change the forms of democracy; it simply expanded the popular nature of state power.

The expansion of popularity paralleled the centralization of state power. As previously discussed, early centralized systems possessed their own legitimacy, but when economic development and differentiation occurred, those factors that had formerly provided legitimacy now lost their effectiveness, and popularity became the most important element in providing legitimacy. As a result, early Western nationalism focused on the nation-state itself, but later the focus shifted to the aspect of popular sovereignty. This shift can be seen in Rousseau's *The Social Contract.*

Democratic politics can mean many different things. Giving the people an institutional channel to participate in politics means, of course, that the people will curb state power. But this is only one aspect of the issue. As far as central governments are concerned, the greatest significance of democracy lies in its ability to provide the government with legitimacy. The paramount leader is elected by the people, and the leader's office is based in the people, thus granting the leader an authority beyond that of any organization within the country. A direct connection between the paramount leader and the people is crucial to the authority of the central government, for without such a direct relationship, the central government's power cannot reach every part of society. Such a relationship allows the central government to consistently maintain the centrality of its power while implementing its policies. This organic connection between the centrality of a government's power and that government's popularity is the biggest difference between the modern state and various types of government in the past—and it is also a major reason why the modern state is stronger than other forms of government.

The Loss of Centrality in State Power

The foregoing brief discussion does not mean that China's political reforms will repeat the path taken by the West. History doesn't simply repeat itself. The discussion here is only suggesting there is a historical logic that clearly explains why we need to face the questions presented at the beginning of this article. The root causes for the existence of a centralized power that lacks power and a decentralization that lacks democracy lie in some deep flaws within China's political system: central power lacks centrality, while the people's power does not provide sufficient political support to central power through democratic means.

How, then, is the centrality of state power lost, and how is it that popularity has not been achieved? This depends on the actual operations of political power in China—particularly on the actual circumstances in central-local relations. The most important factors that have created this situation are the problematic structure of central-local relations, the non-institutionalized or non-standard state of decentralization, and the underdevelopment of democracy.

Structurally speaking, China is a centralized, unitary state, in which all power in principle belongs to the central government. In theory, local government at all levels is nothing more than the executive agency of the central government: Local governments should thoroughly implement national laws, regulations, and policies. But if this were the case, state power would not have gradually lost its centrality. The truth is that local governments do not serve at the beck and call of higher-level government. Local governments have become first-level governments with their own interests, and they govern locales in accordance with the conditions on the ground.

This behavior is also tolerated by the central government. Thus, in its implementation of its power and policies, the central government has no institutions by which it can directly penetrate to the local level; it can only project power and implement policy by relying on the various layers of local governments. Owing to the existence of local interests, the farther down power and policy are pursued in government, the more centrality decreases. Many powers have completely lost centrality by the time they reach the local level, and they become local policies adjusted in accordance with local ideas. Thus, a superficially strong state power is actually divided up among a vast array of local governments.

The decentralization movement has worsened this situation. From the late 1970s to the early 1990s, the central government pursued a strategy of decentralization in order to encourage greater activity in local economic development. This strategy had both its pluses and minuses. On the positive side, decentralization has forcefully driven the development of local economies. In just a few decades, the overall picture of China's economy has completely changed. Without decentralization, China's economy would not have reached its present level, nor would the people's lives have improved so quickly. On a more negative side, decentralization has exacerbated income disparities, and the imbalance in regional development has become difficult to reverse. What's worse, decentralization has had a tremendously negative impact on the central government's power and ability to implement policy. As local government plays a more important role in economic development than the central government does—or, in other words, as local governments take a greater slice of the economic cake—the central government has great difficulty in collecting economic resources from local governments. The reason is quite simple: Decentralization of power away from the central government has meant the withdrawal of central power. After contractions in central power, local governments have become *de facto* autonomous polities, and the central government has lost its ability to influence locales.

The lack of popularity adds fuel to the fire in the state's loss of control over local power. While the Chinese government has already made building democratic politics an objective and has made considerable effort in various regards, it cannot be denied that democracy is still highly undeveloped at the institutional level. Although there are many forms of elections, they are constrained by various factors, and it has been difficult for them to play the role that an electoral system should have. In all aspects, the central government's power is not based in a direct connection with the people. Level after level of government has indirect elections, but while these may feature a certain amount of popularity at the lower levels, at higher levels, there does not seem to be sufficient popularity. Fundamentally speaking, China's is still a top-down system that lacks a direct base among the masses. This means that, during the exercise of power, centrality gradually disappears while localism gradually increases. Since there is no direct connection between central power and the people, the central government experiences difficulty in ensuring that its power reaches the most basic levels of society directly. These circumstances, coupled with the lack of oversight on local power that comes with a lack of democracy, are extremely conducive for enabling local government officials to act arbitrarily and violate national laws and the will of the people.

When state power lacks centrality and popularity, there are many serious consequences. The recent anti-corruption campaigns are an example. Since the 1990s, more and more cases have been uncovered of irregular channels of one kind or another. From the earlier Tai'an Incident and Ningbo Incident to the later Zhanjiang Incident and the Yuanhua Smuggling Case, corruption cases have implicated, at the very least, dozens of Party and government officials, while some have implicated hundreds. These cases have featured very real organizational and institutional corruption. If a local government as a unit becomes corrupt, the central government will never learn what is going on. As a community of common interest, local officials will almost certainly conceal information from the central government. When the central government does not have its own channels for collecting information from local governments, and there are no other mechanisms available such as a relatively free media or democratic mechanisms, the central government may become deaf or blind to local affairs.

This is particularly evident in the Yuanhua Smuggling Case. The handling of this case shows that it's simply not true that the central government has no power. Despite a wide variety of obstacles, the government managed to deal with a large number of officials. But this case also illustrates just how weak the centrality of state power actually is. According to the ringleader, Lai Changxing, the case was only uncovered because the child of a high-ranking cadre was not blackmailed, and submitted an accusation to the central authorities. In other words, it wasn't that the central government itself uncovered the corruption ring, but that it was accidentally discovered through extremely irregular channels. It could be said that the central government cannot uncover such cases on its own strength alone. Lai Changxing had such a wide network at all levels of government that, unless internal conflict within the ring hadn't led to the ring's exposure, the central government would never have been able to learn of its existence.

So what exactly is the relationship like between the central government and local governments? The relationship is multi-faceted, and it includes political, administrative, economic, and legal aspects. But the most important aspect is the system by which the central government appoints local officials—that is, the CCP's cadre management system. If we examine the various relationships between the central government and local governments, we can observe that, except for the power of the cadre appointment system, which is still in the hands of the central government, there is severe localism in every other aspect of the relationship. Administrative localism, judicial localism, and the "duchy economy" (*zhuhou jingji*) are nothing new.

But even the effectiveness of the cadre appointment system in controlling local governments is not beyond reexamination. For starters, we need to make clear that this approach is not a completely modern one. For thousands of years in China, the central government has used primarily this approach to control locales. Today, however, is it still an effective approach that conforms to the political framework of a modern state? In pre-modern societies, the central government's power could not reach locales directly, and central power was extremely weak. In fact, the country was ruled by various scattered local political bodies. And one of the major characteristics of modern society is that central power penetrates deeply into local areas. Since the collapse of the Qing dynasty, Chinese political elites have sought to solve the problem of how a central government's power can penetrate locales, but no effective method has been found that can overcome localism. In addition to the planned economy, the methods used by Mao Zedong included highly stressing principle in organizational appointments, emphasizing ideology, sending central leaders to locales, keeping local leaders out of institutions, and even launching periodic political campaigns to combat localism.

After Deng Xiaoping launched economic reforms, great changes took place in the way the central government controls local politics. In order to maintain political stability, political movements are no longer used as a means of controlling locales. At the same time, Deng Xiaoping's pragmatic principles kept ideology from remaining an important method of control. In terms of organizational appointments, China's cadre system has also undergone considerable changes. When the central government's control over lower administrative levels shrank from two levels below to one level below, the central government's power shrank as well.

These measures obviously helped strengthen local power. At the same time, all of these changes were also conducive to the development of local economies, because these measures increased the flexibility and, to a certain extent, the autonomy of local governments. The rapid development of local economies has further expanded local economic power. Thus Deng Xiaoping's reforms actually increased the political and economic power of local officials.

We should also look at the "rotation" (*jiaoliu*) system of central and local officials. The advantages of sending central officials to local posts are obvious. First of all, doing so can strengthen the central government's direct control over locales and curb the proliferation of localism. Central officials are directly appointed by the central government: Their power comes from the central government, and thus they must obey the central government. Second, sending central government officials to locales is also an important means of promoting reform. Since the interests of the central government are often at odds with those of local governments, local officials will sometimes try to block the central government's reform line and keep central government policy from getting off the ground. Sending central officials to locales has greatly contributed to promoting reforms there.

But the limitations of this approach are also obvious. The purpose of a personnel appointment system is the implementation of central government policy in locales; however, due to the objective nature of local interests, the central government's choices for appointing cadres are limited. There are two primary reasons for this: If candidates are too subservient to the central government, then local interests will be suppressed; and if candidates adhere too closely to local interests, then there will be deviations from central policy. In the former scenario, central cadres have difficulty in winning the cooperation of local cadres in the institutional implementation of central policy; as a result, there is superficial agreement but non-execution of policies. The central officials in some locales view their appointments as only a bridge to higher power and status; thus, they do not work hard to develop localities and only seek stability during their tenure. In the latter scenario, an identification with local interests means that central officials necessarily deviate from central interests. As most officials do not readily find opportunities for career advancement, an inevitable result is that they tend to identify more with local rather than central interests.

There is another aspect of the cadre management system that has implications for central-local relations: the selection of local officials to serve in central leadership.

This approach is profoundly affecting the ways that Chinese politics operates. While China has not experienced any major political reforms, its political system has maintained a relative degree of stability, and this cannot be separated from the cadre rotation system. The entry of local officials into the central government's decision-making processes has improved the exchange of information between central and local governments. If the central government is to effectively lead local governments, then it needs sufficient and accurate information about locales. This has been particularly difficult to achieve in China. China does not have institutions for collecting information that are typical of a modern society—institutions like a free media and periodic elections. Thus, the central government has to rely on the so-called "mass line," require central officials to conduct investigations and research, and rely on local officials to collect information. However, local officials frequently modify or even fabricate information in order to protect local interests. Bringing local officials to Beijing helps to make up for this informational shortfall. Moreover, bringing local officials into central leadership has increased stability in policy. Local officials come from on-the-ground local departments. Thus, they tend to be weak in ideology, and their decisions tend to focus on practical issues rather than ideological factors. This is conducive to problem-solving. Again, since reforms, more and more local officials have come from economically developed regions and have rich experience in reform, thus providing a certain impetus for further reform.

The central government does control locales through personnel appointments, but this does not mean that the central government can effectively lead the locales. An over-reliance on the personnel appointment system reflects a serious misunderstanding of the current relations between the central government and local governments, and this over-reliance is also an important source of conflict between the two. Using personnel systems to control local governments has a very limited effectiveness. In the past thirty-plus years, with the institutional retreat of central power, local governments have developed a set of institutional systems that are in line with local conditions and are intended to enhance local interests. While these have effectively promoted local economic development, they have also strengthened local interests. We need to have an objective understanding of local institutional systems. Local systems are naturally in conformity with local interests, and they may conflict with central interests. But without such local systems, effective national is almost impossible. Factors such as the country's size and regional differences require local governments to establish effective local systems that can locally implement governance.

The central appointment can appoint such officials, but local interests still have an objective existence. Central officials come and go, but local interests remain the same. This means that the central government needs a new way of thinking about its relations with local governments. The question is not whether localism needs to be eliminated, but how central and local interests can be coordinated. When the interests of local and central authorities experience serious conflict, we should not consider employing the central government's superior power to launch movements that restrain local interests. Such movements may work for short periods of time, but once they end, localism will rear its head again. A better approach is to establish a central institutional system independent of local governments that can acknowledge local governments certain autonomous powers while strengthening mechanisms of accountability to the local people. This will transcend all local power and interests and establish a direct link between state power and the people.

The Popularity and Centrality of Selective Centralization and State Power

The most important reason for the lack of centrality in state power is that the central government does not have its own "legs" (institutions) at the local level. When the "legs" are local governments, it is difficult for the central government to achieve centrality and for it to lead effectively. "Legs" for central power are essential for any state power that is to be truly modern. How then can state power reach locales through such "legs"? To put it briefly, the central government must strengthen its building of its own institutions and establish various institutions of its own in locales—that exist outside of local government. On the other hand, however, without democratic politics, it will be extremely difficult for such "legs" to become effective.

How can we go about creating central "legs"? The process of establishing state power in Western societies was a violent one, and at times it was achieved by resorting to war. This history cannot repeat itself in China, nor can we conduct a large-scale centralization movement. What China needs is gradual and stable reforms. The most important thing is to re-examine the various systems involved in central-local relations. Fundamentally speaking, a comprehensive centralization movement is undesirable, while the necessity of a selective centralization movement has become apparent. The creation of some "legs" is entirely the responsibility of the central government. An example here is the unification of the armed forces, national defense, and international affairs and diplomacy, since all of these are among the most important political powers of modern states, and few states allow local governments to share in these responsibilities. At the same time, building these systems does not require much, democratically. This is true, first of all, because these institutions cannot be established through democratic methods, and secondly, because managing these institutions does not require much in the way of democratic methodology. Other institutions, however, such as the administrative system, the taxation system, the financial system, and the judiciary, do require detailed consideration and analysis. Some of these need to be centralized; others need to be decentralized. Furthermore, of these systems, some need the introduction of democratic management methods after they have been established—otherwise they will not be highly effective. Others will need to be both established and managed through democratic methodologies.

We can briefly examine what's in order. Let's first look at the administrative system. Since the mid-1980s, many have placed the blame for various problems in central-local relations at the door of the decentralization of administrative power. They therefore advocate the centralization of administrative power, but this demands careful consideration. A unified administration means that local governments are only the emissaries of the central government, and that local governments must implement central policy without hesitation. But as been previously discussed, this proves extremely difficult in practice. There are vast regional differences in China, and the central government cannot easily apply a unified administrative approach to lead the country. It has to rely on local governments to provide leadership that is in tune with local conditions. Administration must be decentralized so that local leadership can be effective. In other words, local governments cannot be regarded as a "leg" of the central government itself, but as a first-level government, one that can govern in accordance with local circumstances.

What then should the central government do? This is what selective centralization means. The central government must establish a system of its own outside of local governments. Central institutions should establish their own leadership systems independent of and outside of local governments. These institutions will not subject local governments to comprehensive oversight but will centralize those powers that concern the interests of the state, while delegating other powers to local governments completely. The central government will only exercise a legal oversight that reviews the actions taken under these powers. Part of selective decentralization is clearly true decentralization.

One area that needs the central government to have its own "legs" is judicial power. The establishment of a country ruled by law is an important objective for China's political development, but at present localism poses a serious problem for judicial power. Various laws formulated by the central government are not easily implemented at the local level, and local governments always hinder the implementation of laws for one reason or another. One major reason is that the central government itself has not established its own "legs." The court presidents, judges, and even chief prosecutors and prosecutors of local courts at all levels are all appointed and controlled by local party committees and people's congresses. Funds for local courts at every level are essentially paid by the corresponding level of local government, and local government also determines their appropriations. This personal and financial dependence of the judiciary on the local Party and government agencies has turned local courts established by the state into purely local courts. Since central laws need to be implemented by local judiciaries, local protectionism is inevitable. Thus, an effective response will mean strengthening judicial independence and the central government's vertical management of the judiciary, and eliminating the dependence of local courts on local Party and government agencies. For instance, the central government could take on the funding of the judiciary and could appoint its own judges to handle legal affairs across the country.

Heretofore, the central government has seen the most success in extending its "legs" in economic aspects. Economic reforms are ahead of other kinds of reform, and they have also made more rapid progress. One example is the central government's economic reform movement that began in 1993–94. The central government's economic power has been centralizing since the mid-1990s, with the aim of reversing the negative consequences of decentralization. But the comprehensive centralization of the planned economy era is no longer feasible, and the central government has turned to selective centralization, which means strengthening central authority and building and consolidating central power in certain key ways. The year 1994 saw the comprehensive implementation of a tax-sharing system that strengthened the central government's taxation capacity, and the creation of the State Taxation Administration gave the central government its own institution for entering local government. Similarly, a centralized vertical management system for the central bank, a system which began to be implemented after a long period of consideration, is intended to eliminate the intervention of local governments in financial affairs, thereby strengthening the central government's capacity for macro-regulation. In every aspect, the central government's measures that were focused on institution building should, after a period of hard work, be able to effectively strengthen the central government's ability to control the economy.

To speak more generally, to establish effective central-local relations, we have to start with politics. Many of the conflicts between the two are caused by a lack of coordination between economic reforms and political reforms. After decades of economic reform, the economic relationship between the central government and local governments has undergone tremendous upheaval, but, politically speaking, central-local relations have not changed much in theory or in practice. It stands to reason that, with the tremendous changes in the economic relations between the central government and local governments, the political relationship between the two should also be adjusted to adapt to and accommodate the economic changes. But the necessary adjustments have not occurred.

If we want to use institutional means to resolve problems in central-local relations, the central government must make this a political top priority; there should be a comprehensive political transformation of central-local relations. Now that the central government has begun to make institutional adjustments to the economic aspects of central-local relations, why shouldn't it do the same at the political level? If the political relations between the central government and local governments are not reformed, over the long run, these relations will only deteriorate, and the governing capacity of the central government will be further weakened. An increase in central power is not seen in its ability to check local interests but in its ability to effectively accommodate local interests. If we want to incorporate local interests into central institutions, there needs to be a fundamental adjustment in central power itself. For example, some scholars have observed that the tax-sharing system implemented after the mid-1990s has not been as effective as anticipated, mainly because there has not been adjustment in the political power relations between the central government and local governments. Thus, these scholars have called for the introduction of democratic elements to increase the effectiveness of this new system.

As has been previous discussed, if the central government's power is to effectively penetrate locales, there must be an increase in the popularity of central power. And popularity must be achieved through the development of democratic systems. The ultimate ideal is the reduction of indirect elections and the increase of direct elections; this will prevent the loss of power while strengthening a direct connection between the state and the people. However, the necessary conditions for direct democracy in China are not yet mature. At present, the central government is only allowing and encouraging the implementation of various forms of democratic elections at the local level. As Deng Xiaoping once stated, China will not be able to achieve direct elections until the mid-twenty-first century. For many, it seems that democratization in China is moving in a bottom-up direction.

Democratization that moves from the local to the central has its advantages, but it also has its disadvantages. The advantages are gradualism and stability; problems that emerge can be corrected in a timely manner. At the same time, building democracy at the local level can also strengthen accountability mechanisms by which local governments can be held accountable by the people, thereby reducing or even eliminating situations in which "there is decentralization but no democracy." But the disadvantages are also obvious. First, the regime's legitimacy is rapidly shifting downward. When the political legitimacy of local governments outstrips that of the central government, the central government may not be able to control local governments. Second, local experience strengthens the individual characteristics of locales and greatly increases decentralization; that is, the integration of the state may come into question. Third, at a certain level, political resistance will greatly increase. This is due, on the one hand, to local democracy's relationship to local interests, and on the other hand, to local democracy's relationship to central interests. It's hard to imagine how China could develop the village-level election system into a nationwide election system without top-down political reforms.

Thus, the bottom-up development of democratic elections must be accompanied by top-down political reforms. In particular, political reform that aims at democratization needs the unified consideration of the central government. As far as the people are concerned, the only thing they can feel in everyday life is local power and the absence of state power. Since the beginning of the Reform and Opening Up, large-scale decentralization movements have greatly increased this dynamic. I believe that, with the popularization of bottom-up democracy, this trend will become increasingly serious. Bottom-up democracy means that the power of local government is increasingly dependent on the people; it is thus more based on the people and more politically legitimate. If central power cannot base itself in a direct connection to the people, then bottom-up democracy will eventually render central power ineffective.

CHAPTER SEVEN

Decentralization Reform: China's Central Government, Local Governments, and Civil Society

> If it is true that intragovernmental decentralization has shifted from decentralization to "re-centralization," then state-to-society decentralization was from the outset selective, and predicated on firm governmental control. Because of this, the growth of the private economy, the maturation of a civil society, and the expansion of civil participation are facing numerous difficulties.

Many observers have noted that the thirty years passed since China's Reform and Opening Up can be described as a process of continuous decentralization.[1] There are two main forms of decentralization: decentralization of power away from the central government to local governments (that is, intragovernmental decentralization), and decentralization of power away from the government to civil society—what academics call state-to-society decentralization. Intragovernmental decentralization has granted considerable autonomy to China's local governments and become an important institutional reason for the rapid development of the economy. However, intragovernmental decentralization has weakened the central government's macro-regulatory capacity. As a result, beginning in the mid-1990s, the central government re-tightened its power and strengthened its control over locales through the centralization of taxation, finance, and political personnel. On

1 In this text, the terms *fenquan* and *fangquan* are used interchangeably as a translation for the word "decentralization."

the other hand, the central government has also begun to decentralize power to society in the hope that, by strengthening civil society, it can improve its own legitimacy and check the power of local governments. This chapter argues that, owing to an insufficient decentralization of power to society, the implementation of reform policies has not gone smoothly. For China to make headway in reform and development, there must be more decentralization from the state to society.

The Two Kinds of Decentralization

At the close of the Cultural Revolution, China's political system was a classic example of what the academic community calls "totalitarianism." This system is characterized, on the one hand, by a high degree of concentration of political power, in which a certain group or even individual usually controls the powers of the state and dictates to the rest of the country. Government at all levels generally adopts a unitary system instead of a federal system of organization, and each level of government serves on behalf of a higher level of government, implementing the decrees and policies of its superiors.[2] On the other hand, totalitarianism features the state's complete control over society and the economy. Outside of government, no independent social organization exists. Almost all aspects of social life are controlled by the government. The economy is a command economy, and the state controls all economic activities through administrative means. In other words, the private economy, the market, and a civil society essentially do not exist.[3]

In the thirty years following Reform and Opening Up, China essentially promoted reform in two aspects, and the government gradually decentralized its power in these two directions. In the political dimension, the central government delegated a considerable amount of decision-making power to local government at all levels, enabling local governments to enjoy a certain degree of autonomy. This created a framework similar to a federal system, and it has made huge contributions to the rapid growth of the economy. In the economic and social dimensions, a large number of SOEs have been privatized, and the market economy has become the primary driver of economic activity. The government began to tolerate and even encourage the development of some social organizations and a civil society, leading to the rapid growth of a civil society. Table 7.1 summarizes decentralization under these two dimensions.

2 The Soviet Union was a federal republic in form, but in practice the various republics had very little autonomy, and system was highly unitary.

3 Carl J. Friedrich, *Totalitarianism* (Cambridge: Harvard University Press, 1954).

Theoretically speaking, what then are the different results of these two different kinds of decentralization? To put it simply, decentralization from the central government to local governments results in a structure that can be called "*de facto* federalism": Local governments enjoy a certain degree of autonomy and can, to some extent, promote democratic elections at a basic level; NGOs can also achieve a certain degree of development while remaining under the close control of the government; and individual rights also receive some guarantees. Economically, with the decentralization of the central government's SOEs, local governments control the property rights for SOEs, and competition among local officials for economic growth has, to some extent, promoted marketization. At the same time, however, this competition has also led to local-government intervention in the market and local protectionism.

Decentralization from the state to society presents a different picture, as the government's ceding of power to civil society will enhance the protection of individual rights and promote mass participation in the political process. NGOs will grow and mature, and ultimately society will move toward democratization. Economically, the state's concession of power to society means privatizing government-controlled enterprises, protecting private property rights, regulating the economy through market mechanisms, and minimizing government intervention.

In the early stages of reform, the focus was on intragovernmental decentralization and promoting economic development by making adjustments to central-local relations. During this stage, there was practically no substantial decentralization of power from the government to civil society. After the mid-1990s, the government continued to make adjustments to central-local relations on the one hand, while on the other hand, it began to open up to social management, and a civil society began to grow.

Grounded in a high degree of centralization, China's intragovernmental decentralization has produced a unique kind of central-local relationship, one that possesses the characteristics of a federal system. Of course, the constitution states that China is not a federal state, and there is neither decentralization among government at all levels nor power-sharing among different government departments that can be called a separation of powers. After Reform and Opening Up, however, the central government delegated some power to locales in order to promote economic growth; this has made central-local relations more and more federal, leading to a situation that can be described as "*de facto* federalism."[4] This system

4 For additional research into this concept, see Zheng Yongnian, *De Facto Federalism in China: Reforms and Dynamics of Central Local Relations* (London and Singapore: World Scientific Publishing, 2007); "China's De Facto Federalism," in *Federalism in Asia*, eds. Baogang He, Brian

Table 7.1: Two Kinds of Decentralization

	Intragovernmental Decentralization	Decentralization from the State to Society
Political	From the central government to local governments	From the state to society
Results	Local or basic-level democracy	Democratization
	"*De facto* federalism"	Popular sovereignty and individual rights
	Limited individual rights	Political participation
	Government-controlled NGOs	NGOs, civil society, etc.
Economic	From the central government to local governments	From the state to enterprises
Results	Property rights for local governments	Private property rights
	Interregional competition	Privatization
	Limited marketization	Marketization
	Local government intervention	Free competition among enterprises, less government intervention
	Local protectionism	

can be defined as a model of relatively institutionalized decentralization (one that is formed within a unitary state). In this model, the central government stands above the provinces, but provinces have a certain autonomy. Between the central government and provincial governments, there is both open and behind-the-scenes negotiating, and the central government gives provinces either standing or one-time benefits in exchange for the province's compliance with the central government. Of course, this also applies to relations between provincial governments and county and city governments. To be more specific, for a country to feature "*de facto* federalism," it needs to meet the following criteria:

Galligan, and Takashi Inoguchi (Cheltenham: Edward Elgar, 2007), 213–41; "Explaining the Sources of *de facto* Federalism in Reform China: Intergovernmental Decentralization, Globalization, and Central-Local Relations," *Japanese Journal of Political Science* 7, no. 2 (2006): 101–26; "Institutionalizing *de facto* Federalism in Post Deng China," in *China Under Jiang Zemin*, eds. Hung-mao Tien and Yun han Chu (Boulder: Lynne Rienner Publishers, 2000), 215–32.

First, the government system needs to be hierarchical, with levels such as a central government, provincial governments, county governments, and township governments. Within a specific scope, each level of government exercises the power of final decision-making.

Second, intragovernmental decentralization needs to be institutionalized at all levels, making it difficult for the central government to unilaterally impose its will on provinces and change the distribution of power among government at all levels.

Third, provincial governments need to be the party primarily responsible for economic and social affairs within their jurisdictions; to some extent, they are also the party primarily responsible for political affairs, and they exercise considerable autonomy.

There is a generally clear division of power between China's central government and provincial governments. The central government controls areas like foreign affairs, national defense, and population control, and provincial governments have basically no say in these areas. Local governments are responsible for public security, road building, and school building at the local level, and local governments also exercise oversight over the vast majority of economic affairs. Many policies are formulated by the central government but implemented locally. When the central government formulates policy, it often consults local governments.

"*De facto* federalism" is a product of intergovernmental decentralization. This system has made outstanding contributions to the rapid development of China's economy, but it has also brought with it many problems. Owing to their economic strength, wealthy provinces can often resist the central government's policy initiatives, while, owing to insufficient financial resources, poorer provinces often struggle to effectively implement central policy or implement meaningful reforms. As a result, since the mid-1990s, the central government has begun to re-centralize in many ways and strengthen its control over provincial and local governments.

How Intragovernmental Decentralization Sparked Rapid Economic Growth

Among former members of the socialist camp, decentralization has been widely implemented to promote reform and solve a variety of problems generated by the over-centralization of economic planning. Different forms of decentralization have led to different outcomes. In the first stage of Reform and Opening Up, China's government adopted intragovernmental decentralization, which included the decentralization of economic power and the distribution of political power.

Intragovernmental Decentralization of Economic Power

Although China's reforms have been market-oriented, China has not yet completely developed private property rights, commercial law, or the independent judiciaries that are found in developed countries. This prompts a question: Where did China's rapid economic growth come from? An important factor behind this growth can be found in *de facto* federalism (or "market-preserving federalism").[5] The central feature of this form of federalism is the intragovernmental decentralization of power.

From 1979 to the mid-1990s, under the leadership of Deng Xiaoping, the Reform and Opening Up continued to promote decentralization of power to local governments. Many economic decision-making powers were delegated to local governments, and major economic ministries, such as the Planning Commission, the State Administration for Industry and Commerce, the State Administration of Taxation, and the Banking Regulatory Commission, were placed under the control of the pertinent local governments—not under the control of higher-level ministries. Tax policies proved beneficial for local governments, providing local governments with sufficient financial resources to develop local economies.

As some commentators have observed, decentralization directly limits the central government's control over the economy. It also induces competition among local governments, serving both to constrain their behavior and to provide them with a range of positive incentives to foster local economic prosperity. In other words, decentralization eliminates the potential of a single government to monopolize the economy. The authors go on: "If many regions can choose policies for themselves, all can compare the results, including those which do not wish to initiate reform policies."[6] The main players in the Chinese market are not so much individual enterprises but individual local governments. China's market economy is primarily driven by competition among its various regions.

5 Gabriella Montinola, Yingyi Qian, and Barry R. Weingast, "Federalism, Chinese Style: The Political Basis for Economic Success in China," *World Politics* 48 (Oct. 1995): 50–81; Hehui Jin, Yingyi Qian, and Barry R. Weingast, "Regional Decentralisation and Fiscal Incentives: Federalism, Chinese Style" (manuscript, 1999); Yuanzheng Cao, Yingyi Qian, and Barry Weingast, "From Federalism, Chinese Style, to Privatization, Chinese Style" (manuscript, 1997); Yingyi Qian, "The Institutional Foundations of China's Market Transition," paper for the World Bank's Annual Bank Conference on Development Economics (Washington: Apr. 1999).

6 Montinola, G., Yingyi Qian, and Barry R. Weingast, "Federalism, Chinese Style: The Political Basis for Economic Success in China," *World Politics*, 48:1 (October 1995), 79–80.

According to Qian Yingyi, a professor at Tsinghua University, the market economy places a twofold demand on the government. First, the government must be strong enough to protect the economic order through enforcing laws and regulations in the market. Second, the government cannot be so strong that it can arbitrarily plunder the market. To a certain extent, the Chinese government has met these two demands. On the one hand, the central and local governments have sufficient strength to implement laws, regulations, and policies.[7] On the other hand, *de facto* federalism imposes necessary restrictions on central authorities, ensuring that the central government cannot arbitrarily seize wealth. In fact, during the process of economic reform, the central government has consciously refused to obtain access to certain information. This helps keep it from excessively interfering in the economy. For example, the central government permits local governments to retain extrabudgetary or non-budgetary funds that are non-taxable and are not subject to central supervision. This encourages local governments to develop local economies and thereby increase their own revenues.

In fact, many local government-owned enterprises (such as Township and Village Enterprises, TVEs) have outperformed SOEs. What distinguishes these local government-owned enterprises from SOEs is that the income generated by the former returns primarily to the coffers of local governments. Local governments have, in turn, utilized these local enterprises as a check on the power of the central government. Under such conditions, local governments even work to encourage the competitiveness of the market, for capital and resources will quickly flow toward locales that are more conducive to market growth. Therefore, local officials have incentives to increase efficiency, restrict improper intervention in the market, limit asset seizures, and reduce both taxes and government oversight.

Intragovernmental Decentralization of Political Power

In comparison with the socialist systems of the former Soviet Bloc, China's system is more flexible, leaving space for policy innovation. After the commencement of Reform and Opening Up, the central government adjusted the cadres' jurisdiction, from two levels below each cadre to only one level below each cadre. For example, before reform, the central government directly appointed officials at both the provincial and prefectural levels. After reform, the central government was only

7 Douglass C. North, *Structure and Change in Economic History* (New York: Cambridge University Press, 1981).

responsible for appointing provincial-level officials, while provincial governments were given the right to appoint and remove personnel from prefecture-level positions within their jurisdictions. This created conditions in which the provinces could independently formulate and implement strategies for economic reform.

Moreover, senior leaders do not determine policy unilaterally; on the contrary, lower-level departments and regions often have a great deal of say in the decision-making process of their superiors. Every department and region can discuss, negotiate, and bargain with higher-level and other departments with a view toward influencing policies in favor of a department's own interest. The ultimate finalization and promulgation of policy is the result of achieved consensus and compromise among political leadership and its subordinates.[8]

Susan Shirk has pointed out that in post-Mao China, central and provincial officials have formed a system of what she calls "reciprocal accountability." As Shirk observes,

> Yet this relationship between party leaders and subordinate officials is not a pure hierarchy. According to the party rules, the Central Committee has the authority to choose the party leaders, and the Central Committee consists of party, government, and military officials appointed by party leaders. The leaders appoint the officials and the officials in the Central Committee choose (or at least ratify the choice of) the leaders. Government officials are both the agents and the constituents of party leaders; local officials are both the agents and the constituents of central leaders. Officials hold their positions at the pleasure of the party leadership, but party leaders hold their positions at the pleasure of the officials in the selectorate. The lines of accountability run in both directions, turning a hierarchical relationship into one of "reciprocal accountability."[9]

Central and provincial officials have significant levels of reciprocal accountability, for provincial officials form the largest contingent of the Central Committee. This system of reciprocal accountability has been critical in China's economic growth, for it enables central leaders and local officials to work together to establish reforms and promote economic development. On the one hand, as provincial officials look for promotion, the leaders of the central government can use their power of appointment or dismissal as an incentive for mobilizing local officials to support reform. On the other hand, as provincial officials constitute a plurality of the Central

8 Kenneth Lieberthal, "Introduction: The 'Fragmented Authoritarianism' Model and Its Limitations," in *Bureaucracy, Politics, And Decision Making in Post-Mao China*, eds. K. Lieberthal and D. Lampton (Berkeley: University of California Press, 1992).

9 Susan Shirk, *The Political Logic of Economic Reform in China* (Berkeley: University of California Press, 1993), 83.

Committee, their support is indispensable for any central leader. That is to say, provincial officials have the strength to urge the central leadership to promote policies that are conducive to local economic development.

A Centralized Political Structure

Despite the fact that there has been decentralization in economic and political power, and despite the existence of "*de facto* centralism," China remains a unitary state, and it still maintains a centralized political structure. This structure has had positive effects on economic development.

Since reform, local officials have had great autonomy, but they still serve as the behest of the central government. The central government has considerable control over them, especially in its selection and appointment of personnel—the central government has consistently maintained the principle that "the Party manages the cadres," a principle that emphasizes the Party's absolute control over the appointment of cadres. The Party's day-to-day management is rather centralized, and the evaluation, appointment, dismissal, and transfer of cadres at each level must be determined and executed by the Party committee and organization department at the next higher level. Power over personnel appointments is the last trump card that the central government holds over locales, and it is the most fundamental check on local officials.[10]

According to research by American scholars Olivier Blanchard and Andrei Shleifer,[11] the Chinese model of centralization is beneficial for successful economic transition. Although neo-classical politico-economic literature argues that market competition can reward "good" behavior and punish "bad" behavior, market mechanisms alone cannot explain China's transition from a planned economy to a market economy. Political factors have been crucial. Central leadership has been in control of the entire transition process, rewarding and punishing local officials for their actions. The central government has enough authority to implement its own policies and determine the rules of the game. Without this strong central control, localist tendencies will proliferate, and economic and fiscal policy alone cannot prevent this from happening.[12]

10 Yasheng Huang, *Inflation and Investment Controls in China: The Political Economy of Central Local Relations During the Reform Era* (New York: Cambridge University Press, 1996).

11 Olivier Blanchard and Andrei Shleifer, "Federalism with and without Political Centralization: China versus Russia," IMF staff paper, no. 48 (2001).

12 In contrast, Russia's economic transition was accompanied by a collapse in political authority. Because the governors of the provinces and the leaders of the soviet republics were not appointed

The Negative Consequences of Intragovernmental Decentralization and the Re-centralization of Power

Intragovernmental decentralization promotes rapid economic growth, but it also brings with it many problems. The cost of maintaining central authority has grown increasingly high. Although China never collapsed like the Soviet Union did, the forces of localism and local protectionism have often challenged central authority.

The Weakening of Central Authority

Owing to the decentralization of economic power, centrally controlled economic resources have shrunken dramatically. In 1984, the central government's fiscal revenues accounted for 40.5% of the country's total fiscal revenues. By 1994, this figure had fallen to 22%. At the same time, the central government's fiscal expenditure as a percentage of total expenditures fell from 52.5% to 28.3%. Following their growth in economic strength, the provinces began to occasionally issue challenges to central fiscal policy. Efforts by the central government to raise taxes are now often resisted—particularly by the wealthier provinces.

The weakening of central authority has weakened the ability of the central government to coordinate the development of various regions, and so rapid economic growth has increased income inequality between differing provinces and regions. In eastern coastal provinces, such as Guangdong, Zhejiang, Jiangsu, and Shandong, the non-state economy is relatively well developed and brings in large revenues for local governments; it is difficult for the central government to get its hands on these revenues. In contrast, central and western provinces lack both capital and talent, and local governments there do not have many resources available to promote economic growth. Wealthy provinces are reluctant to contribute resources to help poorer provinces develop, while underdeveloped provinces are reluctant to bear the costs of industrialization for the richer provinces—and even think of themselves as being exploited by richer provinces. Under these circumstances, the central government does not have sufficient financial means to coordinate the provinces. As a result, the gap in development continues to widen.

by the central government, it was difficult for the central government to implement its own economic policies through rewarding or punishing these officials.

Furthermore, we must also note that economic decentralization has from the beginning been accompanied by sweeping globalization. Coastal provinces have developed an export-oriented economy, participated in the international division of labor, and neglected economic ties with the provinces of the central and western regions. This has contributed to the interdependence of the provinces and the international community while reducing interdependence among the provinces.

According to a World Bank study, trade between Chinese provinces accounted for only 22% of GDP in the early 1990s. This figure compares to intra-EU trade accounting for 28% of the EU's GDP and internal trade among Soviet republics accounting for 27% of the USSR's GDP. The World Bank has therefore warned that increased foreign trade and declining domestic trade may cause certain provinces in China to behave as if they were independent countries.

The aforementioned problems have attracted the attention of Chinese political and academic circles, with various parties beginning to debate whether it is necessary to re-strengthen central authority, and grant the state the power to regulate the national economy. In the early 1990s, scholars like Wang Shaoguang and Hu Angang advocated re-centralization, arguing that economic decentralization had weakened the power of the central government and might lead to the disintegration of China, as it had in the former Yugoslavia. They held that excessive decentralization was the main obstacle preventing the creation of a unified national market. For Wang and Hu, a highly centralized state is not necessarily a totalitarian or authoritarian regime. On the contrary, a strong democracy must be grounded in a centralized state. Wang Shaoguang and Hu Angang's book on state capacity was widely shared among government officials. In the same year when their book was published, the central government implemented a tax-sharing reform, thereby taking the first steps toward re-centralization.

Selective Re-centralization

In the mid-1990s, China began to re-strengthen central power. Re-centralization was not about returning to the pre-reform status quo but about the central government selectively reclaiming power in certain areas. At first, this re-centralization was primarily concentrated in the economy, with tax reform and reforms to the banking system. Since the beginning of the twenty-first century, as the central government has worked hard to strengthen its governmental and regulatory power, it has expanded its mandate to include more policy areas, as in the environment, product safety, labor, and land. Here we will mainly consider re-centralization in tax reform and banking reform.

Tax Reform

Before the early 1990s, the central government did not have its own tax-collection agency. The provinces assessed their own taxes and then distributed them to the central government in accordance with fixed percentages. In 1994, the "tax-sharing system" was first established. Under the new tax system, taxes were divided into three categories: central taxes (the state tax), local taxes (the local tax), and shared taxes, which were then divided by central and local governments in accordance with previously negotiated agreements. The tax collection system was divided into two parallel systems: Local governments continued to collect taxes in their own jurisdictions through local taxation administrations, while the central government was given an independent taxation agency, the State Taxation Administration, which was responsible for collecting taxes that pertain to the central government. The shared tax is levied by the State Taxation Administration and then returned in part to local governments per agreements.[13]

On the one hand, the new system of taxation recognizes the independent fiscal power of the provinces. Some taxes are completely designated for the collection of either provincial or local authorities; the central government is not permitted to intervene with these taxes. On the other hand, the new system has also greatly strengthened central authority. Under the implementation of the new system, the proportion of revenue collected by the central government vis. total government revenue collected in China jumped from less than 30% to more than 50%. When we also consider that local governments need to submit their various expenses to the central government for review, it becomes clear that the central government now actually collects and distributes most of the country's income, which greatly increases the fiscal dependence of the provinces on the central government. Before tax reform, the central government was constrained by wealthy provinces, but that has now changed.[14]

Reform in the Central Bank

In the early days of Reform and Opening Up, China's central bank was highly decentralized. The People's Bank of China (that is, the central bank) had branches

13 For details on China's tax reform, see Christine P.W. Wong and Richard M. Bird, "China's Fiscal System: A Work in Progress," in *China's Great Economic Transformation*, eds. Loren Brandt and Thomas G. Rawski (New York: Cambridge University Press, 2008), 429–66.

14 Wang Shaoguang, "China's 1994 Fiscal Reform: An Initial Assessment," *Asian Survey* 37, no. 9 (September 1997): 801–17; Hu Angang, "Taxation System: Evaluation and Recommendations," *China Soft Science* 8 (1996), 37–43.

in every province. As local governments controlled the personnel and finances of the Bank's local branches, the Bank's policy was highly influenced by local politics, and the Bank frequently failed to take seriously instructions from the higher authority. Although local branches contributed to economic growth throughout China, the situation in every region could influence the country's economic stability.

From 1992 to 1993, the financial system was destabilized as China experienced wild speculation in real estate, economic development zones, and the stock market.[15] This instability was deeply connected with the lack of central control in the banking system. After Zhu Rongji became premier in 1998, he took drastic steps to reform the financial system. Provincial branches of the central bank were eliminated, and nine trans-provincial regional branches were established. These branches are directly supervised by the central bank, and power over personnel and finances has been decoupled from local governments. This reform has dramatically weakened local governments' ability to intervene in the financial system.[16]

The Re-centralization of Political Power

In the late 1980s and the early 1990s, with the collapse of the Eastern Bloc and the impact of domestic political storms, China's central government decided to re-strengthen the cadre management system.[17] It reiterated the principle that "the Party manages the cadres," and it strengthened the systems for the promotion, appointment, dismissal, transfers, and rotation of cadres. These measures strengthened the Party's central control over local officials.

As the government of China attempts to make adjustments to its development strategy, it has made additional efforts to re-centralize. During Jiang Zemin's tenure (1989–2002), the top priority of the high-ranking leadership was economic growth. But rapid growth has brought with it a whole series of social problems including social differentiation between the rich and the poor, environmental

15 Gu Haibing 顾海兵, Zhou Zhigao 周智高, and Zhang Houming 张厚明, "1992 nian yilai Zhongguo jingji gaosu zengzhang zhong sanci hongguan tiaokong de duowei bijiao" 《1992 年以来中国经济高速增长中三次宏观调控的多维比较》 [A Multidimensional Comparison of Three-tiered Macro-prudential Regulation during China's Post-1992 Rapid Growth], *Jinyang wang*, Guangdong Yangcheng Evening News Digital Media, February 26, 2006.

16 Franklin Allen, Jun Qian, and Meijun Qian, "China's Financial System: Past, Present, and Future," in *China's Great Economic Transformation*, eds. Brandt and Rawski (New York: Cambridge University Press, 2008), 507–68.

17 John Burns, ed., *The Chinese Communist Party's Nomenklatura System* (Armonk: ME Sharpe, 1989).

pollution, and a lack of industrial innovation. These factors jeopardize China's sustainable development. With the arrival of fourth-generation leadership in figures such as Hu Jintao and Wen Jiabao, there has been an emphasis on "scientific development" (*kexue fazhan guan*) and a "harmonious society." This generation has sought to establish a new model for economic development that can cope with the aforementioned problems.

At present, however, it seems that this transition has been difficult, and it has been strongly opposed by the old model's vested interest groups. To overcome local resistance, the central government has re-centralized power in several important areas that include quality inspection, auditing, environmental protection, land management, statistics, and production safety; it has made these departments vertically managed, and it has decoupled them from local government.[18]

The Difficulties Facing State-to-Society Decentralization

Beginning around the mid-1990s, following advances in market reforms, China's government gradually relaxed its oversight over civil society, allowing the development of private enterprise and allowing NGOs to participate in non-political social development projects. Since then, China's private economy and civil society have developed rapidly, and the state's control in these areas is less present.

The space for citizens to participate in public affairs is growing. With the promotion of elections for village committees and residents' committees, more and more Chinese citizens have begun to use their votes to influence affairs in their communities. Civil society and social organizations are growing rapidly, and the government encourages the development of groups related to environmental protection, rural development, and education.[19]

During the 2008 Sichuan earthquake, various volunteer organizations played a significant role in fundraising and disaster relief. The government has also taken some steps to improve human rights—for example, by relaxing the regulation of religious activities, improving education in poorer areas, and protecting the rights of women and children through legislation. In April 2009, the State Council

18 Yongnian Zheng, *Globalization and State Transformation in China* (Cambridge: Cambridge University Press, 2004); Dali Yang, *Remaking the Chinese Leviathan: Market Transition and the Politics of Governance in China* (Stanford: Stanford University Press, 2004).

19 Gao Bingzhong 高丙中 and Yuan Ruijun 袁瑞军, eds., *Zhongguo gongmin shehui fazhan lanpishu* 《中国公民社会发展蓝皮书》 [A Blue Book for the Development of Civil Society in China] (Beijing: Peking University Press, 2009).

issued the 2009–10 National Human Rights Action Plan, which formulated the first national program centered on human rights.[20] This plan calls for measures to be taken to protect the economic, social, and cultural rights of all members of society over the following two years. It strengthens the rule of law, launches education in human rights, and improves the rights and interests of ethnic minorities, women, children, the elderly, and the disabled. Nevertheless, if it's true that intragovernmental decentralization has shifted from "decentralization" to "re-centralization," then state-to-society decentralization was from the outset selective and predicated on firm governmental control. Because of this, the growth of the private economy, the maturation of civil society, and the expansion of civil participation are facing numerous difficulties.

The following two examples illustrate how China's government has decentralized power to society, along with the results of these changes. One example is related to the economy, while the other is political in nature.

The Reform of State-Owned Enterprises

The economic example is the reform of state-owned enterprises (SOEs), a reform which has been at the heart of reforms to the economic system over the past thirty years. Early in the 1980s, reform of SOEs was put on the agenda, but it was not widely enacted until after the 14th Congress in 1992. By making "establishing a socialist market economy" an objective, the 14th Congress removed the institutional and ideological shackles preventing reform of SOEs. So far, this reform can be approximately divided into two stages: the first stage of "grasping the large and letting the small go" under Zhu Rongji, and the second stage, under Wen Jiabao, of the SASAC's oversight over SOEs.

Reform Under Zhu Rongji

In the mid-1990s, Zhu Rongji proposed reforming SOEs by "grasping the large and letting the small go," which officially became party policy at the 15th Congress in 1997. "Grasping the large" means that the government only controls a select few large-scale and vital enterprises. These enterprises are primarily concentrated in seven major industries related to the national welfare or national security—the

20 "Guo xin ban fabu 'Guojia renquan xingdong jihua' (2009–10)" 《国新办发布〈国家人权行动计划（2009—2010 年）〉》 [The State Council's National Human Rights Action Plan (2009–10)], *Xinhuanet.com*, April 13, 2009.

military industry, electricity, oil and petrochemicals, telecommunications, coal, aviation and transportation. The government strives to develop large-scale, competitive enterprises or groups into transregional, cross-industry conglomerates with multiple forms of ownership structures that could even be transnational in size. "Letting the small go" means that the government relinquishes control over small and medium-sized SOEs, allowing their fates to be determined by market forces. Small and medium-sized SOEs have been gradually privatized through joint ventures, mergers and acquisitions, leasing, contracting, proprietary holdings, and public offers.

Under Premier Zhu Rongji, the government designed this strategy along the lines of the experiences of Japan and South Korea.[21] Behind the policy of "grasping the large and letting the small go" is an ambitious strategic objective: the establishment of giant conglomerates that can become the mainstay of the national economy and compete internationally. In some important industries, the state's control over large industries can promote national economic security.

From the government's perspective, privatizing small and medium-sized SOEs was the logical choice. The vast majority of these small and medium-sized SOEs were either inefficient or loss-making. They lacked competitiveness in the market, and they were becoming a financial burden on government at all levels. Since SOEs often had an unsustainable relationship in terms of property rights, management problems were difficult to solve, and the most effective way out was privatization. In addition, privatized SMEs can create a large number of employment opportunities and make society's income distribution more balanced; thus, for the CCP, privatization makes political sense.

However, executing this strategy has proved highly problematic, and its results have not been satisfactory. In terms of "grasping the large," government at all levels has unilaterally pursued "grasping the large" by using political or administrative means to forcibly merge enterprises; governments have been creating enterprises that are large on the surface without taking into consideration their social or economic benefits. The large enterprises created in this way have not had the efficiency, innovation, or competitiveness that was desired. Recently, some SOEs have become well-known international giants, but these rely on the size of their assets rather than on their efficiency. Their vast assets are scraped together from various parts of the government, not from their own profits.

21 For a discussion of Zhu Rongji's reforms, see Zheng Yongnian 郑永年, *Zhu Rongji xinzheng: Zhongguo gaige de xin moshi* 《朱镕基新政：中国改革的新模式》 [Zhu Rongji's New Deal: A New Model for Reform in China] (Singapore: Bafang Culture Company, 1999).

In the wake of "grasping the large," the quantity of SOEs and employees at SOEs have dropped significantly. The government claims that the economic efficiency and competitiveness of SOEs have been greatly improved and that the quality of state-owned assets has also been changed for the better. However, the increase in the profitability of SOEs may partly be due to the fact that "letting the small go" has released many bad assets, and not because of any improvement in the efficiency of SOEs. It may also be partly due to the fact that these remaining SOEs usually control upstream sectors in their industries, giving them monopoly positions. This enables them to easily rake in monopolistic profits; this doesn't mean that they have made any improvements to their efficiency.

"Letting the small go" has also been problematic. The original aims of privatization were the improvement of economic efficiency, the provision of better services for the public, and an increase of benefits for consumers. In developed countries, privatization reforms, like those in the United Kingdom during the 1980s and 1990s, often improve the industrial efficiency of public institutions. But China's governments had no plan for the systematic effectiveness of privatization; they simply forced small and medium-sized SOEs into the market through administrative means. As a result, state-owned assets easily fell into the hands of a large number of entities associated with government officials, while large quantities of workers were laid off, setting off fierce opposition and social unrest. On the other hand, many small and medium-sized SOEs have struggled to survive after being privatized, for the government has not proven very supportive financially, judicially, or policy-wise, and these SMEs have been constrained in their development. After the global financial crisis in 2008, the Chinese government issued a bailout of up to 4 trillion RMB, but the vast majority of these finds went to the state-owned sector, and SMEs got little.[22]

Reform Under Wen Jiabao

After the 16th Congress in 2002, leadership began to initiate further reform for SOEs. Under the new policy, the state now only directly controls a few enterprises, and allows most other SOEs to implement multiple-ownership structures. From the central government to the provincial and city level, governments established specialized agencies for managing state-owned assets on behalf of the state.

22 Sarah Y. Tong and Zhang Yang, "China's Responses to the Economic Crisis," *EAI Background Brief* 438, East Asian Institute, National University of Singapore (March 11, 2009).

In 2003, the State Council's State-Owned Assets Supervision and Administration Commission (SASAC) was founded and given the responsibility of overseeing 196 large SOEs that were directly under the control of the central government; the assets of these enterprises totaled 6.9 trillion RMB (0.9 trillion USD). Since then, SASACs have gradually been established in locales. In accordance with regulations, in addition to serving as the representatives of the state, SASACs are also responsible for the reform and reorganization of SOEs, for organizing the supervisory boards of large SOEs, for monitoring state-owned assets through performing statistical analyses and audits, and for formulating relevant laws and regulations.

This system is designed to solve three important issues in property rights. First of all, it clearly defines the property rights obligations of governments at all levels. This is its vertical orientation. Second, managerial responsibility is concentrated in SASACs. This is the system's horizontal orientation. Previously, a variety of departments could intervene in enterprise operations under the guise of representatives of the state, which owned the enterprises. Such departments could include the Ministry of Finance, the Ministry of Human Resources and Social Security, the Central Enterprise Work Committee, the Central Financial Work Commission, the Economic and Trade Commission, and the Development and Reform Commission. But having multiple departments involved is not conducive to a unified approach to management. Third, the administrative power of the government has been separated from the management of state-owned enterprise properties so that the one doesn't interfere with the other. The founding of the SASACs demonstrates that the government is aware of inefficiencies within and losses incurred by state-owned assets and is looking for ways to remedy the situation.

One important reform measure led by the SASACs has been the reform of the personnel system of SOEs; this reform is an important component of the creation of a modern enterprise system. Managerial positions are openly recruited, and not filled through administrative appointments. From 2003 to 2006, of seventy-eight centrally owned enterprises, eighty-one executive positions were openly recruited.

As reform has progressed, the number of SOEs has been greatly reduced, but their economic strength has been enhanced. By the end of 2006, the number of enterprises under the supervision of the SASAC had been reduced from 196 in 2003 to 159 in 2003, while the assets controlled by these enterprises had grown in value from 6.9 trillion RMB to 12.27 trillion RMB, with annual growth rate of 16.2%. Their annual growth rates in sales revenue, real profits, taxes collected, and net assets were 20.1%, 18.2%, 20%, and 15.2%, respectively. The 1031 SOEs managed by local SASACs have also achieved similar results.

Monopolies and Other Problems with State-Owned Enterprises

These achievements by SOEs did not come from any improvements to their management or efficiency. They largely came from their monopoly positions. SOEs, and particularly large SOEs, are primarily in monopoly industries. At the central level, the oil, natural gas, and telecommunication industries are essentially completely monopolized by SOEs; and the power, heating, coal, and transportation industries are primarily controlled by SOEs. At the local level, SOEs owned by governments at all levels essentially monopolize most profitable industries.

A central issue that faces SOE reform is soft-budget constraints. On the one hand, managers at SOEs do not have sufficient incentive to increase profits and reduce costs because they have no investment in the enterprises they manage. On the other hand, if SOEs are poorly managed, the government cannot simply allow the enterprises to dissolve or go bankrupt. Quite the contrary, the government does everything it can to save troubled enterprises, whether through financial subsidies or the creation of monopolistic profits. For SOEs, it's much easier to ask the state for funding than to fight for profits in the market. Thus, we can hardly expect SOE management to exert itself to improve efficiency. On the contrary, SOEs rely on the assistance of the state and become a burden on public finances. At present, the Chinese government has not found an effective means of solving this problem.

One view is that the high profits of SOEs will greatly enhance the state's fiscal revenues. But this has not yet become a reality. Despite an increase in taxes paid by SOEs, there are also high costs to be paid by over-monopolization. The expansion of these monopolies has grown the inefficient sectors of the Chinese economy. Owing to inefficiency, many SOEs have not done well in competitive industries, so they have gradually moved into monopoly industries—after which they announce that they have turned business around. This has been a tack taken by many local SOEs. Central SOEs can monopolize certain industries while also claiming to serve the country's strategic needs, while local SOEs monopolize the industries they judge most profitable. Their profits increase entirely at taxpayer expense. Thus, the taxes paid for SOEs may not necessarily compensate the losses they cause to ordinary taxpayers.

Furthermore, monopolies result in unfair competition. Monopolistic enterprises operate according to their own rules, often at variance with market principles. More than a decade ago, struggling SOEs were striving to reduce costs so that they could pay employee salaries, and the Chinese government was also striving to "invigorate" and "save" them. SOEs were once synonymous with high wages, high profits, and high dividends, and the wages of employees at monopolistic SOEs are still much higher than those of average wages. This has been an important factor behind the widening wage gap in Chinese society. In large Eastern coastal cities, the average monthly salary of a university graduate is 2000 RMB, but the monthly salary of a toll collector at a highway toll station owned by a monopolistic SOE can reach 8000 RMB. A 2006 survey conducted by the provincial government of Guangdong revealed that many big businesses are increasing their wages even as they lose money.

Departments such as the SASAC and the National Audit Office have tried to take measures to curb the excessively high wages paid by SOEs. Li Rongrong, the then director of the SASAC, required SOEs to resume paying dividends to the Ministry of Finance beginning in 2007 (these had not been paid at all since 1994). But some raised concerns that this would justify the monopolies of the SOEs, since they could argue that their monopolistic profits had been dispensed to the state. What's more, if these measures were to be handled inappropriately, the dividends wouldn't necessarily find equal distribution throughout society, whereas the redistribution of wealth could be performed more efficiently through means such as subsidizing SMEs or funding education or social security.

Corruption is also a common phenomenon among SOEs. In SOEs, the lack of an effective division of powers and the absence of checks and balances have provided many opportunities for corruption. There are two main features of corruption in SOEs: First, most of the individuals involved in corruption cases come from senior management; and second, the amount of assets involved in such cases is staggering. SOE executives usually hold unregulated power, which offers them great incentives for abusing that power. In recent years, the government has focused its anti-corruption efforts on SOEs. But if corruption is going to be completely cured, there need to be major changes in the management systems of SOEs.

Another negative aspect of SOE policy is the way SOEs negatively influence SMEs—standing in the way of the development of SMEs, particularly private SMEs. Currently, SMEs contribute 60% of China's GDP, 50% of tax revenue, and 75% of urban jobs. SMEs have also contributed 65% of China's inventions and patents as well as more than 80% of the country's new product development, but the industrial and financial policies of China's government at all levels are tilted toward SOEs.

Prior to reform, state-owned banks served entirely at the discretion of government and provided loans to SOEs. After the reform of the banking system, state-owned banks were commercialized and could make decisions independently of the government. But, due to the traditional networks and the governmental guarantees standing behind SOEs, banks were still more willing to lend to SOEs than to private enterprises. In 2005, official statistics showed that, while 99% of China's enterprises were SMEs, these enterprises received only 16% of the loans issued in the country. SMEs are also discriminated against in terms of market access, property rights protection, and taxation.

If the government of China can thoroughly "let the small go," once China enters the WTO and commits to completely open its markets, the lack of funding for SMEs might prove too much to cope with in their competition with domestic and international competitors. And these SMEs are the most efficient part of the Chinese economy! If the government thoroughly "grasps the large," it will exhaust limited resources within the coffers of the large-but-inefficient SOEs at a heavy cost for taxpayers. In the long run, this will affect the sustainability of China's economic development and social stability.

The SASAC's role has also been widely criticized, as it is responsible for protecting the rights and interests of state ownership and preventing losses in state assets. On the one hand, as the government investor, it operates state-owned companies and manages state-owned assets; on the other hand, it also participates in formulating market regulations and in regulating the market. Thus, it is both an investor and a regulator. The SASAC also constantly emphasizes the importance of increasing profits at SOEs. This has caused critics to worry that the SASAC's identity as an investor will only further strengthen SOEs' monopolies, while the agency's identity as a regulator will garner profits for certain interest groups by manipulating markets.

The original purpose of SOE reform was the optimization of state-owned assets. But monopolistic positions have made little headway in making SOEs more profitable, and increased profits have not brought concrete benefits to most taxpayers. Monopolizing SOEs also threatens the survival of SMEs. If the monopolistic positions of SOEs are not broken, the country's economic resources will continue to migrate away from the more efficient, non-state-owned sector to the inefficient, state-owned sector, and this will hinder the continued growth of the Chinese economy. At present, it seems that China's leadership still has a long way to go in addressing these issues.

Civic Political Participation and Non-governmental Organizations

This chapter will now turn to the development of local elections and NGOs. With the Chinese government's delegation of power to society, and allowing citizens limited participation in public affairs, a civil society has begun to emerge, and basic-level elections and NGOs have played an increasingly important role in Chinese life. However, the government's decentralization has only been strategic in nature: It has been implemented in order to consolidate political power. Thus, various restrictions prevent a complete delegation of power to society, making it difficult for a civil society to achieve a high degree of autonomy.

Semi-Competitive Local Elections

In the late 1980s, the Chinese government began to implement elections at the village level; the aim was the reconstruction of basic-level authority after the collapse of the people's commune system. In 1987, the National People's Congress passed the Organic Law of Village Committees (Pilot Version), which called for the establishment of village committees in rural areas that would promote village self-government and guarantee the right of villagers to participate in politics. Under this law, cadres on the village committee were directly elected and held responsible by villagers.[23] Since then, village elections have developed rapidly. According to statistics provided by the Ministry of Civil Affairs, in 1997, more than 80% of China's villages held at least one round of elections. By 2001, basically all of the villages in the nation were holding elections.[24]

But this has not meant that the government has abandoned its control over villages. Quite the contrary, this move strengthens the government's administration of villages by introducing mechanisms for democratic competition.[25] With the promotion of elections by the government, the government has put more emphasis on the Party's leading role within villages. The Organic Law of Village Committees that was officially adopted in 1998 clearly stipulates that the village Party branch is the "core leadership" of a village. Studies have shown that, in most villages, the Party secretary controls the most important resources—such as managing collective enterprises, renting out contracted land, and the approval of public funds. At most, the elected village director only serves as an assistant to the village

23 Kevin J. O'Brien, "Implementing Political Reform in China's Villages," *The Australian Journal of Chinese Affairs* 32 (July 1994), 33–59.

24 "China Village Elections Project Fact Sheet," Carter Center.

25 Lianjiang Li and Kevin O'Brien, "Accommodating 'Democracy' in a One-Party State: Introducing Village Elections in China," *The China Quarterly* 162 (June 2000), 465–89; Li and O'Brien, "The Struggle for Village Elections," in *The Paradox of China's Post Mao Reforms*, eds. Merle Goldman and Roderick MacFarquhar (Cambridge: Harvard University Press, 1999), 129–44.

Party secretary.[26] The accountability of villagers to the village assembly has also been greatly reduced.

Reformers within some institutions have also tried out direct elections at the township level. Beginning in the mid-1990s, pilot elections were initiated in several townships in several provinces, and elected offices expanded from the deputy magistrate to the magistrate and sometimes even to the secretary of the township party. But township elections are the result of specific, local decisions, and they lack legal support. At present, elections for township offices are on hold.

The Growth of NGOs

A major component of state-to-society decentralization has been the development of NGOs.[27] In recent years, China's leadership has begun to emphasize social reform, relaxing the state's control over society, and in order to transfer some of the state's functions to NGOs. The number of Chinese NGOs has steadily increased. According to statistics provided by the Ministry of Civil Affairs, in 1978, there were only about 100 nationwide social organizations in the entire country. By the end of 2003, this number was 1736. During the same period, the number of social organizations at the local level increased from 6000 to 142,121. Before the Reform and Opening Up, private non-profits simply did not exist—but by the end of 2003, there were more than 124,491 of them. By the end of 2006, across the country there were 16,800 social organizations, 14,600 private non-profits, and 999 foundations.

Many scholars observe that, in reality, there are far more NGOs than these numbers indicate. For example, Wang Shaoguang holds that, in 2003, the number of social organizations had already reached 8.8 million. Despite rapid growth, the academic community believes that Chinese NGOs have great potential that is yet to be realized. For example, for every 10,000 people in China, there are only 1.45 NGOs, while in France there are 110.45 NGOs per 10,000 people, 51.79 per 10,000 in the United States, 12.66 per 10,000 in Brazil, 10.21 per 10,000 in India, and 2.44 per 10,000 in Egypt.[28]

26 Jean Oi and Scott Rozelle, "Elections and Power: The Locus of Decision Making in Chinese Villages," *China Quarterly* 162 (2000): 513–39.

27 Qiusha Ma, *Non Governmental Organizations in Contemporary China: Paving the Way to Civil Society?* (London and New York: Routledge, 2006).

28 Zengke He, "Institutional Barriers to the Development of Civil Society in China," in *China's Opening Society: The Non-State Sector and Governance*, eds. Zheng Yongnian and Joseph Fewsmith (London and New York: Routledge, 2008), 162–63.

In the West, NGOs operate independently and are not controlled by the government. In China, however, the autonomy of these organizations depends on their relationship with the government, and how distant their fields are from politics. The government stipulates that all social groups must be registered with and be approved by the Ministry of Civil Affairs at levels above the county level while foundations (such as charitable organizations) at levels above the provincial level. All unregistered organizations are illegal.

In addition, all social groups must submit themselves to the oversight of a professional supervisory unit. The supervisory unit must be either a state agency above the county level or a unit authorized by such an authority, and it must be related to the professional field of the social group. Another restriction is that multiple groups with the same expertise are not allowed to operate within the same locality.[29]

Owing to these restrictions, many NGOs cannot register with the government. For the sake of existing legally, other social groups simply register as business organizations with the State Administration for Industry and Commerce, even though they are actually non-profits. There are also a large number of organizations that do not register at all and yet conduct their activities publicly. In such cases, the government generally offers its tacit approval.

NGOs have also not experienced a balanced development across differing professional fields. In the economic domain, since the government is striving to withdraw from direct management of the economy, it is encouraging the development of some intermediate organizations. This provides somewhat greater room for development for social groups, and a large number of trade associations and chambers of commerce have been established. In the fields of social welfare and social development, the government hopes to mobilize society's resources to help it solve some social problems and reduce the burden placed on the government; thus, related social groups have also seen great development. Areas related to politics are essentially under the tight control of the government. NGOs operating in this field are generally not approved—or, if they are approved, their operations are greatly restricted.

The political impact of these NGOs varies with the organization and field of the organization's involvement. In areas such as poverty relief, environmental

29 There are eight large "people's organizations" (*renmin tuanti*) and "mass organizations" (*qunzhong tuanti*) that do not come under the aforementioned regulations. These include the All-China Federation of Trade Unions, the All-China Women's Federation, and the Communist Youth League of China. These organizations are not under the supervision of the Ministry of Civil Affairs, and they do not need to be registered. Their leaders are directly nominated by the Communist Party's Central Committee.

protection, and charity, the government encourages the contributions of social groups, so they often can help promote some public policies. But in fields such as religion, ethnic culture, and human rights, the influence of civil society is much smaller. Commercial organizations usually exert a greater influence, and personnel from these organizations can readily be found in people's congresses and CPPCCs at all levels. However, the industrial working class and farmers have been strictly forbidden from forming their own organizations, and they have no political influence.

Thus we can see, that with the Chinese government's decentralization, both the private economy and civil society have developed considerably. But these various forms of decentralization are as yet incomplete. The government still manipulates the economy through state-owned monopolies while restricting the involvement of its citizenry through various regulatory measures. This has led to a whole series of problems in economic and social development.

A Way Forward for State-to-Society Decentralization

Intragovernmental decentralization has promoted China's rapid economic growth, as both the central government and local governments have incentives for developing their economies. For the central government, rapid economic growth brings more material prosperity for the people, thereby enhancing the legitimacy of its regime. For local leadership, economic growth not only increases the resources they can control but also increases their chances of being promoted. As a result, intragovernmental decentralization is a win-win situation for both the central government and local government.

With intragovernmental decentralization, decision-making power has been delegated to lower-level governments. The SOEs of local governments that haven't been privatized have local governments as their *de facto* property owners. While the central government is gradually withdrawing from the direct management of individual enterprises, local governments are increasing their intervention into SOEs. This intervention does not seriously impede marketization; instead, marketization continues Due to competition among multiple regions and multiple ownership groups, the market economy is given additional stimulus. However, in a classical market, various enterprises compete with each other; in Chinese markets, various regions compete with each other.

Intergovernmental decentralization has strengthened local governments and given them greater power to meet local socioeconomic needs. Decentralization has also changed how the central government and local government interact with each other, making the two parties interdependent. In principle, the central government still wields significant power, but it is often forced to consult and cooperate with various local governments. Local governments not only formulate and implement policies within their own jurisdictions but can also influence central policymaking. Through a series of measures aimed at regaining power, the central government has maintained a dominant position over the provinces, but local governments, and especially provincial governments, still exercise the *de facto* ability to reject the central government's policy initiatives. From time to time, haggling between both parties results in policy deadlock. Also re-centralization has not ensured the smooth implementation of the central government's reform directives.

As local governments enjoy a certain degree of autonomy, they gradually develop interest structures inconsistent with the central government's interests, and local interests may conflict with the central government's interests.[30] While China's local governments clearly possess the characteristics of a "developmental state"—one which is solely dedicated to economic development, they also have the characteristics of a "predatory state"—one that competes for profit with the people.[31] This is particularly evident in the township governments of central and western China, whose behavior in recent years is directly linked to the problems facing farmers and the expropriation of farmland.[32] Such seizures have resulted in general indignation, with mass protests and incidents following one after the other. In order to restrain the illegal behavior of local government, the central government has tried everything in the book, including the re-centralization discussed above—but with little success.

Owing to insufficient state-to-society decentralization, the people lack a channel for participating in public affairs, and they lack a means of holding government accountable. When local governments abuse power and compete for profits, the people have only two choices: They can shut their mouths or protest in the streets. Some studies have shown that when citizens are forced to express their demands through forms such as collective petitions and demonstrations, their support for the government is greatly reduced, which erodes the government's legitimacy.[33]

30 Shaum Breslin, *China in the 1980s: Centre Province Relations in a Reforming Socialist State* (New York: St. Martin's Press, 1996).

31 Peter Evans, "Predatory, Development, and Other Apparatuses: A Comparative Political Economy Perspective on the Third World State," *Sociology Forum* 4, no. 4 (1989): 561–87.

32 Lu Xiaobo, "The Politics of Peasant Burden in Reform China," *Journal of Peasant Studies* 25, no. 1 (Oct. 1997): 113–38.

33 Shan Wei, "How Much Did the Chinese People Trust Their Government," *EAI Background Brief*, East Asian Institute, National University of Singapore (unpublished, 2009).

To change this situation, China needs to promote state-to-society decentralization—that is, to strengthen the power of society and expand citizen participation. On the one hand, the central government's oversight over local governments is far less effective than that which could be exercised by locals.[34] By holding local governments accountable to local voters, voters have the power to stop illegal seizures. This essentially means forming an alliance—between the central government and society to jointly curb the behavior of local governments. On the other hand, expanding citizen participation can give the people greater confidence in the government, increase the legitimacy of government at all levels, and give the central government greater support in implementing its reform policies.

In order to strengthen society's power, the most important thing is increasing society's material strength. In other words, more economic resources should be allowed to flow to the people, thereby promoting the development of private enterprise. The monopolistic positions of large SOEs needs to be brought to an end, and they need to be made to participate fairly, competing in the market; they must be made to improve their efficiency, which will also increase the efficiency of society.

The central government is also aware of the importance of strengthening society. The reform to SOEs under Zhu Rongji was largely aimed at strengthening private SMEs. Under Wen Jiabao, other reforms were also implemented to promote the development of NGOs and local elections. But these steps have been far from adequate. The next step in China's reform requires the CCP's regime to be open to social forces, just as it previously opened itself up to the market economy.

34 Regarding the central government's inability to exercise oversight over local governments, see Kevin J. O'Brien and Lianjiang Li, "Selective Policy Implementation in Rural China," *Comparative Politics* 31, no. 2 (Jan. 1999): 167–86.

CHAPTER EIGHT

Between the State and the Market: The Political Logic of China's Social Policy Reforms

> To a large extent, the scope of reforms remains limited and has failed to meet the public's expectations. At a deeper level, progress in social policy reform will require a broader agenda that includes making adjustments to state-society relations. These necessary adjustments will constitute the political dimension of social reform.

China's post-Mao economic reforms have often been regarded as a textbook case of neoliberal economics.[1] Post-Deng Xiaoping Chinese leadership has given absolute priority to economic growth, and neoliberal economic policies have promoted rapid economic growth. In almost thirty years, the country transformed itself from a planned economy dominated by the agricultural sector to a market economy dominated by vibrant modern manufacturing and service industries.

Over the past thirty years, China's average rate of annual economic growth has been astonishing. Known abroad as the China Miracle, China's growth has demonstrated the powerful vitality that the economic reforms unleashed. However, this growth has also generated massive social problems including a widening income gap, increasing social injustice, and incessant social protests. All of these problems beg for additional progress in social reform and social policy.

1 David Harvey, *A Brief History of Neoliberalism* (Oxford: Oxford University Press, 2005); Manfred B. Steger and Ravi K. Roy, *Neoliberalism: A Very Short Introduction* (Oxford: Oxford University Press, 2010).

During the early stages of reform, "social policy" did not become an independent concept in policy; it was only a term used to describe the welfare-related problems brought about by economic reform. The original aim behind the founding of the vast majority of social security organizations was the management of welfare problems arising from the reform of state-owned enterprises (SOEs) and Township and Village Enterprises (TVEs). It was only when the economic growth guided by neoliberal economics incurred increasingly heavy social costs, and exacerbated social unrest, that the importance of social policy in maintaining social stability and long-term sustainable growth became clear.

In China, the process of formulating social policy is carried out independently by party leadership and political elites. Whenever proposals for social reform have the political priority of economic growth, they are immediately implemented, as with the marketization (or, to adopt Marx's terminology, "commodification") of higher education, healthcare, and housing. Whenever proposals for social reform do not align with economic priorities, such social policies are postponed, and social policy only gets introduced in response to strong social discontent and potential social instability. Although the public's participation in the policymaking process is still quite low, and hasn't been institutionalized, major changes in society, particularly the rise of a middle class, have gradually opened the field of social policy to different voices and social forces.

This chapter attempts to explain the birth and evolution of social policy in China. To begin with, this chapter will look back on the social policy literature of the West. Since social policy was developed in the West and later spread to other parts of the world, including China, this retrospective will provide a comparative perspective on China's social policy issues. Following that, this chapter will outline China's social policy reforms. Lastly, this chapter will provide a political interpretation of the impetus—and also the lack of impetus—behind social policy reform.

A Comparative Perspective on Social Policy

For T. H. Marshall, social policy is the use of political power to replace, supplement, or modify the operation of an economic system to achieve results that the economic system itself is unable to achieve.[2] The "economic system" Marshall is referring to here is the capitalist market economy. In the West, social policy usually means the programs and measures by which the government "corrects" the results

2 T. H. Marshall, *Social Policy* (London: Hutchinson, 1975).

produced by the "invisible hand" of the market. Since World War II, social policy has been at the center of public policy in every Western country.

In the literature, the term "social policy" is often interchangeable with another concept, the "welfare state." In reality, the existence of a welfare state in a country depends on the existence of social policy. Without social policy, there can be no welfare state. A textbook definition of the welfare state includes the state's responsibility to guarantee the basic welfare of its citizens.[3] But the next question is: Why should the state bear this responsibility? Or, is a welfare state reasonable?

In answering this question, another concept, social citizenship, comes into play. Marshall holds that the concept of social citizenship is at the heart of the welfare state, for the conferring of social rights is the only criterion by which a welfare state can be judged.

In Gøsta Esping-Andersen's analysis, for Marx, the birth of social rights is connected with capitalism—for capitalism tends to commodify everything within society. Esping-Andersen holds that conferring social rights is grounded in citizenship rather than in market performance. When the social services of a state are based on rights rather than achieved through performance, individuals no longer depend on money and are no longer "commodified." This decommodification is important for understanding the welfare state. If decommodification is high, the individual is no longer completely dependent on the market and money. In places where social rights are granted by the state, the individual's status as a commodity is reduced, while benefits are available in times of need. In practice, the level of decommodification in a welfare state varies. In some countries (such as Sweden), services are more readily viewed as a matter of rights, while in other countries (such as the United States), welfare is more dependent on individual market performance.

The aims of social policy are also different. Europeans often prefer to use the term "social policy" rather than welfare policy, as the former more appropriately reflects the breadth of policy, categories, and goals connected with the welfare state. Americans in particular tend to think of "welfare" as being to some extent connected with "poverty" and "poverty relief." So different perceptions of social policy may be reflected on a philosophical level. Generally speaking, social policy is a historical product. Europeans now regard it as a component of human social rights, while Americans define social policy more pragmatically, from the perspective of the operations of the capitalist system.

In general, the aims of social policy include:

3 Gøsta Esping-Andersen, *The Three Worlds of Welfare Capitalism* (Princeton: Princeton University Press, 1990), 18–19.

1. The redistribution of wealth: Through various taxes and the subsequent redistribution of public finances, resources are transferred to the poorer classes of society, thereby achieving a more balanced and stable society. Progressive taxation is a major feature of modern welfare states.
2. Subsistence-level income standards: In circumstances such as aging, illness, or a temporary inability to provide for necessary living expenses, social policy allows affected individuals to partially maintain the lifestyle they are accustomed to. This not only makes economic sense, as it allows individuals to continue to participate in the market, but it also strengthens political stability and social cells.
3. Assistance for particularly vulnerable social groups or regions: Certain occupational groups, ethnic minorities, or entire regions may face structural issues that put them at a disadvantage in comparison with other members of society. Many countries have formulated targeted programs that address these disadvantages.
4. A social safety net: In the absence of other resources, social policy can serve as a last resort for maintaining the basics of a decent existence. In every society, some lose their income and eventually exhaust all of their resources, making it impossible for them to support themselves and their families.
5. Poverty relief: Social policies often revolve around poverty relief. In most cases, this includes clearly demonstrating the applicant's needs before benefits are paid. Poverty relief programs rarely receive wide support from the general public, and they tend to provide relief for marginalized and politically powerless groups.
6. Economic governance: Social policy can also play a part in economic governance. Continental European economies are characterized by a more visible role of government in the economy and the collaboration, rather than competition, among economic agents. Powerful (centralized) interest groups such as trade unions and employer organizations fix wage levels or determine work-related issues such as sick leave, overtime pay, weekly working hours, and retirement regulations through large-scale collective bargaining. Under normal circumstances, social policy is expected to complement and facilitate these negotiations, thereby benefiting overall economic organization and stability.

From a historical perspective, social policy is a modern phenomenon. In the early stages of the modern state, the state's main concerns were public order, the military, and the protection of rank and privilege. Today, however, the main concern of modern states is the distribution of welfare. Here arise two key questions about the welfare state: First, where did the modern welfare state come from? And second, how has it evolved to its current level of complexity?

Social policy can be regarded as a logical function of the modern industrial system. With the modernization of society after the Industrial Revolution, traditional models of providing welfare (such as extended families, charitable organizations, church and local community campaigns, and paternalist organizations run by local nobles) proved no longer effective. To this end, modern societies created a modern welfare system that could replace the traditional forms of assistance. In many circumstances, welfare states had to be created in order to save modern capitalism from the primary victims of early industrialization, the restless masses.

Also, democracy is not a necessary condition for the modern welfare state. In Europe, the first welfare systems were created by authoritarian, conservative, and paternalistic governments for a variety of reasons. Under Bismarck, Germany established a blueprint for a modern welfare state that was based on social insurance—but in reality the government was more concerned with fighting the spread of socialism than with redistributing wealth. In the same way, the United Kingdom's Lord Beveridge focused on establishing health programs for military men along with social programs that aimed at providing a basic system of universal welfare. In addition, the French government sought to create welfare policy out of concerns about a declining population. In most continental European countries, the development of early welfare states was deeply influenced by the Catholic Church and its views on the natural order of the family and society.

While there is no causal relationship between democracy and social policy, in many cases democracy does help develop and improve social policy. By expanding democratic mechanisms like extending enfranchisement to the poor, the pressure created by votes forces politicians to develop mechanisms for improving the lives of ordinary citizens.

According to Esping-Andersen's classic research, a welfare state can be classified and analyzed in accordance with the type of regime. Here Esping-Andersen identified three types of welfare states. The first model is a social welfare system or social insurance. In those regions in Continental Europe where the Catholic Church was most influential and autocracy was the strongest, the so-called community welfare state developed. Of these, the most famous was the German welfare model established by Bismarck, a conservative welfare state concerned with maintaining order and the status quo. To achieve these aims, social insurance funds (pensions as well as health, unemployment, and accident insurance) were set up to reward performance and employment. Traditionally, wives could only obtain financial resources from men; this helped ensure the stability of traditional families. These public insurance funds were established and operated by the government or, as in Germany and Austria, by labor associations (for example, miners' insurance funds)—this was a model that originated with medieval guild systems and the nineteenth century's mutual aid societies.

Although such associations were formally independent of the government, they enjoyed social status, meaning that fund contributions were mandatory and usually deducted from wages. Workers' contributions were usually matched by employers, and insurance funds were often grown through transfer payments in government budgets. Social insurance funds often provided different levels of benefits that depended on the status of the labor association (for example, whether it was for blue-collar workers, white-collar workers, or civil servants). Measured in terms of benefits received, the state traditionally ensured that civil servants were the most privileged group, and this led to lasting social differentiation and differing status levels of professional groups.

After World War II, many of these social insurance models were expanded, and left-center governments tried to adjust the level of benefits provided through different funds. The community welfare state remains a system with considerable social stratification. In addition, in a constantly changing economic environment, traditional economic sectors can no longer guarantee lifelong employment, which has torn the social safety net for an increasing number of workers. Those who are particularly affected are women and immigrant workers, who often fail to meet the stipulations for payment periods, as well as workers who take part-time or new jobs.

The second model is the liberal welfare system. This system is characterized by a verification process (tests used to authentic need) and modest universal welfare; this model is based on public services or insurance plans. It usually caters to groups from the low-income to the working class. In this model, the state usually encourages the market to act as a supplier of benefits. Private insurance and savings plans are often supported with national policies such as tax credits and tax avoidance.

The liberal welfare system has two chief characteristics. First of all, most voters fall outside the scope of the benefits it provides, making benefit plans politically unpopular. In other words, benefit plans are usually designed only for those who are poor and politically marginalized. Second, this system tends to create a polarized society in which some rely on poor public services, while the richer middle class can enjoy better services from the market. In liberal welfare states like those found in the United States, Canada, Australia, and Switzerland, the middle class is not compromised by either the state or the market. With its historically dominant position, liberal thought remains skeptical of a powerful state and believes that the middle class is strong enough to find market mechanisms for meeting its needs. Despite its liberal roots, the United Kingdom has developed a model in which universal welfare and services have been greatly expanded through a paternalistic state. This model grew out of its original, basic-level concerns with the health of soldiers and workers. Named after Lord Beveridge, the model lays out a general living standard for every member of society.

The third model is the social democratic or Scandinavian welfare system. Social democracy has long occupied a leading role among the political forces that developed universal welfare systems that could cover all aspects of life. In this system, social rights have been fully achieved, and the enjoyment of benefits and services essentially does not depend on one's market performance but is commensurate with one's own needs. Another characteristic of Nordic welfare states is their extensive range of services (for example, daycare, elderly care, and home help), which caters to the needs of even the most discriminating members of the middle class. Entitlements remain roughly the same across the country, but the system can meet differentiated expectations (for example, by matching welfare with income). Because the level of public services provided is so developed, the state has crowded out all private competition. In addition, Scandinavian welfare tends to reduce class and income disparities while ensuring the highest levels of service possible.

The emergence of the social-democratic welfare state was the result of an alliance between the industrial working class and the smallholder class. Under the control of social democratic parties (leftist parties), it was developed to meet the growing expectations of an increasingly wealthy population. The Protestant tradition of individualism laid the foundation for the universalistic and individualistic welfare system, one which is available to all regardless of individual contribution and is tailored to individual needs.

In East Asia, social policy has traveled a different road than that taken by Western states. Here, countries and regions have played a more important role in the birth and development of social policies. East Asian economies (Japan and the Four Little Dragons of Asia) are typically regarded as economic "miracles," as those societies evolved over several decades from poor "third world" economies into First World economies.[4] However, East Asian countries have also performed

4 The World Bank, *The East Asian Miracle: Economic Growth and Public Policy*, A World Bank Policy Research Report (Oxford: Oxford University Press, 1993); Robert Wade, *Governing the Market: Economic Theory and the Role of Government in East Asian Industrialization* (Princeton: Princeton University Press, 1990).

a social miracle, one which is often overlooked in the literature on East Asian development. The social policies that were born in the West—particularly in Western Europe—involved high costs. And they were the product of violent movements among the working class during the nineteenth and twentieth centuries.

Unlike Western Europe, East Asia's period of rapid economic growth did not experience violent working-class movements. This dissimilarity can be explained by the different roles played by Western European and East Asian states and regions. As described above, in Western Europe, states had to deal with the negative social consequences of capitalism if they wanted to maintain law and order. In contrast, in East Asia, states and regions often took a proactive approach to prevent the rise of a working-class movement. In this approach, one of the most important responses was social policy. In just a few decades, the amount of social policy in East Asian economies was practically that achieved by Western European countries over the course of a century.

China has not followed in the developmental footsteps of other East Asian economies. In terms of economic development, China is often seen as part of the East Asian Miracle. Indeed, as in other East Asian economies, the state has played an important role in promoting China's economic growth. However, China has not yet produced a social miracle. After more than thirty years of rapid economic growth, China still lacks effective and appropriate social policy, and this separates it from other East Asian economies. This lack of social policy will have corresponding social consequences. In today's China, the state is facing fierce social protests that are quite similar to those that occurred in Western Europe in the nineteenth and early twentieth centuries.

To explain the differences between China and other East Asian economies, I need to focus on the role of national policy. I divide China's reform into two periods. During the first stage, the state implemented neoliberal economic policies to achieve rapid economic growth. While these policies have brought strong economic performance, they have also disrupted traditional social policy. What's worse, neoliberal economics has invaded the social sphere and given rise to the commodification of social policy, thereby weakening the social base. Thus, in the second period of reform, the state tried to introduce social policies to address the social consequences of neoliberal economic policy. As of this date, the government has made some gains. However, social policy is still only a response to the consequences of neoliberal economic policy. The government has also had difficulty striking a balance between holding to a neoliberal economic structure while producing appropriate responses in social policy. This demonstrates that contemporary Chinese society has largely been destabilized.

The Social Policy of Mao Zedong

It wasn't until modern times that China produced social policy. Traditionally, the imperial governments' role in this regard had been very limited. This is largely reflected in the Chinese proverb: "Heaven is high, and the emperor is far away." The Communist regime established in 1949 was the first regime to influence every corner of Chinese society. And in accordance with the standard socialist ideology imported into China from the Soviet Union, the regime led by Mao Zedong established a national social policy, but this policy was neither extensive nor particularly effective.

During the Mao era, the Chinese people lived in a highly centralized and isolated social system in which economic, social, and political functions were all bound by the administrative structure of a socialist state. The state implemented a system of low wages. As compensation, the state used rural communes and urban working units to provide social goods such as housing, healthcare, children's healthcare, and education, within prescribed limits. In particular, the employees of all urban work units, along with their families, also enjoyed a certain extent of public healthcare, public education, and public housing through price subsidies.[5] In rural areas, basic communal welfare—particularly basic education and healthcare—were provided through the commune system. However, the low levels of social welfare in the Mao era proved to be unsustainable. At the time, there was an unspoken contract between the state and society—the former provided basic social protections for the latter, and the latter accepted the former's leadership. Under such conditions, there was no dynamic change and development. China under Mao Zedong was a classic example of impoverished socialism.

Neoliberal Economics and Post-Mao Social Policy

The system created in the Mao era experienced a series of crises throughout the 1980s, first in rural areas and then in cities. In rural areas, the decline and collapse of the people's communes caused the rural welfare system to lose its institutional basis, and the rise of the household responsibility system marked the end of supplying basic welfare. Initially, some welfare functions were transferred to TVEs and local governments. But with the decline of TVEs and financial shortfalls

5 Andrew G. Walder, *Communist Neo-Traditionalism, Work and Authority in Chinese Industry* (Berkeley: University of California Press, 1986), 59–67.

in local and basic-level institutions, the rural welfare system became even more irreparable.

In the cities, social reform had an even more complex institutional and historical background. Initial reforms attempted to liberalize SOEs and bring new life to urban markets, but they actually served to strengthen, rather than dispel, employment-based urban welfare.[6]

However, with the introduction of deeper reforms to SOEs and the financial sector under the reformist Premier Zhu Rongji in the mid-1990s, economic reform had to be followed by social reform, for the old system lost even more of the specific institutional support it had had in the traditional SOEs.

During the initial stages of economic reform, China was influenced by the dominant economic thought of the West—particularly Thatcherism and Reaganomics. During the 1980s, China gradually came to adopt neoliberal economics as a guiding principle for economic reform. However, due to the serious ideological constraints that the reformers faced, large-scale privatization did not occur in the 1980s. The reforms of the 1980s were characterized by intragovernmental, economic decentralization and economic decentralization of the SOEs. A fundamental change occurred after the collapse of the Soviet Union and the Eastern Bloc. As the late Deng Xiaoping believed that the collapse of socialism stemmed from the poor performance of communist regimes in providing economic benefits for their peoples, during his famous Southern Tour of 1992, Deng called for radical economic reforms in China. Answering Deng's call, in that same year the 14th Congress ultimately reaffirmed Deng's agenda for reform. For the first time in the history of the Chinese Communist Party, the market was given legal recognition. Congress outlined the reform for SOEs and introduced a new foreign-exchange system along with a modern financial and fiscal system as the keys to shifting toward a market economy. All of these reform agenda items were carried out by the then Deputy Premier Zhu Rongji.

The reform of the SOEs had the largest impact on the social policies that had been established during the Mao era. The reform of SOEs was implemented in two parts. A plan for the radical reform of SOEs allowed the introduction of SMEs under the slogan of "grasping the large and letting the small go." In the 1980s, the principle for enterprise reform was strengthening the entirety of the state sector. Many SOEs—particularly small and medium-sized SOEs—were highly economically inefficient, and these imposed a long-standing and heavy burden on financial and fiscal systems. By the early 1990s reforms to the internal governance and

6 Barry Naughton, *Growing Out of the Plan: Chinese Economic Reform, 1978–1993* (New York: Cambridge University Press, 1995), 101–3.

management of SOEs, reforms that were meant to ensure their sustainability had also stalled.

Zhu Rongji's response was not just a continuation of the reforms of the 1980s, nor was it a sweeping and indiscriminate shift from central planning to the market. Quite the contrary, Zhu adopted selective reforms and restructurings for SOEs. The reform plan was carried out mainly on the basis of the size of the enterprise and the nature of its industry. Ownership reform was applied to SMEs in highly competitive industries, while state ownership restructuring was applied to large enterprises in strategic sectors. In both cases, the goal was to increase the competitiveness of SOEs.

The New Company Law of 1993 provided, for the first time, a legal framework for China's modernized private enterprises. The transformation can be divided into two stages. Beginning in 1994, most small and medium-sized SOEs were corporatized in various ways. Overall, there was a shift from employee stock ownership (ESO) to management buyout (MBO).[7] By 2002, most small and medium-sized SOEs had become either joint ventures or joint-stock companies. The total number of SOEs had fallen from 120,000 in 1995 to only 31,750 in 2004.[8]

As the state withdrew from competitive industries, China witnessed the rise of a non-state sector and, throughout the 1990s, saw its continued economic vitality. The private sector has made tremendous strides in both volume and size. By 1998, the GDP created by the private sector was already on par with that created by the state sector. Since then, the private sector has consistently surpassed the state-owned and collective sectors in terms of job creation and total value added. During the final stages of Zhu Rongji's reforms, the non-public (non-state-owned and non-collective) economy became the primary employer of two-thirds of China's urban labor force.[9]

Under the slogan of "grasping the large and letting the small go," large SOEs were reformed by being developed into powerful conglomerates that operated in sectors with strategic economic and political importance. These enterprises have become dominant monopolies at the national and local level, and some of them, including some ministry-level industrial groups, have become conglomerates. Since 1994, reorganizing and restructuring large SOEs, most of which are in strategic and monopoly sectors, has produced more than 100 central SOEs and 2500 local

7 Ross Garnet, Ligang Song, and Yang Yao, "Impact and Significance of State-owned Enterprise Reform," in *China, Policy Reform and Chinese Markets: Progress and Challenges*, eds. Belton M. Fleischer, et al. (Cheltenham: Edward Elgar, 2006), 40–42.

8 Naughton, *The Chinese Economy*, 313.

9 Jinglian Wu, *Understanding and Interpreting China's Economic Reform* (Mason: Thomson, 2005), 198–99.

SOEs.[10] Considering the political significance of large SOEs, the reform of core SOEs has proceeded very cautiously and incrementally for more than a decade.

The key measure has been the selective refinancing of old debt-ridden SOEs. Zhu Rongji's basic methodology was restructuring and marketization. By retaining only the most productive enterprises and factors of production, most large SOEs have become stronger through restructuring. In fact, most of the surviving SOEs have been allowed to retain some monopoly rights without having to bear responsibility for basic social welfare—with the exception of paying taxes for value-added, resources, and corporate income. The resources for the much-needed refinancing were mainly obtained through the sale of shares in stock markets dominated by state-owned institutions.

The reform of SOEs has successfully strengthened a state-owned sector dominated by central and provincial industrial giants. From 1998 to 2008, the balance sheet of SOEs improved significantly, going from losses of $100 million RMB to after-tax profits of nearly $1.3 trillion RMB in 2009.[11] The seeming success of this policy led to an unintended consequence: the rise of powerful interest groups—in particular, the rise of central SOEs. Large state-owned banks and financial institutions have, without exception, become monopolistic or oligopolistic forces within the domestic market. In product markets, raw material markets, and factor markets, such institutions have significant power.

Another important factor that has exerted a negative impact on social policy has been the decline of TVEs and the surge in migrant workers. At the outset of the 1990s, many TVEs suffered from poor governance and insufficiency, but it wasn't until 1996 that the total value-added and employment share of the TVE sector experienced a decline. The main reasons behind this were ambiguity regarding property rights and the poor financial status of basic-level governments, which were the *de facto* owners of TVEs.[12] Since 1996, in coordination with the reform of small and medium-sized SOEs, the central government has launched a series of reforms in TVEs and collective economic ownership. Most of the inefficient and poorly managed TVEs were converted into joint-stock companies or even private enterprises.

The decline and restructuring of TVEs, along with more rapid rates of urban economic growth, have reshaped the rural economy. At the most basic level, the rural economy, in both its agricultural and modern sectors, has shrunk in GDP and employment share. As far as the agricultural sector goes, total food production and

10 Naughton, *The Chinese Economy*, 313.

11 Ministry of Finance Circular, Xinhua News Agency, January 20, 2010.

12 Linda Yueh, *Economy of China* (Cheltenham: Edwards Edgar, 2010), 51–53.

average yield per *mu* (Chinese acre) stagnated during the first half of the 1990s. Fear of food shortages has even prompted the government to repeatedly increase purchase prices over the past few years and to abolish agricultural taxes in 2005. Although a comprehensive transition to agricultural subsidies will not be enough to improve the competitiveness of the agricultural sector in the labor market, it has so far succeeded in maintaining food protection at adequate levels.

In the 1990s, the decline of the rural economy and the rise of the non-state sector in cities brought tidal waves of labor redistribution from rural to urban areas. Over the course of twenty years, the total number of migrant workers increased from 30 million in 1989 to about 230 million in 2010.[13] More than half of migrant workers have crossed provincial lines to work in coastal industrial centers. These workers, who constitute part of the urban migrant population, have become the mainstay of China's industrial labor force.[14]

The influx of millions of migrant workers into major coastal industrial cities has dramatically realigned China's industrial structure away from a state-owned enterprise system dominated by imports into export-oriented, labor-intensive industries. As a result, behind the rise of China's economically competitive products is the reality of migrant workers. At the same time, migrant workers are increasingly shaping the socioeconomic changes taking place in China's rural hinterlands. From a purely economic perspective, income from wage labor started out by supplementing the income of the farming industry and then gradually evolved into the main source of income for rural residents. The return of successful migrant workers to their rural hometowns has also contributed to regional development. These returning migrant workers bring the skills, know-how, and vision necessary for making a local economy take off. Most rural entrepreneurs in China today have previously made their mark in the developed economic centers of China's coastal cities.

Thus, the first social policy mechanism to be proposed immediately after the reform of SOEs in the early 1990s should come as no surprise. In order to respond to the mass layoffs caused by the contraction or bankruptcy of SOEs, the central government implemented the first round of social reforms in the fields of pensions and unemployment benefits. Thus, the social policy sector mainly concentrated on the problems faced by laid-off workers, and it served as an institutionalized means

13 China National Bureau of Statistics Circular, *Xinhua News Agency*, March 24, 2010.

14 On China's migrant workers, see Rachel Murphy, *How Migrant Labor Is Changing Rural China* (Cambridge: Cambridge University Press, 2002); D. J. Solinger, *Contesting Citizenship in Urban China: Peasant Migrants, the State, and the Logic of the Market* (Berkeley: University of California Press, 1999).

of supporting economic reform and social stability. In 1993, a basic living allowance (known popularly as the *dibao*) was introduced. At first, it targeted elderly workers who had been laid off after the reform of Shanghai's SOEs. At the time, Shanghai was an important industrial center dominated by SOEs.[15]

During his tenure, Zhu Rongji focused on establishing social insurance as an important means of renovating the original socialist welfare system. The main point of the reform was the establishment of social insurance as the cornerstone of a society-based welfare system, one that could replace the old enterprise-based welfare system. Various kinds of employment-related insurance were established: This was first seen in aspects such as employment, healthcare, pension plans, work-related injuries, and maternity leave. Originally a programmatic response to SOE reform, pension insurance (an important program for social insurance), was first established in 1991, and in 2005 it was applied to all urban enterprises as a standardized approach.[16] As more and more financial reforms were rolled out, this part of social policy reform was gradually being placed under the oversight of new state institutions—specifically, the Ministry of Labor and Social Security (later renamed the Ministry of Human Resources and Social Security) and the National Social Security Fund.

As socialist principles gradually gave way to supplementary approaches to social instability, basic policy considerations like welfare provisions and social security also worked alongside market-oriented social reforms in the mid-1990s with specific programs. In policy design, the marketization of the field of social welfare did not exclude the important policy objective of a social safety net. For example, in housing, the central government has designed systems like low-rent housing (LRH) and economical housing (EH) for low- and middle-income families.[17]

At the same time, as with Zhu Rongji's other economic reforms, market-oriented approaches to social reform also have their limitations. Institutions with political strength protect their members from potentially damaging policies while fully accepting the policies of social security and social insurance. Most notably, the politically strong state sector resisted the marketization of the housing sector. With their growing financial resources, streamlined state-owned institutions and

15 "Cong Shibatiao Biaozhun Dao Yitiaoxian: Shanghai Dibao Ruhe Chutai?" [How Did the Minimum Life Guarantee in Shanghai Come About?], *Liberation Daily*, December 4, 2008; Tang Jun, "Chengxiang Dibao Zhidu: Lishi, Xianzhuangyu Qianzhan" ("Urban and Rural MSLS: History, Present Status and Future Prospects") (Beijing: The Institute of Sociology, Chinese Academy of Social Sciences, 2010).

16 Chan Kwan Chan, King Lun Ngok, and David Phillips, *Social Policy in China: Development and Well-being* (Bristol: The Policy Press, 2008), 62–64.

17 Ibid., 173–75.

large monopolies can still provide the most generous subsidies and develop the most comprehensive insurance programs.

Social Policy Reform Under Hu Jintao

When Hu Jintao succeeded Jiang Zemin as the general secretary of the CPC Central Committee in 2002, and Wen Jiabao succeeded Zhu Rongji as the premier of the State Council in 2003, China entered the "Hu-Wen Era." In the field of social policy, the Hu-Wen government inherited three distinct institutional legacies from the previous government. First and foremost was economic reform. At the outset of the Hu-Wen era, China's welfare and social provision systems were very similar to the liberal model—that is, there was a limited scope of state participation, market-based welfare provisions, and high levels of social self-reliance. According to the classic classification of welfare systems by Gøsta Esping-Andersen, China's social policy reforms were in a systematic transition from a static model based on minimal coverage to a liberal model. This model implied assessment-based benefit plans, and most social security was undertaken by social insurance.[18] Under the Zhu Rongji government, neoliberal economics not only dominated the economic sphere (for example, in the reform of the SOEs) but also "invaded" some important social areas. By the late 1990s, two important social fields, healthcare and education, had also been largely commercialized.

The second and perhaps most obvious institutional legacy was the unfair distribution of state-subsidized benefits among different social groups, one that was based mainly on sectoral or regional differences rather than on individual needs or just rewards. After the comprehensive reform of the state-owned sector in the mid- to late 1990s, the central government, the central government's monopolistic SOEs, and various government organizations became powerful business entities that retained the main characteristics of a welfare provision system with their large subsidies.[19] In comparison with other sectors and state employees, after its streamlining, the state-owned sector has become a bastion for corporate welfare programs. Thus, its members have become the social group that enjoys the best protections. At the regional level, the *hukou* system and policies that discriminate against migrant workers constitute another major institutional barrier, one which

18 Gøsta Esping-Andersen, *The Three Worlds of Welfare Capitalism* (Princeton: Princeton University Press, 1990), 24–27.

19 Chak Kwan Chan, Kinglun Ngok and David Phillips, *Social Policy in China*:Development and Well-being (Bristol: Policy Press, 2008) 62–63, 141, and 185.

promotes inequality in the distribution of welfare based on one's residency in rural and urban areas and between migrant workers and local residents.[20]

The last major legacy was post-Maoism. While the institutional arrangements did preserve traces of Mao Zedong's paternalism, ideological indoctrination led to the widespread acknowledgment in China of the basic values of social justice. When society becomes extremely unequal and divided, people begin to call for Maoism. At the social level, China's political discourse, particularly the "New Left," retains important influences from Mao Zedong's paternalistic socialism. After Hu Jintao took office in 2002, one of the first things he did was visit revolutionary sites and reaffirm his agreement with parts of Maoism. In fact, at the practical level, memories of Mao's socialism have provided ideological support for many grassroots activists, reformers in government think tanks, and many vulnerable social groups.

An ever-larger series of worrisome facts has led to social instability, which is why these problems also became an important factor behind the Hu-Wen government's prioritization of social policy reforms. Hu-Wen social policy guidelines were characterized by advances in a market-oriented, hybrid approach, as more countries abroad were also pursuing market regulation and protecting social stability. By emphasizing "scientific development" and a "harmonious society" in ideology, the government has publicly promised to guarantee social harmony and achieve social justice and fairness in the distribution of the benefits and costs of economic development.[21]

The new social policy initiatives have been twofold in nature. First of all, social policy seeks to strengthen and develop the basic social security systems that Jiang Zenmin and Zhu Rongji implemented—systems such as the five employment insurance plans. Second, there is an effort to resolve the problems of excessive marketization in earlier social policy, and state subsidies have been introduced as a means of achieving higher degrees of fairness—these can be seen the provision of direct state subsidies for education, healthcare, and public housing. In summary, Hu-Wen social policy reform has been tasked with achieving higher quality and lower costs in the distribution of social welfare and with creating methods for realizing more equal access to this welfare. Closely related to the social reforms of these two fields is the reform proposal of 2010 which seeks to curb the inequality in income distribution that tends to favor urban workers.

20 Liu Zhiqiang, "Institution and Inequality: The Hukou System in China," *Journal of Comparative Economics* 33, no. 1 (2005): 133–57.

21 Hu Jintao, "Speech on the Harmonious Society," *Xinhua News Agency*, May 24, 2005.

Since social policy reform does not involve making adjustments to the interests of all parties, and only increases government fiscal expenditures to a limited extent, early progress has been relatively smooth. In the Hu-Wen era, the continuance of strong economic growth ensured steady growth in corporate and government revenues. The government observed a marked increase in the coverage of social insurance plans, the total number of people covered, and the total funds involved. Of these, the two most important areas of social insurance, healthcare and pension insurance (retirement plans), have expanded their coverage significantly, with half to two-thirds of urban areas getting coverage. The Hu-Wen government also made significant gains in expanding social security coverage and improving the amount of social security provided. The basic living allowance wasn't put in place until 1993, and it didn't become an effective nationwide institution until the new millennium. In particular, the government effectively extended the basic living allowance to rural areas. From 2003 to 2009, the rural basic living allowance developed from nonexistence until it covered 43.1 million rural poor. The new administration oversaw a significant increase in the coverage provided by the top five insurance companies as well as by other plans.

The second aspect of social policy reform has involved important changes in the market-oriented approach to the provision of social welfare. Most reforms are designed to use the market to address high prices and unfair distribution in key areas such as education, healthcare, and unfair distribution. The government has achieved some concrete successes in these areas.

The government's approach has been to return the state to the provision of basic welfare. It has especially taken care to improve resident income while resolving problems of exclusivity and high pricing in the provision of welfare. The extent of exclusion is at its worst in the healthcare insurance industry. In 2003, 23% to 36% of patients who were from different regions were refused in-patient medical care—in rural areas, this figure was as high as 75%. The main reason was that the cost of seeing such patients was too high.[22] The mission of new healthcare reform is to establish state subsidies while strictly overseeing public hospitals and basic-level medical centers so that the basic needs of citizens can be met.[23] Overall, the Hu-Wen government was able to use state fiscal expenditures in healthcare,

22 Zhao Zhongwei, "Income Inequality, Unequal Health Care Access, and Mortality in China," *Population and Development Review* 32, no. 3 (September 2006): 478.

23 Zhao Litao and Huang Yanjie, "China Moves to Reform Its Healthcare System," *EAI Background Brief*, no. 486, East Asian Institute, National University of Singapore, October 2009.

education, and housing to match the GDP per capita of urban households. Under reform, the share that benefits occupied in rural income grew from 15% to 32% and dipped down slightly in 2008 to 29%.

However, all of these welfare plans have as yet failed to find a comprehensive solution to inequality and exclusion. This is particularly true of those plans which choose to accept market prices. While the government has generally achieved success in monitoring excessive increases in the cost of welfare, as the generations of the 1970s and 1980s grow up and those born in the 1950s and 1960s face retirement, the government also faces many even more pressing issues. The resulting surge in the demand for welfare poses a serious threat to the government, and China's government is still struggling to cope with the younger generation's discontent with unbearable spikes in costs and the rapid rise in housing prices.

The current welfare system adopts a variety of approaches, and the corresponding policies have seen differing levels of success. The policies that have been implemented more systematically have achieved widespread and substantial reforms—one example is the steady increase in social insurance coverage. Other policy reforms have been unsatisfactory and have been beset by rent-seeking behavior—which has occurred in plans for low-rent housing and economical housing. Reform programs like a basic living allowance have been implemented consistently from their inception, but other programs have been implemented in ad hoc or even contradictory ways. This can be seen in the constant back and forth between central regulation and local activism in the housing market. In different fields of welfare, some projects, like the new healthcare reforms, have made progress in drawing clear plans and blueprints—while housing still lacks comprehensive and workable solutions.

These disparities stem from the differing political dynamics of social policy reform, which vary widely among specific policy areas. Some reforms were a direct continuation of early modernization projects and did not become subject to debate or resistance from special interest groups. In urban and social policy areas that were more successfully implemented, employment-related insurance plans encountered minimal resistance and quickly achieved full coverage. Efforts to shore up basic-level compulsory education systems that were subsidized by the state, on the other hand, focused on eliminating high tuition fees and creating more balanced educational opportunities in rural areas. Since 2005, compulsory education in rural areas has been implemented relatively smoothly. These reform efforts are ultimately reflected in the revisions to the new Labor Law and Compulsory Education Law.

Another type of reform is the domestic response to external crises and the pressures of globalization. The best example is the SARS crisis of 2003. A series of serious global criticisms of the state of public health in China prompted the state to reform the public health and information sectors.[24] Moreover, the national "211" university project, along with long-term scientific and technological development plans, involves employing large public funds to establish research universities; this is obviously a response to the challenges of globalization. In 2010, under the impetus of strong domestic social discontent and Sino-American economic exchange, reforms to income distribution systems and to monopolistic SOEs have gained strong momentum.[25]

Although the concept of a "harmonious society" plays a role in social policy reform, economic development and market-oriented reforms still top the agenda for currently ongoing reform. In government at all levels, "GDPism" still dominates the economic policy agenda. To promote growth in GDP, neoliberal economics often invades the social sphere, leading to the commercialization of social policy. This becomes particularly evident in times of crisis. Whenever a global or regional economic recession threatens domestic GDP growth, the social sector is opened up to stimulate domestic demand without first taking into consideration how such measures will influence fairness in distribution or the affordability of welfare. Under Jiang Zemin and Zhu Rongji, market-oriented reforms in higher education and healthcare stalled in 1998; this was a direct result of the 1997 Asian financial crisis. During the Hu-Wen era, policy after the 2008 financial crisis led to wild speculation in the real estate market. The resulting bubble pushed up housing prices, and this in turn threatened future economic and financial stability. The massive social discontent that came as a result also undermined the government's political base.

In the field of social welfare, a series of structural constraints emerged in areas where social policy reform has threatened strong corporate and local interests. At the outset of reform in the Hu-Wen era, the legal barriers to social mobility had already been removed. Yet, in terms of socioeconomic costs and the distribution of benefits, substantial disparities only continued to increase. The new policy package of the Hu-Wen era strictly followed a gradualist approach and was constrained by an unstable society—so that it only achieved limited success in a few areas. This has led to the persistence of social inequality in systematic conditions, for example, in the inadequate levels of basic welfare provided for migrant workers and their dependents.

Most of the reform plans in Hu-Wen social policy still represent an early decision-making stage for Chinese social policy. In comparison with the three

24 L. H. Chan, L. Chen, and J. Xu, "China's Engagement with Global Health Diplomacy: Was SARS a Watershed?" *PLoS Med* 7, no. 4 (2010): e1000266.

25 "Zhongguo chengnuo wanshan shourufenpei geju he longduan gaige" [China's Promise to Reform Monopoly Sector and Income Distribution Pattern], *People's Daily*, May 25, 2010.

legacies of China's previous system of social welfare, the social policy of the Hu-Wen era has avoided abrupt and fundamental change. Significant progress has been made in expanding the coverage of employment-related social insurance and in strengthening labor protections for urban and most migrant workers, but there has not been much progress in achieving universal basic healthcare, equal access to education, and the provision of affordable housing. At the same time, the equality of welfare distribution has actually regressed, making China one of the most unequal countries in the world in the provision of welfare services such as healthcare.

Summary

From a historical perspective, most social discontent originates in social welfare reform in the narrow sense, and social policy reform in the broader sense, of rebuilding "state-society relations." The source of inequality in contemporary Chinese society lies in the unequal and unfair distribution of social welfare. For instance, the new burdens of expensive medicines, education, and housing are a source of discontent among different groups in China's middle class. High crime rates, inadequate social cohesion, and moral decline are largely due to the lack of social security and basic equity in education. The failure of social policy to reduce the cost of essential welfare products or to provide protections for the general public is likely to lead to more social unrest.

Social policy reform and deeper economic reform do not just complement one another; the former is also the key to the latter. Insufficient domestic demand poses a structural problem for the Chinese economy. Structural weaknesses have in turn led to an overreliance on domestic investment and overseas markets, and these themselves are two basic reasons for China's internal and external economic imbalances. Social policy reform is an important remedy for insufficient domestic demand, for effective social reform can provide relief from the burden households carry with overpriced housing, healthcare, and education. Studies show that most of China's middle-class families are drastically cutting their budgets in order to support their mortgages.[26]

The lack of a social infrastructure that protects individuals and families from full exposure to the labor market will also, like the absence of other sources of socioeconomic strength, bring disruptions to economic production. Similar effects can be seen in the state's monopoly on key production factors and market access. Since the late 1990s, the resulting effective domestic demand, private entrepreneurship,

26 "Beixiaoshi de zhongchanjieji" [The Disappearing Middle Class], *China News Weekly* 1, 2010.

and insufficient social sources of economic growth have inexorably led to serious state investment and governmental intervention. Such structural constraints often drive the Chinese economy into industrial overcapacity, staff shortages, monetary inflation, and asset bubbles.

The Hu-Wen government made social policy an important and independent component of the public policy agenda. By expanding the coverage of the social insurance system, strengthening social protections for the poor, and providing market-oriented social benefits, social reform achieved varying degrees of success in various social fields. But the lack of major reform efforts is clearly a serious obstacle. To a large extent, the scope of reform remains limited and has failed to meet the public's expectations. At a deeper level, progress in social policy reform will require a broader agenda that includes making adjustments to state-society relations. These necessary adjustments will constitute the political dimension of social reform.

Today, state-society relations in China are plagued by elites' access—in the name of the state—to privileges and benefits. Elite groups derive huge benefits from market-oriented economies without taking corresponding risks. The existence of various forms of privilege provides elites with an exit (market) route, but it has led to delays and a serious lack of reform. In this sense, progress in reform means converting state-funded privilege and special benefits into various forms of universally shared rights—such as specific employer-sponsored compensation plans that are transparent and legally approved. Besides managing social insurance through law, reform also includes providing social security and state-subsidized welfare for citizens at all levels of society whose needs qualify for the standards determined by professionals.

In particular, the special welfare benefits enjoyed by civil servants and the employees of monopoly industries and SOEs must be adjusted on the basis of current social assessments. By providing exit options for political elites and extending state-funded social benefits to every citizen, significant enhancements will be made in the provision of affordable benefits. An expanded social reform agenda must include the creation of equal access for all citizens to state-funded social provisions.

At the same time, reforms to social policy need to be incorporated into fiscal reforms by increasing central oversight and creating a more transparent and democratic budgeting process. The first mechanism represents a continuation of the Hu-Wen government's approach: It strives to increase welfare spending by increasing the central government's share in welfare programs, and transfers from the central government to local governments. In addition, as an important component of social policy reform, the budgeting process for national social expenditures should be open and subject to wider public scrutiny.

The key to China's economic success depends on a twofold impetus: the mutual strengthening of economic growth and social stability. But the current GDP-centered model of economic growth under direct state control and the static state of social stability are both replete with controversy and internal contradictions. One of the main sources of these contradictions is the lack of a clear vision for or the timely implementation of social policy. Social policies can both protect and provide compensation for those social groups that are adversely affected by economic reforms and the current socioeconomic system. A lack of reform in social policy will lead to an increase in distrust between the state and society. Most people will end up losing confidence in the state, and this will produce far-reaching political consequences. Without proper reform in social policy, along with other important reforms that work together to resolve fundamental structural predicaments, social and economic development will become unsustainable, and China will enter a vicious cycle. These are the primary challenges facing a new generation of leadership.

CHAPTER NINE

Mao Zedong and the Rise of the Market Economy in Contemporary China

> Simply put, there are a variety of obstacles standing in the way of the development of a market economy, and these obstacles cannot be overcome by capital alone. To overcome these obstacles, capital needs the help of state power. After Mao Zedong's thirty years of continuous revolution, it can be said that everyone changed, and became a new people. And all systems were restructured with political power. But once political ideology was removed, capital was let loose. It was free to penetrate every nook and cranny of Chinese society without any resistance, piercing even to the depths of the individual soul.

Why Do We Need to Discuss Mao Zedong's Connection to China's Market Economy?

No matter how you look at it, the rise of the market economy in contemporary China has been a major event in world economic history. In just over thirty years, China transformed itself from a poor country isolated from the world economy into an integral part of the world economy—and, in fact, the second largest economy in the world. As part of the world economy, China is also the world's largest trading nation, and Chinese capital is making its way into every corner of the globe. At the same time, there have been even more striking changes in the domestic operations of China's economy. In terms of economic structure, China has transformed itself from a pre-reform agricultural-based economy into the world's greatest manufacturing country; it has transformed from a monolithic state-owned and collective economy into a system in which both state-owned companies and multiple-ownership companies coexist. In China, any kind of ownership economy can find the space to survive and thrive. In terms of social structure, China has transitioned from a pre-reform, generally poor but egalitarian country into a highly differentiated and highly divided society. All of these changes have been inseparable from the operation of markets and capital—that is, they have been inseparable from the emergence and development of capitalist modes of production.

However, all of this seems to be the exact opposite of what Mao Zedong said and did during his lifetime; in fact, it is hard to mentally associate the market and capital with Mao Zedong. For Mao Zedong's system of thought, socialism and a market economy are contradictory and mutually antagonistic—as since the birth of Marxism, the ultimate aim of socialism has been the abolition of capitalism. The Chinese Communist Party has been no exception to this stance. Both capitalism and capitalists have been seen as the enemies of the Communist Party, and during his lifetime, Mao's deepest worry was that the Communist Party would evolve into a party of the bourgeoisie. Thus, he deployed political means to launch, time after time, political movements against those within the Party who would take the capitalist road, thereby resisting the so-called "capitalist roaders." Moreover, before Reform and Opening Up, there was a flood of criticism and attacks on capitalism—for all economic, political, and social forms that did not agree with socialist ideology were equated with capitalism. As an ideology, Maoism was also reflected in China's foreign policy—that is, China long practiced an isolationist policy and opposed China's integration into the capitalist world as represented by the West.

But in the thirty years since Reform and Opening Up, all of this has been turned on its head. China has achieved rapid economic growth and development. Future world economic historians will discover that the development of China's market economy was a milestone in the history of global capitalist economics. Historically speaking, China has developed much faster than early market economies and societies did, faster even than the other Asian market economies (namely Japan and the Four Little Dragons), and faster than most developing capitalist societies. The reason China has been growing faster is simple: China's economy has been more market-oriented than the economies of all these other countries.

It's obvious that social welfare in any European country far surpasses that of China, and that the social welfare of the Asian economies also outstrips China's.

Even those developing countries that have not matched China's pace in development have welfare that is better than China's. At the social level, Western civil society is also effectively resisting the monetization and marketization of social relations. And in developing countries, traditional forces can resist the monetization and marketization of social relations. But all social relations in China, including interpersonal relationships, have been monetized—also this monetization has not received much resistance. The modern market economy originated in the West; the expansion and spread of the market economy from the West to the rest of the world was only accomplished with great hardship. To this day, the market economy has not entered most parts of many developing countries. So why is it that China has been a rising star capable of becoming the center of a modern market economy within just a few decades?

For such an important issue to receive the neglect of the academic and policy research communities is highly unacceptable. The causes of this neglect lie in the nature of the academic world itself and in the political environment. As far as the academy goes, the primary reason for this neglect lies with the fact that changes in contemporary academic paradigms have made it difficult for scholars to explore such issues. The grand narratives of Western sociology primarily have their origins in the eighteenth and nineteenth centuries, and they are reflected in the works of social thinkers such as Marx, Weber, Durkheim, and Smith. These narratives all constructed imposing systems of sociology.

By World War II, the meso-narrative of Western sociology was essentially complete; this meso-narrative is the theory that is discussed today. As a result, most contemporary sociologists focus on micro-level or methodological research, for these are the two fields where one can make discoveries. But if we apply contemporary micro-sociology to the study of Chinese society, we will have great difficulty in answering macroscopic or even meso-scopic questions. In its thousands of years of history, China has not developed a sociology like that of the West.

After the May Fourth Movement, groups of scholars who had traveled to the West or had been influenced by Western sociology began to employ Western sociological methods to build the sociology of China. This stage happened to occur at the precise moment that Western scholars were striving to build a meso-narrative of sociology.

We will pass over the question of whether these sociology pioneers were successful in their efforts—after 1949, their work was completely abandoned due to war and other political factors. After 1949, the only thing that dominated Chinese sociology was Marxism—as understood by the Chinese. Marxism itself is not problematic, and it is still considered one of the methodologies of sociology. The problem is that China didn't truly understand Marxism, and it employed Marxism as a rigid way to interpret everything in China. As a result, not only was the formation of sociological theory stunted but also China itself was greatly misunderstood.

In the West, Marxism originally formed amidst the process of criticizing and interacting with other theories. But once Marxism became regarded as the only "science," all other theories were completely forced out—and this nearly amounted to declaring the death of Marxism itself. After the Reform and Opening Up, a large number of Chinese students and scholars visited the West, but by then Western sociology had entered the stage of micro-level research. But because there was no meta-level or meso-level theoretical backdrop, an excessive focus on micro-level research made it difficult for these scholars to really know China. Some foreign scholars have remarked that the Western study of China today can be summarized as "the more you study, the less you know." Why should we think that this isn't true for Chinese scholars as well? People often "see the trees but not the forest." In a word, micro-level research methodologies cannot raise, much less answer, macro- and meso-level questions.

Outside of research methodologies, the study of China has been excessively politicized, both in the West and in China. Many social phenomena, such as capitalism, socialism, the market, democracy, and even Mao Zedong have been highly ideological; they can no longer be regarded as "social things." Once these "social things" have become ideological, researchers proceed to conduct their research from a "politically correct" position, and it is difficult to achieve the "value neutral" position of which Max Weber spoke. Clearly, if there can be no de-ideologicalization, it will be difficult for Western and Chinese scholars alike to obtain informed knowledge of China.

Nevertheless, it is both a theoretical and practical reality that addressing the question of the relationship between Mao Zedong and the Chinese market is one of great importance. Why is this so? This can be explored on at least three levels.

First, this issue concerns the historical continuity of political and economic development between Mao Zedong and contemporary China. The existence of continuity or change between the thirty years before and the thirty years after reform has been one of the loci of debate between the left and the liberals (or the right) in recent years. It has also been a point of interest in the international academic community. At a policy level, this issue is moreover a theoretical conundrum facing China's ruling party. The thirty years prior to reform are generally labeled "the Age of Mao," while the thirty years after the reform are frequently held to be "the Age of Deng Xiaoping." As a result, in official ideology, there has been a split between Maoism and "Deng Xiaoping Theory."

Generally speaking, the left agrees with Maoism, while liberals approve of Deng Xiaoping Theory. Although, in official discourse, Maoism and Deng Xiaoping

Theory are an interconnected, organic entity, with the latter being regarded as the continuation and innovation of the former, the left and the right clearly disagree with official discourse on this point, and they regularly attack each other. Why is this? The central issue here is that both the left and the right pay too much attention to ideological distinctions between Maoism and Deng Xiaoping Theory, while they ignore the organic connections between the two at the practical level.

Is it really true that the post-Reform and Opening Up market economy is just a product of Deng Xiaoping Theory? Can it really be said that the development of the past thirty years has nothing to do with the history that preceded the Reform and Opening Up? In the past few years, the ruling party's leadership has argued that the history of the thirty years prior to and after the Reform and Opening Up cannot be divorced from each other. This is certainly a factual judgment. However, as a factual judgment, if it cannot be expressed at the conceptual and theoretical level, it remains unable to address the issue. If we can clarify the connection between Mao Zedong and the rise of the market economy in contemporary China, then this question will not be difficult to answer. Of course, this issue could be addressed with many other approaches, but they are beyond the scope of this chapter.

Second, this issue is concerned with Mao Zedong and decisions made about China's developmental path. The issue also involves an interpretation of Mao Zedong and Maoism. From a discursive perspective, there certainly is an antagonistic relationship between Maoism and the market economy. Yet many questions can still be raised: Did Mao reject the market economy merely for the sake of rejection? The market economy had not yet substantially developed in China: On what grounds did Mao base his rejection of it? Similarly, at the time, China lacked substantial practical socialist experience. On what basis did Mao affirm and accept socialism?

We can say with certainty that Mao's attitude toward the market economy and socialism was essentially a value judgment, and this was mostly based on his contemporaries' understanding of the Western developmental experience. In fact, Mao never offered a systematic treatment of the Western market economy, and he was not well versed in the actual circumstances of the Western market economy. However, just as he knew well during the Chinese Revolution that Marxism in a rigid sense could not guide the revolution, he also knew that, during the construction of the Chinese state, he could not use the Western market economy to develop and build China in an equally mechanical way. What he needed was to find an approach that was suitable for China's economic and social development.

Historically speaking, since the May Fourth Movement, all of China's political elites have sought a way forward for China's modernization. Before Mao, however, most people generally equated modernization with "Westernization." It was only under Mao that China set out on the path of "internal modernization" that conformed to China's own realities. It was this foundation laid by Mao's "internal modernization" that made possible Deng's "external modernization"—which was an approach that conformed to the world economy. In that sense, there is not much difference between the approach to modernization taken by China and that taken earlier by countries like Germany, the United States, and Japan (this will receive more detailed treatment below).

Third, at the international level, this issue touches on how developing countries should go about adopting a developmental model. A serious and longstanding problem facing the modern world is that wealthy nations get wealthier while poor nations get poorer—this is what is frequently described as the "the North-South problem." Since the advent of modernity, why have the vast majority of non-Western countries (the "South") failed to develop, while Western countries (the "North") succeeded? In non-Western developing countries, only a few economies have developed into high-income societies—these have primarily been Japan and the Four Little Dragons, along with some oil-supplying countries. In many developing countries, it is difficult to find any development at all. Some of them are at a low-level development, while others, after achieving some development at earlier stages, have stagnated and fallen into the "middle-income trap." The question for these countries is: How can they escape their low levels of development? Or how can they break out of the "middle-income trap"? The remedy the West prescribes is centered around free markets (without government intervention), openness, and democracy. In recent years, there has been a constant debate about the "Washington Consensus," focusing on whether the solutions offered by the Washington Consensus can solve the problems of low-level development and the middle-income trap in developing countries.

Yet the Washington Consensus is only a summary of the developmental experience and practice of the West—it is not a summary of the developmental experience conducted outside of the West. To argue that the Washington Consensus applies to developing countries is to work from an unfounded assumption. Since the advent of modernity, the West has dominated the world economy, and for long periods of time, many developing countries have also been reduced to colonies of the West. The underdevelopment or "middle-income trap" experienced by these countries is closely connected with the Western rule and interference. Over long historical periods, neither free markets (with less or no government intervention) and openness (interpreted as "openness to the West") nor democracy (Western-style multiparty systems and elections) have been able to help those countries achieve development.

In fact, if we take a closer look, those things which the West regards as "cures" are, to a large extent, precisely the main reason why these countries fail to develop or fall into the middle-income trap. In Latin America, it has long been recognized that low-level development is related to the "dependent development" of Latin American countries. Of course, this phenomenon exists, not only in Latin America but also around the world. And the West's introduction of democratic politics into these countries has actively pushed them into low-level development and the middle-income trap.

It is not difficult to understand the reason. In the West itself, the basic state systems of modernity were established during earlier periods of political autocracy, thereby laying the institutional foundations for subsequent sustainable economic development. But in later developing countries, modern state systems do not exist, and democratic politics—particularly mass democracy—has been introduced prematurely, thereby hindering the construction of basic state systems in those countries. It's easy to see that economic and social development will not readily be put on the agenda for political elites. Their agenda remains a perpetual political struggle, one in which political forces of all persuasions compete for a slice of the country's limited resources, and no party can focus making a cake that can serve the interests of the country and society as a whole. As a result, the state is often plunged into dictatorship or anarchy.

The extreme opposite of "dependent development" is "disconnected development," which means breaking away from the Western world and developing behind closed doors. This developmental model primarily describes the developmental models of the Soviet Union and the Eastern Bloc during the Cold War. Today, only a few countries, such as Cuba and North Korea, continue to adhere to this model. The "disconnected model" was first derived from Lenin's revolutionary theory, in which Lenin held that if a revolution in an underdeveloped country were to succeed, it had to first break free of the chains of Western imperialism. This represented a major innovation of Marxist theory on Lenin's part. Marx called on the workers of the world to unite and oppose capitalism together, but Lenin advocated just the opposite.

Later practice proved Lenin right. Under the guidance of Lenin's theory, the Soviet revolution was successful. However, due to war, the Cold War, and other factors, this revolutionary model gradually evolved into a model for economic development. During the Cold War, the development of the Soviet Union and Eastern Europe experienced a total break with the West. This developmental model operated in a manner exactly opposite to that of the West: There was no market, no freedom, and no democracy. While this model of "disconnected development" achieved considerable development in its early years, experience has shown that if this model cannot transform itself with time, sustainable development cannot be achieved. To make matters worse, this model quickly lost out in competition with the West. From our current perspective, this model in many ways appears to be even worse than the model of "dependent development."

In the wake of the Reform and Opening Up, some Westerners summarized China's developmental model as a "Beijing Consensus" to correspond to the Washington Consensus. However, the Beijing Consensus is only a partial reflection of the developmental experience after the Reform and Opening Up, and it ignores the thirty years of the Mao era. If we compare the "dependent model" to the "disconnected model," we'll discover that the Chinese model is an organic combination of "disconnection" and "connection"—that is, a successful integration of the "break" during the Mao era and the "connection" of the Deng era. And here, "disconnection" is a precondition for the success of "connection."

It must be observed that, in Maoism, "disconnection" is not an end in itself, but is only a means of "connection." In other words, the "internal modernization" of the Mao era laid the foundations for the "external modernization" of the Deng era. Although, as an ideology, Maoism contains many anti-Western elements, Mao was not anti-Western himself but opposed a simplistic adoption of the Western model. What he was looking for was his own developmental model. It can be said that this model actually pursued Western goals with non-Western means. However, in many respects, this model was similar to the early modernization model in the West, and it also had similarities to the East Asian Model (that of Japan and the Four Little Dragons). In other respects, it also transcended both models. To explore or summarize the China Model is not necessarily tantamount to substituting Western or other models, but it does undoubtedly have value as a practical reference for countries that are still in a state of low development.

Today, China defines its economic system as a "socialist market economy," and a market economy is inseparable from capital. Markets and capital are two inseparable components: Markets need capital, and capital needs markets. Markets are a platform, and capital is the primary driver of the operations on the platform. Of course, the forms of capital are diversified—for example, there is private capital, state capital, and foreign capital, or any combination of the three. China's mixed economy implies a combination of various forms of ownership—this means the combination of various kinds of capital. Thus, the "capitalism" discussed in this book refers to the ways in which China's economy operates, not to capital at an ideological level.

In an economic sense, the contemporary world economy has become so complex that no single "-ism" or ideology can provide a generalized interpretation for all of reality. Obviously, even the classic capitalist economies of the West long ago developed considerably socialist elements. In some of the West's welfare states (such as in Northern Europe), socialist elements have even outgrown capitalist elements. At the same time, even a country like China that is defined as socialist has developed considerable capitalist elements, and in some areas, capitalist elements have even outgrown socialist elements.

Deng Xiaoping once emphasized that the market economy is a mode of economic operation, and that it can be used under both capitalism and socialism. This assessment closely matches the reality of economic operations. The same can be said of capital. Differing forms of capital take a leading role on the stage of the market. Whether an economy is socialist or capitalist, it still needs capital. Without capital, there can be no market economy. I have offered this simple explanation in order to forestall an overly ideological interpretation of either "Mao Zedong" or "capitalism."

The State and the Market Economy: The Western Experience

How are we to understand capitalism? There are three elements to any form of capitalism: markets, capital, and rules. To put it simply, the operational modes of a capitalist economy consist of at least three elements: the platform of the market, market roles, and trading rules among market roles. These three elements are indispensable. Economic activities are trades between economic actors, and the market is the place where the trades take place—it is the platform for those trades. This platform can be either natural or artificial. The agent who trades on the market is the trader—this is the subject of market activity. Without a platform, traders cannot trade; without traders, a platform is useless. Trades occur between economic actors—trades involve buying or selling. Relationships of supply and demand are balanced through trade. Among the masses of traders on a market, the most important group is the owners of capital. Moreover, without market trading, there can be no market. Markets are the platform by which economic agents can turn their funds (wealth) into capital. At present, people can have wealth without that wealth being capital. It is only when people invest their wealth in trading markets that their wealth can be transformed into a market. More importantly, however, transactions between traders must be regulated. Without rules, traders cannot trade. Rules can be things that form naturally and evolve into "cultural rules," or they can be *a posteriori* formulated as rational objects like laws and regulations.

Thus, for capital to operate, a market must first be built. In any society, three basic markets can be distinguished. The simplest kind of market is the localized, basic market. This kind of market has existed in various social forms during differing historical periods. Local and regional markets are composed in a bottom-up fashion. They are formed spontaneously by local traders and rarely bring in the role of the government. Generally speaking, as long as the government does not prevent the occurrence or development of this kind of market, it will operate quite effectively. The basic market has several distinctive features. First, its platform is formed either spontaneously or with limited assistance of the government. Second, it is an open and inclusive market, with very low barriers to market entry. This ensures that it has many traders. Third, trading roles are formed spontaneously from the free trades of traders, and all elements, including price, are regulated by the market. Because there are many traders, the market cannot be easily manipulated by a small number of people. Thus, people generally believe in the fairness of the trades occurring on this market platform.

If it is true that the formation and development of the basic market does not demand governmental oversight, then the formation of a unified domestic market and an international market needs the role of the government. At these two levels, market platforms do not readily emerge in a bottom-up manner, and government intervention is necessary. As far as a unified domestic market is concerned, it is difficult for capital alone to overcome the various obstacles to its expansion. If these obstacles are to be overcome and a national market is to be formed, capital needs the help of the state, which controls the monopoly on violence. Moreover, maintaining the market requires the government, most critically in the establishment and implementation of infrastructure, laws, and regulations.

In most countries, the construction of large-scale infrastructure, especially facilities for transportation, often involves the government. Of course, some infrastructure can be built by the business community itself. But at any given time, the law must be provided by the state. As far as international markets go, the principles behind their formation and maintenance are the same, except that governments need to be play an even greater role, for the international market exists among sovereign states, and the resistance encountered by the market in the process of its formation is even more powerful. Similarly, sovereign states have taken on a major role in the formulation and implementation of the international laws and regulations that manage international economic activities. Entrepreneurs can participate in this process, but they must do so through the medium of sovereign states.

The formation of Western markets and the formulation and implementation of market rules help us clearly see the intimate relationship between the state and capital. We can see how the state was from the first an integral element in modern capitalism—not the liberalism that is proclaimed by mainstream modern economic schools. In the West, opposition to or resistance against capitalism has often included religion, local communities, castle politics, and feudalism—and state power has often played a large or even decisive role in removing such resistance. The developmental process in the West demonstrates that capitalism needs the support of state power.

The formation of the modern Western market economy has its origins in the fall of the Roman Empire. While this formation was a bottom-up process, the power of the state in this process cannot be underestimated. After the collapse of the Roman Empire, as there was no "central power," autonomous cities arose in Western Europe, and the primary actor or even ruler of the city was often a merchant. A city dominated by markets is an ideal platform for markets. However, urban markets were only the spontaneous basic markets that were later emphasized by Adam Smith. They were small in size and far from being unified national markets. In a highly decentralized feudal system, despite the existence of these localized, free markets, markets remained fragmented. It was the unification of the state that led to the formation of the unified national markets of Europe.

The unification of European states could be said to be the product of cooperation between political elites and merchants (that is, capital). National unification was often achieved through war, and political elites thus needed the support of merchants. At the same time, the unification of the country meant the formation of a unified national market, and merchants thus supported the unification of the country. After a unified market was formed, capital could penetrate every aspect of society. In Karl Polyani's *The Great Transformation*, we can observe how capital permeated all of society and exerted a gigantic impact on traditional social and economic life. The expansion of the market and the deep penetration of capital could be said to have promoted the transformation of the West from a traditional society into a modern society.

The process of forming unified markets in the West was also a process of establishing relations between capital and the state. This was a process of both centralization and decentralization. To begin with, unifying a country is a process of centralization. To unify a country is to establish a centralized system and eliminate, even destroy, political obstacles like various local political communities, castle politics, and feudal territories. Decentralization, on the other hand, meant that, during this process, merchants obtained political power by funding the state, thus achieving a separation of power between the merchants and the king. In order to obtain the economic support of merchants, kings had to share political power with them. This was primarily seen in the parliamentary powers of merchants or property owners. The establishment of private property rights and the rule of law was inseparable from the dominance of merchants in parliamentary politics. Since merchants had to support the kings in their unification of their countries, they also had to find ways to prevent kings from infringing on the interests of capital and thus protect the interests of capital. How could they go about doing so? By controlling parliaments, and thus, controlling legislative power, for the rule of law was in the best interest of the merchants. From this perspective, the establishment of private property rights and the rule of law was an interactive process between political and economic power. In this process, we can also see that it was the power of capital (that is, of the merchants) that tamed the power of politics (that is, of the king).

Religious reforms were also an important spiritual and cultural factor in the rise of Western market economies. As a cultural spirit or form of power, religion often hinders the development of a commercial economy. The reason for this is simple: The heart of religion is spiritual, while the heart of business is material interests. Although there were many factors behind the rise of religious reforms in the West, these reforms provided an objective legitimization of the market economy, thereby enabling economic activity and profit to escape the taint of "sin." In his *The Protestant Ethic and the Spirit of Capitalism*, Max Weber discusses how reformed religion promoted the rise of Western capitalism. Today, we can still see how religion and the sociopolitical order it embodies continue to hinder secular economic activity in the modern Islamic world, India, and some societies that maintain their traditions. The rise of Western capitalism had an even greater impact on society itself. It can easily be said that capitalism rebuilt Western society. In other words, this was a process in which traditional society was first destroyed and then modern (contemporary) society was built.

The birth of modern sovereign states with the assistance of capital demonstrates that a new type of nation-state or national community had been formed. It was a baptism of blood and fire. The state and capital freed people from all kinds of traditional restraints; people lost their traditional attachments and gained a new freedom. The first social groups to win this new freedom were merchants and the capitalist class. Freed from the fetters of religion, at the same time, they relied on the power of their capital to subdue royal power and protect their interests with the rule of law. Merchants as a group composed the earliest civil society. This explains why, in the works of Marx, "civil society" refers to both the merchant and capitalist classes. Other social groups still lacked rights, so to speak.

However, with the advent of industrialization and urbanization, on the one hand, the capitalist class won gigantic markets, but on the other hand, they needed the political power of the state to provide and maintain the order necessary for the operation of capital, which is what is often referred to as law and order. The process of industrialization was also the process of the formation of the modern working class. Marx, Dickens, and Hugo—each in his own way described a world dominated by capital. For a long stretch of time, capital and state power were integrated, interdependent, and mutually supportive. While vigorously promoting economic development, they also stratified society. As a result, Marx held that the state was only representative of the interests of capital.

But as elite democracy gradually transitioned into mass democracy, the relationship between political power and the power of capital—that is, between political elites and capitalists—also changed. Marx held that, without the bourgeoisie, there can be no democracy. The bourgeoisie was the first social group to struggle for democracy. This was the aforementioned power-sharing between merchants (capital) and kings (politics). The bourgeois democracy that Marxism depicts is also an elite democracy—that is, it is a democracy in which the bourgeoisie and political elites share political power. Most of the two hundred years of Western democracy was characterized in practice by this elite democracy. During the stage of elite democracy, the interests of capital and politics generally went hand in hand, and society (or social groups other than political and economic elites) was dominated by elite classes.

The working class was the product of industrialization. As the working class rose and grew in strength, there was a change in the relationship between politics and capital. During the stage of elite democracy, politicians served as the agents of capital. In other words, political elites were supported by capital. But the development of mass democracy demonstrates how the power base of political elites gradually shifted away from capital to votes—that is, to the enfranchised working class. (After the bourgeoisie, industrial workers were the second social group to become involved in the political process. At the time, women and ethnic minorities were not granted the right to participate in politics.) Elections gradually emancipated political elites from their dependence on capital and won a large decree of "autonomous" power. Moreover, there was a need to reconcile the power of capital with the power of society (that is, votes), and elections became a balancing force.

At the same time, the emergence of mass democracy also began the transition of Western economies away from primitive capitalism to welfare capitalism. Under the primitive capitalism depicted by writers such as Marx, Dickens, and Hugo, the only aim was profit and the expansion of capital. The purpose of capital was capital itself—nothing else. As Polanyi depicts it, capital destroyed traditional societies, leading to social uncertainty and a revolutionary disorder. During the nineteenth century, Europe experienced the rise of the socialist movement. Clearly, the socialist movement was both a product of capitalism and a looming threat to capital itself. Without an orderly society (that is, a market), capital has difficulty achieving normal operations. This led to the first welfare policy.

Early welfare policies still existed to serve capital: They were a product of the union of capital and state power. Welfare was provided in a top-down manner in order to circumvent working-class movements; this welfare was thus conservative in nature. The most classic example was the social policy adopted by Bismarck. But by the middle of the twentieth century, as mass democracy expanded to more and more social groups including women and minorities, the concept of welfare itself experienced radical changes: It evolved into a "right" that everyone ought to have. In any case, the evolution of Western economies away from primitive capitalism to welfare capitalism was not driven by capital itself but was the result of social and political reforms. The state played a key role in this process, acting as a mediator between capital and social forces, thus ensuring order in markets and providing the political and institutional conditions for the regular operation of capital.

The state has played an even greater role in the West-driven formation of an international market. The formation of unified markets in nation-states had already been a violent process, and the formation of an international market was even more so. The expansion of Western capitalism around the world was supported by state power. An international market involves relations among sovereign states; it involves relations between the West and the non-West. Such a market was not easily established. It faced not only various social forces in other countries but also the state power itself of other countries. As a result, in the process of establishing an international market that involved sovereign states, Western countries often opened the way for capital with their cannons. In other words, after the use of force to eliminate resistance, capital could successfully reach those places it wanted to go.

Historically speaking, the West's creation of an international market has primarily followed several approaches. The first is colonialism. Over a long span of time, many countries in the West flourished as colonizers, while vast swathes of the non-Western world also saw the establishment of a wide variety of colonies. Colonies often directly served the markets of colonial powers. On the one hand, they provided new markets for the goods of colonial powers, while on the other hand, they provided the raw materials needed for industrialization. In the wake of global anticolonial movements, many colonial nations became independent sovereign states. But achieving political sovereignty did not necessarily mean that these colonies had also won their economic independence. On the contrary, political independence has not changed the economic relationship between colonies and their colonizers, and this has led to the "dependent development" model that was discussed above. More important, however, was the struggle of Western countries to build various international economic organizations that could form and maintain world markets.

Despite the openness of these international organizations, as Western states were the ones who laid down their rules, the formation of world markets occurred primarily in order to serve the West and not the rest of the world. In many cases, international economic organizations have also been exclusive. For example, during the entirety of the Cold War, the Western Bloc and the Soviet Bloc were mutually exclusive, and economic and commercial performance was often strategic in nature, with economic exchanges occurring only within those blocs and not between them. The "world-systems theory" of Western Neo-Marxism has done penetrating research into this world market, depicting how Western state power and capital power have worked together to create an international market whose center lies in the West and which extends to non-Western peripheries. This theory has also depicted how this market serves Western countries.

The State and the Market Economy: The Non-Western Experience

How did capitalism develop within the non-Western world? Here, the term "non-Western" refers primarily to developing countries. In this regard, the emergence and development of capitalism have been very different from the experience of the West. To begin with, it should be noted that, before the arrival of Western-style capitalism, these societies featured a variety of markets and kinds of capital operation. Yet, most of these markets were spontaneous, localized markets that were small-scale in nature. Before the arrival of Western capitalism, these countries were mostly traditional agricultural economies that operated on a subsistence level—that is, they maintained their residents' survival. In fact, both ideologically and culturally speaking, the aim of economic activities in these societies was not profit or economic expansion and reproduction, but simply the regular operation of local societies.

Western-style endogenous capitalism is quite rare in the non-Western world. In the non-Western world, the emergence and development of markets and the expansion of capital were mostly influenced by outside, mainly Western, forces. The aforementioned international markets were primarily established by the West in non-Western developing countries when many countries in Asia, Africa, and Latin American became Western colonies. The colonial powers brought modern economic activity to these countries and injected vitality into their economic development. Marx's assessment of the colonizers' role has been borne out: He held that, without the colonizers, the economies of these societies would have remained stagnant and in a traditional stage.

However, many factors suggest that the capitalism developed within colonialism was limited. This was because the colonizers were not interested in developing the economies of colonized societies. Instead, they primarily sought to open new markets for their own products and access the raw materials needed for domestic production. This also demonstrates that the domestic markets formed and developed by colonialism were often misshapen—that is, they concentrated in the areas that the colonizers needed. As far as the international market is concerned, colonizers broke through the isolation of these countries, connected their domestic markets with the colonizers' markets, and created international markets. At the same time, however, this international market was also lopsided in shape, for it often formed the previously discussed models of "dependent development"—that is, the high degree of dependency of developing countries on colonizing countries. Although these countries would later win their political independence, their model of economic dependency was retained. After the model of colonialism, there was also an "occupation model"—for example, as with the American occupation of the Philippines and Japan. The aim of the occupation model primarily touched on political considerations, not economic considerations.

The exogenous capitalist economies promoted by external force were not only misshapen in nature but were also not highly developed. Political changes were often for the worse. It's not hard to notice that when these countries do not experience sufficient development in their industrialization, it is because, under the influence of Western colonial powers, democratic politics has been introduced. In these countries, there are two forms of democratic politics. First, there is the one which was imposed by colonial powers and remained after the cessation of the colonial rule. India is an example of this kind of democratic politics. The second was established by local political elites after the end of the anti-colonial resistance. Most of these political elites were educated by Western colonial powers and accepted Western democratic ideas, and they often linked the success of the West with the democratic system implemented by the West. However, establishing democratic politics exerted a tremendously complex impact on the development of capitalism in developing countries. This can be seen, first of all, in the nature of democracy itself.

Democracy means the coexistence of multiple political forces within a country, and this is primarily seen in a multiparty system. But multiparty systems require a relatively open political system, and this openness keeps these countries connected to the West and prevents them from being isolated. This connection can also be seen in how the economies of these countries are easily affected by economic changes in the West.

Second, the introduction of democracy made it difficult for these countries to effectively establish state power and thereby promote the country's economic development. Previously, we discussed how Western political practice was long dominated by elite politics—that is, by an alliance of political elites and economic elites (capital). It was this alliance that effectively promoted the development of capitalism. But the early introduction of democracy made it difficult for these countries, unlike the early days of the West, to carry out large-scale industrialization and infrastructure construction through the alliance of state power and capital. As a result, capitalism has often faced strong resistance that has included various traditional political machines and traditional modes of production.

As democracy is competition among political forces, competition for the state's limited economic resources often leads to the plundering of a nation's economy, not its construction. In other words, the political forces of all factions mobilize their own support in a struggle for the country's limited economic cake, while no political force can effectively focus its power on developing the economy and making the cake bigger. Excessive competition among various political forces also frequently contributes to endless violence among social groups, thereby dragging a society into anarchy.

It also needs to be pointed out that, when colonizers introduced capital and democracy into developing countries, they also introduced Western social organizations. Most of these countries had not yet been baptized by modern capitalism—that is, they had been in traditional states. In some places which, during the modern period, experienced Western influence, there began to develop Western-like social forces. No matter whether a social force was traditional or Western-style, once it was combined with democracy, it had a highly complex impact on these developing countries.

Democracy means that elections are important, and that, for political figures to hold power, they need to first win enough votes. As a result, politicians cannot simply stand on the side of capital and ally themselves with capital in order to promote economic development. Quite the contrary, democracy must protect social forces. Seen from this perspective, democracy has a twofold nature. On the one hand, democracy can effectively limit the extent to which political power and capital power combine, thus protecting society. In these countries, laws are not as capital oriented as they were in early Europe; instead, they tend to aim at protecting society.

On the other hand, it is precisely because of this that political power and capital power are restrained by social forces and cannot come completely into play.

This prevents the market economy from developing. In these countries, capitalist means of production are often limited to certain domains, and large amounts of economic space remain occupied by traditional modes of production and traditional society. India is a classic example of this. To this day, India's modern market economy occupies a limited space; most of the economy remains in traditional economic forms. The market economies in most developing countries face resistance from at least three different forces: religion, traditional local communities, and modern civil society.

In developing countries, outside of the aforementioned capitalist developmental model left behind by colonizers, there are also two typical developmental models, the East Asian Model and the socialist model. The East Asian model—primarily that of Japan and the Four Little Dragons—has its unique characteristics, and its market economies have been very successful. In these economies, domestic and international markets are developing well, demonstrating that there is sufficient space for capital to operate and promote economic development.

Japan was the first country in Asia to modernize; it was also the first to introduce capitalist modes of production. The Meiji Restoration was essentially after the same things as the establishment of unified nation-states in Europe: the elimination and destruction of various local political communities and social forces, along with the establishment of a unified market within a nation-state. However, Japan went on to copy the West and attempted to develop overseas markets through colonial means through the creation of the so-called "Greater East Asian Co-Prosperity Sphere."

This resulted in acts of aggression against other Asian countries. In the wake of World War II, Japan's international market has developed rapidly. Both because the United States was occupying Japan and also because, during the Cold War, the U.S.-led West sought to compete geopolitically with the Soviet Union, the West generously opened its markets to Japan. With seemingly little effort, Japan entered the markets established by the West.

The markets and capital development of the Four Little Dragons in East Asia have much in common with Japan. First is the colonial factor. Singapore and Hong Kong were British colonies. These two places have always been associated with their colonizers and have never been isolated from the international market. Moreover, these two cities are themselves small, and their domestic markets are not large; thus, their development depends primarily on the international market. As in Japan, the formation of the international market within the Four Little Dragons cannot be isolated from the geopolitics of the Cold War. During the Cold War, the Four Little Dragons all belonged to the Western Bloc, which made it easy for these economies to integrate into Western markets. Without international markets, there could have been no formation or development of export-oriented economies in the Four Little Dragons.

However, the more important factor was that Japan and the Four Little Dragons all established highly centralized political systems strong enough to build various institutions conducive to the development of a market economy. Hong Kong was a colony, and before its reunification in 1997, local residents never had any political power—and the British authorities had absolute political power. Prior to democratization, the political systems of South Korea, Singapore, and Taiwan were all highly centralized. That these countries and regions were able to achieve the equivalent of a century of the West's economic development within a brief span of time is intimately related to the establishment of centralized political systems. Owing to the unique developmental experience of these countries and regions, they have received the label the "East Asian Model."

The East Asian Model can be simplified as follows: "economy first, society second, politics third"; or "production first, distribution second, political rights third." In other words, the economy needs to be developed first; then, social policy (public services) must be developed; and finally, politics can be opened up. To say "production first" means that these countries and regions established very "pro-business" economic policies. As in the early West, they combined political power and capital power to vigorously develop their economies. "Distribution second" means that, in these countries and regions, when the economy had developed to a certain stage, the government took the initiative in society building, providing social services, and protecting society. In this respect, East Asian societies have performed better than Europe. European governments did not take the initiative. It was only after the rise of socialist movements threatened the capitalist modes of production that Europe formulated social policy. East Asian societies appear very proactive, and governments work to engage in society building. As a result, socialist movements like those of Europe have been avoided.

In just over thirty years, the East Asian Model has not only produced economic miracles but also performed a social miracle—that is, it has generated a vast middle class. This has provided democratic politics with a relatively solid socioeconomic foundation. Without the wealth created and the political systems established during their authoritarian periods, it's hard to imagine the democratic process functioning more peacefully in East Asia. Of course, this is not to say that there are no contradictions between democracy and capital in East Asian society. In today's globalized context, the contradictions between East Asian capital and mass democracy have become ever more apparent. Simply put, democracy means local interests but capital needs to operate on a global scale. And globalization has exacerbated contradictions between capital and democracy. Of course, this is a global phenomenon that is not limited to East Asia.

The contradictions between democracy and capital also reveal that, in East Asian economies, capital and social forces are still maintaining a relative equilibrium. This is seen first of all in traditional areas—primarily in agriculture. In Japan, the interests of farmers have been effectively protected by the ruling party in order to prevent the entry and the excessive influx of Western capital. Politicians need the votes of farmers, and farmers need the government to protect their economic interests. This alliance between politicians and farmers is still playing a large role today. Outside of the urban economies of Hong Kong and Singapore, the situation in agriculture in both South Korea and Taiwan is practically the same. If governments and capital want to open up agricultural markets, they will encounter strong social resistance.

Second, the equilibrium can be seen in the relations between capital and modern social forces. As in Western societies, modern social forces are primarily the products of industrialization and urbanization—they include industrial workers, the middle class, students, and NGOs. These social forces have played an increasingly important role in balancing the forces of capital, and the political radicalization in some parts of East Asia can be seen in the resistance of modern social forces to capital. These social movements often revolve around the idea of an anti-market economy.

For developing countries, there needs to be added a brief discussion of the "disconnected model" that was previously mentioned—that is, the socialist model. During their socialist period, countries such as the Soviet Union and those of the Eastern European Bloc implemented planned economies; there was no market to speak of. After their collapse, they began to transition toward a market economy model. Understandably, under the planned economy model, these countries eliminated all traditional forces, and thus there was no strong resistance to the formation of unified domestic markets. At the same time, the collapse of the Soviet Bloc demonstrated that these countries no longer opposed the West; in response, the West accepted them into its system.

In theory, therefore, there should have been no problems in the development of modern capitalist modes of production. However, this has not been the case. With the exception of a few societies that were originally Western cultures and kept close contact with the West, the development of a market economy in many post-socialist societies did not go as well as expected. In many societies, the national economy often evolved into oligarchic economies, in which the oligarchs divided and controlled entire national economies. Oligarchic economies cannot easily unify domestic markets, and domestic economic development and industrial structures are also maladjusted. In the international market, some of these countries have emerged as what might be termed "colonial-like economies"—economies in which Western capital controls the national economy. In the analysis below, we will observe how, although there were many similarities between China and these countries during their rule by Communist Parties, the development of the market economy in China since the Reform and Opening Up has gone much more smoothly and has been more dynamic than in these post-socialist countries. We hold that the main reason for this lies in the absence of strong political power after these countries' democratization. Not only were they unable to convert conditions created by their socialist regimes into advantages for the development of a market economy but these conditions actually turned into disadvantages. In China, however, a system of one-party governance and multiparty political participation has avoided this predicament.

The State and the Market Economy: The Chinese Experience

Our previous discussion of the development of market economies in the West and in later developing countries primarily served to explain how the market economy grew and developed amidst the interaction of political power and capital. How is it, then, that we can connect Mao Zedong with the rise of the market economy in contemporary China? Simply put, there are a variety of obstacles standing in the way of the development of a market economy, and these obstacles cannot be overcome by capital alone. To overcome these obstacles, capital needs the help of state power. In China, it was Mao Zedong and the revolution that he led that helped overcome all the obstacles that capital would have inevitably encountered. Regardless of Mao's private aims, he created the material, institutional, and ideological conditions that were objectively necessary for the contemporary Chinese market economy. To be more specific, after the founding of the People's Republic in 1949, Mao conducted three domestic revolutions—a material revolution, an institutional revolution, and an ideological revolution. The thoroughness and success of these three revolutions provided all the conditions for the development of a market economy after Mao; they enabled the market economy to directly penetrate Chinese society for long periods of time; and they completely changed Chinese society.

To begin with, it should be explained that religious forces have never offered resistance to the development of China's market economy, whether during the Mao era or after the Reform and Opening Up. Culturally, China has always been a secular country. It has had religious forces (folk religion, Buddhism, etc.), but traditionally these have been rather weak. So, religion has never presented any contradictions to commercial production. Moreover, religious forces, psychologically, can be conducive to the development of commerce. In the West, as has been earlier discussed, religious reform demonstrated that capital gains were no longer "evil," while the social services (such as charity) provided by religious forces also assisted the capitalist modes of production. In other words, religion resolved some of the problematic aspects produced by the development of a market economy.

In the Mao era, with the exception of some officially sanctioned religious activities, the space for religion was limited. Mao did not hold anti-religious attitudes in order to develop the economy, but to build the socialist society he believed in. Since the Reform and Opening Up, religious forces have recovered. While the emergence and development of new religious forces (religions not officially recognized) have produced many contradictions with Chinese politics, the development of religion and a market economy are not necessarily contradictory. Since there are political constraints, in modern China religious forces primarily come into play in the social services and charity sectors, and this provides assistance for the operation of the market economy. In the West, it's easy to observe the symbiotic nature of charitable organizations and the market economy, and China is no exception. Moreover, religion is also conducive to the development of a market economy: It provides motivation for the winners and comfort for the losers.

Mao Zedong's revolution restructured the organization of Chinese society. In Chinese history, "revolutions" are only "dynastic change"—that is, one dynasty replaces another, while the overall structure of the country (including politics, the economy, society, and culture) does not experience significant change. Mao's revolution, however, was a true revolution, one which led to massive changes in all of those areas. It was a social revolution that began by eliminating traditional local communities.

To begin with, the foundation of the traditional local community was the family, the extended family, and the clan. Under Mao, these foundations were either destroyed or rendered less important. To put it in historical perspective, no revolution has reached every corner of Chinese society in the way Mao's did. Before Mao, Sun Yat-sen and Chiang Kai-shek also carried out revolutions, but these were only political revolutions, not social revolutions. After Chiang Kai-shek's victory in the Northern Expedition and the establishment of the Nanjing government, he initiated the "New Life Movement" during the 1930s. But the New Life Movement had nothing new about it, for its primary objective was the restoration of the structures and values of traditional Chinese society. Under Mao, traditional local communities were eliminated, making it impossible for the people to resist external forces—including state power and the market economy. After the Reform and Opening Up, traditional social communities have recovered somewhat, but they are far from being strong enough to combat the entry of the market economy.

As Mao's revolution was destroying traditional local communities, it also restructured social organizations. Since modernity, with the development of industry and commerce and concomitant urbanization, China has seen the emergence of the social force known in the West as "civil society"—primarily spontaneous organization. After the founding of the New China, spontaneous social organizations were controlled or even destroyed. Those social organizations that were not eliminated, such as religious organizations, have been functionally reorganized by the Communist Party. The Party has employed state power to organize them into a component of the regime—in other words, it has made them highly dependent on state organizations, and they are bereft of any autonomy.

More importantly, the Communist Party provides functional organizations for society. Typical examples are the Communist Youth League, the All-China Federation of Trade Unions, and the Women's Federation. In fact, these organizations are not so much social organizations as extensions of the government into society.

The most important way in which Mao's revolution influenced Chinese society was the reconstruction of administrative and economic systems. In Chinese tradition, the monarch is, in theory, autocratic—but in practice, society is difficult to govern and holds a high degree of autonomy. This was completely changed with Mao's revolution. A classic example can be seen in the extension of administrative systems. For thousands of years, China basically had only three levels of government: the central government, the provinces, and the counties. Before the Yuan Dynasty, the provinces were also units within the central government. Even the Kuomintang era still featured a three-tier government. After Mao's revolution, however, the three levels of government evolved into five levels: the central government, the provinces, the counties (cities), communes, and production brigades. In fact, there were many more, for we need to add to the list of government organizations such as administrative offices (*xing shu*) and production teams. This expansion of administrative organizations was unprecedented. It can easily be said that Mao's revolution made it possible for state power to penetrate every aspect of society for the first time.

The reconstruction of the economy was mainly reflected in the establishment of a planned economy. Mao did not invent the reorganization of economic activity through government power; this is the theme and general tendency of modern economic life. From the government-led Westernization Movement of the late Qing to the economic policies of the Kuomintang and the Republic, to the planned economy of Mao, the theme has been the same. However, the planned economy differed from all previous economic systems in its rejection of markets.

A planned economy is a completely governmental economy. Without markets, economic activities are organized by administrative departments, and all economic resources are allocated by administrative departments. This leads to the sectorization of economic activity, for all economic activity is carried out by different bureaucratic departments. It is a kind of vertical economic activity that can be labeled a "vertical feudal system." From the central to the local level, there is one economic domain unified from end to end—what China has called a "lined economy" (*tiao tiao jingji*). However, as was mentioned above, because the administrative system is divided into five levels, and these administrative departments are all responsible for economic activity, there was formed what is known in Chinese as a "lumped economy" (*kuai kuai jingji*). And as the vast sweep of rural area has been the most important vehicle of Chinese tradition, all rural economic activity was also organized through the people's commune system. This included production teams, production brigades, and the people's communes.

In terms of material conditions, the revolution primarily touched on industrialization and infrastructure construction. During the Mao era, China carried out its first large-scale, state-mobilized industrialization movement. Mao rejected Western capitalist methods of production primarily because he did not think that these methods could help China industrialize. He observed from the experience of the Soviet Union and other countries that development through state mobilization was faster and more effective. Instead, Mao's objective was to regain economic parity with developed Western nations such as Britain and the United States.

The major features of Mao's industrialization were the replacement of the market with the state, the replacement of Western mobilization via capital with mobilization via the state, and the replacement of the external colonialism of the West with internal colonialism. Considering both that China had to modernize as fast as possible and that China found itself in a specific domestic and international context, it's easy to see why Mao formulated the strategy he did. At that time, markets were underdeveloped, and market forces could not be relied upon to develop the economy. Domestic private capital was negligible, and it could not be relied upon in the task of modernization. External colonialism was even less acceptable, since the Chinese revolution was itself anti-colonialist (China was what Mao described as "semi-colonial"), and colonialism lacked any ideological legitimacy. Thus, deploying the state's power in a political mobilization that would replace capital and using methods such as sacrificing farmers' interests to replace external colonialism with "internal colonialism" became the effective means for Maoist industrialization.

Furthermore, the industrialization of the Mao era penetrated every corner of the country. In both developed Western countries and in developing countries, industry was concentrated in few areas and regions. In Mao's China, on the other hand, while industry was concentrated in coastal regions and the northeast, in comparison with other countries, China's industrial concentration was still quite diffuse. This could especially be seen in "Third Front construction" (*san xian jianshe*). "Third Front construction" was necessary primarily because of national defense considerations, but, objectively speaking, it promoted industry and thus also extended infrastructure such as transportation into the interior.

State mobilization also took place in rural areas. Rural land reform, collectivization, and large-scale farmland water conservation all reflected the state's power to mobilize. In any society, the rural landlord class always offers strong resistance to modern capitalism. Through land reform, China eliminated the landlord class, thereby clearing the way for the development of the market economy in the future. While rural land was owned by "collectives," the land was actually in the hands of those in power in rural areas. When these power brokers themselves accepted capital, individual farmers were not powerful enough to resist the inroads of capital.

Mao's ideological initiatives went on to produce the exact opposite results of his intentions, reaching the peak in the Cultural Revolution. Mao's ideology was highly complex, but in simple terms, the most important element was the introduction of "class struggle." In Europe, class struggle was a product of the development of capitalist modes of production. Classes, as understood by Marx, were economic in nature. But in traditional Chinese society, there was no concept of class. After the introduction of the concept of class, however, relations between traditional social groups and interpersonal relations were completely destroyed.

During the Cultural Revolution, even relations between father and son, between mother and daughter, and among siblings were ruptured. By the end of 1976, official ideology could hardly affect the people. In other words, China faced an ideological vacuum. Thus, at the outset of the Reform and Opening Up, with the introduction of capital, people quickly turned toward the other extreme: money. Just as Marx observed, the most important feature of capital is its monetization of all social relations; this has been completely borne out in contemporary China.

Thus, with the death of Mao Zedong, in addition to a defunct official ideology, China was completely prepared for the development of a market economy. After Mao Zedong's thirty years of continuous revolution, it can be said that no Chinese is still a "natural" person; everyone is a changed, new person. It turns out that no system is traditional; all systems can be restructured with political power. During the Mao era, it was only a reliance on political power that could achieve a market-free, monetization-free situation.

Once political ideology was taken away, capital was let loose. No religion, no traditional political community, and no modern civil society could stand in its way. Capital was free to penetrate every nook of Chinese society without any resistance, piercing even to the depths of every individual soul.

The Reform and Opening Up and China's Market Economy

The Reform and Opening Up changed China's economy, transforming it from a planned economy into a market economy. As a result, people have separated the thirty years prior to reform from the thirty years following it, whereas the reality is that these two periods are inseparable. What was the main point of "reform"? Reform was the introduction of markets and the role of capital. Mao's rejection of the market economy was rooted in his rejection of the modes of operation of capital in a market economy: He believed that this mode could not help China develop. He did not reject alternative methods of capital operation, and China's large-scale industrialization was itself the result of the operation of the state's capital. Sacrificing the interests of farmers, political mobilization, and the high accumulation of capital along with low consumption can all be understood as the accumulation of seed capital, for the only reason for taking these steps was economic development and industrial expansion.

We can well imagine what might have happened to China's economic structure if it had relied solely on the power of capital and not on state power. Similarly, we also need to understand what is essential to "openness." "Openness" is, on the one hand, the use of foreign capital, and on the other hand, it is a connection to the Western world. Mao never opposed contact with the Western system. In fact, after the founding of the New China, he wanted to work with the U.S.-centered West. But during the Cold War, the East and the West were in conflict, and China was forced into isolation.

China never even rejected the use of foreign capital. The early New China practiced "leaning to one side" (*yibian dao*), relying on the Soviet Union—Soviet capital was also foreign capital. After the breakdown in Sino-Soviet relations, the unreliability of foreign support forced China to embark on a "disconnected" developmental path of self-sufficiency. But contact with the West had already begun before Deng Xiaoping launched the Reform and Opening Up. The "Foreign Leap

Forward" (*yang yuejin*) of the 1970s was external openness, and the use of foreign capital to develop the national economy.

As previously discussed, a market economy means capital plus the platform of the market. Economically speaking, the changes brought to China by the Reform and Opening Up were a diversity of capital and markets. This was a change from the Mao era's sole reliance on state capital and lack of markets. Because of the state's administration-style centralism and management during the Mao era, if a market economy was to be developed, the only thing to be settled was the relationship between the government and the market.

Here we can analyze the development of China's market economy under the headings of the previously discussed three types of markets, namely local markets, unified national markets, and the international market. First, let's turn to the development of basic markets. Having existed in China for thousands of years, basic markets are deeply entrenched. There is no difficulty attached to bringing back basic markets. In fact, even during the Mao era, with the exception of a brief period of promoting an extreme "leftist" line, basic-level markets (for example, open-air markets) have always existed. With the Reform and Opening Up, this kind of market was unleashed—and has developed extremely rapidly. Such markets are now found throughout the country. It could be said that, if there is any economic activity, there will be basic markets. In locations that are thriving, these markets are already connected with the international market. The most famous of these is the small commodities market in Yiwu, Zhejiang. This kind of market and the economic transactions that occur on it make significant contributions to the national economy. While local markets occupy a small share of GDP, they provide employment for a vast number of people. At the same time, as mentioned earlier, local markets are the most equitable kind of market.

At the other end of the spectrum, China's international market is also developing well. This is mainly the result of the interplay between the government and international capital. The formation of China's international market is the result of not only the international market expanding into China with the entry of foreign capital but also China's quest to integrate into the international market. Because this market is an extension of the Western market, and Western market economies are generally more developed, the rules on this market platform are quite mature and clear-cut. While, on this market, political factors cannot be avoided, its openness and diversity mean that it is rarely manipulated by a few individuals, and the market's rules generally remain in effect. As a result, this market is widely welcomed by a variety of market players in China. Both SOEs and private enterprises want to enter this market. This explains many aspects of China.

It has long been known that the interdependence of trade among China's provinces is vastly lower than that of every province with the international market. In other words, the degree of integration between the economy of an individual Chinese province and the international economy is higher than among the provinces themselves. Again, small commodities markets like that in Yiwu have not been able to effectively expand domestically, but they have successfully developed international markets and integrated with the international market. In fact, most Chinese companies are much happier to do business with international companies than with their domestic counterparts. This status quo is due, not only to China's export-oriented economy but also to the relative difficulty in developing credit relationships between domestic companies. They can, however, develop credit with international companies.

The popularity of international capital in China also explains why international capital has been able to penetrate to every corner of Chinese society in a brief span of time. In China, apart from the theoretical concerns of some intellectuals, international capital has encountered little resistance. Throughout the world, few governments have embraced international capital with as much enthusiasm as Chinese government at all levels. For the government, the question is whether international capital can help China develop its economy, and not whether international capital should occupy the Chinese market. The model for China's early economic growth was export-oriented, with foreign trade and foreign investment as the driving forces. Competition in economic development among governments at all levels also means that they are competing for foreign trade and foreign investment. In many countries, whether out of an ideology of economic protectionism or under pressure from domestic capital and society, governments are often a barrier to the entry of international capital. China, however, is the exact opposite. Governments do everything they can to clear away obstacles to international capital. As was previously mentioned, Mao's revolution had already cleared away all obstacles from non-governmental entities. Once the government came down on the side of international capital, the entire Chinese market was open to international capital.

This is in stark contrast to the difficulties encountered by Chinese capital "going out" (*zou chuqu*) today. In a brief span of little over thirty years, China has transformed from a country extremely short of capital to a country overflowing with capital. As a result, at the beginning of the twenty-first century, the government advocated the slogan of "going out," asking Chinese enterprises to go global. But Chinese enterprises, both state-owned and private, face a variety of difficulties here, and the resistance they encounter comes not only from the governments representing sovereign states but more so from traditional and modern social forces. Sovereign states often use "national security" and laws and regulations as a means of checking Chinese capital, while various social forces resort to forms of direct action to resist Chinese capital. This makes China feel that Chinese capital is not all that popular. In reality, as has been discussed previously, the expansion of capital in developing countries requires many conditions. The countries where Chinese capital is flowing do not have the same conditions as China itself. These countries resist not only Chinese capital but also capital from other countries.

So how can we go about developing a national domestic market? At this level, market platforms do not just spontaneously emerge in bottom-up processes; they need government interventions. The most important means of intervention is the establishment of infrastructure and laws. If some infrastructure can be provided by the business community itself, then the state needs to provide laws. Such market-platforms have existed before in Chinese history, as with Shanxi banks, and the Huizhou merchants of Anhui. These market platforms were difficult to establish and operate without governmental permission and assistance, and in today's China, such platforms are hard to create, for a variety of reasons. Since China has an administration-oriented political system, it is often difficult to distinguish between the administration and the market. A unique feature of this administration is its segmentation—that is, each district is governed by a different administrative unit. Because politics and the economy are not separate, administrative segmentation naturally determines the segmentation of the market. This has led to a phenomenon often labeled as a "mayoral economy" rather than a "market economy." In the 1980s, local protectionism prevailed in China, and this prevented the development of interprovincial markets. Of course, this protectionism originated in the administrative power of the government, not from society.

While local market protectionism is not as strong today as it was in the 1980s, intergovernmental competition still plays a more important role in economic development than does competition among enterprises. There are also serious problems with the role of the market. At this level, the primary driver of the market has long been SOEs. Later, with the development of private enterprise, this changed. Thus far, however, the major players in interregional and national economic sectors have been SOEs and a few private enterprises.

In some industrial fields, while private enterprises have emerged, they are weak and have difficulty competing with SOEs and international corporations. Simply put, at this level, while the market does exist, it is often monopolized and closed. The market's role is limited, and the barriers to market entry are high, making it inaccessible to ordinary enterprises. As a result, up till now, the main players on this market platform are still SOEs, a small number of private enterprises, and international corporations.

This dynamic also means that the market rules in this field are immature and unclear, and transactions lack fairness. The reason for this is simple. In this field, trading rules must present themselves as laws and regulations, and laws and regulations must be formulated and implemented by the government. At the same time, because the major players are SOEs, there will be some major contradictions. For example, how can the government treat its own enterprises and those of other enterprises on an equal footing? How can the government regulate its own businesses? How can the government prevent itself from intervening in the daily operations of its own enterprises?

In terms of cultivating the role of markets, China has also been more effective than other developing countries. During the Mao era, the economy played a role in the cities in the SOEs of various administrative levels and in rural areas in the communes (the people's communes, production brigades, and production teams). Reform was first implemented in rural areas: The household responsibility system was implemented for rural production, making the individual farmer the main driver of the rural economy. The creation of this system soon led to the collapse of the people's communes, replacing them with a system of rural village autonomy. Economically speaking, vast rural areas, particularly in coastal areas, developed a massive number of TVEs in just a short span of time. After the Reform and Opening Up, TVEs became the forerunners of China's industrialization, and they once garnered a great deal of attention in the international community. Once reform began in urban areas, TVEs gradually fell into decline, with most of them being restructured and privatized.

In urban areas, the government did not begin with a reform of SOEs; rather, it cultivated a non-state-owned sector outside of the SOEs. Sole proprietorships and other forms of urban private enterprise began to emerge, and they developed rapidly. At the same time, since government at all levels had enterprises, beginning in the 1980s, governments began to act as enterprises in what the academic community often labels a "corporate government," in which the government directly manages business activities. As in the West, China's economic growth comes from competition. But unlike the West, this competition does not occur among enterprises, but among local governments. While intra-governmental competition is national in scope, in some locations, local governments have chosen to withdraw from direct economic activity on the basis of their own economic structures, and they have allowed enterprise to become the main player in the market.

Since the 1990s, economic reform has used administrative power to propel the development of the market economy. Here there are several critical aspects. First, there's the restructuring to SOEs that began in the mid-1990s. Reform of SOEs proceeded along two lines: "grasping the large" and "letting the small go."

"Grasping the large" meant assembling large SOE conglomerates and learning from the experience of early Japan and South Korea so that international competitiveness could be improved. "Letting the small go" meant privatizing many small and medium-sized SOEs (particularly those that were losing money at the time)—this was a Chinese-style privatization. Privatization went a long way in promoting the development of private enterprise and changing the landscape for SOEs and private enterprise in the Chinese economy.

Second, after restructuring, SOEs employed capital to develop and manage themselves—this was state capitalism. State capitalism is quite effective, and SOEs quickly transitioned from generally incurring losses to becoming the most profitable enterprises in the country. Today, large SOEs occupy a dominant and monopoly position in all the key areas of the national economy, and they are also playing a leading role in the implementation of the Chinese government's "going out" strategy.

Finally, the government has also reformed the financial system to serve the operations of the market economy—this has included the reformation of the banking system, and particularly the formation of commercial banks and the establishment of a central banking system. The government also directly influences investment through the China Development Bank. These financial reforms have benefited the development of the real economy. In addition, building off of these reforms in the financial system, China has also started to develop a modern financial capitalism similar to that of the West—one that pursues profitability through the operations of finance itself. Although China's financial capitalism is not as well developed as that of the West, it has experienced rapid development in a short span of time. However, it's clear that this is a risky situation. A good example can be found in the rapid development of shadow banking in recent years and the damage it has done to the national financial system.

The development of a market economy also demands a change in administrative organization or the bureaucracy. If we can say that Mao's organizational methodology for the administration and the bureaucracy are more about controlling society through political mobilization and economic development, changes to administrative organization after the Reform and Opening Up are more about developing a market economy. Starting with the 1980s, China has conducted many reforms to the administrative system. From the 1980s to the mid-90s, reforms in the administrative system sought to cancel and abolish bureaucratic agencies that directly operated and managed the economy; the aim was for the government to withdraw from the economy and grant space to markets and enterprises.

Reforms to the administrative system from the late 1990s to the present have sought to establish a regulatory government—that is, the governmental oversight of enterprise. Early institutional reform was about decentralizing power to enterprises, but a failure to supervise enterprise has produced many problems in the economy—particularly in food and drug safety, environmental protection, production safety, etc. While this is still an ongoing process, it generally approximates a market economy approach—that is, the government is transitioning from a "corporate government" into a regulatory government that manages the economy through the rule of law. Administrative-level reforms have had a similar effect. In the 1980s, a system in which cities govern counties was introduced, and this helped to strengthen the role of cities. Subsequently, administrative offices were made prefecture-level cities and cities with independent planning status (*jihua danlie shi*). These changes were made to promote economic development—or at least, that was the original intention.

The Future of China's Market Economy

Just as there is no single model for the Western market economy, China's market economy differs from its Western counterpart. While the Chinese-style market economy has come under considerable criticism today, it still must be admitted that it is a variant of the market economy. As far as market platforms are concerned, there is nothing to distinguish China from other countries—that is, the market platform is composed of local basic markets, a unified national market, and international markets. Because China's economy is continental in scale, domestic trans-provincial and regional markets have also come into being. The difference between the Chinese market economy and the Western market economy lies in the role and rules of the market. However, the difference between these two aspects is only a matter of time and space. When it comes to the role of the market, China has gigantic SOEs. Yet, the West, particularly Europe, also has a large public sector, and the proportion that the public sector occupies is not lower than that in China.

The difference is that, in many areas, private companies dominate the West, while SOEs dominate China. Moreover, China's SOEs are evolving. There is no contradiction between SOEs and a market economy as long as SOEs are part of the market and not part of politics. China's market-oriented reforms to SOEs are going to make SOEs part of the market. In terms of market rules, China has not yet developed an effective set of rules—but this is only a matter of time. It took the West centuries to develop an economy under the rule of law. As long as China continues to move toward a market economy, it will eventually develop effective market rules.

The biggest difference between China's market economy and the West's lies in the social sphere, not in the economic sphere. China's economy is more market oriented than the West's, and it's also more market oriented than the economies of many developing countries. This is primarily due to the capitalization and monetization of the social sphere. As was previously discussed, during the Mao era, China eliminated any resistance that could be posed by religion, traditional society, or local political communities; this meant that there were no obstacles in the way of the market economy after the Reform and Opening Up. After the Reform and Opening Up, the government implemented a pro-business policy that stood in solidarity with capital, and the government's control has prevented the development of a modern civil society. This has created massive imbalances between the economy and society, and between capital and society. Compared with other developing countries, this imbalance has allowed China to achieve faster economic development while simultaneously inflicting greater and more insidious damage on Chinese society.

Although marketization reform has been a tortuous road, the general outline of overall economic reform has been neoliberal economics. China's Reform and Opening Up began during the 1980s when the Reagan Revolution and the Thatcher Revolution were at their height. Neoliberal economics was peaking at the same time. Thus, China's reforms could not but be influenced by this international context. And after thirty years of Mao's planned economy, people yearned for a neoliberal economy—and accepted one without thinking. To be more specific, neoliberal economics has exerted a tremendous influence over China's economic reform. Unfortunately, however, neoliberal economics has also occupied the social sphere without any resistance. It's clear now that China's reformers did not distinguish between the economic and social spheres, and that they simplistically applied economic policy to the social sphere.

In the 1980s, China's economic reforms were still subject to a traditional ideology, in which the planned economy and the market economy were interconnected. It wasn't until the 14th Congress in 1992 that, in the wake of Deng Xiaoping's Southern Tour, a "socialist market economy" was established and market-oriented reforms experienced a massive breakthrough. However, marketization also rapidly entered the social sphere. The reform to SOEs soon undermined social welfare—that is, the unit-based system—that had been originally established under the planned economy. The government, however, did not intend to replace it with a new system. The government hoped to use "socialization" (that is, marketization) to solve the problem of social welfare. The problem was that neither the market nor society was in a position to undertake social welfare. For example, both private enterprises and SOEs have discarded social welfare as a "burden." In many countries, including the classic kind of capitalism of the United States, companies provide many social benefits for their employees. China, however, has taken on an extremist understanding of welfare, which has led companies to the extreme of discarding every form of welfare.

Even worse, neoliberal economics has entered what had originally been the social sphere. The healthcare system was the first to bear the brunt of this in the late 1990s, as hospitals and healthcare began to be marketized, and hospitals became a get-rich-quick industry. Similar things happened in education. After the Asian financial crisis occurred in 1997, China carried out educational reforms centered around commercializing education in order to cope with the crisis. This reform was implemented in order to maintain GDP growth, for Chinese citizens have a high savings rate and families are willing to invest in their children's education. This led to rapid growth in higher education and a sharp increase in tuition. To this day, China's educational system is one of the most highly marketized in the world.

In 2008, the global financial crisis hit. Working with the same understanding, the government turned its attention to the development of real estate in order to respond to the crisis. In a brief span of time, real estate practically became the backbone of the Chinese economy. Here it must be noted that, in more and more countries, fields like healthcare, education, and housing are being considered part of the social sphere, rather than as purely part of the economic sphere. It could be said, in other words, that these are economic fields with a high degree of sociality. The developed countries of the West also looked at these fields as economic fields in earlier days, and this led to tremendous social cost. After the rise of welfare policies, these fields have entered the social sphere and become main drivers of the public sector. In many developing countries that were originally Western colonies, the West's influence has also made these fields part of society, and these fields do not feature high levels of marketization. In Japan and the Four Little Dragons of East Asia, as has been previously discussed, while governments actively promote economic development, they also take the initiative to lay the foundations for social stability in social construction.

China approaches social areas as if they were economic and are fields for amassing wealth. This in itself illustrates the extent of the damage done to society's base. Here it should also be emphasized that the reason why these areas have been so easily marketized is primarily because Chinese society lacks the ability to resist marketization and monetization. As we have previously discussed, since the Mao era, Chinese society has lost its ability to resist markets and capital.

This is in stark contrast to Western society. For instance, when Thatcher attempted to privatize education and healthcare, she failed completely. The reason was simple: The people resisted the government's efforts with their votes. Today, in all welfare states, while state finances cannot afford excessive welfare, and this is also affecting national economic development, it is practically impossible to reform welfare systems. Even in developing countries, society is much stronger than in China. Thus, while many developing countries, like India, have lower levels of economic development than China, they provide higher levels of social welfare than China. As there is no social resistance, China has successfully introduced neoliberal economics into the social sphere, making China's marketization more successful than it has been in any other country and spurring economic development. But society has actually become the victim of economic development.

It can be said that all of this has been a social failure, for social failure is intimately connected to many of the serious problems facing China's market economy. Economically, it's hard for China to create a society with high domestic demand. A society with high domestic demand is essential to China's sustainable economic development. But across the globe, sound and effective policies are the systemic foundation for high domestic demand. Without this institutional foundation, the people will not consume, even when they have large amounts of savings. Most Chinese cannot save to buy a home, send their children to school, or see the doctor. Even more importantly, social policy is an effective way for the government to regulate income distribution and ensure basic fairness in society.

The sheer size of China's income gap is abnormal, and it has created a highly differentiated society. In terms of social development, the high degree of monetization and marketization in these social fields has actually destroyed and shaken the foundations of society. The ensuing social instability is not hard to understand. Since the aim of social policy is social stability, without an effective social policy, the common people feel tremendous uncertainty, and society becomes increasingly violent. In other words, China could see political radicalization at any moment.

Economic success and social failure have made China's development differ from the East Asian Model and that of many developing countries, while it is very similar to that of the West during the late nineteenth and early twentieth centuries. Might China solve the problem by adopting a European approach? Europe approaches problems with a democratic-socialist model—that is, through democratization. In China, this is not very likely. Unless massive political radicalization causes premature democratization, China will not yet have the conditions necessary for democratization for some time to come. Moreover, a democratization caused by radical politicization will push China into an impoverished democracy.

As a component of East Asian society, China needs to return to the East Asian Model to solve its problematically unbalanced marketization. It needs to change society-state relations in order to promote a virtuous circle in the relationship between capital and society. Of course, the East Asian Model and the

European Model are not mutually exclusive, for the former contains European elements within it, but East Asian governments have been more proactive in social construction than European governments were during the late nineteenth and early twentieth centuries. Social forces are key to changing relations among capital, government, and society. In China, as reform moves forward, traditional social forces such as religion and the family will recover, but they will never be as powerful as they once were. This is primarily because conditions have changed: A market-oriented economic development has produced vast changes in social structures—that include social mobility, urban-rural integration, and the nuclear family. However, new social forces are also growing rapidly. These include NGOs and professional organizations.

The rise of these new social forces is likely to lead to democratization. But in an era of globalization, even democratization will not do much to help social forces effectively constrain capital. As we can see from the democratic experience of some Western, post-development countries, it's hard to use votes to constrain capital.

The blame for this can be laid at the feet of globalization. Globalization has spurred capital flow, and capital has no country—it can choose to go wherever it wants. In other words, governments have already lost their sovereignty.

Democratization can of course exert tremendous pressure on governments, but governments do not readily put the same pressure on capital itself. Whenever capital faces pressure, it can pick up its bags and move somewhere else. As a result, some have called on the governments of the world to unite and impose an "international law" on circulating capital. But this is a utopian idea. As long as sovereign states continue to exist, the unification of the world's governments will only be a dream. Of course, previous methods of eliminating capital are no longer feasible as well. The history of the Soviet Union and China both prove this.

For China to achieve a balance among capital, government, and society, besides learning from the European and East Asian experience, the country can also resort to traditional means. In Chinese tradition, there is a professional ruling class which, situated as it is in a relatively independent and autonomous position, can regulate relations between capital and society. And when democratization is not feasible, a professional ruling class can be quite effective.

The early successes of Japan and the Four Little Dragons of Asian in achieving fair economic growth are connected with the governance of these economies by professional ruling classes. At the same time, in comparison with other countries and regions, China also has an advantage in its gigantic SOEs. In other countries and regions, governments can only regulate capital through fiscal and monetary policies. But in China, in addition to its control over fiscal and monetary policy, the government also controls a large number of SOEs.

For thousands of years, SOEs in China have served to "stabilize the market," and they have also been an effective means of regulating markets. This approach will still prove effective today. Thus, if China wants to find a balance among capital, government, and society, there is a long agenda of items for the government to choose from. These include cultivating social forces to resist excesses in the operation of capital, building a professional ruling class that is open enough to prevent it from turning into an oligarchy, implementing market-oriented reforms of SOEs in order to regulate markets and prevent them from competing with the interests of the people, and creating rule of law and regulations that can protect the interests of capital. These reforms will help China create a new market economy that can absorb the advantages of the market economy while overcoming the abuses found in contemporary marketization.

CHAPTER TEN

Chinese Nationalism and Liberalism

> Democracy is an essential condition for the modernity of a state; without democracy, it's difficult to have a modern nation-state. But in the process of transmitting nationalism to China, as there were changes in conditions, there were also changes in the two kinds of sovereignty. Clearly, nationalism is about China's construction, and not about an emotional response to international pressure. In other words, emotional responses are inevitable, but they are not what makes nationalism.

Western Nationalism and Democracy

Why do we need to discuss Western nationalism before we turn to Chinese nationalism? Because modern nationalism is essentially a Western concept. Without the spread of Western nationalism to China, China would probably have never seen the rise of modern Chinese nationalism. Pre-modern China was dominated by "culturalism," and not by nationalism—the former being identified with culture, while the latter is based on race.[1] However, it has been argued that China's traditional "culturalism" also contained racial factors, meaning that it also contained

1 For a comprehensive discussion of this distinction, see James Townsend, "Chinese Nationalism," in *Chinese Nationalism*, ed. Jonathan Unger (Armonk: ME Sharpe, 1996), 1–30.

factors of modern nationalism. According to this line of reasoning, culturalism and nationalism are not mutually exclusive, but can be mutually complementary.[2] I hold that the distinction between culturalism and nationalism is still basically valid, for even if traditional Chinese cultural identity contained factors such as race, it was far away from being comparable with the nationalism of Western Europe. Furthermore, this distinction provides a useful perspective on the evolution of Western nationalism after its introduction to China as well as the causes behind that evolution.

Literature on the definition of nationalism is so vast that I'd rather not spend much time on it. Working from a political perspective, this chapter defines nationalism as the emergence and development of a nation-state and the political identification of a people with that nation-state. Specifically, nationalism has two important levels: The first is the objective, institutional level, the institutions of the nation-state; the second is the subjective level, the national consciousness and passion of the members of a nation-state.

This second level is seen in the supreme loyalty given to the state, a loyalty which prompts members of the nation-state to give their lives for it. After nation-states were formed, the national consciousness of the second level was found in state ideologies or value systems. Nation-states created nationalist value systems that sought to cultivate the self-awareness, attitudes, and behaviors of the nation-state's members, and that urged them to advance and defend the interests of the nation. As a result, nationalism under the nation-state system was highly political. For the leaders of a nation, nationalism meant patriotism, and it was a people's duty to fight for and defend the state's sovereignty and dignity on the international political stage.

The nation-state system and a people's identification with the nation-state were intertwined, for a people's identification with the nation-state and the degree of their identification with it were closely related to the formation of nation-states. As different nation-states went through different processes of formation, popular identification with the state also differed. Because modern nationalism first formed in the West and then was transmitted to other countries, in order to understand the original significance of a nation-state, we must also examine the role played by peoples in the formation of nation-states.

To put it simply, the formation and development of Western nation-states (and thus nationalism) was an interactive process between two kinds of

2 For example, Prasenjit Duara, "De-Constructing the Chinese Nation," in *Chinese Nationalism*, ed. Jonathan Unger (Armonk: ME Sharpe, 1996), 31–55; Frank Dikotter, *The Discourse of Race in Modern China* (Stanford: Stanford University Press, 1992).

sovereignty—namely, national sovereignty and popular sovereignty.[3] Nationalism has deep-running historical origins, but as a political force that helped bring about the birth of the nation-state, it is a modern product. Here, special mention should be made of the French Revolution. Before the French Revolution, there were national issues, but the French Revolution introduced a completely new factor into national issues so that various national elements were reorganized, thereby forming a brand-new ideology. This new factor was democratic politics. After democracy became an important element in nationalism, nationalism was no longer for a few elite figures alone but became relevant to millions of ordinary people. From then on, nationalism and popular sovereignty were inseparable—that is, during the formation of a nation-state, the people were no longer politically passive but became active participants. Seen in this light, nationalism and liberalism are actually the same thing. The idea of nationalism is intimately connected with the idea of freedom.

According to the American political scientist Morgenthau, "nationalism as a political phenomenon must be understood as the aspiration for two freedoms, one collective, the other individual: the freedom of a nation from domination by another nation and the freedom of the individual to join the nation of his choice."

Nationalism first meant that the nation itself was called on to defend its freedom. But more importantly, it meant the triumph of individual liberty. The rise of nationalism occurred not only because absolute monarchy betrayed the nation abroad but also because it oppressed the individual at home. Morgenthau elaborates:

> Individual freedom was taken as a precondition of national freedom and the later, in turn, was regarded as a mere extension of the former to the international scene. The political and legal principles, originally formulated to support and guarantee the freedom of the individual, were applied to the nation.[4]

By the end of the eighteenth century, monarchies were no longer able to protect the nation-state. In Europe, some kings colluded with foreign powers against their own countries in order to further their own interests. The interests of the king were placed above the interests of the nation. As a result, nationalism was born: The nation had to rise up to protect its own interests.

3 For the convenience of my analysis, I have omitted here the various elements that constituted nationalism before the birth of the modern nation-state, for the aim of this chapter is not a discussion of nationalism itself.

4 Hans J. Morgenthau, "The Paradoxes of Nationalism," *Yale Review* 46, no. 4 (June 1957), 481–83.

After the French Revolution, nationalism became a revolutionary ideology and rapidly mounted the international and domestic stage. In domestic politics, popular sovereignty meant that the traditional rulers of the state, such as absolute monarchs and the aristocracy, lost their legitimacy. Nationalism instead emphasized that a country's citizens are equal, that they all have the right to participate in a country's political processes, and that they cannot be excluded from these political processes. No one class or political group may organize or manage national politics on behalf of the rest of the nation. Here, the concept of "nation" approaches the concepts of "political equality" and "democracy."

Then how is nationalism reflected in the political systems of liberalism—that is, in the systems of democratic politics? Here we need to examine how nation-states transitioned to democracies and how they embodied the principles of popular sovereignty. Nationalism emphasizes that all citizens have the right to participate in a country's political processes—that the foundation of a state's power is the people. Of course, this is only an ideal, because it is impossible for all people to participate equally in the political processes of a country. In fact, when democracy became an important aspect of nationalism during the French Revolution, it only appeared as a political ideology or as an ideal. The transformation from an ideal into a political reality—or the externalization of the ideal into a political system—would go on to experience an extremely complex political process.

The process of the institutionalization of the principle of popular sovereignty was a process in which the people entered a country's political life, while the process of transitioning from monarchy to democratic politics was a process in which various political forces struggled for power. First came the bourgeoisie. In Marx's analysis, the emergence of a monarchy or an autocracy is itself inseparable from the bourgeoisie, for neither imperial regimes nor decentralized, localized feudal regimes could satisfy the demands of the emerging bourgeoisie. When autocracies unified states, the principle of national sovereignty was institutionalized, and this served the bourgeoisie by providing a unified market. However, contradictions between monarchies and the bourgeoisie were soon exposed after the establishment of autocratic regimes. The bourgeoisie not only wanted to enjoy the domestic order provided by monarchies but also wanted to become active players in national politics. Since monarchical sovereignty was based on unnatural qualities such as personal identity and parentage, the bourgeoisie demanded for regimes to be built on a more natural footing—that is, on "common people" with property, the bourgeoisie. The bourgeoisie used their economic power to win the right of power-sharing and ultimately came to control power through a variety of routes (in reform, as in the United Kingdom, or in revolution, as in France). Simply put, this was the first victory for popular sovereignty in the West, and the foundation of this victory was economic power.

The second victory for popular sovereignty was the entry of the working class into national political processes. Because the rise of the bourgeoisie also created a working class, the growing working class also demanded that it share the state's political power with the bourgeoisie. Unlike the bourgeoisie's participation in politics through economic power, the working class based its participation in politics on its organization and numbers. In the end, universal suffrage successfully brought the working class into national political processes. Formally speaking, the entry of the working class into politics has been the "universalization" (*pingminhua*) of popular sovereignty. While popular sovereignty is still in development in terms of political reality, the establishment of various institutions has allowed more and more of the people to enter the political processes of the state.[5]

The Evolution of Nationalism in China and Its Relationship to Liberalism

At the close of the 1960s, the American scholar James Harrison summed up the contemporary academic consensus—particularly that of American academic Sinology—that in traditional China, emphasis was placed on a culturalism rooted in shared historical traditions and common beliefs. This culturalism was fundamentally different from the nationalism that was based in the modern concept of the nation-state. According to this line of argument, since Qin and Han times, Chinese culture has had a political sense of national superiority and loyalty, but the Chinese people primarily identified with Chinese culture. They did not have to identify with or feel any loyalty to an independent state, and they did not distinguish culture from nationality. In other words, the Chinese reserved their highest loyalties for culture—not for the state. For the Chinese, there was no reason to abandon or change their culture in order to strengthen the loyalties to the state.[6]

In this interpretation of Chinese culture, there are two elements to the Chinese idea that humanism or culture was supreme. First of all, this culturalism contained

5 This chapter is not offering a thorough discussion of the actual impact of the universalization of popular sovereignty on the democratic political system of a country, but this does not mean that the issue is not important.

6 James Harrison, *Modern Chinese Nationalism* (New York: Hunter College of the City of New York, 1969).

the belief that China is the only true civilization, and that China's culture is undoubtedly superior to that of others. Other nations may be stronger than China militarily and thus pose a threat to China, but they are not true competitors with China. Unless these nations accept Chinese culture, they cannot truly rule China. Chinese humanism took shape because, for long stretches of time, Chinese culture never encountered any competitors or challengers. The Chinese had no concept of nationalism because there had never been any external pressure placed on the Chinese nation. Second, rulers needed to receive a Confucian education and govern the country in accordance with Confucian principles. Moreover, Confucian thought was universal. Because the legitimacy of a ruler depended on education, if other nations were willing to be guided by Chinese culture—that is, the Confucian spirit—they could also possess the legitimacy to rule China. Politicians were loyal to Confucian culture, not to a particular government or nation.

This culturalism was also reflected in the Chinese perspective on international politics, one which does not recognize an equality among nations. What culturalism emphasizes is the superiority of Chinese culture, not the greater acquisition of material wealth. With the arrival of modernity, China's greatest minds realized that Chinese culture was not enough to deal with the material progress of the West, so they abandoned culturalism and turned to nationalism.

There is a lot going for this line of argument. When Westerners forced their way into China, and Chinese intellectuals began to come into contact with the Western world, they immediately discovered that the culturalism of China differed from the nationalism of the West. At the beginning of the twentieth century, Liang Qichao observed that the Chinese had a deep-running culturalism but no nationalism like that of Europeans. For the Chinese, China was the world, not a country in the world. In Liang Qichao's view, this profound sense of identity was preventing the Chinese from developing their patriotic spirit. As a result, if a new kind of country were to be created, there had be created a "new person."[7] Working from a different perspective, Liang Shuming argued that the differences between culturalism and nationalism ran as follows: Traditional Chinese government was characterized by rule without law, and that it fundamentally could not perform the functions of a modern state.[8]

7 Liang Qichao 梁启超, "Xin min shuo" 《新民说》 [On a New People], and "Yinbinshi wenji" 《饮冰室文集》 [Collected Works of Yinbinshi] "New People's Talk." (Hong Kong: Tianhang Press, 1974).

8 Liang Shuming 梁漱溟, *Zhongguo wenhua yaoyi* 《中国文化要义》 [The Substance of Chinese Culture] (Taiwan: Zhongzheng Bookstore, 1975).

After the imperialist invasions of China, the Chinese people also began to accept Western nationalism. This acceptance was a complex process. It has been emphasized here that, in Western societies, the formation and development of modern nation-states was an interactive process between national sovereignty and popular sovereignty. Again, democracy is an essential condition for the modernity of a state. Without democracy, it's hard to have a modern nation-state. But in the process of transmitting nationalism to China, as there were changes in conditions, there were also changes in the two kinds of sovereignty. This could be seen specifically as follows: The two kinds of sovereignty were separated from each other, with national sovereignty gradually coming to occupy the dominant position, while popular sovereignty morphed into state sovereignty and democracy morphed into statism.

Thus, a strong state and not democracy became the necessary condition for China's modernity. This transformation was not freely chosen by some individuals; rather, it depended on the international and domestic context of China's state-building—that is, on China's status as a developing country among other nation-states. When China began the work of building a nation-state, it had already been reduced to a semi-colonial state. As a result, the first task was the struggle for national sovereignty. Without national sovereignty and state sovereignty, there could be no state-building. In addition, after achieving national sovereignty, the next question facing China's political elites was how to go about building a nation-state. As has been previously discussed, the Chinese identified with their culture, not with a nation. This meant that, even after winning national sovereignty, political methods needed to be employed to establish a political nation-state. In other words, the transition from traditional culturalism to modern nationalism was a political process, and it was this political process that gave rise to the nationalism of modern China.

On the international political stage, the primary characteristic of the Chinese people's pursuit of national sovereignty was the pursuit of sovereignty. Sovereignty means independence, autonomy, and equal status in the international community. It is the primary marker of a country's modernity. As soon as the concept of sovereignty entered China, it quickly exerted a tremendous impact on Chinese society. In a statistical analysis of the "Archives of the Qing Ministry of External Affairs, from 1875 to 1911," one Western scholar searched for the frequency of the concept of sovereignty and discovered that it had appeared in China as early as the 1860s. From 1875 to 1894, the term "sovereignty" only appeared about once per 100 pages of documents. From 1895 to 1899, it appeared 2.5 times per 100 pages; from 1890 to 1901, it appeared 8.8 times per 100 pages; from 1902 to 1910, it appeared about 22 times per 100 pages. In 1909, the frequency of usage reached its highest, with the term appearing on average 37 times per 100 pages. Sovereignty had not only become a new concept that Chinese scholars could use to analyze current events but was also being implemented in China's international affairs.[9] It can well be said that no concept has had such a profound impact on the political development of modern China as sovereignty, for sovereignty implies the existence of an independent nation-state. From Sun Yat-sen and Chiang Kai-shek to Mao Zedong, political figures, despite their differing political ideals and their differing views and approaches to questions about the kind of nation-state to be built and the means by which it was to be organized, had a great deal of common ground concerning the importance of the independent sovereignty of this nation-state.[10]

China's political elites agreed in their pursuit of national sovereignty, but they had different visions and strategies for how a new political nation-state was to be built. Not only did Western nationalism influence the Chinese concept of national sovereignty but it also influenced the Chinese concept of popular sovereignty. What's interesting is that, while Chinese had differing views on the role of the people in the construction of a nation-state, they all leaned toward statism. This is not to say, however, that Chinese nationalists rejected liberalism and democracy, but that the international context did not allow China to use liberal methods to construct a nation-state. When we say that popular sovereignty gave place to state sovereignty, we mean that priority was given to the state's power and not the individual's power in the process of creating and constructing a nation-state.

The ultimate incarnation of nationalism is the state, which centers a complete set of political institutions—but the Chinese understanding of these institutional forms of Western nationalism underwent a complex process. The Chinese first learned about the military institutions of the West and then about the West's political organizations. After the Western invasions of China, the weakness of traditional Chinese political organizations became obvious. By the middle of the nineteenth century, there was great concern within China concerning its future and even its survival. National revival became the most pressing priority. The Chinese discovery of Western military organizations and technology, known in historical circles as the Tongzhi Restoration of the 1860s, led in its turn to the Self-Strengthening Movement, which saw the beginning of the first stages of modernization. The Self-Strengthening Movement sought to strengthen the

9 John E. Schrecker, *Imperialism and Chinese Nationalism: Germany in Shantung* (Cambridge: Harvard University Press, 1971).

10 Mr. Liao Guangsheng offers a more detailed discussion of this. See Liao Guangsheng 廖光生, *Paiwai yu Zhongguo zhengzhi* 《排外与中国政治》 [Anti-Foreignism and Chinese Politics] (Taiwan: San Min Book Company, 1988).

country by cultivating talent that had both education in traditional morality and ability in modern politics, by training experts in the mastery of Western technology, and by organizing and planning construction efforts in fields such as the military, the economy, and diplomacy. But the Self-Strengthening Movement only aimed at reforming the military. At the time, elites did not have a strong grasp on the context and domestic political systems behind the West's power. This is understandable, for, on the international stage, Western nationalism was immediately visible in its military strength and military systems.

During the 1894–95 Sino-Japanese War, China was defeated by a Japan on the rise. Before the war, China's elites had believed that, as long as China had a strong military, it could resist the aggression of the great powers. The Sino-Japanese War demonstrated that the modernization of national defense and the military was not in itself capable of resisting foreign enemies who were superior to China in other respects. From government officials down to intellectuals, there was the feeling that the Self-Strengthening Movement was far from adequate for the creation of a strong nation-state. Political change had made Japan strong. If China were to be strong, it also needed to plan on political reform. Critics of the Self-Strengthening Movement believed that it hadn't erred in emphasizing state-building, but that it had neglected the state's base in the masses—and morality. Thus, it was necessary to carry out an ideological revival that could connect the emperor with the people. Only when the government and its officials were able to listen to the voice of the people and make decisions that expressed the people's will would there be hope for China's revival. Only then could China hope to compete with foreign powers on the international stage.

In the wake of the Sino-Japanese War, many sought to strengthen the state's connection to the people. On the one hand, such thinkers held that, if China were to catch up with Western nations, it must have a strong state. On the other hand, they also emphasized that the foundations of a strong state lie in the people. Wang Tao said that, of all the misfortunes in the world, the greatest was the people's lack of confidence in their rulers. China was misfortunate because there was no communication between the rulers and the governed; there was no relationship between sovereignty and the people. For Wang Tao, in order to combine the two, there had to be institutional reform, and this could only be affected by political means.[11] For Kang Youwei, on the other hand, while imperial power was important, the emperor's power base also needed reform. Without innovative reforms, the state's power could not be strengthened. Kang Youwei proposed that, in addition

11 Paul A. Cohen, *Between Tradition and Modernity: Wang Tao and Reform in Late Ch'ing China* (Cambridge: Harvard University Press, 1974).

to stressing the importance of reforms in fields such as the economy, the military, and education, attention must be paid to training the people—otherwise the state would lack a foundation.[12]

While there were many suggestions for reforming moribund national institutions and creating a new nation-state, in the midst of a harsh international context, the country was still fully in decline. By the time of the May Fourth Movement, many Chinese realized that political revolution alone could not make China strong; social and economic revolutions were also necessary. As various revolutionary ideologies spread, reform became impossible. And in many ways, revolution posed a contradiction to state-building, for revolution means that, in order to save the state, it must first be destroyed. But many of the ideologies that appeared around the time of the May Fourth Movement—ideologies like anarchism and federalism—eventually vanished, for they did not provide feasible solutions for building a nation-state. Only the nationalism of the Kuomintang and the early Communist Party survived, grew, and became systematized, eventually providing effective organizational structures for state-building.

Sun Yat-sen, Chiang Kai-shek, and Mao Zedong all emphasized using nationalism to save China, and their first efforts were to arouse nationalistic sentiments among the Chinese. Sun Yat-sen observed that the traditional loyalties of the Chinese lay with the clan and the household—while the traditional state could not govern, for it did not perform the functions of a state. Thus, the people's loyalty to the state was very weak. If the people's loyalty could not be transferred away from the clan and the family to the state or the government, the state would lack a psychological base in the people. Having a modern nation-state meant that the people were emotionally connected to the state. In other words, nationalist sentiments must be institutionalized as a support to the state—that is, nationalism must become an institution. And for citizens to have a sense of national identity or loyalty, there must first be a state.

Only a state as an organization could make nationalism an institution; only when nationalism was institutionalized could its political power be realized. The Chinese had a strong sense of family, but they lacked a group or collective consciousness, while nationalism is itself a collective consciousness, and the nation is itself a collective. Sun vividly compared China to a pile of sand on a plate. The Chinese people could only be called masses, not modern citizens. They were individuals, not a collective. Thus, the two overriding priorities were the formation

12 Michael H. Hunt, "Chinese National Identity and the Strong State: The Late Qing Republic Crisis," in *China's Quest for National Identity*, eds. Lowell Dittmer and Samuel S. Kim (Ithaca: Cornell University Press, 1993).

of a nationalistic national consciousness among the masses and the establishment of a state. In other words, after the state is first created, it must create a national consciousness or organize the national consciousness of the disorganized masses. Just how to organize Chinese nationalism was the most important political issue facing Chinese political elites from Sun Yat-sen to Mao Zedong.

In the early days of his revolutionary career, Sun Yat-sen gave greater emphasis to popular democracy, believing that a republic based on a Western multiparty system could provide an effective way for the people to participate in politics. But the ineffectiveness of the republican government established after the 1911 revolution prompted Sun Yat-sen to reconsider popular sovereignty. He realized that, without a strong political system, no form of democracy could help China build a strong state. Sun Yat-sen therefore turned to the organizational aspects of the nation-state.

Working from his understanding of Chinese society, Sun Yat-sen proposed a three-stage strategy to state-building: first, military government, then a government of training for constitutional government, and finally a constitutional government. But this sequencing was unable to consolidate the republic. After the October Revolution in Russia, Sun Yat-sen turned to the Soviet Union. The Soviet Union was the first country to break away from the capitalist system and establish a modern political system different from that of the West, and it had exerted a major influence on many Chinese—including Sun Yat-sen. For Sun, the appeal of the Soviet Union did not lie in Lenin's systematic treatment of issues surrounding nations and colonialism, but rather in the party organization of Leninism. In 1994, at the First National Congress of the Kuomintang, Sun emphasized that the Kuomintang (KMT) had to do two things: first, to reorganize the KMT, and second, to use the power of the KMT as a political power to transform the country. Transforming the country involved a vast number of areas: It was not limited to the government, but establishing a new kind of government was its first task. Establishing a party and using the party to transform the country was a completely new approach. The significance of applying this line of thought to nationalism was clear: China's first task was the organization of various political forces, or the institutionalization of political forces, and then the transformation or even reconstruction of a brand-new nation-state.

Organization and a political party became Sun's most effective weapons in building China's nation-state. He once made it clear that he "had always advocated governing the country through a party."[13] But in Sun, the concept of a party had

13 The Institute of Modern History of the Chinese Academy of Social Sciences, ed., *The Complete Works of Sun Yat-Sen*, vol. 8 (Beijing: Zhonghua Book Company, 1986), 281.

undergone a change. In his earlier years, he had copied his idea of using parties to govern a country from the West. For the younger Sun, political parties meant multiple parties in political competition. After Yuan Shikai's seizure of power, Sun wanted to use political parties to check Yuan's authoritarianism. Song Jiaoren organized the party and worked toward a parliamentary politics and a party-based cabinet. In the end, however, Song failed and was assassinated. As a result, Sun Yat-sen later advocated imitating the Soviet Union's political party, and he no longer advocated the party politics of the West. For Sun, the Russian Revolution was successful because "it put party above country." This "is also our model—that is, in Russia, a party completely governs the country. In this system, political parties hold more power than they do in Britain, America, or France." He also further observed that it was too early for China to be governed by a party, for the country was still in chaos and society in decline. Thus, "we currently have no state that we can govern; we can only say that the Party must build a state. Once a state is built, then we can govern it."[14]

The CCP is also committed to ruling the country with a party. In terms of the state's structure, there is not much that separates the KMT from the CCP. So why is it that the CCP was eventually able to replace the KMT and rule the country? This was primarily because the two parties used differing nationalist methodologies and strategies. The KMT employed an elitist strategy, relying on local elites and not the people. At the local level, the KMT excluded local people from the regime. As local elites failed to improve the lives of the local people and officials became corrupt, Chiang Kai-shek's regime, although highly centralized, was actually extremely fragile. In contrast, the CCP matured in the marginal regions of China. As most local elites had been brought into the fold of the KMT regime, the primary resources available to the CCP were the masses. This enabled the CCP to approach nationalist state-building from the bottom up.

As Joseph Whitney has observed, what was more important was that the KMT was not able to develop a nationalism that was understood and accepted by the common people. In other words, the KMT's ideology was aimed at elites within every class, and not at ordinary Chinese. As a ruling party, the KMT only emphasized the concentration of power, and it did not allow bottom-up political participation. Moreover, as the KMT was pursuing an urban-centered policy, it lacked the tools necessary for conveying its state-building ideology to the lowest levels of Chinese society. Unlike the KMT, the CCP successfully transmitted its ideology to the people through methods such as sending cadres to rural areas.[15]

14 Ibid., 103–4.

15 Joseph B. R. Whitney, *China: Area, Administration and Nation Building* (University of Chicago, Department of Geography Research, 1969).

From the foregoing discussion of the development of modern nationalism in China, we can observe the complexity of the interaction between nationalism and liberalism. As liberalism has always been an important part of nationalism, in the development of Western politics it was only when democratic thought and nationalism were combined that the latter won massive political power. Because Western nation-states were in a relatively peaceful international context during their development, democratic politics and the building of nation-states has been a relatively balanced process. Once democracy became an important principle in the building of nation-states, conflicts and wars among Western countries have only served to promote and strengthen democratic principles—for rulers must mobilize the people's resources through democratic principles.

The same has not been true for China. Faced with a harsh international environment, the most important issue facing political elites has been that of the nation's survival and the power of the state became much more important. Without the power of the state, the nation's survival was in jeopardy. Furthermore, as culturalism dominated traditional Chinese society and the people identified with their culture and not with the state, the role of political elites was only enhanced. They not only had to fight for national sovereignty but also had to create a nation-state and produce a sense national identity among the people. In this process, the power of the state superseded the power of the people. Thus, I argue that popular sovereignty was replaced by state sovereignty—that is, collective power superseded the political power of individuals. For it was only with the state's organization that the individual strength of the people could be gathered into a collective force; only this collective force could guarantee the survival of the nation. As the people are organized by the state, the state naturally ranks higher than the people, or society.

Popular sovereignty thus evolved into nationalism, with popular sovereignty taking secondary status. It's clear, however, that an antagonistic understanding of the relationship between popular sovereignty (or democracy) and nationalism ignores the complexity of the relationship. In the West, the nation-state represents the externalization of popular sovereignty, while in China, popular sovereignty could not be made to create a new nation-state. Thus, if the development of Western nation-states and Western democratic politics was a unified process, in China, the development of the two faced a problem of chronological precedence. In other words, political methods had to establish a nation-state first, and then the state could be adjusted in accordance with popular sovereignty. Just how the state can now reform itself to reflect popular sovereignty remains another matter that needs to be discussed.

Economic Development and the Building of the Nation-State

Among Western scholars who argue that China represents a threat, it is often claimed that China's leaders are using economic development to promote a revival of nationalism, which will pose a threat to the world order. Thus, we must discuss the relationship between economic development and nationalism—that is, the relationship between the economy and the nation-state.

There's nothing new in the idea that economic development will lead to a nationalistic revival. Scholars of international relations, from Marx to Lenin and even the contemporary realist school, have all emphasized that economic factors determine a country's international status. For example, Yale historian Paul Kennedy, in his celebrated *The Rise and Fall of the Great Powers*, holds that the impetus behind changes in international relations is economics and its related technological progress. He believes that economic and technological progress determine the imbalance in development among countries and that it thus influences every country's international standing; it determines whether a country poses a threat to another country.[16]

Why is it, then, that economic development drives a country's nationalism into imperialism (in which imperialism is the expression of a country's nationalism within the international community)? To begin with, the pursuit of economic interests is the highest priority for any country. If the existing structure of international relations cannot supply the economic interests of a country, it will do everything it can to change this structure. And the economic strength of a country determines whether it is capable of challenging the existing international order. Second, the hierarchical structure of international relations is ultimately determined by the economic base of the country. A country's economic growth reflects commensurate increases in its wealth and other resources. As a country's economic efficiency improves, its industrial structure and approach to international trade also change—which will also produce changes in its international actions. The reason why economic interests have become the most basic impetus behind international relations is primarily because there is a scarcity of global economic resources. If any country wants to survive, it needs to acquire more resources. Thus, every country wants to organize international relations in accordance with its own desires whenever possible.

16 Paul Kennedy, *The Rise and Fall of the Great Powers: Economic Change and Military Conflict from 1500 to 2000* (New York: Vintage Books, 1989).

But we need to go one step further and discuss how economic growth leads to a country's expansion, and whether economic growth itself contains enough power for this expansion. Economic determinists explain expansion in accordance with three main factors. The first is the development of economies of scale. Because an economy of scale can improve economic efficiency and reduce transaction costs, countries will do everything they can to expand their economies into other countries. The second factor is the internationalization of economic activity. Every country—particularly a large country—always wants to exploit other countries by controlling international relations, thereby forcing them to bear the cost of maintaining the status quo in international relations. The third factor is the law of diminishing returns. According to this law, if economic growth is to be maintained, all of the necessary elements in production must also increase proportionally; otherwise, economic output will decline. If this ratio cannot maintain a balance in the domestic market, new markets need to be opened internationally to supply domestic demand.

Although it's clear that these laws are primarily interpretations of phenomena associated with the development of the Western capitalist market economy, it's also true that these laws continue to play a role in the international relations of today. Yet the interpretation offered by economic determinism is not without its challengers. Princeton Professor Robert Gilpin also stresses the important influence of economic factors in international relations, but he goes on to find that international conflicts are closely associated with the organizational forms of a state.[17] Over the course of human history, we have experienced three main kinds of states: that is, various forms of localized politics, imperial politics, and the modern nation-state. One form replaces another form because the old form was unable to meet the demands of economic development.

For example, empires disappeared from the international political stage for three reasons. First, the rise of modern nation-states replaced the empire as the driver of international relations. Second, industrialization promoted transition in economic forms, and modern economic growth does not depend on an agricultural economy but on the development of science and technology. Third, there was the formation of a global market.

While Gilpin takes the form of a state into consideration, he still puts too much emphasis on the relationship between the economy and the state. In Gilpin, the economy still plays a major role, and the form of the state is only a reflection of economic development. This interpretation still does not help us understand the expansion of nationalism. We can boil down the question to the precise

17 Robert Gilpin, *War and Change in World Politics* (Cambridge: Cambridge University Press, 1981).

relationship between the organizational form of a country's domestic government and its international behavior.

Some German historians long ago observed that, on the one hand, external pressure exercises a decisive influence on the domestic structures of a country, and on the other hand, the internal organization of a country also has a major impact on the country's international behavior. For a country to succeed in international competition, it has to start with the establishment of effective national organizations.[18] There are also American scholars who study diplomatic behavior, especially war, by beginning with state systems. For example, Jack Snyder holds that war offers tremendous benefits for various domestic interest groups such as the military, diplomats, and big business; thus, these groups control the state's machinery and wage war to increase their own interests.[19] This theory is quite similar to Lenin's theory of imperialist expansion.

In fact, advocates of "threatism" can all find the substantiation for their arguments in the aforementioned theories. As early as the opening years of the 1990s, international organizations such as the World Bank used actual purchasing power to predict that China's economy would surpass Japan in the early years of the 2000s and become the world's second largest economy. This economic growth has meant that, on the one hand, those who emphasize the relationship between economic growth and nationalism see a potential influence of China's rapid economic growth on the global power structure. That is, China's economic strength will disrupt the status quo in international relations: With the growth in China's economic power, the nation's international ambition must necessarily grow with it. On the other hand, those who emphasize the government's influence on expansionism in nationalism believe that China's "non-democratic" government will exert a negative influence on international relations. In Western international relations theory, it is assumed that war will not occur between democratic countries. When this theory is extended to China, it will naturally pose a threat to the existing world order.

Here it should be noted that these theories are also controversial in the West's academic community. Regardless of whether these theories are correct, using them to explain Chinese nationalism has led to some severe misunderstandings, for these theories have been derived from Western experience, and they reflect

18 For example, Otto Hintze, "Military Organization and the Organization of the State", in Felix Gilbert (Editor), *The Historical Essays of Otto Hintze* (New York: Oxford University Press, 1975), 183.

19 Jack Snyder, *Myths of Empire: Domestic Politics and International Ambition* (Ithaca: Cornell University Press, 1991).

the developmental trajectory of Western nation-states. As a developing country, China has not and will not follow the same developmental trajectory experienced by Western nationalism. This is evident simply from the foregoing analysis of the evolution of modern Chinese nationalism. Furthermore, in comparison with Western nationalism, Chinese nationalism tends to react more than act. That is, it is not native and spontaneous but is a response to environmental changes. And this is true, first of all, because of China's international context. Nationalism is both "imported" and a response to "exporting countries." Secondly, China's nationalism is a response to changes in the domestic context. As nationalism was "imported," it necessarily exerted a tremendous impact on China's home-grown systems and institutions; at the same time, it also set off a chain reaction in those systems and institutions.

Seen in this light, the rise of Chinese nationalism in the 1990s was not due to the rapid growth of the national economy, although this growth did enable China to bring change to the status quo of international relations. Instead, the rise in Chinese nationalism was the product of two different responses.[20] The first was a response to pressure from the international community. Western society believed that China's economic rise was bound to challenge the status quo in the international order. Thus, beginning in the 1990s, theories of the "China threat" and "containing China" began to emerge one after the other. At the same time, to varying degrees, China was regarded as an imaginary enemy in the practice of international relations.

It should be pointed out that these changes in the West were a response to China's economic development, a response that was itself based in the West's own developmental experience. But this response in turn set off the rise of Chinese nationalism. If we consider the differences in the popular mood between the 1980s and the 1990s, we can clearly observe the reactive side of this nationalism. In the 1980s, the Chinese generally entertained positive feelings about the Western world, and the entirety of Chinese society called for "learning from the West." But since the outset of the 1990s, as Western societies brought pressure on China, the public no longer entertained fantasies about the West; instead, the intellectual climate was rampant with nationalistic criticism. This could particularly be seen in response to the series of "anti-China" books and articles published in the United States.

20 For a detailed discussion, see Yongnian Zheng, *Discovering Chinese Nationalism in China: Modernization, Identity and International Relations* (Cambridge: Cambridge University Press, 1999).

Equally importantly, Chinese nationalism was also a response to China's domestic problems. The economic reforms started under Deng Xiaoping brought, on the one hand, rapid economic growth, but on the other hand, they also caused many negative effects. Because the main focus of reform in the 1980s was decentralization, the Chinese government's capacity—particularly in the economic domain—experienced a significant decline. This has been the subject of the so-called "crisis in state capacity" that has been debated in the mainland since the early 1990s.

As rapid economic growth does indeed pose serious challenges to the old nation-state system, without effective responses to these challenges, the survival of a unified nation-state will be brought into question. Under these circumstances, many scholars have called once again for re-building the nation-state, and a wide variety of political philosophies have emerged. In this context, nationalism has become one of the major schools of thought.

Chinese nationalism is a response to the new international and domestic environment. Western scholars, on the other hand, have reached almost the opposite conclusion: The rise of nationalism means that, with its growth in economic power, China has begun to use its "muscle" to test its power. This misunderstanding is widely prevalent in the West. Most obviously, political figures often deliberately misunderstand Chinese nationalism in pursuit of their own political interests. But why is this true of academia as well? Many people are influenced by their emotions, and when they view Chinese nationalism, they bring many emotional elements to their understanding. More importantly, in analyzing China, they have brought with them preexisting Western concepts. Sociology should not be divorced from useful concepts, but concepts also have their own cultural and historical backgrounds. When the concepts developed within a Western context are used to approach Chinese questions, such misunderstandings will be inevitable.

The Future of Chinese Nationalism

We have discussed the complexity of Chinese nationalism from an academic perspective. Here we need to re-emphasize several important issues that were raised above. To begin with, Chinese nationalism is not a reflection of China's economic power, and economic growth does not necessarily lead to an outward expansionism. On the contrary, if China's economic development has served to promote nationalism, it is only because economic development has damaged pre-existing systems, thereby threatening the old institutions and structures of the nation-state. Second, Chinese nationalism is not necessarily antagonistic to democracy (popular sovereignty). Quite the contrary, not only is it true that the two can be complementary but nationalism can even play a role in advancing democratic politics. Third, Chinese nationalism is a response to external pressure. The level of internal nationalism depends on the amount of external pressure. Fourth, for nation-states on the international stage, the level of organization within nationalism is just as important as economic development. Economic growth itself does not turn into international power. If economic power cannot be organized into the power of the nation-state, it cannot play a role in the international arena. In the same way, where there is no sound political system that can organize economic power, nationalism can only remain at the level of the emotions.

These preliminary conclusions also indicate the developmental future of Chinese nationalism. While we must oppose the use of Western concepts to explain Chinese nationalism, we must also be clear that Chinese nationalism has a long way to go. Clearly, nationalism is about China's construction and not about an emotional response to international pressure. In other words, emotional responses are inevitable, but they are not what makes nationalism. At the beginning of this chapter, it was clearly stated that the essence of nationalism lies in providing an institutional foundation for the nation-state. This is why the various revolutions in modern China from Sun Yat-sen to Mao Zedong all sought to establish such an institutional foundation. Without this institutional foundation, the nation-state cannot survive.

It should also be observed that, while seeking an institutional foundation for the nation-state, many elements of nationalism have been rearranged, with some getting prioritized and others being assigned secondary status. When state power is supreme, popular sovereignty can only take the subordinate position. Now, after many battles, China has not only won its national sovereignty but also created an institutional foundation for the nation-state. But nationalism has not yet completed its task, and the institutional foundations of the nation-state need further consolidation and strengthening. During this process, just how to restructure the relationship between state power and popular sovereignty is going to become more important.

Furthermore, the precise ways in which the nation-state can be adapted to new circumstances, and enable the people to enter the national political process, will become the major concern for Chinese nationalism in the future. At the same time, in international politics, nationalist feeling must be transformed into a force for domestic construction, into a sense of identification with the nation-state. Without this transformation, the state will not have a consistent set of nationally beneficial principles for international relations. It will only get momentary bursts of national pride.

CHAPTER ELEVEN

Rural Democracy and the Chinese Political Process

> Class consciousness is grounded in social communication, while the *de facto* and *de jure* inequalities of various classes under the state have further strengthened rural class consciousness. And it is this class consciousness constructed by society that is often more effective than the class consciousness formed by the state's mobilization. What's most important is that rural democracy gradually uses institutionalized forms to fill the institutional vacuum that emerged after the retreat of state power, and this effectively prevents the multiplication of other localized institutions.

In discussions of China's modernization and political development, we must not ignore questions regarding the relationship between farmers and democracy. From a world-historical perspective, peasants (farmers) have essentially been a force against the modernization and democratization of the state. However, because every country begins modernizing at its own historical moment, and because the institutional environments that pre-existed modernization have also differed from one another, it is difficult to understand the modernization of any country with a general theory of the relationship between farmers and democracy. The role of a particular class in the modernization of an earlier developing country is likely to be different from that of one in a later-developing country. Thus, while peasants have not played a positive role in the democratization of European and American countries, this does not mean that they cannot play a positive role in developing countries and serve to help promote democracy.

This chapter seeks to explore the questions around the relationship between farmers and democracy through the case of Chinese rural democracy since the reforms of 1978. We are going to argue two basic points. First, we will argue that the development of rural democracy has given shape to the class consciousness of China's farmers. Owing to the constant organization of their political life, China's peasant class has, unlike peasant classes in earlier-developing countries, become a constructive force in the democratization of China. Second, we will argue that the fact that rural democracy has been given priority in development among all other classes and social strata in China has largely determined the path available to Chinese democratization and its future development.

Peasants and Democracy

There is no place for peasants in existing Western theories of democracy, for modern Western democracies emerged after the Industrial Revolution, and it was the bourgeoisie, not peasants, who served as the founders of democracy. As a result, the major theories about democratic development offer us little in understanding the role that peasants can play in the process of democratization.

Out of the great mass of theories about democratic development, three can prove of great benefit in helping us understand what democracy means. The first theory holds that democracy as a form of government can only be generated amidst markets and capitalist economies. The second theory emphasizes that democracy can only survive and develop in rich and economically developed societies. The third theory holds that whether democracy can emerge and develop depends on the preexistence of a tradition of political compromise and mechanisms that restrict central power. Below, I'd like to offer a brief discussion regarding the internal logic of these three theories.

Let's begin with the first theory. Among contemporary scholars, Lindblom, Huntington, and Moore all agree that there is a historical and logical relationship between capitalism and democracy.[1] In their research on the development of Western democratic politics, they have discovered that rise of the industrial bourgeoisie enabled countries to transition successfully into democracies. As an economic system based on private ownership, capitalism provides a mechanism

1 Charles E. Lindblom, *Politics and Markets: The World's Political Economic Systems* (New York: Basic Books, 1977); Samuel P. Huntington, "Will More Countries Become Democratic?" *Political Science Quarterly* 99, no. 2 (Summer 1984), 193–218; Barrington Moore, *Social Origins of Dictatorship and Democracy: Lord and Peasant in the Making of the Modern World* (Boston: Beacon, 1966).

for restricting state power and producing a private sphere separate from the public sphere. And the separation of public and private spheres is a necessary condition for democracy as a form of limited government.

The second theory emphasizes the positive correlation between democracy and economic development and argues that democracy is not a "native species" peculiar to capitalist, industrialized countries.[2] This theory emphasizes that, once democracy is introduced, industrialized capitalism will provide it with a favorable institutional environment. But why is an industrial society conducive to democracy? Here, American political scientists believe that industrial capitalist societies are relatively wealthy, at least economically speaking, and this helps reduce political conflict among different groups of elites, within groups of elites themselves, and between politics and the general public. Again, in these societies, political struggles are not "zero-sum games."[3] Economic prosperity provides a baseline for power struggles among political elites, and it is this baseline that proves critical for the stability of a democracy. For if elites bet their lives on political power, then a democracy will overflow with violence.

The third theory argues that the emergence of democratic institutions can be attributed to a tradition that is conducive to democracy.[4] In Great Britain, for example, the feudal systems of medieval Britain actually laid the foundations for the democracy that was to follow. Such a tradition gives the politically powerful a mindset that tolerates differing systems of political interest, and this mindset is essential for democracy.

Moore's analysis of the incompatibility of agricultural society with democracy is the most widely known, but the focus of his analysis was on the role of peasants and landowners in the process of democratization. According to Moore's theory, socialist revolutions occurred in countries that had high population density, a weak bourgeoisie, landlord classes that depended on political rights granted to them by the state, and opportunities for collective action that arose from weakened relations between the peasant class and the landlord class. Moore's analysis here also includes China. But why is it that China didn't move toward a democratic

2 For the most famous exposition, see Seymour M. Lipset, "Some Social Requisites of Democracy: Economic Development and Political Legitimacy," *The American Political Science Review* 53 (1959): 69–105.

3 In addition to Lipset, see Karl Deutsch, "Social Mobilization and Political Development," *The American Political Science Review* 55 (September 1961): 493–514; Alex Inkles, "Participant Citizenship in Six Developing Countries," *The American Political Science Review* 63 (December 1969): 1120–41.

4 For example, Reinhard Bendix, *Kings or People: Power and the Mandate to Rule* (Berkeley: University of California Press, 1978).

revolution or a socialist revolution? The answer is that although China's peasant class had a weak relationship with the landlord class, and it had a certain amount of independence and democratic potential, the landlord class's use of state power prevented peasants from finding an opportunity to develop a class consciousness or engage in the collective action that could lead to a bottom-up socialist revolution.[5]

Recently, some comparative research has begun to challenge mainstream theories about democracy, and re-evaluate the relationship between peasants and democratization. This comparative research has found that whether the peasant class or the rural middle class play an active role in democratization depends largely on their ability to form autonomous organizations and resist the influence of the ruling class. In countries where landlord classes are very strong, peasants tend toward authoritarianism, whereas agricultural workers in family-oriented countries tend to be the promoters of democracy. An even more important finding of these researchers is that class consciousness is not a purely objective thing: It has a highly subjective element.[6] Thus, the formation of a class consciousness does not depend entirely on the class itself but also on other factors, such as the relationship between the state and the peasant class, the interactions between peasants and urban residents, and the development of education.

The New Characteristics of Chinese Farmers

To summarize, among many theories of democracy, the theory about the relationship between farmers and democracy is in a relatively poor state, and the comparative political theory we currently have cannot easily explain China's rural development. Thus, in order to interpret the development of rural China, we must develop a theory about peasants and politics that is grounded in China's realities. Rural policy under Deng Xiaoping changed the lives of China's farmers, differentiating them from both those of traditional peasants and of those in most Western countries. Below we will make only a few observations that touch on the intimate relationship between farmers and democratic politics.

In comparison with other classes in China, the peasant class has had greater independence. This independence wasn't part of traditional China itself but came with state action. The Land Reform Movement of the early 1950s eliminated

5 In addition to Moore, see Jeffrey M. Paige, *Agrarian Revolution: Social Movements and Export Agriculture in the Underdeveloped World* (New York: Free Press, 1975).

6 For example, Dietrich Rueschemeyer, Evelyne H. Stephens and John D. Stephen, *Capitalist Development and Democracy* (Chicago: University of Chicago Press, 1992).

China's landlord class, severing any dependency of China's peasants on that class. Rural areas no longer had a ruling class. Moreover, China's initial industrialization was directed by the state. This meant that Chinese peasants no longer depended on the state either. Instead, because industrialization was based on the premise of sacrificing the interests of peasants, the state's actions created a new dependent class: the working class. At the same time, they also created an independent class, the peasant class. This also strained relations between the state and peasants. At various times over subsequent years, peasants would go on to pose a threat (whether explicit or implicit) to the state's power. In other words, China's industrialization increased the independence of the peasant class, and peasants as a class were not assimilated by the state.

The decentralization-focused reform movement greatly deepened the independence of the peasant class and gave it institutionalized autonomy. At the heart of rural reforms was the reduction of the scope of the state's control over rural areas. This contraction of state control created some institutional space that was filled by the rural autonomy system. Although current basic-level organizations are still deeply influenced by and restricted by Mao-era institutions, their revival has been the result of farmers' autonomy. In this sense, China's rural areas are moving toward privatization, and privatization is at the essence of autonomy.

The results of reform have strengthened the level of organization among China's farmers. After the state's power was withdrawn, farmers were forced to reorganize their own lives. Although the system has not developed evenly across different regions, every region has seen the development of various autonomous organizations—especially in democratic institutions such as village assemblies. The development of urbanization within rural areas (as in the development of small towns) has not turned farmers into true urban residents, but the rapid development of rural markets has forged connections between communities across the country. In addition, the increase in social mobility (as with the migrant population) has also strengthened farmers' sense of identity as a greater community or class.

The results of this organization have led to class consciousness. In the increasing number of interactions they have with other classes (such as with urban residents), farmers have developed a "who am I?" sense of personal identity and a "who we are?" sense of collective identity. Class consciousness is grounded in social communication, while the *de facto* and *de jure* inequalities of various classes under the state have further strengthened rural class consciousness. And it is this class consciousness constructed by society that is often more effective than the class consciousness formed by the state's mobilization.

It is the class consciousness and collective identity among farmers that provide the foundations for group behavior. For democracy is not merely individual behavior; it is much more class behavior. The most successful instance of giving shape to the peasant class's group behavior can be found in the pre-1949 Mao Zedong.[7] After reform, the rapid development of rural self-government has been building an institutional framework for farmers' collective action. The collective action that the farmers of several Sichuan counties took in 1993 reflected these new characteristics of the farming class in many ways. Rural elections had been held in Sichuan's Renshou County as early as the 1980s, but most of them were merely a formality. Farmers lacked the opportunity to truly express their own wishes, and local officials still set quotas for the farmers in accordance with their own wills. From the perspective of local cadres, they were completely focused on the needs of local residents. However, their decisions did not involve local participation, and they lacked transparency. Finally, on June 5, 1993, a storm broke as thousands of farmers protested in collective action against local governments. Local governments immediately responded with force. The antagonisms between farmers and local governments were now on full display.

The movement quickly spread to the surrounding areas, with nearby counties such as Bazhong, Wanyuan, Nanjiang, and Santai all seeing collective action. The provincial government and the central government quickly intervened, releasing the farmers' leaders and abolishing some of the problematic local regulations. Interestingly enough, in Renshou County's neighboring Pengshan County, the local government was collecting proportionately much more in taxes than in Renshou. But since Pengshan County was a pilot county for rural autonomy in Sichuan, and its rural democracy was already relatively well in place, farmers did respond sharply to the government's actions. This demonstrates that democratically based government decisions, even when there was some compulsoriness to their implementation, had found greater acceptance among farmers. Thus, after this incident, the Sichuan provincial government decided to extend the Pengshan County experience to other counties with the hope of creating a new order and environment.

The relations we are discussing between China's farmers and democracy have been undergoing a variety of transitions precisely like the one just outlined. In the process of democratization, then, just how are farmers to relate to the state? Various current theories in comparative politics have emphasized that the important question is whether the farmers can act as an autonomous force that shares political rights with the state. However, during the process of democratization,

7 It should be pointed out that, except for a few intellectuals like Mao who made peasants the focus of revolutionary theory, Chinese intellectuals have rarely focused on the importance of peasants in their theories regarding the construction of China. At present this remains true.

farmers do not necessarily have to come into conflict with the state. I think that taking a unique approach to democratizing rural China will ease tensions between farmers and the state, and the two will eventually be able to cooperate with each other within an institutional framework. It is in this sense that we can say that rural democracy is in the process of advancing democratization for the entire country. And this is what we intend to discuss next.

Forms of Basic-Level Organization in Rural China

The current system of rural democracy in China takes its form from the commune committees and commune congresses of rural production cooperatives and production brigades. In 1987, the central government stipulated that the objective for village committees was the expansion of villagers' democratic rights under the people's commune system. At the village level (that is, at the level of the production brigades), commune committees were abolished, and village committees similar to the old commune congresses were established, allowing villagers to exercise direct decision-making in village affairs. At present, rural democracy in China consists of three interconnected institutional forms: the village assemblies (*cunmin dahui*), village representative assemblies (*cunmin dabiao dahui*), and villagers' committees (*cunmin weiyuanhui*). Let's take a look at how these three forms relate to each other.

According to the Organic Law of Village Committees, the village assembly is the highest decision-making body for village self-government, and major matters in the village must be decided by the village assembly. In principle, the members of the village assembly are directly elected by villagers and manage the village's daily affairs: The assembly is the "administrative organ" of the village. However, in actual performance, the village assemblies are not very efficient. Institutionally speaking, the current village assemblies and villagers' committees are based on the pre-reform production brigade system; this was characterized by a large scale and a large population. Generally speaking, a village assembly has jurisdiction over one to three thousand people, with the largest reaching eight to nine thousand. With such a large population to manage, village assemblies tend toward more formalism.

This problem is compounded by geographical factors, as rural residents are scattered across large areas. After Reform and Opening Up, many villagers have become migrant workers who work in other parts of the country, making it difficult for the village assemblies to organize. Furthermore, some matters that, in principle, should be decided by village assemblies are actually controlled by the Party's village committees, so the villagers are not actually participating in the political process. Under these circumstances, the villages of many regions have seen institutional innovation in which the village representative assemblies have emerged. This has transformed the direct democracy laid down by the central government into an indirect democracy. When it is hard to convene a village assembly, village representative assemblies implement decision-making on the village assembly's behalf. According to statistics from the Ministry of Civil Affairs, by 1994, more than half of the country's villages had established village representative assemblies. At the same time, the central government also recognized the legitimacy of this system.

What then is the democratic basis for the village representative assemblies? This depends on the relationship of the representative assembly with its villagers. According to research by the Ministry of Civil Affairs, there are currently three major ways of constituting village representative assemblies: First, the village representative assembly is composed only of villagers directly elected by other villagers; second, the assembly is composed of representatives elected by the village and other representatives selected by the county and township people's congresses; and third, the assembly is composed of representatives elected by the village, other representatives elected by the county and township people's congresses, and the secretary of the village Party committee. Thus, the way village representative assemblies are formed differs from place to place. Generally speaking, candidates are nominated by villager groups convened by a previous session of the village committee, and they are then elected as formal representatives by either a show of hands or secret ballot. In summary, village representative assemblies are not produced through a strictly democratic process, but they more or less reflect the traditional and pre-reform institutional environment of rural China.[8]

The functions of the village representative assemblies are mostly modeled on the powers of the people's congresses at all levels. The power of congresses comes under four heads: legislative power, decision-making power over major matters, control over personnel, and supervisory power. Other than legislative power, the other three powers can all be found in village representative assemblies, while legislative power has evolved into the power of the village assembly and village representative assembly to determine village regulations and non-governmental agreements. The year 1988 saw the first general election for rural villagers' committees nationwide. By 1992, more than twenty provinces, cities, and autonomous regions had held the second round of general elections. By the end of 1992, there were 1,004,399

8 For an introduction to rural village representative assemblies, see Zhongguo jiceng zhengquan yanjiu hui 中国基层政权研究会 [The Institute for Chinese Basic-Level Government] and Zhongguo nongcun cunmin zizhi zhidu yanjiu ketizu 中国农村村民自治制度研究课题组 [Task Force on China's System of Rural Village Autonomy], *Zhongguo nongcun cunmin diabiao huiyi zhidu* 《中国农村村民代表会议制度》[China's Rural Village Representative Assemblies] (Beijing: Chinese Society Publishers, 1994).

villagers' committees across the country. There were 43,088,780 members of these committees.[9]

Let's now turn to the "administrative organs" of autonomous rural villages, the villagers' committees, and the relations between villagers' committees and villagers. According to the 1982 constitution, rural villagers' committees are basic-level autonomous organizations, and the chairman, vice chairman, and committee members are elected by villagers. As the 1987 Organic Law of Villagers' Committees (Pilot) stipulates, the committee chairman, vice chairman, and other committee members should be directly elected by villagers. Simply put, the relationship between villagers and the villagers' committees is the relation between the elector and the elected. It is this institutional element that shows us that villagers' committees are actually an institutional expression of Chinese rural democracy. And it is also the existence of this system of regular elections that makes today's basic-level organizations different from those of the pre-reform days. Thus, the effectiveness of this electoral system directly demonstrates the effectiveness of rural democracy.

Rural Democracy and the Construction of the Nation-State

Here, we will focus on how rural democracy promotes the progress of Chinese politics. This is not to suggest that China's democratization can only begin in rural areas—we only want to emphasize that if China's political progress does not include farmers, it will be hard for China to achieve democratization. This does not mean, however, that other classes or social strata are unimportant.

China is currently building a nation-state, and democracy will eventually become a component of this nation-state. To be specific, the modern nation-state is the product of the interactions between national sovereignty and popular sovereignty. Without democracy, it is difficult to have a modern nation-state. In the process of spreading democracy from earlier developing countries to later developing countries, however, the two kinds of sovereignty were separated from each other, and national sovereignty gradually achieved dominance, while popular sovereignty was transformed into state sovereignty. The main reason behind this was the status of later developing countries within the international system.

If we judge from the history of global modernization, the development of democracy in various regions and countries has been extremely uneven. This

9 Ibid., 3.

imbalance has often meant that the state plays a greater role in the democratization of later developing countries than it did in earlier developing countries. In later developing countries, the state was not only charged with the task of political transition but also had to bear the burdens of socioeconomic transition. And later developing countries were often at a disadvantage within the international system. Thus, it was not enough for the state to pursue rapid domestic development—it had to survive international competition.[10]

The modern nation-state demands not only that its inhabitants become the political animals that Aristotle spoke of but also that every member of society be included in the political process through political participation. Citizenship demands that citizens have a sense of national identity. And here it should be said that the CCP's struggle to build a nation-state in the early days after the founding of the People's Republic were quite successful. This is primarily evident in the Party's centralization of political power and its expansion of the scope of the state to every member of society. Under Mao Zedong, the CCP established a system of effective peasant-centered revolutionary theory, while the Party transmitted its ideas to the peasants through means such as sending cadres to rural areas. This laid the foundations for the political mobilization of the peasants. The CCP's state-building was implemented through top-down coercive mobilization, and this was the key to its success.[11]

From 1949 to 1978, this mobilized "democratic construction" involved the greatest possible mobilization of the people's participation in every aspect of political and social life, and every few years another round of political struggle had to be initiated to strengthen such participation. This mobilized participation was also institutionalized. People's communes became the basic-level organization for rural areas. This institutionalization of mobilization spread downwards into production brigades and production teams. Farmers became commune members (*she yuan*)—that is, members of an organization. The consequences of this military-communistic, organizational mobilization directly contributed to the pre-reform economic crisis. In the political realm, excessive mobilization and the infinite expansion of the state's scope actually reduced the effectiveness of state power.

10 For further discussion of this topic and its relevance for China, see Yongnian Zheng, "Development and Democracy: Are They Compatible in China?" *Political Science Quarterly* 109, no. 2 (Summer 1994): 235–59.

11 For a discussion of this, see Joseph B. Whitney, *China: Area, Administration and Nation Building* (Chicago: University of Chicago, 1970); Chalmers A. Johnson, *Peasant Nationalism and Communist Power* (Stanford: Stanford University Press, 1962); Paul A. Cohen, "Post Mao Reforms in Historical Perspective," *Journal of Asian Studies* 47, no. 3 (1988): 519–41.

What concerns this chapter is that, today, decentralization has not only provided the impetus for China's modernization but has also led to many different problems. So, should we use centralization to solve these problems? Should China's construction of a nation-state be carried out through a top-down mass democracy? In a nutshell, what kind of nation-state do we want to build in China?

China's reforms have been dominated by decentralization. This can be seen in the relationship between the state and society. First of all, there was a retreat in the scope of the state—that is, society moved from excessive to low-level mobilization. Through economic decentralization, local and individual economic forces were also brought into play. At the same time, rural residents also established a system of autonomy—that is, rural democracy—and they have begun what can be truly said to be a local democratic life.

To a certain extent, however, decentralization has created an obstacle to the rebuilding of the Chinese nation-state—this obstacle is the shrunken scope of the state. A nation-state needs every member of society to become an "imperial person" (*huang min*)—it needs a local awareness to become a national consciousness. Now, in a certain sense, decentralization is the institutional retreat of state power. Not only has the state relaxed political control over localities and local residents but it has also in fact abandoned some of the systems that represent and symbolize the state—systems like the cooperative medical system and the educational system.

With decentralization, economic development has not been even across various regions, and institutional development is still extremely imbalanced. It is also difficult for the central government to coordinate the development of various regions with a unified policy. Thus, it is hard to say that all of the country's residents live within a common nation-state. In fact, they live under different local political systems. This has allowed local officials and local residents to develop a strong sense of local identity or local consciousness, while their national consciousness has been relatively weakened.

These are indeed major issues in nation-state construction, and these problems are only getting worse with reforms to the political system. But must we use top-down, centralized mobilization to destroy some of these newly born local systems and thereby politicize China once again. Must we recreate a politicized nation? We have previously rejected this idea from the perspective of central-local relations. Here we will attempt to give it further discussion in connection with the new system of rural democracy.[12]

12 Wu Guoguang 吴国光 and Zheng Yongnian 郑永年, *On Central and Local Relations: An Axial Issue in China's Institutional Transformation* (Hong Kong: Oxford University Press, 1995).

First, no matter the path of political development that we choose, political stability will always be the most important premise of that political development. This is the only place where the state and society will both agree on. Besides, using top-down mobilization to create a political democracy often ends up in authoritarianism (as was previously discussed), and mobilization is itself an unstable material to work with. High degrees of political mobilization often lead to political turmoil, for it is almost impossible for developing countries to rapidly achieve the high degree of institutionalization that can absorb the unstable elements released by political mobilization. There is always a major chronological disparity between the mobilization of participation and institutionalization.[13] On the other hand, centralized power often leads to a situation in which the state monopolizes economic resources, thereby inviting corruption among government officials. And corruption leads to tensions between the state and society. Thus, a distinction needs to be made between centralization and state capacity. There is no necessary connection between the two.

But let's turn back to Chinese rural democracy. Rural democracy can help maintain China's current political stability in many ways, and it also offers an extremely institutionalized method of achieving this stability. To begin with, the emergence of rural democracy has created a buffer zone between the state and farmers, one that avoids direct confrontations between the state and rural society. Without the villagers' committees and village assemblies, issues like family planning and taxation (that cadres cannot solve) would have to be resolved by higher-level government agencies with forceful diktat. Villagers' committees and village representative assemblies, however, are elected democratically, and their power has greater legitimacy than that of higher-level governments. Second, while rural democracy cannot eliminate corruption altogether, it can effectively curb it. Since village committees are regularly elected and one of the functions of the representative assemblies is economic supervision, the economic behavior of the village committees needs to be transparent and open. Under this electoral system, property is "public," for without the approval of villagers, minorities cannot use or abuse properties. In addition, since rural democracy is an effective mechanism for recruiting local elites, it reduces factors that could lead to political instability. What's most important is that rural democracy gradually uses institutionalized forms to fill the institutional vacuum that emerged after the retreat of state power, and this effectively prevents the multiplication of other localized institutions.

13 Samuel P. Huntington, *Political Order in Changing Societies* (New Haven: Yale University Press, 1968).

While rural democracy only occurs at the most basic level of China, it is nevertheless an effective place for training a civic spirit.

Second, rural democracy has become an institutional structure that cultivates a civil spirit and is laying the foundations for Chinese political nationality. Recent research has shown that nation-states are in reality a kind of "imagined community,"[14] and it is only residents with a civic spirit that hold them in their imagination. Civic spirit can only be generated in the face-to-face interactions of local communities.

In many ways, China's rural democracy is helping to develop this spirit. To begin with, since the representatives of the villager representative assemblies are elected by differing "constituencies" or groups, they represent the interests of the constituencies and groups they belong to. Since electoral districts are not divided in accordance with traditional units such as families or relatives, village representative assemblies have actually helped in breaking through the limitations of traditional organizations, and delegates have been liberated from these traditional organizations, while new groups (that is, voters) have been formed. In addition, direct village elections are changing villagers' political consciousness. As rural China has experienced two different direct elections for village committees, and voting is no longer mandatory as it was previously, the attitude of villagers toward voting has changed greatly. In one survey, when asked, "Do the cadres on village committees need to be directly elected?", answers were distributed as follows: 80.4% answered, "They need to be elected"; 10.8% answered, "They do not need to be elected; they can be appointed by the township or village party cadres"; and 6.7% answered, "Regardless of whether they are elected, it has nothing to do with me anyway." When they were asked, "Are village committee elections just a formality? Do they mean anything?", answers were distributed as follows: 62.6% answered, "It's not just a formality; elections are very important"; 22.3% answered, "Elections are a formality, but they do have some value"; and 11% answered, "Elections are only a formality; they don't have any value."[15] Again the voting behavior of villagers has also changed greatly. Since village elections are directly connected to the interests of villagers, they have added motivation to vote. According to a Ministry of Civil Affairs survey on voting behavior during the second general election, participation

14 Benedict Anderson, *Imagined Communities: Reflections on the Origin and Spread of Nationalism* (London: Verso, 1991).

15 Zhongguo jiceng zhengquan yanjiu hui 中国基层政权研究会 [The Institute for Chinese Basic-Level Government] and Zhongguo nongcun cunmin zizhi zhidu yanjiu ketizu 中国农村村民自治制度研究课题组 [Task Force on China's System of Rural Village Autonomy], *Zhongguo nongcun cunmin diabiao huiyi zhidu* 《中国农村村民代表会议制度》 [China's Rural Village Representative Assemblies] (Beijing: Chinese Society Publishers, 1994), 9–10.

rates averaged above 80%.[16] Since there was a secret ballot, even when villagers were compelled to vote, they could still complete their ballots as they chose. When asked, "What is it that brought you to vote?", 4.5% answered, "Village cadres made us go vote"; 4.7% answered, "Everyone was going to vote, so I came too"; and 88% responded, "Voting is my right, and I want to cast my vote seriously."[17]

Third, rural democracy is increasingly driving China's overall process of democratization. It's clear that rural democracy is gradually reducing the amount of political coercion in state power. Regular elections prevent village committees from governing as they please. They must administer the village in accordance with village law (village regulations and non-governmental agreements); otherwise, committee leadership will lose its legitimacy, and their "political career" will end with the next round of elections. This has proven effective, not only for village committees but also for higher-ranking government officials.

In the traditional system, village cadres were only tools used to execute directives issued by higher authorities. Now higher-ranking officials are gradually finding it more difficult to dismiss the elected members of village committees, for doing so will arouse the ire of villagers. Take one example. In Jiangsu province, a conflict between an important township cadre and a village committee chairman within his jurisdiction led the township government to try to dismiss the village chairman. However, since the chairman had been elected in a general election in accordance with the Organic Law of Villagers' Committees (Pilot), the township government's actions drew villagers' ire. The village chairman appealed to the county court, sued the township government, and won his case. It is because of this that, while China's political system is highly hierarchical, it also features what we call "sagging legitimacy." That is to say, lower-level officials are elected by the people, so they possess democratic legitimacy; higher-level officials are based in traditional legitimacy (that is, in their appointments) and lack a base in public opinion. Thus, tensions develop between differing tiers of government. Because the leadership of lower-level governments has a stronger base among the masses, and thus a greater legitimacy than the governments above them, the higher-level government cannot change their decisions, while the lower-level government can exert the pressure of legitimacy on higher-level governments. The solution to this tension is either the abolition of existing rural democracy or the acquisition of greater legitimacy through additional democratization.

The moment rural democracy came into being, it gained a great deal of traction and performed many of the indispensable functions of political governance.

16 Ibid., 89.
17 Ibid., 90.

Abolishing rural democracy now seems virtually impossible. If there is to be further democratization, then the legitimacy of higher-level governments will also need to be based in democracy.

Summing Up

The rapid economic development resulting from decentralization has given China another opportunity to rebuild the nation-state. But just how the nation-state should be rebuilt is a subject worthy of further study. As a developing country, China needs to maintain its long-term economic development, and it also needs institutional political stability. In addition, democratization is one of the goals that needs to be achieved in state-building. The answers to the problems that have arisen since decentralization go far beyond the traditional dispute between "decentralization" and "centralization."

The process of building a nation-state is a process of both centralizing and decentralizing power. It is a process of decentralization because the decentralization is institutionalized: that is, the current and recently built institutions that can help in state-building (for example, rural democracy) should be institutionalized through nationwide laws, thereby promoting further democratization and achieving a certain amount of decentralization. It is a process of centralization, not because the state is using social mobilization to destroy the newly formed local institutions, but because the state itself is strengthening its political legitimacy through institutional reforms, because the state strengthens state capacity, and because new institutions of legitimacy enable the state's policies to reach every member of society, thereby fostering a national consciousness among every individual in society. A cooperative approach between higher- and lower-level governments—at least in the case of rural democracy—seems to be on the table.

CHAPTER TWELVE

What China Needs to Learn from the Singapore Model

The decentralization of power is not a good in itself. The key is how power is concentrated and, after it is concentrated, what is done with it. In that respect, Singapore has experience that China should take into account. This experience addresses the following key questions: How do political parties organize power? How is power maintained? How is power wielded effectively? To a large extent, many aspects of the Singaporean experience discussed are manifestations of Singapore's political system. Without an understanding of this political system, it's hard to understand how these specific systems came about in the first place.

Can We Learn from Singapore?

Is there anything China can learn from Singapore? I ask this question because the answer isn't always clear. On the one hand, since Deng Xiaoping, Chinese leadership has attached great importance to Singapore's experience. During his 1992 Southern Tour, Deng himself specifically emphasized studying Singapore's experience with economic development and social governance. Since then, many national leaders, including Jiang Zemin, Zhu Rongji, Zeng Qinghong, and Wen Jiabao, have expressed a variety of views on Singapore's experience. Generally speaking, earlier there was an emphasis on learning from Singapore's experience with economic and social development, but now China not only continues to study the Singaporean economy and its society but also has a deep interest in the developmental experience of Singapore's politics and political parties. Since the Reform and Opening Up, China has been learning from other countries, and, amidst this process, there has been a greater emphasis on Singapore's experience than that of any other country.

Yet there is a great gulf fixed between leadership's emphasis on learning from Singapore and what local officials actually do. Leadership doesn't just want to learn from Singapore's specific experience. Much more importantly, China needs to learn from the forward-looking spirit of Singapore's reforms. As a small country with no resources and less than a century of history, Singapore has undergone a massive transformation, from "Third World" to the "First World." This is an inherently valuable experience. In fact, not only is China studying Singapore but other countries such as Russia have also shown great interest in Singapore's experience. While Singapore previously was hailed as one of the "Four Little Dragons" of East Asia, the Singapore Model now seems to have separated itself from that of the Four Little Dragons and become the focus of attention. In Singapore, people of Chinese descent are the majority, making it essentially a Chinese country. This seems to indicate that Singapore's experience has greater relevance for China than for other countries.

In the wake of Deng Xiaoping's Southern Tour, Chinese government at all levels sent large numbers of delegations to Singapore for professional development. However, it's not uncommon to hear local officials in China questioning whether there is anything to learn from Singapore. Some officials argue that Singapore's experience is well and good, but that the country is too small for any substantial lessons. If one must study it, the most one can glean is a lesson in city administration.

For other local officials, it's unclear how Singapore's experience can or should be studied. To them, learning means copying or "rote repetition." Since Singapore is so small, there is nothing to learn. But they're off the mark. Across the globe, many poorly governed countries are small countries, and many failed states are also small countries. Small countries do not necessarily feature good governance. Similarly, large countries are not necessarily hard to govern. The United States is large—does this mean it is not well governed? Large countries can absorb mistakes, and one or two missteps don't make much of a difference. But in small countries, if there is a major policy mistake, the entire country may be done for. What I'm trying to say is that size is completely irrelevant to whether or not a country is worth studying.

I am not an expert in Singapore, but I have studied it, and worked in Singapore, for many years. After these years of observation, I can offer something of an analysis. Generally, it seems to me that many people have limited their understanding of Singapore to a few specific areas—like the Central Provident Fund, public housing, industrial parks, Temasek, and financial oversight. Very few discuss Singapore's political system, and this may be due to the fact that political issues are a more sensitive topic. However, there are some in Chinese senior leadership who are interested in Singapore's actual political experience. And, to a large extent, many aspects of the Singaporean experience that people talk about are manifestations of Singapore's political system. Without an understanding of this political system, it's hard to understand how these specific systems came about in the first place.

The Effective Centralization of Power

Singapore is usually described as an authoritarian system with centralized power. But every modern state features the centralization of power. In and of itself, centralized power is neither good nor bad. It cannot be used to assess the strength of a particular political system. For example, power is also centralized in democratic countries. The United States is a democracy, but its president wields supreme power, a power that many scholars have called emperor-like. In my opinion, the American president actually wields greater and more substantial power than did the traditional Chinese emperors. Traditional Chinese imperial power was often symbolic in nature, with rule but not governance. Imperial power was quite weak in its implementation, but the power of the American president has extremely strong executive force.

As far as centralization of power goes, there are three questions that we need to ask. One is how power is concentrated—that is, by what means is power concentrated? The second is how the concentration of power is maintained. And the third is reasons for that concentration of power—that is, why is power concentrated? In comparison with many other countries, in Singapore, power is quite concentrated. The ruling party, the People's Action Party (PAP), has a Leninist party structure and assumes what is often referred to as a "one-party dominant" system. While Singapore has many opposition parties that play some political role, they cannot be compared to the opposition parties in other countries.

It's also often said that concentration of power means corruption, but this has not happened in Singapore. Very few existing theories in social sciences can explain how it is that in Singapore there is both concentration of power and the "cleanness" of that power. Moreover, in Singapore, the concentration of power also means that policies and plans can be implemented. In other words, in Singapore, power is centralized, but those who have power do not waste any of their power. Power is used to get things done.

The situation is quite different in China. Centralization and decentralization are intertwined, yet power invisibly slips away. While it is true overall that the political system remains highly centralized, nobody in the government feels empowered. The common people feel powerless; leadership feels powerless; society feels powerless; and governments feel powerless. The departments have great powers, but they never feel sufficient. This is a systemic problem. There are contradictions between the Party and the government, contradictions among departments, contradictions between the central government and local governments, and contradictions between the state and society. Among all these tensions, power is frittered away.

The United States is a democracy, and the power to create leaders is quite decentralized. But once a president is elected, he wields emperor-like powers. Conversely, on the surface, China appears highly centralized, but the moment leaders try to do anything, resistance crops up everywhere. Governments at the central, provincial, and city level are all trying to concentrate their own powers. Formally and theoretically speaking, there is highly concentrated power. But this power is not substantial. In the past, it was said that decrees do not leave Beijing. But now there's a new turn on the old saying: Decrees do not leave Zhongnanhai. If nothing is done to change the status quo, we may reach the point where there are no decrees at all. There were many times in traditional China in which there were no decrees, in which there was rule but no government. But if this proves the case, China will experience a terribly weak government or even anarchy. In fact, at the basic level, large swathes of the country are already covered by anarchy.

Power can do good. Nor is the decentralization of power a good in itself. The key is how power is concentrated and, after it is concentrated, what is done with it. In these respects, Singapore has three kinds of experience that China should take into account. This experience addresses the following key questions: How do political parties organize power? How is power maintained? And how is power wielded effectively?

Blending the Political Party into Society

It is not a simple matter to concentrate power, maintain power, or wield power effectively. Power needs a vehicle; it needs an organizational structure. There are more than 80 million members of the CCP, more than the total populations of many countries—greater than populations of France, Britain, or Iran. And from the central government to local governments, there are a plethora of Party organizations. The Party's gigantic size and scope has historical roots. During the Revolution, the CCP needed to have many members, for at the time the Party was playing a mobilizing role—mobilizing the power of the masses and other forms of support. To this day, the CCP is still essentially a party for mass mobilization. In recent years, the CCP has been trying to transition away from being a revolutionary party to becoming a ruling party, but in terms of the total number of Party members and the Party's operations, this is a task that is far from complete.

Things are different in Singapore's PAP. The PAP is an elite party. Party members are either cadres or ordinary party members, but there are not many ordinary party members, and even fewer cadres. In society at large, the party's existence is hardly noticed. The party is hidden from sight, and acts as an "invisible hand" in the political arena. This is to say, the political party has blended into society. In fact, political parties must be part of society—the elite part of society—and this is the chief characteristic of Leninist parties. Political figures are to be from the people. If a party becomes a self-contained, vested interest group that is distinct from society at large, then the party is already in crisis.

The way the PAP's cadres are trained also differs from China. The CCP's elites are cultivated from within the Party's system. In many cases, owing to imperfections in the system, the training system for elites has evolved into a *de facto* system of negative selection, in which the thoughtful and talented are eliminated by others. Since the Party's talents are mainly recruited from within the Party, those who are trained are essentially bureaucratic officials. Excessive bureaucratization turns the other officials-in-training into bureaucrats as well—not into political figures. At the same time, bureaucratization prevents the political party from being sufficiently open to society.

This stands in sharp contrast to Singapore. Although Singapore has a system of one-party dominance, its political system is open to society. From the country's founding, the leaders of Singapore realized that, in a country with no resources, political talent was the key to the country's survival, development, and growth. Unlike the developed nations of the West, in which those with the greatest talent go into business, Singapore wants its best to go into politics. As a result, one of the critical functions of the ruling party is searching for and cultivating rare talent from across society and the world at large.

In Singapore, the civil servants for the government's bureaucracy are selected internally, but many political elites are recruited from society at large—and then trained. In other words, many political leaders are not cultivated from within the ruling party itself but are drawn in from society at large. In the 1970s, the PAP recruited Goh Chok Tong and Tony Tan Keng Yam, who would go on to serve as prime minister and deputy prime minister, respectively. In the 1980s and the 1990s, the party also brought in talents like the current Prime Minister Lee Hsien Loong and Deputy Prime Minister Wong Kan Seng. Before they became leaders of the ruling party, they had all been elites from other areas in society. The ruling party invited them to join the party and serve the nation from the fields in which they had already been successful.

As a result, in Singapore there is very little talk about "party standing" (*dang ling*). Today you might not be a party member, but tomorrow the party may need you, and you can then become a party member. This has solved a problem that many Leninist parties have had: promotion according to seniority. It is essential that a Leninist party recruit elites from the rest of society, but once the party becomes organized, it often evolves into a vested interest group. Singapore has effectively resolved this problem. Its solution is: keeping the party transparent and open to society.

For a ruling party to recruit talents cultivated by society is a matter of far-reaching significance. To begin with, when a ruling party's cadres come from society, the ruling party can maintain organic connections with society. Since such talents come from a variety of fields in society, they can better understand the needs of society, express those needs, and represent the interests of society as a whole. More importantly, as these talents come from society, society can closely identify with them—and after they enter the party, they strengthen the ruling party's legitimacy. This is an effective way for the ruling party to preserve its power. To summarize, a ruling party needs to keep political power open to society.

Furthermore, keeping a party open to talent from society helps prevent corruption. As talented people are already economically well off, the possibility of their being corrupted is greatly reduced. That is, they don't enter the ruling party and hold public office for any economic benefit, but to serve society. In many countries, democracies included, those who hold public office often engage in rent-seeking—that is, seeking power for personal gain. In Singapore, however, this seldom happens. Furthermore, there are lower costs involved in training. Training a cadre is not easy, and when society can train cadres, this greatly reduces the costs involved in training.

In the multiparty governments of the West, government policy can be easily transformed. Rotating political parties keeps the ruling party in power from having to pay the price for the actions of other ruling parties. Under one-party rule, however, policy transitions happen slowly, and the long-term challenge is always how to go about upgrading talent and policy. This demands that the party be integrated with society so that it can gain a first-hand experience of society and recruit society's elites.

Here, we can observe traditional Chinese elements at play in Singapore. In pre-modern China, there were no political parties, but the state's administrative power remained essentially transparent and open to society, as scholars were recruited through civil service examinations. In some respects, the current system of governance in China could be described as more closed than it was in pre-modern China, as political elites need to climb step-by-step up from the basic level. In comparison, U.S. citizens who meet the conditions set forth in the Constitution can run for president, but in China you have to be progressively promoted.

The Party's cadres climb a ladder from section member to department head to bureau head. It's simply impossible to reach high office in your thirties. You've got to be really lucky to make it to the ministerial level when you're young, and at every step, you really need a lucky break. In fact, it's only possible to make it to senior leadership positions around the age of fifty or sixty. The system's lack of vitality is due to the closed and limited nature of the system itself. But if we turn to Singapore's experience, we can see that the limitedness of this system is not insurmountable. The CCP has now begun to use social elites (such as figures from various Democractic Parties of China), and this is a good start. But there is much that still needs to be done. We need to reform the system and establish direct channels between the ruling party and the outstanding talents of society.

Here there is another problem that needs special emphasis: Singapore's system of high salaries. Singapore's ministers are famous for their high salaries. Seen in the light of current world trends surrounding the corruption of government officials, the high salaries in the Singapore government have proven very far-sighted. In Asian countries, low salaries for government officials are a major source of corruption in both democratic and non-democratic systems. Large-scale corruption has occurred in countries such as the Philippines and Thailand, as well as in Taiwan. The suicide of the former South Korean president Roh Moo-hyun also shows that morals alone will not maintain politicians' integrity; in fact, relying on morality will create massive political problems. This is true even in well-functioning democracies, as subsidy scandals in the United Kingdom demonstrate; in the past, the vast majority of people involved in politics were either nobles or celebrities. These often had comfortable economic backgrounds, and they did not get into politics for the sake of economic benefit. But in this modern era of mass democracy, anyone can get into politics as long as he or she has enough votes or political appointments. For many of these people, their economic background is not comfortable, and government salaries alone cannot provide a decent living. Under such circumstances, rent-seeking will occur, and corruption will become inevitable.

It's common to associate high salaries with anti-corruption efforts. But it should also be pointed out that personal integrity is only one of the objectives here.

There is another important—even more important—consideration: High salaries can create competition with society for elite talent. Many of Singapore's political talents originally came from society. They could make millions in business, so why should they come to the government to get a lower salary? Thus, in order to attract these talents, they need to be provided with some basic compensation. Of course, one reason Singapore can offer them high salaries is because of how it structures its cadre system. With few high-ranking cadres, Singapore can muster enough funds to provide high salaries for all of them.

Government-Society Relations

Singapore is a small urban country. The members of the PAP regularly meet with voters to discuss their concerns; this brings the ruling party together with society. In China, however, Party representatives, Congress members, and members of the Chinese People's Political Consultative Conference have no organic mechanism for connecting with society. They have no direct relationship with the common people. If these representatives have no direct connection to society and the people, how can they represent the interests of the people?

Singapore combines democracy with a political system of single-party dominance. Westerners say that Singapore is an illiberal democracy, but the name is beside the point. What matters is that a democracy can produce a good, effective government. Liberal democracy does not necessarily produce good and effective government, as the recent crises in democracies across Asia demonstrate. In Western countries, the ability of democratic politics to function effectively depends on the establishment of basic state systems prior to democratization, and democracy also benefits from relatively high levels of social and economic development. But in many Asian countries, the emergence and development of democratic politics have been overly influenced by either colonialism or the United States, and this has led some countries and regions to democratize before they could establish basic state systems and achieve socioeconomic development. This in turn has often created problems for their democratic politics. The problem is exacerbated by the fact that democratic politics is characterized by irreversibility: Once a country is democratized, it's hard to establish many basic state systems. Countries that democratize too soon can be weakened for a long time thereafter.

Thus it needs to be emphasized that good government is possible within any political system. China has also had good emperors and good governments, but in these situations, good government has depended on the individual qualities of leaders. Where there are good leaders, there is good government. This is precisely why to this day many Chinese cherish a hope that there will one day be a "wise king" (*ming jun*) and good leadership. But China does not have an effective system for protecting itself against bad politicians.

Singapore has responded to this problem by using democracy to ensure good government. Every five years, the ruling party must pass a "big test"—that is, a general election; for the many opposition parties, while they are individually small, do constitute positive, competitive pressure. The opposition parties themselves cannot substantially check the ruling party: They only control a few seats in Parliament. But if the people are dissatisfied with the ruling party, they can, in principle, support an opposition party during the general elections. Thus, the ruling party is always under pressure, and the ruling party's behavior must always satisfy a majority of the people.

Governments need to ensure that real talent is being hired, but China's *de facto* system of negative selection keeps those who are critical of the government or its politics from being hired or rehired. In fact, if you look at Chinese officialdom, you'll see quite a few who deceive their superiors and delude their subordinates: They are only flatterers. This stands in stark contrast with some of Singapore's officials, who were consistently critical of the government before they entered politics. But the ruling party is very open, and the government needs people who can offer constructive criticism. As long as this criticism is reasonable, the ruling party is happy to recruit them. What the ruling party hates the most is mediocre people who can only flatter others. If you are talented, perform well, and offer constructive ideas, the party can take you. The ruling party is also not fond of people who only criticize without offering constructive suggestions.

As was mentioned above, China's traditional imperial system opened up its regime through the imperial examinations. Now the State Council has appointed two members of democratic parties as ministers (the Minister of Health and the Minister of Science and Technology), but this is far from adequate. In the early days of the founding of the New China, Mao Zedong chose a large number of figures from democratic parties to serve as ministers, making the government something like a coalition government. Since then, this has not been well managed. Currently, the CCP is the only ruling party, and the concept of a coalition government is a thing of the past. But how can we keep the regime open to represent society's interests? This is a problem that the ruling party needs to fix; otherwise, it will itself become a vested interest group.

It is important that a ruling party represents the people's interests. Here, Singapore's government has been able to do things that many advanced democracies cannot, and it has done so in a highly Chinese way. While there are never-ending debates about the relative role of the government and the market, about the role of capital and the people, Singapore has been able to find a balance in these respects.

The founding spirit of the Singaporean government is people-centeredness (*minben zhuyi*): an authentically Chinese, traditional spirit. In this spirit, the government has found a balance between being "business-friendly" and "people-friendly." Being "business-friendly" means favoring business and valuing the role of capital. Now, development requires valuing the role played by capital, businesspeople, and entrepreneurs. Without entrepreneurs or capital, there can be no development. And as far as I know, Singapore invented the concept of being business-friendly. For example, China's concept of "being business-friendly" was borrowed from Singapore: In China, the concept first entered the country via the China-Singapore Suzhou Industrial Park and then spread to the rest of the country.

Meanwhile, the West had no concept of being business-friendly because it was never necessary: The West's development was originally led by businessmen. In Singapore, however, it was realized early on that the government must provide a favorable environment for business and capital: It must allow them to play a role in promoting economic and social development. It was this understanding that was behind the emergence of Singapore's industrial parks and the government's devotion to attracting foreign capital. Without the government's business-friendly policies, Singapore would have never achieved today's achievements in national construction.

However, being business-friendly and developing are not ends in themselves; they exist in order to be "people-friendly." That is, the former is the means, and the latter is the end. This is why Singapore is also far ahead of many democratic countries in its provision of basic government services. For in order to govern over the long term, it is essential to provide services for society. Being business-friendly exists in order to provide an economic basis for a service-oriented government. Many of the ideals of traditional Chinese culture—for example, universal home ownership—have never been achieved in China, but they have been realized in Singapore. (Of course, many other countries besides China, democracies included, have never been able to solve this problem.)

A case in point of these government services can be seen in Singapore's approach to housing and workers' pay. Many Chinese who visit Singapore come away thinking that Singapore's housing policy is a form of poverty relief, but this is a major misunderstanding. The vast majority of people in Singapore, including the middle class, live in government housing. Furthermore, whenever an economic crisis hits, the government always has to take into account the interests of both employers and workers—and strike a balance between the two. On the one hand, employers need help in surviving the crisis, for once employers go under, then it will be hard to find employment for workers. Thus, in the aftermath of the most recent financial crisis, the government subsidized employers to prevent employers from arbitrarily laying off their workers. On the other hand, the government stints at nothing to help workers, but instead of aimlessly throwing money at the poor, the government provides them with various kinds of job training and employment opportunities.

In China, the relationship between being business-friendly and people-friendly has not yet been straightened out. But in the light of Singapore's experience, it's clear that the two are not mutually contradictory. Development means being business-friendly, but sustainable development, the construction of a harmonious society, and long-term governance all demand that there also be people-friendliness.

Opposition Parties Are Not the Only Sign of Democracy

Politics can be concentrated, and power can be concentrated, but it must be ensured that those who control power are the best that society has to offer. This is something that Singapore's leaders take seriously. History has often shown that, in many cases, liberal democratic politics cannot keep bad people from getting elected. It has also been proven that democracy doesn't necessarily find the best people for the job.

Again, many often associate democracy with a multiparty politics or even equate the existence of opposition parties with democratic politics. But this doesn't fit the facts. Opposition parties do serve to provide a check on ruling parties, but there are other, more effective means of checking a ruling party. In Singapore, the most effective check on the ruling party are not the opposition parties, but society—that is, the people.

It's also said that only multiparty competition can provide voters with rational choice, for under a multiparty politics, different political parties will propose different policies and voters can make rational choices among different policies. But this assumption may not actually fit the evidence. Whether a candidate is elected depends, not only the strength of his or her policies but also on many other factors. Moreover, this theory assumes that voters are rational agents, which is not always exactly the case. Elections can depend on good looks, wealth, and the ability to speak well. When it comes to giving a speech, lawyers like Chen Shui-bian can go on and on. Nor should we forget that Hitler was elected, and that many corrupt presidents have also been elected.

Furthermore, if both candidates up for election are "bad apples," then it doesn't matter which you choose. The West has seen this happen repeatedly over the years. When several candidates are essentially the same, or everyone thinks that the candidates are all bad, voter turnout is low. In my observation, one benefit of Singapore's system is that it combines "selection" with "election." In this system, the PAP ensures that several "good apples" have been selected before the people can vote for them. Since selection is traditional in China, and elections are Western, Singapore has managed to combine the two well.

It should be also noted that selection does not mean appointment. In particular, current leaders should be prevented from designating their own successors. If successors are designated, then there is no democratic politics but dynastic politics. Rather, selection means intra-party democracy and intra-party competition. For the leadership of Singapore, the intra-party acceptance of leaders is highly important. Lee Kuan Yew once remarked that, between Goh Chok Tong and Tony Tan Keng Yam, the former would not have been his first choice. But, with the party's internal support for Goh, it was the party's internal acceptance, and not his own personal independence, that was decisive. It wasn't about who Lee liked.

Singapore also demonstrates that the essence of democracy is not multiparty competition but competition itself. Democracy has nothing to do with the number of political parties. In Japan, it was long true that factional competition within the Liberal Democratic Party (that is, intra-party democracy within the LDP) was far more important than competition among parties. This kind of intra-party competition is selection, and it is crucial. Moreover, some countries in Europe have many political parties within them, and thus they feel that the United States is not sufficiently democratic; for in the United States, there are only two political parties that hold power. And not only is there not much to distinguish the two but also neither of them is sufficiently representative. Some Americans have tried to forge third parties only to discover that a third party doesn't have enough power to achieve anything.

In reality, the number of parties in a country has nothing to do with the essence of democracy. In game theory, there are no basic differences in the rules of the game and the results when you have competition between two parties versus when you have competition among three, four, or five parties. This is because the essence of democracy is competition. There can be competition among multiple parties, but there can also be competition among leadership within one party. Political parties are just a platform for organizing competition. In the past, it was true that political parties were the main platform for organizing political competition, but it's also possible that other platforms could emerge that are more effective and fairer than any political party could be. In the West, more and more candidates are paying attention to the platform of the Internet. The current U.S. President, Barack Obama, has made full use of this platform.

When a one-party system or a system of one-party dominance is implemented, intra-party competition becomes critical. As with Japan's Liberal Democratic Party, compromise among a party's elites means institutional competition among elites. Of course, the most ideal situation is intra-party elections. These elections can involve all party members voting directly or indirectly. And along these lines, China has also made great progress, and the 17th Congress has been gradually experimenting with this approach. Intra-party democracy can also be seen in the United States, as candidates for the Democratic and Republican parties are also the products of a variety of forms of intra-party competition. Once this process is concluded, the common people are then allowed to choose from among these candidates. Furthermore, the nomination of candidates for British political parties has also adopted a "selection" system in disguise.

It is only when the character and talent of candidates are ensured can the vote of the common people have any significance. And Singapore excels at this. As members of Parliament must be selected through voting, the party first chooses someone who has done well in a particular field as a candidate for a specific constituency, and then sees whether the people will elect him or her. In this regard, the candidate must first win the approval of society through success in society, and then the candidate must gain the approval of the political party. When the party is on top of things, it directly recruits candidates into the party so that they will be easily elected. The opposite holds true in China. In China, first you win the Party's approval, and then you go to win society's approval. But in Singapore, if society does not approve of you, the ruling party will not recruit you.

Another truth Singapore teaches us is that, in democracy, a noisier opposition does not necessarily make for a better democracy. Instead, the key is competition. Political parties exist in order to benefit the country, not to hold power for the sake of holding power—this is why opposition parties in the United Kingdom are referred to as "Her Majesty's most loyal opposition." But in many countries and regions across Asia, opposition parties have evolved for the sake of opposition, and this is not in keeping with the original intent of democracy.

In fact, Singapore is currently implementing political reforms that are mainly aimed at providing more democracy, and increasing the proportion of opposition parties in Parliament. The government has decided to revise electoral provisions so that the number of seats for opposition parties in Parliament is increased—that is, the seats for non-constituency members of Parliament have been increased from three to nine. Regardless of how many votes opposition candidates receive, they will hold at least nine seats in Parliament, which increases the proportion of seats held by opposition parties in Parliament to 20%. Prime Minister Lee Hsien Loong has said that this reform aims at maintaining political stability and a strong public mandate for the government. But the government emphasizes that proportional representation is not on the table for political reform, for this would produce a weak government. In other words, developing greater democracy does not necessarily demand copying the West.

Many Western practices are relatively fair in theory, while actual practice remains unfair, and many of these practices aren't practical in Asian countries. The spirit of the Singaporean approach is to provide greater space for differing interests and voices within the system, to digest and coordinate differing interests within the system.

The Role of Leadership

If the United States didn't have a Washington, would it have experimented with monarchy? This is a frequently asked question. Founding fathers of a country are incredibly decisive, and Lee Kuan Yew played such a decisive role in Singapore's history.

It's frequently true that under strongman politics there is no political competition, and that strongmen can appoint their successors. Lee was also a political strongman. What was different about him was that he could transform his worldview and policies into a set of institutions, and establish a ruling party and anti-corruption systems. Lee had studied law, and knew that, in order to maintain long-term stability, he had to transform his ideas into institutions. In the same way, Mao Zedong and Deng Xiaoping were also strongmen. Under Mao, China didn't achieve much as far as institution building. Deng transformed some of his ideas into systems, as in the mandatory retirement system, and these have gone far in maintaining China's political stability up through the present day.

Generally speaking, Singapore is a classic example of the combination of Western democratic constitutionalism with Chinese cultural traditions. Singapore isn't interested in ideology, but in shared values. In combining its own culture with a constitutional system, it has taken second place among Asian countries in integrating Eastern and Western civilization. In my opinion, Japan has had the greatest success in combining its traditional culture with Western political democracy. Japan is not a completely Western-style democracy. Instead, Japan combines its traditional culture, especially its Confucian culture, with Western democratic constitutional government. The way that factions within the LDP achieve consensus is inseparable from that traditional culture. Japanese politicians also have the fortitude to assume responsibility for their actions, which is another aspect of traditional culture. Through their own efforts, Singapore's leaders have also embarked on a political path that accords with the country's own characteristics. What happened in Singapore was not institutional transplantation but institutional innovation.

The American system has two hundred years of history; it has taken deep roots and appears indestructible. But in Asia, Africa, and Latin America, many democracies function problematically, and these issues have become the source of social instability. The original spirit of democracy is that of mutual compromise, but these countries often feature mutual aggression. In Asia, many countries have been implementing democracy for many years, but their political situations remain chaotic, and neither society nor the economy is highly developed. Singapore, however, managed to avoid the political detours experienced by many developing democracies. And in this process, institutional innovation played a critical role. Now, Singapore faces the question of a "post-Lee era." To my mind, in a post-Lee era the systems created by Lee will continue to provide the institutional guarantee for systemic continuity. At the same time, the system is also largely imbued with a spirit of institutional innovation.

The Singapore Model and China's Prospects for Political Reform

In China today, the key to all reform begins with determining the main drivers of reform—that is, who is doing the reforming. No one can deny the importance of reform, and there are various ideas about how to reform. The crux lies in who is going to do the reform. Why was Singapore able to find success? The main thing was careful thought and authority: Lee Kuan Yew could turn his ideas into institutions. Under Deng Xiaoping, in the 1980s, when problems occurred during reform or new policies could not be carried forward, questions were raised concerning the authority of leadership—this was what was then called the "neo-authoritarian movement."

Today, while neo-authoritarianism itself is not mentioned, the central government still lacks authority. And because of a history of strongman politics, this problem is getting increasingly worse. As has been previously discussed, China has a lot to learn from how Singapore establishes authority. If the CCP can truly bring together the Party's elites and social elites, authority can also be established. Moreover, Chinese tradition places the most emphasis on selection, but now the system places greater emphasis on negative selection. This negative selection primarily exists because there are no formal mechanisms for competition. When

Chinese compete, 30% of the competition is driven by talent and 70% is driven by relationships. Those who can participate in competition are not necessarily the cream of the crop, and those with the best performance are not necessarily those who get promoted.

In Singapore, those who enter competition are those who are already highly recognized by society, for if a ruling party wants to attract real talent, it needs to be open to society. In contrast with the PAP, China's level of openness is still quite low. If we take into account China's unique circumstances, China might still implement openness in different sectors. In some sensitive sectors (for example, those related to politics and security), openness will be difficult to achieve, and once it is achieved, problems will arise. But in other sectors—such as education, scientific research, society, and the economy—great efforts should be made to create openness to society's talents, the true elites of society.

Here it needs to be emphasized that if China is to attract real talent, it needs to change its "administerization" approach. In Singapore, the existence of administrative levels is limited to governmental sectors, and many sectors have no administrative levels at all. Banking, government enterprises, schools, and research institutions—which all have their own sets of administrative levels in China—have no administrative levels in Singapore. An absence of specific administration is conducive to developing talent. With administrative levels, these positions become political, and this often prevents talent from coming into full play. At the same time, linking talent to administrative level does not make use of talent but rather wastes it. Those who are employed often give most of their attention to administration, and little time to their professions themselves.

More importantly, an "administerization" approach and professionalism are mutually contradictory. In terms of talent, Singapore has been the most successful at cultivating talent in two fields: political talent and professional talent. In Singapore, we can say that cultural progress has been achieved by the efforts of professionals, while politicians have provided an ideal developmental environment for these professionals.

In order to make the ruling party the driver of reform, in addition to making use of talent, China must also devote considerable attention to democracy. Without a strongman in charge, if the Party wants to establish its authority, in addition to opening up to society, it must also prioritize intra-party democracy. If the Party's leaders are elected from within the Party, then a truly democratic authority can be established. This is the route China must take. At the 17th Congress a few years ago, a very important step was taken in this direction. Once the Party's leaders cannot be internally appointed, they can only be produced through intra-party democracy and elections.

Once established, intra-party democracy will only grow ever more rapidly. In fact, elite democracy and intra-party democracy will develop much more rapidly than social democracy or a people's democracy would, for, as the 17th Congress accurately suggests, intra-party democracy is a means of guiding the country toward a people's democracy. Without intra-party democracy, it will be hard for social democracy to develop from the bottom up. But intra-party democracy must be coordinated with social democracy; otherwise, people will ask, "If you weren't elected, and I was elected, would I listen to you?" Under the status quo, there is a certain amount of contradiction between the village committees and the village party committees that are at the same level. Thus, top-down democracy and bottom-up democracy need to be combined.

In fact, this is actually how things play out in the West. Parties arrange matters internally and then let the common people vote for which candidate they approve—for the true essence of Western democracy is competition among elites. But elite democracy and social democracy must both be based on the rule of law; without it, democracy will descend into anarchy.

When there is greater intra-elite competition, some basic rules will develop. These rules can be written or unwritten. For example, holding democratic elections within a party involves technical requirements for office such as age, level of education, and work experience at the central and local levels. Furthermore, basic premises—such as what can be debated, what cannot be debated, what can be adjusted, and what cannot be adjusted—all serve as the boundaries of and constraints on democracy. The rule of law means that, as a variety of political forces enter into political competition, all participants, whether individuals and parties, must obey the law and operate within the framework established by the law. Without the rule of law, there can be no political stability. And if political forces do not recognize the rule of law, and each political force only recognizes a state on its own terms, there will never be peace in a country or in society.

China must first establish rule of law and then promote intra-party democracy and social democracy. Of course, this is not to say that China has no rule of law. The ruling party has played a very important role in promoting progress within the legal system, and the Party also uses the law to govern society. But just how the Party should use the law to govern itself still needs a lot of work.

Thus, we need to consider how it will be possible to implement judicial reform without political reform. It is hard to see the CCP as a Western-style political party, for the Party is the founder of the state and its owner, and it administers the government. But as in the economic sphere, managers and owners can either be the same or distinct from each other, while the Party can either be the same as the government or distinct from it.

In the Chinese context, a completely independent judiciary is not going to happen all at once, but the judiciary must have some autonomy. Of course, even in the West, the appointment of judges by presidents (as by the president of the United States) can also exert a certain impact on the administration of justice. However, we must not interfere with the autonomy of the judiciary, and the independence and professional spirit of judges and lawyers must be maintained. If judges and lawyers cannot win some independence from politics, they will not gain the confidence of society, for society always reserves the right to judge.

Instead, the ruling party can participate in politics through the People's Congress system, just as it does in Singapore. The Party holds the vast majority of seats in the people's congresses; it simply must not directly administer or directly intervene in the judiciary. Rather, it should use the people's congresses to form relations with the government and the judiciary. Already, in local government, many Party secretaries are also the chairmen of the standing committees of the people's congresses. Given all this, the ruling party must adopt a reasonable mechanism for governing and participating in politics.

China must promote the rationalization of its systems. Here, many forces come into play, but the Party itself is quite important. The Party must administer society by adopting reasonable methodologies that are consistent with changes in socioeconomic conditions.

China's political development needs not only chronological analysis but also a point-by-point analysis. In comparison with the times before the Reform and Opening Up, China's politics has made great progress. And this is true in terms of a point-by-point analysis as well. If the Party weakens, China will not be strong enough to consolidate the entire country. Of course, in the eyes of Westerners, the Philippines is a liberal democracy while Singapore is an illiberal democracy. But which one would most people rather live in? In many countries across Asia, Africa, and Latin America, democracy is in dire straits. What most people want to know is: What can democracy give me?

Reform is the product of the interactions of various forces, and the Party cannot be separated from other forces. Moreover, the modern Party has changed considerably from the Party of Mao's time. While it is still a Leninist party, much of what it stands for has changed. China must look for ways to democratize within this structure. Again, although Party's top priority is its long-term governance, this does not really set it apart from any other political party. Given this priority, democracy can contribute to the long-term governance of the ruling party.

Since the Reform and Opening Up, the ruling party has demonstrated openness. As long as this openness is sustained, it will eventually lead to democracy.

Epilogue: The China Model and Intellectual Emancipation[1]

Since the time of the May Fourth Movement, the movement was destined to become the main motif of modern Chinese history. Since then, every development in Chinese history can seemingly be linked back to the May Fourth Movement. Whether we're talking about politics or culture, it's hard to imagine a China that never experienced the May Fourth Movement. As a result, the interpretation and evaluation of it has been unending. There have been ideological interpretations, political interpretations, Party-related interpretations, and a variety of cultural interpretations that have been imbued with the zeitgeist in which they were produced. However, regardless of whether these interpretations were positive or negative in their assessments, they are all inseparable from the stuff of reality. Optimists can find positive elements within the May Fourth Movement, while critics can just as easily find negative elements.

For example, in the 1980s, mainland China entered a period in which political reform was widely advocated. Whether in the political realm or the intellectual sphere, there were widespread calls for the progressive, reform-minded, and even revolutionary spirit of the May Fourth Movement. By the 1990s, however, there were very different views on the movement, and some simplistically connected the movement to radicalism. Chinese academia wanted to "bid farewell to the

1 This article is co-authored with Wang Gungwu.

Revolution" (*gaobie geming*), and academic circles undertook an intellectual reassessment of the Revolution and radical social movements. Soon thereafter, China's leadership also formally proposed that the Communist Party should transition away from being a revolutionary party to becoming a ruling party. This interpretation holds that, during the Revolutionary period, the spirit of the May Fourth Movement was needed, but in an era of peaceful governance, circumstances are different. Thus, while the May Fourth Movement was a product of radicalism and was also associated with the Revolution, our times do not call for a return to the spirit of the May Fourth Movement. This attitude may be one of the reasons behind the low-key approach to commemorating the movement's anniversary in mainland China.

It is still too early to draw any simple conclusions about this landmark movement of modern Chinese history—much less form any political conclusions. Yet the attitudes found in the various assessments of the movement also show that, while the movement has become history, it still retains a profound modernity. Regardless of whether modernity is approached through the lens of the May Fourth Movement or the movement is approached from the vantage point of modernity, it's easy to observe the movement's greatness and profound historical significance.

It needs to be noted that, from the outset, the May Fourth Movement exerted a global impact, with its influence extending to the Chinese societies of mainland China, Taiwan, Hong Kong, and Macau. But while these Chinese societies all originated in Chinese tradition, since the advent of modern times, the movement had differing impacts on them, owing to each one's unique historical development under various social, economic, and political forms. As a result, different Chinese societies offered differing assessments of the value of the movement. It is not possible here to offer a thorough discussion of the impact that the movement has had on all of these social developments. Instead, this chapter will focus on the birthplace of the movement, which was mainland China. Yet, even when we focus on mainland China, it will not be easy to offer a straightforward analysis of China's intellectual development in the wake of the May Fourth Movement: It is both a gigantic and a serious task. At the same time, it is impossible to draw any conclusive assessments of the movement, for the evaluation of the movement needs to be open. History is open, and the evaluation of history should be open, too. Thus, this chapter aims to discuss the profound influence of the movement on modern China, along with its significance for future development.

The era of the May Fourth Movement can be described as a historical period in which "a hundred flowers bloomed." In many respects, contemporary China seems very similar. Owing to the existence of objective socioeconomic and political questions, debates among various "-isms" have erupted from time to time in a variety of ways. In the struggle among "isms," people are looking for an "-ism" that offers an effective approach to understanding and solving practical problems. Among the people, we have only seen the beginning of these debates—but officials still adhere to Deng Xiaoping's policy of "no debate" (*bu zhenglun*). While at the practical level the Chinese government's policy of Reform and Opening Up has considerable continuity and consistency, the ideological or intellectual underpinning implied by this policy often goes unaddressed. This has led to our current problem of "ideological decline" among officials.

It is also because this holds true that another May Fourth Movement might have some viability. From the perspective of the debate over "isms," one of the most salient characteristics of the May Fourth movement was that, at the time, no one could control debate, nor was anyone afraid of debating. During the May Fourth period, a vast multitude of "-isms" appeared, but the vast majority of them quickly disappeared. These "-isms" did not disappear under external pressure—for instance, because of political or administrative power—but because many of the philosophies did not find suitable soil in China. At the same time, some of those "-isms" have survived and developed in the midst of competition, and the main reason is that they found good soil in China.

The mainstream of socialist ideology of contemporary China was established and developed during and after the May Fourth period. Why was it that socialism became China's dominant ideology during the May Fourth period? Socialism's success stemmed from how competitive socialist thought was at the time. During that period, socialist thought lacked any political, administrative, legal, or economic support, and it was frequently regarded as deviant. But socialist thinkers were clearly unafraid of competition, and their thought quickly took the reigns. There were many reasons for this. Socialist thought began by winning acceptance from many intellectuals, and this group of intellectuals played an important role in disseminating and developing socialist thought. To borrow the terminology of the Italian Marxist theorist Antonio Gramsci, these people were the "organic intellectuals" of socialism.

Socialist thought also achieved a leading position because it more strongly corresponded to China's political and economic realities than other ideologies did. On the one hand, it could explain China's realities, and, on the other hand, it could also solve China's problems. As a result, in China, socialism was not only a theoretical philosophy but also a practical philosophy. Another important factor was the spirit of free intellectual competition in the universities and schools. All formal thought needs vehicles, and universities and schools are the primary vehicles of thought. If the period's universities had not accommodated the intellectuals who believed in socialist thought, it would have been much more difficult for socialism to achieve leadership in China. At the time, university leaders—particularly at Peking University—did not accept socialism themselves, but they were brave and strong enough to confront competition amidst a variety of ideas. Thus, socialism was able to go mainstream because of competition.

From the May Fourth period to the present day, socialist thought and practice has passed through several historical stages, each with its own characteristics. To summarize, it has gone from openness to closedness and then back to openness. During the May Fourth period, socialism was a product of openness, but once it had developed into the mainstream ideology of China, it became a closed and rigid dogma. In the wake of the Reform and Opening Up, socialism has once again become open and regained its vitality.

When socialism first arrived in China, it kept pace with various popular "-isms" such as liberalism, democracy, capitalism, nationalism, and anarchism. The first generation of early communist leaders, including Li Dazhao and Mao Zedong, chose socialism because the main goal at the time was the creation of an independent sovereign state. As a tradition of political thought, European socialism sought to rectify the inhumane conditions produced by primitive capitalism. Thus, European socialism emphasizes social justice and social welfare. Once socialism had arrived in China, however, it underwent a tremendous transformation and was merged with nationalism. After the founding of the New China, the content of this socialism did not change much. At that time, a planned economy was implemented in order to establish an independent sovereign state. Socialism's focus was not on individuals and individual rights, but on state power. When this was mixed with factors such as the Cold War, the leadership ended up overemphasizing public ownership and making an artificial distinction between socialism and capitalism.

After the Reform and Opening Up, the second generation of CCP leadership as represented by Deng Xiaoping undertook a deep rethinking of socialism. The extreme forms of socialism of the Mao era had produced a country with strong sovereignty but a poor people. This led Deng Xiaoping to propose the slogan "Poverty is not socialism" and implement a policy of "letting some get rich first." After the collapse of the Soviet Union and the Eastern Bloc, China undertook a comprehensive introduction of the market economy. This was done, on the one hand, to engage in economy-building and escape from an impoverished socialism, and on the other hand, to use the market economy to attack the restraints that the rigid political system posed on economic reform. This period achieved great success in developing the market economy, and it also prompted Chinese society to begin to undertake a comprehensive transformation. The old system was washed away, but it took a while to establish a new system. Outside of the desperate pursuit of economic interests, every aspect of Chinese life experienced unprecedented disorder, as no one knew where society was headed.

Since its entrance into the twenty-first century, Chinese socialism has begun to enter yet a new state of development. It has been observed that Chinese leadership is currently promoting transformation within all aspects of Chinese society, and Chinese officials have officially proposed the establishment of a "harmonious society." Thus, it could well be said that what is currently emerging is a new wave of socialism. This new wave is reflected in many aspects. First of all, in terms of developmental orientation, the theme has been "human-centeredness." "Human-centeredness" was originally at the heart of the European socialist movement, and the aim was to rectify many of the abuses brought by the capitalist system. But for a long stretch of time before the Reform and Opening Up, the practice of socialism in China was directly opposed to human-centeredness. Until the 1980s, it was also regarded as a major facet of bourgeois liberalization, and it came under criticism. Today it has become a touchstone for the development of Chinese society, and this represents a major advance in politics. Second, at the policy level, human-centeredness focuses policy on the needs of society's majority. While legal means are used to protect emerging social classes, the interests of laborers and farmers, who account for the majority of society, have also been recently reaffirmed. Many of the new ideas proposed by leadership—ideas such as "The New Three Principles of the People" and "scientific development"—are manifestations of a human-centered outlook. At the policy level, leadership has also begun to bring greater focus to the pursuit of social equity. In recent years, using social reforms to establish social systems and thereby achieve social equity has become a major trend in China's reform, and the government has concentrated its efforts in the fields of social security, healthcare, education, and environmental protection.

Thus, this is a new wave of socialism. It is not a return to traditional socialism, but a synthetic product. It inherits many reasonable ideas, like social justice, human-centeredness, and coordinated development, from traditional socialism, but it uses completely different methods to realize these ideas. In many respects, this new wave of socialism has completely abandoned the Cold War's Soviet-style socialism, and it is much more similar to European versions of socialism. Of course, this new wave of socialism is grounded in China's social realities. In the European sense, the establishment of an industrialization based on a market economy has only just begun in China. Together with factors such as globalization, social mobility, farmer problems, and class, China seems to have a stronger base for socialism. In other words, if the problems of the laborers, farmers, and migrant workers who account for society's majority cannot be solved, no "-ism" will long survive in China. This is why socialist ideas like social justice and human-centeredness have brought socialism back to life in China. In fact, in contemporary Chinese society there are a variety of intellectual movements, such as liberalism and the New Left. While many of these have different ideas, none of them denies the core beliefs of socialism. With the exception of a few basic doctrines, it is not their ideas about society that divide them, but rather the means by which these ideas are to be realized.

In summary, the proposal of new ideas, like human-centeredness, and the introduction of new means of development, has injected new life into Chinese socialism. But how should human-centered systems be represented and established at the political level? In other words, how should we go about building a socialist democracy? As with the economic sphere, this is both a theoretical issue and a practical question. Socialism is a system that achieves social justice and realizes human-centered values through the people's participation in the political process. Now that China's market economy has been established and consolidated, more attention is being paid to creating political democratization and social democracy in China. It is in this question of democratization that the disputes and disagreements between the people and the government come to light.

It should be noted that this new wave of socialism as promoted by the government has not become the ideology accepted by most Chinese. Quite the contrary, for many years, China has seen a decline in its official ideology and the rise of various ideologies within society. In other words, official ideology is being challenged by many other "-isms" and social ideologies, creating a competitive environment in which each "-ism" seeks growth at the expense of all others.

The rapid economic development that has occurred since the Reform and Opening Up has led to a pluralistic society. As income inequality between social groups and regions is growing, a plurality of interests is quickly evolving into a differentiated society. Of course, every economy experiences a stage of widening inequality in income distribution during the early stages of development; the political impact of inequality in income distribution depends on the degree to which society accepts it. In China, income inequality has not only objectively exceeded typical international levels (as measured by the Gini coefficient) but has also exceeded Chinese society's ability to accept it. Many have moved from dissatisfaction to rage at the inequalities of income distribution. In fact, inequality in income distribution and its political and social impacts have also held the attention of Chinese officials for many years. While the Chinese government has made great efforts to reshape socialism, reduce income inequality, and achieve social equity, there is no sign that these efforts have checked the widening of income inequality. On the contrary, because the government has not yet developed enough effective capacity to manage capital, inequality in income distribution continues to increase. The differentiation of interests naturally leads to ideological differentiation.

With the term "ideological differentiation," we are referring to the reality of ideology at the level of Chinese society. A considerable contingent of people agree with one "-ism" or understanding, while another group accept a different doctrine or understanding. And while officials still control the media in China, this has not hampered the spread of a variety of "isms." In many respects, the intellectual environment in modern China mirrors other historical periods, such as the late Qing and the early Republic. A wide variety of "-isms" have emerged: "-isms" like "leftism," "rightism," "conservatism," "nationalism," and various other indigenous or Western "-isms" and religious beliefs. Now, such intellectual understandings are a reflection of social realities, so the rise of various "-isms" in China is normal. But these "-isms" are also seeking to combine with social forces in various ways, and they are seeking results at both the policy level and the political level.

For many years, Chinese economic reform has been dominated by the discourse of neoliberal economics. This school of economics has played an irreplaceable role in promoting China's transition from a planned economy to a market economy. But today's neoliberal economics finds itself in a very embarrassing situation. While it has contributed to the differentiation of Chinese society, it does not offer any effective policies for improving the situation. Instead, it seems to many that neoliberal economics has become the tool of vested interest groups. At the other end of the spectrum, some social classes are suffering under or have become the victims of reforms dominated by neoliberal economics. These classes do not see any way forward under reforms centered around neoliberal economics. And in recent years, some have begun to reject *in toto* the policies of the Reform and Opening Up. They have begun to be skeptical of Deng Xiaoping's reform line and are demanding a reconsideration of and an improvement of the reform line, for market-oriented reforms have created many problems. These groups often look to the past. China's social groups that constitute its "New Left" and "Old Left," along with what outsiders refer to as "Maoists," all exhibit this tendency to varying degrees. Of course, here we can also find some intellectuals who approach reality and criticize it from an idealistic point of view.

Meanwhile, every major "-ism" is experiencing radicalization. In some circumstances, "-isms" also manifest some of the characteristics of populism. The term "populism" often refers to a situation in which the grassroots of a society are mobilized. In today's China, there is both a "leftist" populism that bases itself in the bottom rungs of society and vulnerable groups and a "rightist" populism that bases itself in vested interests and privileged classes. It seems highly unlikely for the two sides to find common ground for compromise, and thus the two oppose each other. On the one hand, the attitude of the vested interests is "to hell with the poor." They mobilize everything they have available to protect the basis of their vested interests and expand their interests by every means possible. On the other hand, it is increasingly difficult for the lower classes of society to tolerate a society that is daily becoming more and more unjust, and these classes regard vested interests as holding ill-gotten gains. These classes and their spokespersons, of course, also need to mobilize their own support.

Between the two, the power of the middle ground is very small and weak. China's middle class has never been big, and now this still small and frail middle class faces a dilemma. Because wealth is rapidly transferring from the majority and concentrating in the hands of the minority, a small portion of the middle class has already accumulated enough wealth to enter the ranks of the vested interests, but there is also a considerable portion of the middle class—particularly urban residents—who have been re-impoverished and become the new poor. While economic development continues to create a middle class, the current economic structure of China is preventing China's middle class from experiencing rapid growth.

The ruling party certainly does not want to see radicalization in society. Government officials are also quite aware of the radicalization ongoing among ideologies in society. Moreover, they continue to control the media and ideology. But with the pluralizing of interests, the effectiveness of this control has now come into question. Even within the ruling party itself, there is already a pluralizing of thought. This has made it crucial that there be established an ideology that everyone can accept. Of course, what official ideology currently emphasizes is compromise between interests. But although all social strata can see the benefits of compromising on social interests, it's hard for the lower classes to accept the injustices in contemporary society without any concrete systems or policies that can create sufficient compromise in social interests.

The radicalization of society's ideology has begun to manifest itself in some aspects of social activism. The most obvious are the group protests of recent years. Earlier group protests were set off by specific economic and social issues, and participants also appeared to be struggling for specific benefits. In recent years, however, group protests have begun to go beyond the economic and social realms and have become political in nature. Nor can it be denied that some group protests are beginning to be shaped by ideals. In other words, society's ideology is beginning to play an important role in the occurrence and development of group protests. If highly differentiated interests cannot find compromise among each other, we may eventually see social upheaval that neither the left nor the right want to see.

The current environment of Chinese society shows that the ruling party must recapture the spirit of the May Fourth Movement and establish a mainstream ideology for China in competition with the various "isms." Instead of officials controlling the people, what the ruling party now needs is the movement's spirit of open competition. Official worries that intellectual movements will radicalize are understandable, for no ruling party ever wants to see any intellectual radicalization. But we need to take a reasonable look at the radicalization of thought during the May Fourth period. Like all other intellectual movements, the May Fourth Movement did have a radical side to it, one which mainly involved a radical criticism of traditional Chinese culture. But this doesn't mean that radical movements are without their own reasonableness. As far as the ruling party is concerned, using intellectual competition to establish mainstream values and ideology—not using political or administrative force to suppress thought—can serve as an effective approach to governance. The twentieth century offers profound lessons in this regard. In the 1930s and 1940s, after the Kuomintang established its regime, it began to criticize and attack the May Fourth Movement. This was ironic, for the development of the KMT was inseparable from the May Fourth Movement, but once the KMT became a ruling party, it lost the May Fourth spirit and showed intellectual conservatism. However, the Chinese intellectual community responded to the many problems of their times by maintaining the May Fourth spirit and making penetrating criticisms of social realities. The ruling party obviously was averse to this, so it used various means to control and suppress intellectuals. This necessarily led to attacks on the May Fourth Movement itself. But this approach backfired, and official control led to greater radicalization of thought and behavior among students and the intellectual community, for they believed that only radicalization could resolve the profound crisis that China faced. Losing the acceptance and support of students and intellectuals was a key cause of the KMT's failure.

This history ought to offer contemporary significance. Ideologically speaking, the hegemony of socialism was established in China through the May Fourth Movement, and the manner in which the movement established ideological hegemony still offers profound significance for China's mainstream thought and values. In the ruling party's relationship to society, two different concepts need to be distinguished: "hegemony" and "domination." According to Gramsci, "hegemony" and "domination" are two interconnected but substantially different political concepts. Ideological hegemony is the status obtained by a particular ideology through free competition with other ideologies. Members of society freely choose this ideology, voluntarily accept and agree with this ideology, and accept the guidance and direction of this ideology in action. But ideological domination differs in this respect. Ideological domination often involves a political party or political organization that imposes its own thought or ideology on other groups after seizing power. This ideology maintains its dominance, not necessarily through free competition but by using political, administrative, legal, and economic force to impose itself on social groups. Although ideological domination does not necessarily exclude hegemony, the difference between the two is clear. Hegemony is not coercive, while domination includes coercion. Thus, generally speaking, ideological hegemony has greater rationality and sociality than does domination.

The spirit of intellectual competition embodied in the May Fourth Movement still offers referential significance for the intellectual frontlines in China today. The CCP is now the ruling party and possesses domination. With this domination, some officials who supervise intellectual and ideological fields either rarely consider or even ignore intellectual and ideological hegemony. Because they have a strong political base and control every aspect of economic, social, and administrative power, they often seem extremely arrogant. Some are just afraid of competition—they cannot tolerate competition, so they frequently use their power to suppress others and solve problems. While this is true for many fields, it is even more true in terms of thought. And while every official can see the importance of intellectual and ideological hegemony, many do not want to fight for intellectual hegemony through competition. Instead, they always want to use the domination available to them to achieve this kind of "hegemony."

To gain hegemony in thought and ideology, and not just possess and make use of domination, we need to think about the status of intellectuals—particularly the Party's intellectuals. Every political party—especially a ruling party—needs its own organic intellectuals. If a political party cannot cultivate its own organic intellectuals, it will have difficulty in achieving and maintaining ideological hegemony. In multiparty states, a party is itself just an organization with organizational interests and that is in competition with other parties. In China, however, the reality is that the CCP is the only ruling party. Under these circumstances, what are the Party's interests? This is an issue that needs careful consideration. People often refer to the "interests of the Party and the state"—this is to say that the Party has its own interests. So, what are these interests? No matter how complex the Party's interests may be, it cannot be ignored that the Party must depend on the interests of the majority in society.

In other words, the Party is an organism representing the entirety of society. The Party is dependent on society as a whole, but society is not dependent on the Party. This means that the Party's organic intellectuals should first serve as organic intellectuals on the behalf of the entirety of society, intellectuals who reflect the voice of society and represent society's interests. The Party's intellectuals must be part of society, come from society, and serve society. Intellectuals, along with other Party cadres, are the organic point of contact between the Party and society as a whole. If intellectuals, particularly the Party's intellectuals, become the spokespersons for certain special interests, then the Party's intellectual and ideological hegemony will come into question. When a "soft" hegemony experiences problems, a hard domination will emerge. When domination is overly relied on or is abused, there will be tension between the Party and the masses.

At present the CCP leadership has raised the question of the Party's transition from a revolutionary party to a ruling party, and it has also made governing capacity an item on the political agenda. This has deep significance for China's future. With ongoing socioeconomic transition, transition within the Party is now inevitable. In recent years, the CCP has made many efforts in respect to intra-party democracy and anti-corruption campaigns, but thus far it has mainly focused on organizational and administrative transition, and this is far from adequate. Intellectual and ideological transition is equally important. If the Party continues to disallow competition among various ideas and does not, on the basis of this competition, merge with shared values that the majority in society can recognize and accept, then the ruling party will continue to experience an ideological decline. For many years, it was not that the ruling party did not offer policies that could promote the interests of society's majority, but that these policies have lacked ideological understanding and consensus among cadres and Party members. This has prevented these policies from winning effective support from cadres and Party members, and the implementation of policy has continued to be a major problem. Even worse, if society lacks shared values, society will experience ever lower degrees of cohesion. Such developmental trends are obviously not conducive to the realization of China's goal of a harmonious society.

Today, China is facing unprecedented change. Great change creates great problems, and solving great problems calls for a great intellectual emancipation. Since the Reform and Opening Up, all walks of life have called for intellectual emancipation. But how we are truly going to achieve intellectual emancipation? Here the contemporary relevance of the May Fourth spirit comes into play. It is precisely in this sense that China needs to recover the May Fourth Movement, rather than say goodbye to it.

www.ingramcontent.com/pod-product-compliance
Ingram Content Group UK Ltd.
Pitfield, Milton Keynes, MK11 3LW, UK
UKHW021836100926
8556IPUK00004B/373

9 781433 172007